StampWorks

Experiments and BASIC Stamp Source Code

Version 1.2

PARALLAX

Internet Access

We maintain internet systems for your use. These may be used to obtain software, communicate with members of Parallax, and communicate with other customers. Access information is shown below:

E-mail: info@parallaxinc.com
Web: www.parallaxinc.com and www.stampsinclass.com

Internet BASIC Stamp Discussion List

We maintain two e-mail discussion lists for people interested in BASIC Stamps (subscribe at www.parallaxinc.com under the technical support button). The BASIC Stamp list server includes engineers, hobbyists, and enthusiasts. The list works like this: lots of people subscribe to the list, and then all questions and answers to the list are distributed to all subscribers. It's a fun, fast, and free way to discuss BASIC Stamp issues and get answers to technical questions. This list generates about 40 messages per day.

The Stamps in Class list is for students and educators who wish to share educational ideas. To subscribe to this list go to www.stampsinclass.com and look for the E-groups list. This list generates about 5 messages per day.

Table of Contents

Table of Contents

StampWorks **Preface**

Dear Friends:

There are probably as many ways to learn a new subject or skill as there are students and yet, most will agree that *learning by doing* produces the longest lasting results. And, quite frankly, learning by doing is almost always the most satisfying way to learn; it involves more of the senses. That's what this text and the StampWorks kit is all about: learning to program the BASIC Stamp by actually writing programs for it. The theory sections are short and concise. You'll learn programming theory by putting it into practice. There's not a lot of hand holding here; there's work – fun work that will teach you about microcontroller programming with the Parallax BASIC Stamp.

Why take up the challenge? Why learn to write programs for the BASIC Stamp microcontroller? The answer is simple, if not obvious: microcontrollers are everywhere. They're in our television sets, our microwave ovens and our sprinkler controllers – even our cars. The fact is that most new cars today have ten or more microcontrollers managing everything from the engine, the interior climate, wheel spin (traction control), the braking system (anti-lock braking) and many other functions. In short, today's cars are safer and more comfortable due, in large part, to the use of microcontrollers.

With microcontrollers we can build "smart" circuits and devices. In the past, we would have to change wiring or components in a circuit to modify or create a new behavior. The advantage of using a microcontroller over other approaches is that changing its program can modify the behavior of our circuit or device. The advantage of using the BASIC Stamp is that writing and modifying a program is very easy and the StampWorks kit will show you just how easy it can be.

Have fun with these projects and think about how you could apply the concepts while building each one. I appreciate your feedback anytime by e-mail to jwilliams@parallaxinc.com.

Jon Williams

StampWorks   Introduction

Getting the Most from Your StampWorks Lab

This book is divided into two major sections: the StampWorks experiments and the BASIC Stamp II manual. Throughout the use of this course, you will be moving between the two sections frequently as you work with the experiments. Additional reference materials are available from download on the StampWorks page at www.parallaxinc.com, including datasheets, updates and technical details released after this publication.

Three Steps to Success with StampWorks:

1. Read Section 1 of the BASIC Stamp II manual. This section will introduce you to the BASIC Stamp II and guide you through the installation of the programming software. Another helpful resource is <u>Robotics</u> chapter 1 from www.stampsinclass.com.

2. Read "Prepare your StampWorks Lab for Experiments," the next section of this manual. This section walks you through the simple steps of preparing the experiment board for the projects that follow.

3. Work your way through the experiments, referring to the BASIC Stamp Manual syntax guide as needed. This is the fun part – working with the Stamp by building simple circuits and writing code.

By the time you've worked your way through all the experiments you'll be ready to develop your own Stamp projects, from the very simple to the moderately complex. The key here is to make sure you understand everything about a particular experiment before moving on to the next.

One last reminder: Have fun!

StampWorks **Preparing Your StampWorks Lab**

Before moving into the experiments, you need to take inventory of your kit and prepare your StampWorks lab. Once this is done, you'll be able to build a wide variety of Stamp-controlled circuits with it.

The StampWorks kit includes the following items from Parallax:

Stock Code#	Description	Quantity
28135	NX-1000 board and 2x16 LCD	1
750-00007	12V 1A wall pack power supply	1
BS2-IC	BASIC Stamp II module	1
800-00003	Serial programming cable	1
27220	StampWorks Manual	1
27000	Parallax CD-ROM	1
150-01020	1K ohm resistor, ¼ watt, 5%	4
150-01030	10K ohm resistor, ¼ watt, 5%	8
150-02210	220 ohm resistor, ¼ watt, 5%	3
150-04720	470 ohm resistor, ¼ watt, 5%	1
150-04720	4.7 k resistor, ¼ watt, 5%	2
200-01040	0.1 uF capacitor	4
201-01061	10 uF capacitor	1
201-03080	3300 uF capacitor	1
251-03230	32.768 kHz crystal	1
350-00009	Photoresistor	2
602-00009	74HC595	2
602-00010	74HC165	2
602-00015	LM358 dual op-amp	1
603-00001	MAX2719 LED display driver	1
604-00002	DS1620 digital thermometer	1
604-00005	DS1302 timekeeping chip	1
604-00009	555 timer	1
604-00020	24LC32 4K EEPROM	1
ADC0831	ADC0831 8-bit A/D converter	1
900-00001	Piezo Speaker	1
900-00005	Parallax standard servo	1
27964	12 VDC / 75 ohm stepper motor	1
451-00301	3-pin single row header	1
700-00050	22 gauge wire roll – red	1
700-00051	22 gauge wire roll – white	1
700-00052	22 gauge wire roll – black	1
28162	Digital multimeter	1
700-00065	6-piece tool set	1
700-00066	Wire cutter/stripper	1

To setup the StampWorks for experiments that follow, you'll need these items:

- BASIC Stamp II module
- StampWorks (INEX-1000) lab board
- 12-volt wall transformer
- Programming cable
- Red and black hookup wire
- Wire cutter/strippers

Start by removing the BASIC Stamp II module from its protective foam and carefully inserting it into the StampWorks socket. You'll notice that the BASIC Stamp II module and the StampWorks lab board socket are marked with semi-circle alignment guides. The BASIC Stamp II module should be inserted into the socket so that the alignment guides match.

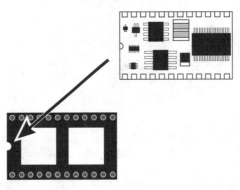

Use the programming cable to connect the StampWorks lab board to your PC. It is best to select a serial (com) port that is not already in use. If, however, you're forced to unplug another device, for example, a PDA or electronic organizer from your computer, make sure that you also disable its communication software before attempting to program your BASIC Stamp. If you haven't installed the Stamp programming software, refer to Section 1 of the Stamp II programming manual for instructions.

Ensure that the StampWorks lab board power switch is set to OFF. Connect the 2.1 mm power plug to the DC INPUT jack. Plug the 12-volt wall transformer into a suitable (120 VAC) outlet.

On the center portion of the breadboard is a solderless breadboard where you will build circuits that are not integral to the StampWorks lab board itself (a variety of parts are included in the StampWorks kit). It's important to understand how this breadboard works. With a little bit of preparation, it will be even easier to use with the experiments that follow.

The innermost portion of the breadboard is where we will connect our components. This section of the breadboard consists of several columns of sockets (there are numbers printed along the top for reference). For each column there are two sets of rows. The rows are labeled A through E and F through J, respectively. For any column, sockets A through E are electrically connected. The same holds true for rows F through J.

Above and below the main section of breadboard are two horizontal rows of sockets, each divided in the middle. These horizontal rows (often called "rails" or "buses") will be used to carry +5 volts (Vdd) and Ground (Vss). Our preparation of the breadboard involves connecting the rails so that they run from end-to-end, connecting the top and bottom rails together and, finally, connecting the rails to Vdd and Vss. Here's what the breadboard looks like on the outside:

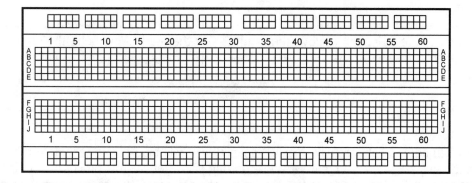

If we X-Rayed the breadboard, we would see the internal connections and the breaks in the Vdd and Vss rails that need to be connected. Here's a view of the breadboard's internal connections:

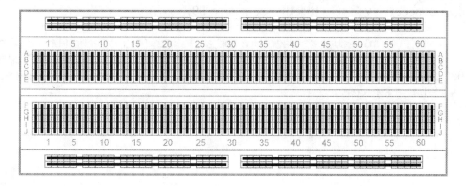

Start by setting your wire stripper for 22 (0.34 mm^2) gauge. Take the spool of black wire and strip a ¼-inch (6 mm) length of insulation from the end of the wire. With your needle-nose pliers, carefully bend the bare wire 90 degrees so that it looks like this:

0.25 inch
(6 mm)

Now push the bare wire into the topmost (ground) rail, into the socket that is just above breadboard column 29 (this socket is just left of the middle of the breadboard, near the top). Hold the wire so that it extends to the right. Mark the insulation by lightly pinching it with the diagonal cutters at the socket above column 32. Be careful not to cut the wire.

Remove the wire from the breadboard and cut it about ¼-inch (6 mm) beyond the mark you just made. With your wire strippers, remove the insulation at the mark. Now bend the second bare end 90 degrees so that the wire forms a squared "U" shape with the insulation in the middle.

If you've measured and cut carefully, this "U" shaped wire will plug comfortably into the ground rail at sockets 29 and 32. This will create a single ground rail. Repeat this process with black wire for the bottom-most rail. Then, connect the two rails together using the same process at column 60 (right-most sockets on each rail).

With the red wire, connect the top and bottom inside rail halves together. These rails will carry +5 volts, or Vdd. Connect the Vdd rails together at column 59.

Now take a 1½-inch (4 cm) section of black wire and a 1½-inch (4 cm) section of red wire and strip ¼-inch (6 mm) insulation from the ends of both. Bend each wire into a rounded "U" shape. These wires are not designed to lie flat like the other connections, making them easy to remove from the StampWorks lab board if necessary.

Carefully plug one end of the red wire into any of the terminals sockets of the +5V block (near the RESET switch) and the other end into the Vdd (+5) rail at column 1. Then, plug one end of the black wire into any of the sockets of the GND block and other end into the ground rail at column 19. BE VERY CAREFUL with these last two connections. If the Vdd and Vss rails get connected together, damage will occur when power is applied to the StampWorks lab board. When completed, your StampWorks breadboard will look like this:

Move the StampWorks lab board power switch to ON. The green ON LED (green) should illuminate. If it doesn't, make sure that wall transformer is plugged into a live socket and that there are no wiring errors with your setup.

Start the BASIC Stamp II software editor and enter the following lines of code:

```
' {$STAMP BS2}
DEBUG "The StampWorks lab is ready!"
```

Now run the program. If all went well, the program will be downloaded to the Stamp and a DEBUG window will appear on screen.

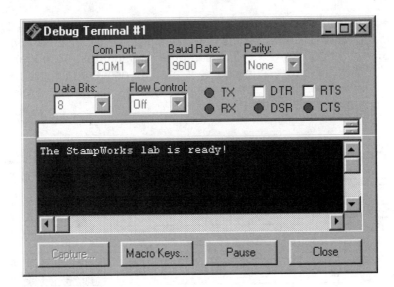

If an error occurs, check the following items:

- Is the BASIC Stamp II plugged into the NX-1000 board correctly?
- Is the StampWorks lab board power switch set to ON? Is the green ON LED lit?
- Is the programming cable connected between the PC and the StampWorks lab board?
- Have you (manually) selected the wrong PC com port?
- Is the PC com port being used by another program?

When the DEBUG window appears and tells you that the StampWorks lab is ready, it's time to talk about Stamp programming.

Connecting a Chip

There are two ways to draw a schematic. One way is considered "chip-centric" in which I/O pins appear on the chip according to their physical location. StampWorks has drawn schematics for efficiency, meaning that I/O pins are placed to make the schematic legible. I/O pins on all chips are counted according to their indicator, starting with Pin 1 and counting in a counter-clockwise direction.

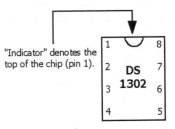

"Indicator" denotes the top of the chip (pin 1).

StampWorks **Programming Essentials**

Contents of a Working Program

In Section 1 of the BASIC Stamp II manual you were introduced to the BASIC Stamp, its architecture and the concepts of variables and constants. In this section, we'll introduce the various elements of a program: linear code, branching, loops and subroutines.

The examples in this discussion use *pseudo-code* to demonstrate and describe program structure. *Italics* are used to indicate the sections of pseudo-code that require replacement with valid programming statements in order to allow the example to compile and run correctly. You need not enter any of the examples here as all of these concepts will be used in the experiments that follow.

People often think of computers and microcontrollers as "smart" devices and yet, they will do nothing without a specific set of instructions. This set of instructions is called a program. It is our job to write the program. Stamp programs are written in a programming language called PBASIC, a Parallax-specific version of the BASIC (Beginners All-purpose Symbolic Instruction Code) programming language. BASIC is very popular because of its simplicity and English-like syntax.

A working program can be as simple as a list of statements. Like this:

```
statement 1
statement 2
statement 3
END
```

This is a very simple, yet valid program structure. What you'll find, however, is that most programs do not run in a straight, linear fashion like the listing above. Program flow is often redirected with branching, looping and subroutines, with short linear sections in between. The requirements for program flow are determined by the goal of the program and the conditions under which the program is running.

Branching – Redirecting the Flow of a Program

A branching command is one that causes the flow of the program to change from its linear path. In other words, when the program encounters a branching command, it will, in almost all cases, not be running the next [linear] line of code. The program will usually go somewhere else. There are two categories of branching commands: *unconditional* and *conditional*. PBASIC has two commands, GOTO and GOSUB that cause unconditional branching.

Here's an example of an unconditional branch using GOTO:

```
Label:
  statement 1
  statement 2
  statement 3
  GOTO Label
```

We call this an *unconditional* branch because it always happens. GOTO redirects the program to another location. The location is specified as part of the GOTO command and is called an address. Remember that addresses start a line of code and are followed by a colon (:). You'll frequently see GOTO at the end of the main body of code, forcing the program statements to run again.

Conditional branching will cause the program flow to change under a specific set of circumstances. The simplest conditional branching is done with IF-THEN construct. The PBASIC IF-THEN construct is different from other flavors of BASIC. In PBASIC, THEN is always followed by a valid program address (other BASICs allow a variety of programming statements to follow THEN). If the condition statement evaluates as TRUE, the program will branch to the address specified. Otherwise, it will continue with the next line of code.

Take a look at this listing:

```
Start:
  statement 1
  statement 2
  statement 3
  IF (condition) THEN Start
```

The statements will be run and then the condition is tested. If it evaluates as TRUE, the program will branch back to the line called Start. If the condition evaluates as FALSE, the program will continue at the line that follows the IF-THEN construct.

As your requirements become more sophisticated, you'll find that you'll want your program to branch to any number of locations based on a condition. One approach is to use multiple IF-THEN constructs.

```
IF (condition_0) THEN Label_0
IF (condition_1) THEN Label_1
IF (condition_2) THEN Label_2
```

This approach is valid and does get used. Thankfully, PBASIC has a special command, BRANCH, that allows a program to jump to any number of addresses based on the value of a variable. This is very handy because the conditions we've referred to in the text are often checking the value of a control variable. BRANCH is a little more complicated in its setup, but very powerful in that it can replace multiple IF-THEN statements. BRANCH requires a control variable and a list of addresses

In the case of a single control variable, the previous listing can be replaced with one line of code:

```
BRANCH controlVar, [Label_0, Label_1, Label_2]
```

When controlVar is zero, the program will branch to Label_0, when controlVar is one the program will branch to Label_1 and so on.

Looping – Running Code Again and Again

Looping causes sections of the program to be repeated. Looping often uses unconditional and conditional branching to create the various looping structures. Here's an example of *unconditional looping*:

```
Label:
  statement 1
  statement 2
  statement 3
  GOTO Label
```

By using GOTO the statements are unconditionally repeated, or looped. By using IF-THEN, we can add a conditional statement to the loop. The next few examples are called *conditional looping*. The loops will run under specific conditions. Conditional programming is what gives microcontrollers their "smarts."

```
Label:
  statement 1
  statement 2
  statement 3
  IF (condition) THEN Label
```

With this loop structure, statements will be run so long as the condition evaluates as TRUE. When the condition is evaluated as FALSE, the program will continue at the line following the IF-THEN statement. It's important to note that in the previous listing the statements will always run at least once, even if the condition is FALSE.

To prevent this from taking place, you need to test the condition before running the statements. The code can be written as follows so that the statements (1 – 3) will only run when the condition is TRUE. When the condition evaluates as FALSE, the program continues at Label_2.

```
Label_1:
  IF NOT (condition) THEN Label_2
  statement 1
  statement 2
  statement 3
  GOTO Label_1

Label_2:
  statement 4
```

The final example of conditional looping is the programmed loop using the FOR-NEXT construct.

```
FOR controlVar = startVal TO endVal STEP stepSize
  statement 1
  statement 2
  statement 3
NEXT
```

The FOR-NEXT construct is used to cause a section of code to execute (loop) a specific number of times. FOR-NEXT uses a control variable to determine the number of loops. The size of the variable will determine the upper limit of loop iterations. For example, the upper limit when using a byte-sized control variable would be 255.

The STEP option of FOR-NEXT is used when the loop needs to count increments other than one. If, for example, the loop needed to count even numbers, the code would look something like this:

```
FOR controlVar = 2 TO 20 STEP 2
   statement 1
   statement 2
   statement 3
NEXT
```

Subroutines – Reusable Code that Saves Program Space

The final programming concept we'll discuss is the subroutine. A subroutine is a section of code that can be called (run) from anywhere in the program. GOSUB is used to redirect the program to the subroutine code. The subroutine is terminated with the RETURN command. RETURN causes the program to jump back to the line of code that follows the calling GOSUB command.

```
Start:
   GOSUB MySub
   PAUSE 1000
   GOTO Start

MySub:
   statement 1
   statement 2
   statement 3
   RETURN
```

In this example, the code in the MySub is executed and then the program jumps back to the line PAUSE 1000.

The Elements of PBASIC Style

Like most versions of the BASIC programming language, PBASIC is very forgiving and the compiler enforces no particular formatting style. So long as the source code is syntactically correct, it will compile and download to the Stamp without trouble.

Why, then, would one suggest a specific style for PBASIC? Consider this: Over two million BASIC Stamps have been sold and there are nearly 2500 members of the BASIC Stamp mailing list (on Yahoo! Groups). This makes it highly likely that you'll be sharing your PBASIC code with someone, if not co-developing a BASIC Stamp-oriented project. Writing code in an organized, predictable manner will save you – and your potential colleagues – time; in analysis, in troubleshooting and especially when you return to a project after a long break.

The style guidelines presented here are just that: guidelines. They have been developed from style guidelines used by professional programmers using other high-level languages such as Java™, C/C++ and Visual Basic®. Use these guidelines as is, or modify them to suit your needs. The key is selecting a style the works well for you or your organization and sticking to it.

1. Do It Right The First Time

Many programmers, especially new ones, fall into the "I'll slug it out now and fix it later." trap. Invariably, the "fix it later" part never seems to happen and sloppy code makes its way into production projects. If you don't have time to do it right, when will you have time to do it again?

Start clean and you'll be less likely to introduce errors in your code. And if errors do pop up, clean formatting will make them easier to find and fix.

2. Be Organized and Consistent

Using a blank program template will help you organize your programs and establish a consistent presentation.

3. Use Meaningful Names

Be verbose when naming constants, variables and program labels. The compiler will allow names up to 32 characters long. Using meaningful names will reduce the number of comments and make your programs easier to read, debug and maintain.

4. Naming Constants

Begin constant names with an uppercase letter and use mixed case, using uppercase letters at the beginning of new words within the name:

```
AlarmCode       CON     25
```

5. Naming Variables

Begin variable names with a lowercase letter and use mixed case, using uppercase letters at the beginning of new words within the name. Avoid the use of internal variable names (such as B0 or W1):

```
waterLevel      VAR     Word
```

6. Naming Program Labels

Begin program labels with an uppercase letter, used mixed case, separate words within the label with an underscore character and begin new words with an uppercase letter. Labels should be preceded by at least one blank line, begin in column 1 and be terminated with a colon (except after GOTO and THEN where they appear at the end of the line and without a colon):

```
Print_String:
  READ eeAddr, char
  IF (char = 0) THEN Print_String_Exit
  DEBUG char
  eeAddr = eeAddr + 1
  GOTO Print_String

Print_String_Exit:
  RETURN
```

7. PBASIC Keywords

All PBASIC language keywords, including VAR, CON and serial/debugging format modifiers (DEC, HEX, BIN) should be uppercase:

```
Main:
  DEBUG "BASIC Stamp", CR
  END
```

8. Variable Types

Variable types should be be in mixed case and start with an uppercase letter:

```
status          VAR    Bit
counter         VAR    Nib
ovenTemp        VAR    Byte
rcValue         VAR    Word
```

9. Indent Nested Code

Nesting blocks of code improves readability and helps reduce the introduction of errors. Indenting each level with two spaces is recommended to make the code readable without taking up too much space:

```
Main:
..FOR outerLoop = 1 TO 10
....FOR innerLoop = 1 TO 10
......DEBUG DEC outerLoop, TAB, DEC innerLoop, TAB
......DEBUG DEC (outerLoop * innerLoop)
......PAUSE 100
....NEXT
..NEXT
```

Note: The dots are used to illustrate the level of nesting and are not a part of the code.

10. Be Generous With Whitespace

Whitespace (spaces and blank lines) has no effect compiler or BASIC Stamp performance, so be generous with it to make listings easier to read. As suggested in #6 above, allow at lease one blank line before program labels (two blanks lines before a subroutine label is recommended). Separate items in a parameter list with a space:

```
Main:
  BRANCH task, [Update_Motors, Scan_IR, Close_Gripper]
  GOTO Main

Update_Motors:
  PULSOUT leftMotor, leftSpeed
  PULSOUT rightMotor, rightSpeed
  PAUSE 20
  Task = (task + 1) // NumTasks
  GOTO Main
```

An exception to this guideline is with the bits parameter used with SHIFTIN and SHIFTOUT. In this case, format without spaces:

```
  SHIFTIN A2Ddata, A2Dclock, MSBPost, [result\9]
```

11. IF-THEN Conditions

Enclose IF-THEN condition statements in parenthesis:

```
Check_Temp:
  IF (indoorTemp >= setPoint) THEN AC_On
```

The StampWorks files (available for download fromwww.parallaxinc.com) include a blank programming tempalate (Blank.BS2) that will help you get started writing organized code. It's up to you to follow the rest of the guidelines above – or develop and use guidelines of your own.

StampWorks Time to Experiment

Learn the Programming Concepts

What follows is a series of programming experiments that you can build and run with your StampWorks lab. The purpose of these experiments is to teach programming concepts and the use of external components with the BASIC Stamp. The experiments are focused and designed so that as you gain experience, you can combine the individual concepts to produce sophisticated programs.

Building the Projects

This section of the manual is simple but important because you will learn important programming lessons and construction techniques using your StampWorks lab. As you move through the rest of the manual, construction details will not be included (you'll be experienced by then and can make your own choices) and the discussion of the program will be less verbose, focusing specifically on special techniques or external devices connected to the BASIC Stamp.

What to do Between Projects

The circuit from one project may not be electrically compatible with another and could, in some cases, cause damage to the BASIC Stamp if the old program is run with the new circuit. For this reason, a blank program should be downloaded to the Stamp before connecting the new circuit. This will protect the Stamp by resetting the I/O lines to inputs. Here's a simple, two-line program that will clear and reset the Stamp.

```
' {$STAMP BS2}
DEBUG "Stamp clear."
```

For convenience, save this program to a file called CLEAR.BS2.

StampWorks   Experiment #1:
Flash An LED

The purpose of this experiment is to flash an LED with the BASIC Stamp. Flashing LEDs are often used as alarm indicators.

New PBASIC Elements/Commands:

- CON
- HIGH
- LOW
- PAUSE
- GOTO

Building The Circuit

All StampWorks experiments use a dashed line to show parts that are already on the NX-1000 board. The LED is available on the "LED MONITOR 16 CHANNELS" part of the board.

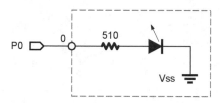

Since the StampWorks lab board has the LEDs built in, all you have to do is connect one to the BASIC Stamp.

1. Start with a six-inch (15 cm) white wire. Strip ¼-inch (6 mm) of insulation from each end.
2. Plug one end into BASIC Stamp Port 0.
3. Plug the other end into LED Monitor Channel 0

```
' =============================================================================
'
'   File...... Ex01 - Blink.BS2
'   Purpose... LED Blinker
'   Author.... Parallax
'   E-mail.... stamptech@parallaxinc.com
'   Started...
'   Updated... 01 MAY 2002
'
'   {$STAMP BS2}
'
' =============================================================================


' ---------------------------------------------------------------------------
' Program Description
' ---------------------------------------------------------------------------

' Blinks an LED connected to P0


' ---------------------------------------------------------------------------
' I/O Definitions
' ---------------------------------------------------------------------------

LEDpin          CON     0                       ' LED connected to Pin 0


' ---------------------------------------------------------------------------
' Constants
' ---------------------------------------------------------------------------

DelayTime       CON     500                     ' delay time in milliseconds


' ---------------------------------------------------------------------------
' Program Code
' ---------------------------------------------------------------------------

Main:
  HIGH LEDpin                                   ' turn LED on
  PAUSE DelayTime                               ' pause for a bit
  LOW LEDpin                                    ' turn LED off
  PAUSE DelayTime                               ' pause while off
  GOTO Main                                     ' do it again

  END
```

Behind The Scenes

Each of the Stamp's I/O pins has three bits associated with its control. A bit in the `Dirs` word determines whether the pin is an input (bit = 0) or an output (bit = 1). If the pin is configured as an output, the current state of the pin is stored in the associated bit in the `Outs` word. If the pin is configured as an input, the current pin value is taken from the associated bit in the `Ins` word.

`HIGH` and `LOW` actually perform two functions with one command: the selected pin is configured as an output and the value is set in the `Outs` word (1 for `HIGH`, 0 for `LOW`).

For example, this line of code:

```
HIGH 0
```

performs the same function as:

```
Dir0 = 1                                    ' make Pin 0 an output
Out0 = 1                                    ' set Pin 0 high
```

StampWorks

Experiment #2:
Flash An LED (Version 2)

The purpose of this experiment is to flash an LED with the BASIC Stamp. The method in this experiment adds flexibility to the LED control.

New PBASIC elements/commands to know:

- VAR
- Out0 – Out15
- Dir0 – Dir15
- Byte
- Bit0 – Bit15

Building The Circuit.

Use the same circuit as in Experiment #1.

```
' ==========================================================================
'
'   File...... Ex02 - Blink2.BS2
'   Purpose... LED Blinker - Version 2
'   Author.... Parallax
'   E-mail.... stamptech@parallaxinc.com
'   Started...
'   Updated... 01 MAY 2002
'
'   {$STAMP BS2}
'
' ==========================================================================


' --------------------------------------------------------------------------
' Program Description
' --------------------------------------------------------------------------

' Blinks an LED connected to Pin 0.  LED on-time and off-time can be set
' independently of each other.
```

```
' --------------------------------------------------------------------
' I/O Definitions
' --------------------------------------------------------------------

MyLED            VAR     Out0                ' LED connected to Pin 0


' --------------------------------------------------------------------
' Constants
' --------------------------------------------------------------------

DelayOn          CON     1000                ' on-time time in milliseconds
DelayOff         CON     250                 ' off-time in milliseconds

On               CON     1
Off              CON     0


' --------------------------------------------------------------------
' Initialization
' --------------------------------------------------------------------

Initialize:
  Dir0 = %1                                  ' make LED pin an output


' --------------------------------------------------------------------
' Program Code
' --------------------------------------------------------------------

Main:
  MyLED = On
  PAUSE DelayOn                              ' pause for "on" time
  MyLED = Off
  PAUSE DelayOff                             ' pause for "off" time
  GOTO Main                                  ' do it again

  END
```

Can you explain what's going on?

Since MyLED is a bit-sized variable, Bit0 of cntr will control it. It works like this: When cntr is odd (1, 3, 5, etc.), Bit0 will be set (1), causing the LED to light. When cntr is an even number, Bit0 will be clear (0), causing the LED to be off.

Experiment #3:
Display a Counter with LEDs

The purpose of this experiment is to display a byte-sized value with LEDs. Multiple LEDs are frequently used as complex status or value indicators.

New PBASIC elements/commands to know:

- OutL, OutH
- DirL, DirH
- FOR-NEXT

Building The Circuit.

These LEDs are denoted by the "LED MONITOR 16 CHANNELS" notation on the NX-1000 board.

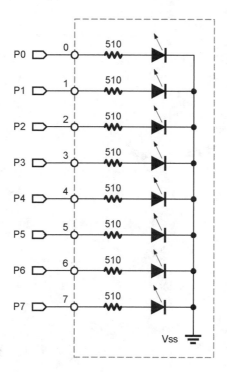

Since the StampWorks lab board has the LEDs built in, all you have to do is connect one to the BASIC Stamp.

1. Start with eight, six-inch (15 cm) white wires. Strip ¼-inch (6 mm) of insulation from the ends of each.
2. Plug one end of a wire into BASIC Stamp Port 0.
3. Plug the other end into LED Monitor Channel 0.
4. Repeat Steps 2 and 3 for LED Monitor Channels 1-7 (Stamp pins 1– 7) using more wire.

```
' ===============================================================================
'
'   File...... Ex03 - LED Counter.BS2
'   Purpose... Binary Counter
'   Author.... Parallax
'   E-mail.... stamptech@parallaxinc.com
'   Started...
'   Updated... 01 MAY 2002
'
'   {$STAMP BS2}
'
' ===============================================================================


' -------------------------------------------------------------------------------
' Program Description
' -------------------------------------------------------------------------------

' Displays a binary counter on Pins 0 - 7


' -------------------------------------------------------------------------------
' I/O Definitions
' -------------------------------------------------------------------------------

LEDs            VAR     OutL                    ' LEDs on Pins 0 - 7


' -------------------------------------------------------------------------------
' Constants
' -------------------------------------------------------------------------------

MinCount        CON     0                       ' counter start value
MaxCount        CON     255                     ' counter end value
DelayTime       CON     100                     ' delay time in milliseconds
```

```
' -------------------------------------------------------------------
' Variables
' -------------------------------------------------------------------

counter          VAR      Byte


' -------------------------------------------------------------------
' Initialization
' -------------------------------------------------------------------

Initialize:
  DirL = %11111111                          ' make pins 0 - 7 outputs


' -------------------------------------------------------------------
' Program Code
' -------------------------------------------------------------------

Main:
  FOR counter = MinCount TO MaxCount        ' loop through all count values
    LEDs = counter                          ' show count on LEDs
    PAUSE DelayTime                         ' pause before next number
  NEXT
  GOTO Main                                 ' do it again

  END
```

Behind The Scenes

As explained in Experiment #1, the state of the BASIC Stamp's output pins are stored in a memory area called outs (OutL is the lower byte of the outs word). Since OutL is part of the BASIC Stamp's general-purpose (RAM) memory, values can be written to and read from it. In this case, copying the value of our counter to outL (alias for LEDs) causes the value of the counter to be displayed on the StampWorks LEDs.

Challenge

Modify the program to count backward.

Experiment #4:
Science Fiction LED Display

The purpose of this experiment is to "ping-pong" across eight LEDs to create a Sci-Fi type display. Circuits like this often are used in film and television props.

New PBASIC elements/commands to know:

- << (Shift Left operator)
- >> (Shift Right operator)
- IF-THEN

Building The Circuit

Use the same circuit as in Experiment #3.

```
' ==========================================================================
'
'   File...... Ex04 - Ping Pong.BS2
'   Purpose... Ping-Pong LED Display
'   Author.... Parallax
'   E-mail.... stamptech@parallaxinc.com
'   Started...
'   Updated... 01 MAY 2002
'
'   {$STAMP BS2}
'
' ==========================================================================


' --------------------------------------------------------------------------
' Program Description
' --------------------------------------------------------------------------


' "Ping-Pongs" an LED (one of eight).


' --------------------------------------------------------------------------
' I/O Definitions
' --------------------------------------------------------------------------

LEDs            VAR     OutL                    ' LEDs on Pins 0 - 7
```

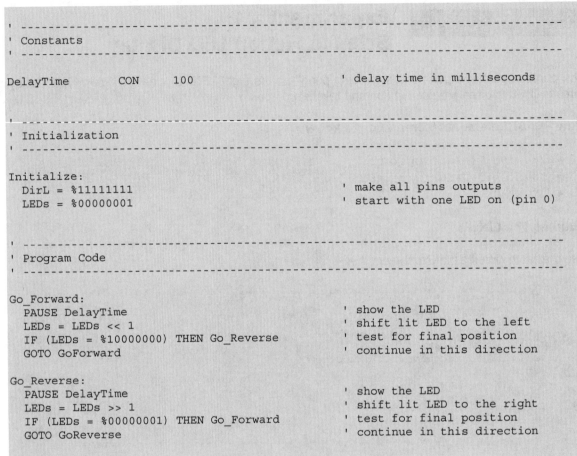

```
' ----------------------------------------------------------------
' Constants
' ----------------------------------------------------------------

DelayTime       CON     100                 ' delay time in milliseconds


' ----------------------------------------------------------------
' Initialization
' ----------------------------------------------------------------

Initialize:
  DirL = %11111111                          ' make all pins outputs
  LEDs = %00000001                          ' start with one LED on (pin 0)


' ----------------------------------------------------------------
' Program Code
' ----------------------------------------------------------------

Go_Forward:
  PAUSE DelayTime                           ' show the LED
  LEDs = LEDs << 1                          ' shift lit LED to the left
  IF (LEDs = %10000000) THEN Go_Reverse     ' test for final position
  GOTO GoForward                            ' continue in this direction

Go_Reverse:
  PAUSE DelayTime                           ' show the LED
  LEDs = LEDs >> 1                          ' shift lit LED to the right
  IF (LEDs = %00000001) THEN Go_Forward     ' test for final position
  GOTO GoReverse                            ' continue in this direction

  END
```

Behind The Scenes

This project demonstrates the ability to directly manipulate the BASIC Stamp's outputs. The program initializes the LEDs to %00000001 (LED 0 is on) then uses the shift-left operator (<<) to move the lit LED one position to the left. With binary numbers, shifting left by one is the same as multiplying by two. Shifting right by one (>>) is the same as dividing by two.

Both major sections of the code use IF-THEN to test for the limits of the display, causing the program to branch to the other section when a limit is reached.

Experiment #5: LED Graph (Dot or Bar)

The purpose of this experiment is to create a configurable (dot or bar) LED graph. This type of graph is very common on audio equipment, specifically for VU (volume) meters. The value for the graph in the experiment will be taken from the position of a potentiometer.

New PBASIC elements/commands to know:

- Word
- RCTIME
- */ (Star-Slash operator)
- GOSUB-RETURN
- DCD

Building The Circuit

Add this circuit to Experiment #4.

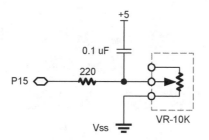

1. Using red wire (cut as required), connect the Vdd (+5) rail to socket A15.
2. Plug a 0.1 uF (104K) capacitor into sockets B14 and B15.
3. Plug a 220-ohm (RED-RED-BROWN) resistor into sockets C10 and C14.
4. Using white wire, connect socket A10 to BASIC Stamp Port 15.
5. Using white wire, connect socket E14 to the wiper of the 10K potentiometer
6. Using black wire, connect the Vss (ground) rail to the bottom terminal of the 10K potentiometer.

```
' ==============================================================================
'
'   File...... Ex05 - LED Graph.BS2
'   Purpose... LED Bar Graph
'   Author.... Parallax
'   E-mail.... stamptech@parallaxinc.com
'   Started...
'   Updated...
'
'   {$STAMP BS2}
'
' ==============================================================================


' ------------------------------------------------------------------------------
' Program Description
' ------------------------------------------------------------------------------

' Displays a linear (bar) or dot graph using 8 LEDs


' ------------------------------------------------------------------------------
' I/O Definitions
' ------------------------------------------------------------------------------

LEDs            VAR     OutL                    ' LED outputs
PotPin          CON     15                      ' pot wiper connects to pin 15


' ------------------------------------------------------------------------------
' Constants
' ------------------------------------------------------------------------------

DotGraf         CON     0                       ' define graph types
BarGraf         CON     1
GraphMode       CON     BarGraf                 ' define current graph mode
```

```
On              CON     1
Off             CON     0

Scale           CON     $005F                   ' scale value to make 0 .. 255

' Scale         CON     $0028                   ' scale for BS2sx
' Scale         CON     $0027                   ' sclae for BS2p


' -----------------------------------------------------------------------
' Variables
' -----------------------------------------------------------------------

rawValue        VAR     Word                    ' raw value from pot
grafValue       VAR     Byte                    ' graph value
bits            VAR     Byte                    ' highest lighted bit
newBar          VAR     Byte                    ' workspace for bar graph


' -----------------------------------------------------------------------
' Initialization
' -----------------------------------------------------------------------

Initialize:
  DirL = %11111111                              ' make low pints outputs


' -----------------------------------------------------------------------
' Program Code
' -----------------------------------------------------------------------

Main:
  HIGH PotPin                                   ' discharge cap
  PAUSE 1                                       '   for 1 millisecond
  RCTIME PotPin, 1, rawValue                    ' read the Pot

  grafValue = rawValue */ Scale                 ' scale grafVal (0 - 255)

  GOSUB Show_Graph                              ' show it
  PAUSE 50
  GOTO Main                                     ' do it again

  END


' -----------------------------------------------------------------------
' Subroutines
```

```
'   --------------------------------------------------------------

Show_Graph:
    IF (GraphMode = BarGraf) THEN Show_Bar      ' jump to graph mode code

Show_Dot:
    LEDs = DCD (grafValue / 32)                 ' show dot value
    RETURN

Show_Bar:
    bits = DCD (grafValue / 32)                 ' get highest bit
    newBar = 0

Build_Bar:
    IF (bits = 0) THEN Bar_Done                 ' all bar LEDs lit?
    newBar = newBar << 1                        ' no - shift left
    newBar.Bit0 = On                            ' light low end
    bits = bits >> 1                            ' mark bit lit
    GOTO Build_Bar                              ' continue

Bar_Done:
    LEDs = newBar                               ' output new level
    RETURN
```

Behind The Scenes

After initializing the outputs, this program reads the 10K potentiometer (located on the StampWorks lab board) with RCTIME. Using DEBUG to display the raw value, it was determined that RCTIME returned values between zero (pot fully counter-clockwise) and 685 (pot turned fully clockwise). Since grafVal is a byte-sized variable, rawVal must be scaled down to fit.

To determine the scaling multiplier, divide 255 (largest possible value for grafVal) by 685 (highest value returned in rawVal). The result is 0.372.

Dealing with fractional values within PBASIC's integer math system is made possible with the */ (star-slash) operator. The parameter for */ is a 16-bit (word) variable. The upper eight bits (high byte) are multiplied as a whole value. The lower eight bits (low byte) are multiplied as a fractional value.

To determine the value of the fractional byte, multiply the desired decimal fractional value by 255 and convert to hex.

Example:

 0.372 x 255 = 95 (or $5F)

Since the multiplier in the experiment is 0.372, the */ value is $005F.

The program uses the DCD operator to determine highest lighted bit value from grafVal. With eight LEDs in the graph, grafVal is divided by 32, forcing the result of DCD to output values from %00000001 (DCD 0) to %10000000 (DCD 7).

In Dot mode, this is all that is required and a single LED is lit. In Bar Mode, the lower LEDs must be filled in. This is accomplished by a loop. The control value for the loop is the variable, bits, which also calculated using DCD. In this loop, bits will be tested for zero to exit, so each iteration through the loop will decrement (decrease) this value.

If bits is greater than zero, the bar graph workspace variable, newBar, is shifted left and its bit 0 is set. For example, if DCD returned %1000 in bits, here's how bits and newBar would be affected through the loop:

```
bits   newBar
1000   0001
0100   0011
0010   0111
0001   1111
0000   (done - exit loop and display value)
```

The purpose for the variable, newBar, is to prevent the LEDs from flashing with each update. This allows the program to start with an "empty" graph and build to the current value. With this technique, the program does not have to remember the value of the previous graph.

Experiment #6: A Simple Game

The purpose of this experiment is to create a simple, slot machine type game with the BASIC Stamp.

New PBASIC elements/commands to know:

- RANDOM
- & (And operator)
- FREQOUT
- BUTTON
- LOOKUP

Building The Circuit

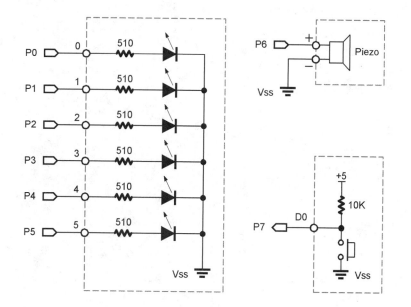

Note: Later versions of the StampWorks lab board come with a built-in audio amplifier. Attach an 8-ohm speaker to the output of the amplifier to get the best sound from this project.

You may wish to substitute the piezo speaker on the StampWorks lab board with the one in the kit, which seems to have a higher volume.

1. Using white wires, connect BASIC Stamp Ports 0 – 5 to LEDs 0 – 5.
2. Using white wire, connect BASIC Stamp Port 6 to the + side of the Piezo speaker.
3. Using black wire, connect the – side of the Piezo speaker to ground.
4. Using a white wire connect BASIC Stamp Port 7 to Pushbutton D0.

```
' ==============================================================================
'
'   File...... Ex06 - Las Vegas.BS2
'   Purpose... Stamp Game
'   Author.... Parallax
'   E-mail.... stamptech@parallaxinc.com
'   Started...
'   Updated... 01 MAY 2002
'
'   {$STAMP BS2}
'
' ==============================================================================


' ------------------------------------------------------------------------------
' Program Description
' ------------------------------------------------------------------------------

' Stamp-based slot machine game that uses lights and sound.


' ------------------------------------------------------------------------------
' I/O Definitions
' ------------------------------------------------------------------------------

LEDs            VAR     OutL            ' LED outputs
Speaker         CON     6               ' speaker output
PlayBtn         CON     7               ' button input to play game


' ------------------------------------------------------------------------------
' Variables
' ------------------------------------------------------------------------------

randW           VAR     Word            ' random number
pattern         VAR     Byte            ' light pattern
tone            VAR     Word            ' tone output
```

```
swData              VAR     Byte              ' workspace variable for BUTTON
delay               VAR     Word              ' delay while "spinning"
spin1               VAR     Byte              ' loop counter
spin2               VAR     Byte              ' loop counter


' --------------------------------------------------------------------------
' Initialization
' --------------------------------------------------------------------------

Initialize:
  DirL = %00111111                            ' make LEDs outputs


' --------------------------------------------------------------------------
' Program Code
' --------------------------------------------------------------------------

Main:
  GOSUB Get_Random                            ' get a random number and tone
  FREQOUT Speaker,35,tone                     ' sound the tone
  PAUSE 100
  BUTTON PlayBtn, 0, 255, 10, swData, 1, Spin ' check for play
  GOTO Main

Spin:
  LEDs = %00111111                            ' simulate machine reset
  PAUSE 750
  LEDs = %00000000
  PAUSE 500
  delay = 75                                  ' initialize delay

  FOR spin1 = 1 TO 25                         ' spin the wheel
    GOSUB Get_Random                          ' get random number
    FREQOUT Speaker, 25, 425                  ' wheel click
    PAUSE delay                               ' pause between clicks
    delay = delay */ $0119                    ' multiply delay by 1.1
  NEXT

  IF pattern = %00111111 THEN You_Win         ' if all lit, you win
  FREQOUT Speaker, 1000, 150                  ' otherwise, groan...
  LEDs = %00000000                            ' clear LEDs
  PAUSE 1000
  GOTO Main                                   ' do it again

You_Win:                                      ' winning lights/sound display
  FOR spin1 = 1 TO 5
```

```
      FOR spin2 = 0 TO 3
         LOOKUP spin2, [$00, $0C, $12, $21], LEDs
         LOOKUP spin2, [665, 795, 995, 1320], tone
         FREQOUT Speaker, 35, tone
         PAUSE 65
      NEXT
   NEXT

   LEDs = %00000000                            ' clear LEDs
   PAUSE 1000
   GOTO Main                                   ' do it again

   END


' --------------------------------------------------------------
' Subroutines
' --------------------------------------------------------------

Get_Random:
   RANDOM randW                                ' get pseudo-random number
   tone = randW & $7FF                         ' don't let tone go too high
   pattern = randW & %00111111                 ' mask out unused bits
   LEDs = pattern                              ' show the pattern
   RETURN
```

Behind The Scenes

This program demonstrates how to put more randomness into the pseudo-random nature of the RANDOM command. Adding a human element does it.

The program waits in a loop called Attention. The top of this loop calls Get_Random to create a pseudo-random value, a tone for the speaker and to put the new pattern on the LEDs. On returning to Attention, the tone is played and the button is checked for a press. The program will loop through Attention until you press the button.

The BUTTON command is used to debounce the input. Here's what gives the program its randomness: the time variations between button presses. When the button is pressed, the LEDs are lit and cleared to simulate the game resetting. Then, a FOR-NEXT loop is used to simulate the rolling action of a slot machine. For each roll, a "click" sound is generated and the delay between clicks is modified to simulate natural decay (slowing) of the wheel speed.

If all six LEDs are lit after the last spin, the program branches to You_Win. This routine uses LOOKUP to play a preset pattern of LEDs and tones before returning to the top of the program. If any of the LEDs is not lit, a groan will be heard from the speaker and the game will restart.

Challenge

Modify the game so that less than six LEDs have to light to for a win.

Experiment #7:
A Lighting Controller

The purpose of this experiment is to create a small lighting controller, suitable for holiday trees and outdoor decorations. The outputs of this circuit will be LEDs only (To control high-voltage lighting take a look at Matt Gilliland's Microcontroller Application Cookbook).

New PBASIC elements/commands to know:

- DATA
- MIN
- // (Modulus operator)
- BRANCH

Building The Circuit.

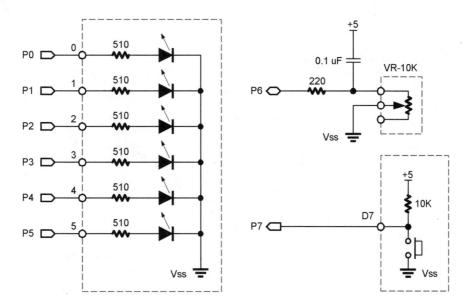

1. Using white wires, connect BASIC Stamp Ports 0–5 to LEDs 0– 5.
2. Using red wire, connect the Vdd (+5) rail to socket A15.
3. Plug a 0.1 uF (104K) capacitor into sockets B14 and B15.
4. Plug a 220-ohm (RED-RED-BROWN) resistor into sockets C10 and C14.
5. Using white wire, connect socket A10 to BASIC Stamp Port 6.
6. Using white wire, connect socket E14 to the top terminal of the 10K potentiometer.
7. Using black wire, connect the Vss (ground) rail to the wiper (middle terminal) of the 10K potentiometer.
8. Using a white wire connect BASIC Stamp Port 7 to Pushbutton D7.

```
' ===============================================================================
'
'   File...... Ex07 - Light Show.BS2
'   Purpose... Simple lighting controller
'   Author.... Parallax
'   E-mail.... stamptech@parallaxinc.com
'   Started...
'   Updated... 01 MAY 2002
'
'   {$STAMP BS2}
'
' ===============================================================================


' -------------------------------------------------------------------------------
' Program Description
' -------------------------------------------------------------------------------

' Mini light show controller with variable speed and multiple patterns.


' -------------------------------------------------------------------------------
' I/O Definitions
' -------------------------------------------------------------------------------

Select          CON     7               ' pattern select input
PotPin          CON     6               ' speed control Pot input
Lights          VAR     OutL            ' light control outputs


' -------------------------------------------------------------------------------
' Constants
' -------------------------------------------------------------------------------

Scale           CON     $018A           ' convert pot input to 0 - 1000
```

```
' Scale          CON     $00A0                       ' scale for BS2sx
' Scale          CON     $009E                       ' scale for BS2p


' -------------------------------------------------------------------------
' Variables
' -------------------------------------------------------------------------

delay           VAR     Word                        ' pause time between patterns
btnVar          VAR     Byte                        ' workspace for BUTTON
mode            VAR     Byte                        ' selected mode
offset          VAR     Byte                        ' offset into light patterns
randW           VAR     Word                        ' workspace for RANDOM


' -------------------------------------------------------------------------
' EEPROM Data
' -------------------------------------------------------------------------

SeqA            DATA    %000001, %000010, %000100, %001000, %010000, %100000
SeqB            DATA    %100000, %010000, %001000, %000100, %000010
                DATA    %000001, %000010, %000100, %001000, %010000
SeqC            DATA    %000000, %001100, %010010, %100001
SeqD            DATA    %100100, %010010, %001001
SeqE            DATA    %0

AMax            CON     SeqB - SeqA                 ' calculate length of sequence
BMax            CON     SeqC - SeqB
CMax            CON     SeqD - SeqC
DMax            CON     SeqE - SeqD


' -------------------------------------------------------------------------
' Initialization
' -------------------------------------------------------------------------

Initialize:
  DirL = %00111111                                  ' LED control lines are outputs


' -------------------------------------------------------------------------
' Program Code
' -------------------------------------------------------------------------

Main:
  HIGH PotPin                                       ' discharge cap
  PAUSE 1
```

```
  RCTIME PotPin, 1, delay                    ' read speed pot
  delay = (delay */ Scale) MIN 50            ' calculate delay (50 ms ~ 1 sec)
  PAUSE delay                                ' wait between patterns

Switch_Check:
  BUTTON Select, 0, 255, 0, btnVar, 0, Show  ' new mode?
  mode = mode + 1 // 5                        ' yes, update mode var

Show:
  BRANCH mode, [ModeA, ModeB, ModeC, ModeD, ModeE]
  GOTO Main


' ---------------------------------------------------------------------------
' Subroutines
' ---------------------------------------------------------------------------

ModeA:
  offset = offset + 1 // AMax                 ' update offset (0 - 5)
  READ (SeqA + offset), Lights               ' output new light pattern
  GOTO Main                                  ' repeat

ModeB:
  offset = offset + 1 // BMax
  READ (SeqB + offset), Lights
  GOTO Main

ModeC:
  offset = offset + 1 // CMax
  READ (SeqC + offset), Lights
  GOTO Main

ModeD:
  offset = offset + 1 // DMax
  READ (SeqD + offset), Lights
  GOTO Main

ModeE:
  RANDOM randW                               ' get random number
  Lights = randW & %00111111                 ' light random channels
  GOTO Main
```

Behind The Scenes

Overall, this program is simpler than it first appears. The main body of the program is a loop. Timing through the main loop is controlled by the position of the potentiometer. RCTIME is used to read the pot and during development the maximum pot reading was found to be 648. Multiplying the maximum pot value by 1.54 (delay */ $018A) scales the maximum value to 1000 for a one-second delay. The MIN operator is used in the delay scaling calculation to ensure the shortest loop-timing delay is 50 milliseconds.

The code at Switch_Check looks to see if button D7 is pressed. If it is, the variable, mode, is incremented (increased by 1). The modulus (//) operator is used to keep mode in the range of zero to four. This works because the modulus operator returns the remainder after a division. Since any number divided by itself will return a remainder of zero, using modulus in this manner causes mode to "wrap-around" from four to zero.

The final element of the main loop is called Show. This code uses BRANCH to call the code that will output the light sequence specified by mode. Modes A through D work similarly, retrieving light sequences from the BASIC Stamp's EEPROM (stored in DATA statements). Mode E outputs a random light pattern.

Take a look at the code section labeled ModeA. The first thing that happens is that the variable, offset, is updated – again using the "wrap-around" technique with the modulus operator. The value of offset is added to the starting position of the specified light sequence and the current light pattern is retrieved with READ. Notice that the DATA statements for each sequence are labeled (SeqA, SeqB, etc.). Internally, each of these labels is converted to a constant value that is equal to the starting address of the sequence. The length of each sequence is calculated with these constants. By using this technique, light patterns can be updated (shortened or lengthened) without having to modify the operational code called by Show. ModeE is very straightforward, using the RANDOM function to output new pattern of lights with each pass through the main loop.

Challenge

Add a new lighting sequence. What sections of the program need to be modified to make this work?

StampWorks **Building Circuits On Your Own**

With the experience you gained in the previous section, you're ready to assemble the following circuits without specific instruction. These projects are fairly simple and you'll find them electrically similar to several of the projects that you've already built.

Proceed slowly and double-check your connections before applying power. You're well on your way to designing your own Stamp-based projects and experiments.

Let's continue with 7-segment displays....

StampWorks Using 7-Segment Displays

A 7-segment display is actually seven (eight counting the decimal point) standard LEDs that have been packaged into a linear shape and arranged as a Figure-8 pattern. The LEDs in the group have a common element (anode or cathode).

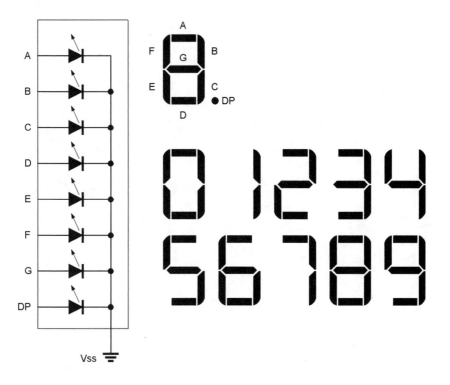

By lighting specific combinations of the LEDs in the package we can create digits and even a few alpha characters (letters and symbols). Seven-segment LEDs are usually used in numeric displays.

The StampWorks lab has four, common-cathode seven-segment displays. The experiments in this section will show you how to get the most from these versatile components.

Experiment #8:
A Single-Digit Counter

The purpose of this experiment is to demonstrate the use of seven-segment LED module by creating a simple decimal counter.

New PBASIC elements/commands to know:

* Nib

Building The Circuit.

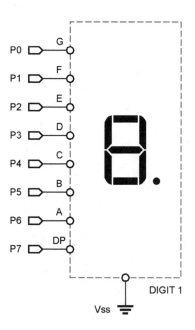

```
' ===============================================================================
'
'   File...... Ex08 - SevenSegs.BS2
'   Purpose... 7-Segment Display
'   Author.... Parallax
'   E-mail.... stamptech@parallaxinc.com
'   Started...
'   Updated... 01 MAY 2002
'
'   {$STAMP BS2}
'
' ===============================================================================


' -------------------------------------------------------------------------------
' Program Description
' -------------------------------------------------------------------------------

' Displays digits on a 7-segment display.


' -------------------------------------------------------------------------------
' I/O Definitions
' -------------------------------------------------------------------------------

Segs            VAR     OutL                    ' 7-segment LEDs


' -------------------------------------------------------------------------------
' Constants
' -------------------------------------------------------------------------------

Blank           CON     %00000000               ' clears the display


' -------------------------------------------------------------------------------
' Variables
' -------------------------------------------------------------------------------

counter         VAR     Nib


' -------------------------------------------------------------------------------
' EEPROM Data
' -------------------------------------------------------------------------------
```

```
' Segments               .abcdefg
'                        --------
DecDig        DATA    %01111110              ' 0
              DATA    %00110000              ' 1
              DATA    %01101101              ' 2
              DATA    %01111001              ' 3
              DATA    %00110011              ' 4
              DATA    %01011011              ' 5
              DATA    %01011111              ' 6
              DATA    %01110000              ' 7
              DATA    %01111111              ' 8
              DATA    %01111011              ' 9


' --------------------------------------------------------------------
' Initialization
' --------------------------------------------------------------------

Initialize:
  DirL = %11111111                           ' make segments outputs


' --------------------------------------------------------------------
' Program Code
' --------------------------------------------------------------------

Main:
  FOR counter = 0 TO 9                       ' count
    READ (DecDig + counter), Segs            ' put 7-seg pattern on digit
    PAUSE 1000                               ' show for about one second
  NEXT
  GOTO Main                                  ' do it all again

  END
```

Behind The Scenes

This program is very similar to the light show program: a pattern is read from the EEPROM and output to the LEDs. In this program, sending specific patterns to the seven-segment LED creates the digits zero through nine.

Challenge

Update the program to create a single-digit HEX counter. Use the patterns below for the HEX digits.

StampWorks Experiment #9: A Digital Die

The purpose of this experiment is create a digital die (one half of a pair of dice).

Building The Circuit.

Add this pushbutton to the circuit in Experiment #8.

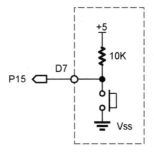

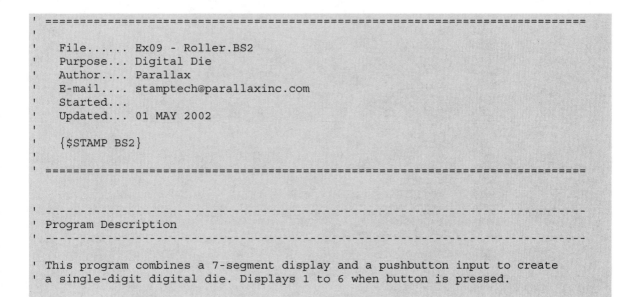

```
' =============================================================================
'
'   File...... Ex09 - Roller.BS2
'   Purpose... Digital Die
'   Author.... Parallax
'   E-mail.... stamptech@parallaxinc.com
'   Started...
'   Updated... 01 MAY 2002
'
'   {$STAMP BS2}
'
' =============================================================================


' -----------------------------------------------------------------------------
' Program Description
' -----------------------------------------------------------------------------

' This program combines a 7-segment display and a pushbutton input to create
' a single-digit digital die. Displays 1 to 6 when button is pressed.
```

```
' -----------------------------------------------------------------------------
' I/O Definitions
' -----------------------------------------------------------------------------

RollBtn          CON     15                       ' roll button on Pin 15
Segs             VAR     OutL                     ' 7-segment LEDs


' -----------------------------------------------------------------------------
' Variables
' -----------------------------------------------------------------------------

swData           VAR     Byte                     ' data for BUTTON command
dieVal           VAR     Nib                      ' new die value
spinPos          VAR     Nib                      ' spinner position
doSpin           VAR     Nib                      ' spinner update control


' -----------------------------------------------------------------------------
' EEPROM Data
' -----------------------------------------------------------------------------


'                        abcdefg
'                        -------
DecDig           DATA    %01111110                ' 0
                 DATA    %00110000                ' 1
                 DATA    %01101101                ' 2
                 DATA    %01111001                ' 3
                 DATA    %00110011                ' 4
                 DATA    %01011011                ' 5
                 DATA    %01011111                ' 6
                 DATA    %01110000                ' 7
                 DATA    %01111111                ' 8
                 DATA    %01111011                ' 9

Bug              DATA    %01000000                ' spinning bug
                 DATA    %00100000
                 DATA    %00010000
                 DATA    %00001000
                 DATA    %00000100
                 DATA    %00000010


' -----------------------------------------------------------------------------
' Initialization
' -----------------------------------------------------------------------------
```

```
Initialize:
  DirL = %01111111                              ' create output pins


' --------------------------------------------------------------------
' Program Code
' --------------------------------------------------------------------

Main:
  GOSUB Get_Die                                 ' update die value
  PAUSE 5
  ' is the button pressed?
  BUTTON RollBtn, 0, 255, 10, swData, 1, Show_Die
  GOTO Main                                     ' no

Show_Die:
  READ (DecDig + dieVal), Segs                  ' show the die
  PAUSE 3000                                    ' - for 3 seconds
  GOTO Main                                     ' go again

  END


' --------------------------------------------------------------------
' Subroutines
' --------------------------------------------------------------------

Get_Die:
  dieVal = (dieVal // 6) + 1                     ' limit = 1 to 6
  READ (Bug + spinPos), segs                    ' show spinner pattern
  doSpin = (doSpin + 1) // 7                     ' time to update spinner?
  IF (doSpin > 0) THEN Get_DieX                  ' only if doSpin = 0
  spinPos = spinPos + 1 // 6                     ' update spinner

Get_DieX:
  RETURN
```

Behind The Scenes

This program borrows heavily from what we've already done and should be easy for you to understand. What we've done here is added a bit of programming creativity to make a very simple program visually interesting.

There is one noteworthy point: the use of the variable, `dospin`. In order to create a random value, the variable `dieVal` is updated rapidly until the button is pressed. This rate of change, however, is too fast to allow for a meaningful display of the rotating "bug." The variable `dospin`, then, acts as a delay timer, causing the LED "bug" position to be updated every seventh pass through the `Get_Die` routine. This allows us to see it clearly and creates an inviting display.

Experiment #10: LED Clock Display

The purpose of this experiment is create a simple clock display using four, seven-segment LED modules.

New PBASIC elements/commands to know:

- OutA, OutB, OutC, OutD
- DirA, DirB, DirC, DirD
- In0 - In15
- DIG

Building The Circuit

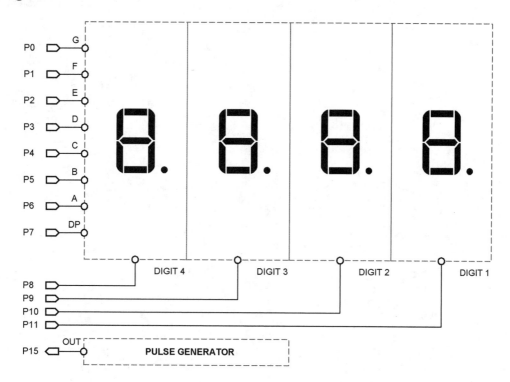

```
' ==============================================================================
'
'   File...... Ex10 - Clock.BS2
'   Purpose... Simple software clock
'   Author.... Parallax
'   E-mail.... stamptech@parallaxinc.com
'   Started...
'   Updated... 01 MAY 2002
'
'   {$STAMP BS2}
'
' ==============================================================================


' ------------------------------------------------------------------------------
' Program Description
' ------------------------------------------------------------------------------

' This program monitors a 1 Hz input signal and uses it as the timebase for
' a software clock.


' ------------------------------------------------------------------------------
' I/O Definitions
' ------------------------------------------------------------------------------

Segs            VAR     OutL                    ' segments
DigSel          VAR     OutC                    ' digit select
Tic             VAR     In15                    ' 1 Hz Pulse Generator input


' ------------------------------------------------------------------------------
' Constants
' ------------------------------------------------------------------------------

DecPoint        CON     %10000000               ' decimal point bit
Blank           CON     %00000000               ' all segments off

Dig0            CON     %1111                   ' digit select control
Dig1            CON     %1110
Dig2            CON     %1101
Dig3            CON     %1011
Dig4            CON     %0111

IsLow           CON     0                       ' Tic input is low
IsHigh          CON     1                       ' Tic input is high
```

```
' -----------------------------------------------------------------------
' Variables
' -----------------------------------------------------------------------

secs            VAR    Word                      ' seconds
time            VAR    Word                      ' formatted time
digit           VAR    Nib                       ' current display digit


' -----------------------------------------------------------------------
' EEPROM Data
' -----------------------------------------------------------------------

'                       .abcdefg
'                       --------
DecDig          DATA    %01111110                 ' 0
                DATA    %00110000                 ' 1
                DATA    %01101101                 ' 2
                DATA    %01111001                 ' 3
                DATA    %00110011                 ' 4
                DATA    %01011011                 ' 5
                DATA    %01011111                 ' 6
                DATA    %01110000                 ' 7
                DATA    %01111111                 ' 8
                DATA    %01111011                 ' 9


' -----------------------------------------------------------------------
' Initialization
' -----------------------------------------------------------------------

Initialize:
  DirL = %11111111                                ' make segments outputs
  DirC = %1111                                    ' make digit selects outputs
  DigSel = Dig0                                   ' all digits off


' -----------------------------------------------------------------------
' Program Code
' -----------------------------------------------------------------------

Main:
  GOSUB Show_Time                                 ' show current digit
  IF (Tic = IsHigh) THEN Inc_Sec                  ' new second?
  GOTO Main                                       ' do it again
```

```
Inc_Sec:
  secs = (secs + 1) // 3600              ' update seconds counter

Waiting:
  GOSUB Show_Time                        ' show current digit
  IF (Tic = IsLow) THEN Main             ' if last tic gone, go back

  ' additional code could go here

  GOTO Waiting                           ' do tic check again

  END


' --------------------------------------------------------------------------
' Subroutines
' --------------------------------------------------------------------------

Show_Time:
  time = (secs / 60) * 100               ' get minutes, put in hundreds
  time = time + (secs // 60)             ' get seconds, put in 10s & 1s
  Segs = Blank                           ' clear display
  ' enable digit
  LOOKUP digit, [Dig1, Dig2, Dig3, Dig4], digSel
  READ (DecDig + (time DIG digit)), Segs ' put segment pattern in digit
  IF (digit <> 2) THEN Skip_DP
  Segs = Segs + DecPoint                 ' illuminate decimal point

Skip_DP:
  PAUSE 1                                ' show it
  digit = (digit + 1) // 4               ' get next digit
  RETURN
```

Behind The Scenes

The first two projects with seven-segment displays used only one digit. This project uses all four. A new problem arises; since the segment (anode) lines of the four displays are tied together, we can only show one at a time. This is accomplished by outputting the segment pattern then enabling the desired digit (by making its cathode low).

The goal of this program though, is to create a clock display, which means we want to see all four digits at the same time. While we can't actually have all four running at once, we can trick the human eye into thinking so.

The human eye has a property known as Persistence Of Vision (POV), which causes it to hold an image briefly. The brighter the image, the longer it holds in our eyes. POV is what causes us to see a bright spot in our vision after a friend snaps a flash photo. We can use POV to our advantage by rapidly cycling through each of the four digits, displaying the proper segments for that digit for a short period. If the cycle is fast enough, the POV of our eyes will cause the all four digits to appear to be lit at the same time. This process is called multiplexing.

Multiplexing is the process of sharing data lines; in this case, the segment lines to the displays are being shared. If we didn't multiplex, 28 output lines would be required to control four seven-segment displays. That's 12 more lines than are available on the BASIC Stamp.

The real work in this program happens in the subroutine called show_Time. Its purpose is to time-format (MMSS) the seconds counter and update the current digit. Since the routine can only show one digit at a time, it must be called frequently, otherwise display strobing will occur. This program will update the display while waiting for other things to happen.

The clock display is created by moving the minutes value (secs / 60) into the thousands and hundreds columns of the variable time. The remaining seconds (secs // 60) are added to time, placing them in the tens and ones columns. Here's how the conversion math works:

Example: 754 seconds

754 / 60 = 12
12 x 100 = 1200   (time = 1200)
754 // 60 = 34
1200 + 34 = 1234 (time = 1234; 12 minutes and 34 seconds)

Now that the time display value is ready, the segments are cleared for the next update. Clearing the current segments value keeps the display sharp. If this isn't done, the old segments value will cause "ghosting" in the display. A LOOKUP table is used to enable the current digit and the segments for that digit are READ from an EEPROM DATA table.

The StampWorks display does not have the colon (:) normally found on a digital clock, so we'll enable the decimal point behind the second digit. If the current digit is not a second, the decimal point illumination is skipped. The final steps are a short delay so the digit illuminates and the current digit variable is updated.

The main loop of this program watches an incoming square-wave signal, produced by the StampWorks signal generator. When set at 1 Hz, this signal goes from LOW to HIGH once each second. When this low-to-high transition occurs, the seconds counter is updated. The modulus operator (//) is used to keep seconds in the range of 0 to 3599 (the range of seconds in one hour).

When the seconds counter is updated, the display is refreshed and then the program waits for the incoming signal to go low, updating the display during the wait. If the program went right back to the top and the incoming signal was still high, the seconds counter would be prematurely updated, causing the clock to run fast. Once the incoming signal does go low, the program loops back to the top where it waits for the next low-to-high transition from the pulse generator.

Challenge

If the decimal point illumination is modified as follows, what will happen? Modify and download the program to check your answer.

```
  segs = segs + (DPoint * time.Bit0)              ' illuminate decimal point
```

StampWorks   **Using Character LCDs**

While LEDs and seven-segment displays make great output devices, there will be projects that require providing more complex information to the user. Of course, nothing beats the PC video display, but these are large, expensive and almost always impractical for microcontroller projects. Character LCD modules, on the other hand, fit the bill well. These inexpensive modules allow both text and numeric output, use very few I/O lines and require little effort from the BASIC Stamp.

Character LCD modules are available in a wide variety of configurations: one-line, two-line and four-line are very common. Screen width is also variable, but is usually 16 or 20 characters for each line.

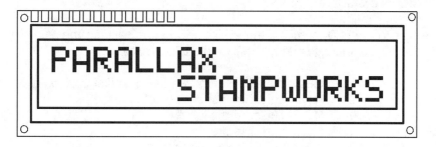

The StampWorks LCD module (2 lines x 16 characters).
Datasheet is available for download from www.parallaxinc.com.

The StampWorks LCD module connects to the lab board by a 14-pin IDC header. The header is keyed, preventing the header from being inserted upside-down.

Initialization

The character LCD must be initialized before sending information to it. The projects in this document initialize the LCD in accordance with the specification for the Hitachi HD44780 controller. The Hitachi controller is the most popular available and many controllers are compatible with it.

Modes Of Operation

There are two essential modes of operation with character LCDs: sending a character and sending a command. When sending a character, the RS line is high and the data sent is interpreted as a character to be displayed at the current cursor position. The code sent is usually the ASCII code FOR the character. Several non-ASCII characters also are available in the LCD, as well as up to eight user-programmable custom characters.

Commands are sent to the LCD by taking the RS line low before sending the data. Several standard commands are available to manage and manipulate the LCD display.

Clear	$01	Clears the LCD and moves cursor to first position of first line
Home	$02	Moves cursor to first position of first line
Cursor Left	$10	Moves cursor to the left
Cursor Right	$14	Moves cursor to the right
Display Left	$18	Shifts entire display to the left
Display Right	$1C	Shifts entire display to the right

Connecting The LCD

The StampWorks LCD has a 14-pin IDC connector at the end of its cable. The connector is "keyed" so that it is always inserted correctly into the StampWorks lab. Simply align the connector key (small bump) with the slot in the LCD socket and press the connector into the socket until it is firmly seated.

![StampWorks]

Experiment #11:
A Basic LCD Demonstration

This program demonstrates character LCD fundamentals by putting the StampWorks LCD module through its paces.

New PBASIC elements/commands to know:

- PULSOUT
- HighNib, LowNib
- ^ (Exclusive OR operator)

Building The Circuit

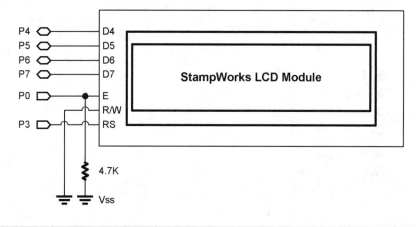

```
' ================================================================================
'
'   File...... Ex11 - LCD Demo.BS2
'   Purpose... Essential LCD control
'   Author.... Parallax
'   E-mail.... stamptech@parallaxinc.com
'   Started...
'   Updated... 01 MAY 2002
'
'   {$STAMP BS2}
'
' ================================================================================
```

```
' -----------------------------------------------------------------
' Program Description
' -----------------------------------------------------------------

' This program demonstrates essential character LCD control.
'
' The connections for this program conform to the BS2p LCDIN and LCDOUT
' commands.  Use this program for the BS2, BS2e or BS2sx.  There is a separate
' program for the BS2p.


' -----------------------------------------------------------------
' I/O Definitions
' -----------------------------------------------------------------

E               CON      0                    ' LCD Enable pin  (1 = enabled)
RS              CON      3                    ' Register Select (1 = char)
LCDbus          VAR      OutB                 ' 4-bit LCD data bus


' -----------------------------------------------------------------
' Constants
' -----------------------------------------------------------------

ClrLCD          CON      $01                  ' clear the LCD
CrsrHm          CON      $02                  ' move cursor to home position
CrsrLf          CON      $10                  ' move cursor left
CrsrRt          CON      $14                  ' move cursor right
DispLf          CON      $18                  ' shift displayed chars left
DispRt          CON      $1C                  ' shift displayed chars right
DDRam           CON      $80                  ' Display Data RAM control


' -----------------------------------------------------------------
' Variables
' -----------------------------------------------------------------

char            VAR      Byte                 ' character sent to LCD
index           VAR      Byte                 ' loop counter


' -----------------------------------------------------------------
' EEPROM Data
' -----------------------------------------------------------------
```

```
Msg             DATA    "THE BASIC STAMP!", 0    ' preload EEPROM with message


' --------------------------------------------------------------------
' Initialization
' --------------------------------------------------------------------

Initialize:
  DirL = %11111101                              ' setup pins for LCD

LCD_Init:
  PAUSE 500                                     ' let the LCD settle
  LCDbus = %0011                                ' 8-bit mode
  PULSOUT E, 1
  PAUSE 5
  PULSOUT E, 1
  PULSOUT E, 1
  LCDbus = %0010                                ' 4-bit mode
  PULSOUT E, 1
  char = %00001100                              ' disp on, crsr off, blink off
  GOSUB LCD_Command
  char = %00000110                              ' inc crsr, no disp shift
  GOSUB LCD_Command


' --------------------------------------------------------------------
' Program Code
' --------------------------------------------------------------------

Main:
  char = ClrLCD                                 ' clear the LCD
  GOSUB LCD_Command
  PAUSE 500
  index = Msg                                   ' get EE address of message

Read_Char:
  READ index, char                              ' get character from EEPROM
  IF (char = 0) THEN Msg_Done                   ' if 0, message is complete
  GOSUB LCD_Write                               ' write the character
  index = index + 1                             ' point to next character
  GOTO Read_Char                                ' go get it

Msg_Done:                                       ' the message is complete
  PAUSE 2000                                    ' wait 2 seconds
  char = CrsrHm                                 ' move the cursor home
  GOSUB LCD_Command
  char = %00001110                              ' turn the cursor on
```

```
GOSUB LCD_Command
PAUSE 500

char = CrsrRt
FOR index = 1 TO 15                    ' move the cursor accross display
  GOSUB LCD_Command
  PAUSE 150
NEXT

FOR index = 14 TO 0                    ' go backward by moving cursor
  char = DDRam + index                 '  to a specific address
  GOSUB LCD_Command
  PAUSE 150
NEXT

char = %00001101                       ' cursor off, blink on
GOSUB LCD_Command
PAUSE 2000

char = %00001100                       ' blink off
GOSUB LCD_Command

FOR index = 1 TO 10                    ' flash display
  char = char ^ %00000100              ' toggle display bit
  GOSUB LCD_Command
  PAUSE 250
NEXT
PAUSE 1000

FOR index = 1 TO 16                    ' shift display
  char = DispRt
  GOSUB LCD_Command
  PAUSE 100
NEXT
PAUSE 1000

FOR index = 1 TO 16                    ' shift display back
  char = DispLf
  GOSUB LCD_Command
  PAUSE 100
NEXT
PAUSE 1000
GOTO Main                              ' do it all over

END
```

```
' -----------------------------------------------------------------------
' Subroutines
' -----------------------------------------------------------------------

LCD_Command:
  LOW RS                                      ' enter command mode

LCD_Write:
  LCDbus = char.HighNib                       ' output high nibble
  PULSOUT E, 1                                ' strobe the Enable line
  LCDbus = char.LowNib                        ' output low nibble
  PULSOUT E, 1
  HIGH RS                                     ' return to character mode
  RETURN
```

Behind The Scenes

This is a very simple program, which demonstrates the basic functions of a character LCD. The LCD is initialized using four-bit mode in accordance with the Hitachi HD44780 controller specifications. This mode is used to minimize the number of BASIC Stamp I/O lines needed to control the LCD. While it is possible to connect to and control the LCD with eight data lines, this will not cause a noticeable improvement in program performance and will use four more I/O lines.

The basics of the initialization are appropriate for most applications:

- The display is on
- The cursor is off
- Display blinking is disabled
- The cursor is automatically incremented after each write
- The display does not shift

With the use of four data bits, two write cycles are necessary to send a byte to the LCD. The BASIC Stamps' HighNib and LowNib variable modifiers make this process exceedingly easy. Each nibble is latched into the LCD by blipping the E (enable) line with PULSOUT.

The demo starts by clearing the LCD and displaying a message that has been stored in a DATA statement. This technique of storing messages in EEPROM is very useful and makes programs easier to update. In this program, characters are written until a zero is encountered. This method lets us change the length of the string without worry about FOR-NEXT control settings. With the message displayed, the cursor position is returned home (first position of first line) and turned on (an underline cursor appears).

The cursor is sent back and forth across the LCD using two techniques. The first uses the cursor-right command. Moving the cursor back is accomplished by manually positioning the cursor. Manual cursor positioning is required by many LCD programs for tidy formatting of the information in the display.

With the cursor back home, it is turned off and the blink attribute is enabled. Blink causes the current cursor position to alternate between the character and a solid black box. This can be useful as an attention getter. Another attention-getting technique is to flash the entire display. This is accomplished by toggling the display enable bit. The Exclusive OR operator (^) simplifies bit toggling, as any bit XOR'd with a "1" will invert (1 XOR 1 = 0, 0 XOR 1 = 1).

Using the display shift commands, the entire display is shifted off-screen to the right, then back. What this demonstrates is that the display is actually a window into the LCD's memory. One method of using the additional memory is to write messages off-screen and shift to them.

Experiment #12:
Creating Custom LCD Characters

StampWorks

This program demonstrates the creation of custom LCD characters, animation with the custom characters and initializing the LCD for multi-line mode.

Building The Circuit

Use the same circuit as in Experiment #11.

```
' ===============================================================================
'
'   File...... Ex12 - LCD Characters.BS2
'   Purpose... Custom LCD Characters
'   Author.... Parallax
'   E-mail.... stamptech@parallaxinc.com
'   Started...
'   Updated... 01 MAY 2002
'
'   {$STAMP BS2}
'
' ===============================================================================


' -------------------------------------------------------------------------------
' Program Description
' -------------------------------------------------------------------------------

' This program demonstrates custom character creation and animation on a
' character LCD.
'
' The connections for this program conform to the BS2p LCDIN and LCDOUT
' commands.  Use this program for the BS2, BS2e or BS2sx.  There is a separate
' program for the BS2p.


' -------------------------------------------------------------------------------
' I/O Definitions
' -------------------------------------------------------------------------------

E              CON      0                      ' LCD Enable pin   (1 = enabled)
RS             CON      3                      ' Register Select (1 = char)
LCDbus         VAR      OutB                   ' 4-bit LCD data bus
```

```
' -----------------------------------------------------------------------------
' Constants
' -----------------------------------------------------------------------------

ClrLCD          CON     $01                     ' clear the LCD
CrsrHm          CON     $02                     ' move cursor to home position
CrsrLf          CON     $10                     ' move cursor left
CrsrRt          CON     $14                     ' move cursor right
DispLf          CON     $18                     ' shift displayed chars left
DispRt          CON     $1C                     ' shift displayed chars right
DDRam           CON     $80                     ' Display Data RAM control
CGRam           CON     $40                     ' Custom character RAM
Line1           CON     $80                     ' DDRAM address of line 1
Line2           CON     $C0                     ' DDRAM address of line 2


' -----------------------------------------------------------------------------
' Variables
' -----------------------------------------------------------------------------

char            VAR     Byte                    ' character sent to LCD
newChar         VAR     Byte                    ' new character for animation
index1          VAR     Byte                    ' loop counter
index2          VAR     Byte                    ' loop counter


' -----------------------------------------------------------------------------
' EEPROM Data
' -----------------------------------------------------------------------------

Msg1            DATA    "THE BASIC STAMP "       ' preload EEPROM with messages
Msg2            DATA    " IS VERY COOL! ", 3

CC0             DATA    $0E, $1F, $1C, $18, $1C, $1F, $0E, $00  ' character 0
CC1             DATA    $0E, $1F, $1F, $18, $1F, $1F, $0E, $00  ' character 1
CC2             DATA    $0E, $1F, $1F, $1F, $1F, $1F, $0E, $00  ' character 2
Smiley          DATA    $00, $0A, $0A, $00, $11, $0E, $06, $00  ' smiley face


' -----------------------------------------------------------------------------
' Initialization
' -----------------------------------------------------------------------------

Initialize:
  DirL = %11111101                              ' setup pins for LCD
```

```
LCD_Init:
  PAUSE 500                          ' let the LCD settle
  LCDbus = %0011                     ' 8-bit mode
  PULSOUT E, 1
  PAUSE 5
  PULSOUT E, 1
  PULSOUT E, 1
  LCDbus = %0010                     ' 4-bit mode
  PULSOUT E, 1
  char = %00101000                   ' multi-line mode
  GOSUB LCD_Command
  char = %00001100                   ' disp on, crsr off, blink off
  GOSUB LCD_Command
  char = %00000110                   ' inc crsr, no disp shift
  GOSUB LCD_Command

Download_Chars:                      ' download custom chars to LCD
  char = CGRam                       ' point to CG RAM
  GOSUB LCD_Command                  ' prepare to write CG data
  FOR index1 = CC0 TO (Smiley + 7)   ' build 4 custom chars
    READ index1, char                ' get byte from EEPROM
    GOSUB LCD_Write                  ' put into LCD CG RAM
  NEXT


' --------------------------------------------------------------------
' Program Code
' --------------------------------------------------------------------

Main:
  char = ClrLCD                      ' clear the LCD
  GOSUB LCD_Command
  PAUSE 250

  FOR index1 = 0 TO 15               ' get message from EEPROM
    READ (Msg1 + index1),char        ' read a character
    GOSUB LCD_Write                  ' write it
  NEXT

  PAUSE 2000                         ' wait 2 seconds

Animation:
  FOR index1 = 0 TO 15               ' cover 16 characters
    READ (Msg2 + index1), newChar    ' get new char from 2nd message
    FOR index2 = 0 TO 4              ' 5 characters in animation cycle
      char = Line2 + index1          ' set new DDRAM address
```

```
        GOSUB LCD_Command
        LOOKUP index2, [0, 1, 2, 1, newChar], char
        GOSUB LCD_Write                          ' write animation character
        PAUSE 50                                 ' delay between animation chars
      NEXT
    NEXT
    PAUSE 1000
    GOTO Main
                                                 ' do it all over

    END


  ' ---------------------------------------------------------------------
  ' Subroutines
  ' ---------------------------------------------------------------------

LCD_Command:
    LOW RS                                       ' enter command mode

LCD_Write:
    LCDbus = char.HighNib                        ' output high nibble
    PULSOUT E, 1                                 ' strobe the Enable line
    LCDbus = char.LowNib                         ' output low nibble
    PULSOUT E, 1
    HIGH RS                                      ' return to character mode
    RETURN
```

Behind The Scenes

In this program, the LCD is initialized for multi-line mode. This will allow both lines of the StampWorks LCD module to display information. With the display initialized, custom character data is downloaded to the LCD.

The LCD has room for eight, user-definable customer characters. The data is stored for these characters in an area called CGRAM and must be downloaded to the LCD after power-up and initialization (custom character definitions are lost when power is removed from the LCD). Each custom character requires eight bytes of data. The eighth byte is usually $00, since this is where the cursor is positioned when under the character.

The standard LCD font is five bits wide by seven bits tall. You can create custom characters that are eight bits tall, but the eighth line is generally reserved for the underline cursor. Here's an example of a custom character definition:

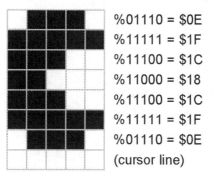

%01110 = $0E
%11111 = $1F
%11100 = $1C
%11000 = $18
%11100 = $1C
%11111 = $1F
%01110 = $0E
(cursor line)

The shape of the character is determined by the ones and zeros in the data bytes. One in a given bit position will light a pixel; zero will extinguish it.

The bit patterns for custom characters are stored in the BASIC Stamp's EEPROM with DATA statements. To move the patterns into the LCD, the CGRam command is executed and the characters are written to the display. Before the characters can be used, the display must be returned to "normal" mode. The usual method is to clear the display or home the cursor.

Interestingly, the LCD retrieves the bit patterns from memory while refreshing the display. In advanced applications, the CGRam memory can be updated while the program is running to create unusual display effects.

The heart of this program is the animation loop. This code grabs a character from the second message, then, for each character in that message, displays the animation sequence at the desired character location on the second line of the LCD. A LOOKUP table is used to cycle the custom characters for the animation sequence. At the end of the sequence, the new character is revealed.

Challenge

Create your own custom character sequence. Update the initialization and animation code to accommodate your custom characters.

Experiment #13: Reading the LCD RAM

This program demonstrates the use of the LCD's CGRAM space as external memory.

New PBASIC elements/commands to know:

- InA, InB, InC, InD

Building The Circuit

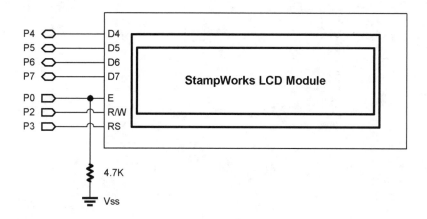

```
' =============================================================================
'
'   File...... Ex13 - LCD Read.BS2
'   Purpose... Read data from LCD
'   Author.... Parallax
'   E-mail.... stamptech@parallaxinc.com
'   Started...
'   Updated... 01 MAY 2002
'
'   {$STAMP BS2}
'
' =============================================================================
```

```
' --------------------------------------------------------------------
' Program Description
' --------------------------------------------------------------------

' This program demonstrates how to read data from the LCD's display or CGRAM
' areas.
'
' The connections for this program conform to the BS2p LCDIN and LCDOUT
' commands.  Use this program for the BS2, BS2e or BS2sx.  There is a separate
' program for the BS2p.


' --------------------------------------------------------------------
' I/O Definitions
' --------------------------------------------------------------------

E              CON      0              ' LCD Enable pin  (1 = enabled)
RW             CON      2              ' LCD Read/Write pin (1 = write)
RS             CON      3              ' Register Select (1 = char)
LCDdirs        VAR      DirB
LCDbusOut      VAR      OutB           ' 4-bit LCD data bus
LCDbusIn       VAR      InB


' --------------------------------------------------------------------
' Constants
' --------------------------------------------------------------------

ClrLCD         CON      $01            ' clear the LCD
CrsrHm         CON      $02            ' move cursor to home position
CrsrLf         CON      $10            ' move cursor left
CrsrRt         CON      $14            ' move cursor right
DispLf         CON      $18            ' shift displayed chars left
DispRt         CON      $1C            ' shift displayed chars right
DDRam          CON      $80            ' Display Data RAM control
CGRam          CON      $40            ' Custom character RAM


' --------------------------------------------------------------------
' Variables
' --------------------------------------------------------------------

char           VAR      Byte           ' character sent to LCD
index          VAR      Byte           ' loop counter
rVar           VAR      Word           ' for random number
addr           VAR      Byte           ' address to write/read
tOut           VAR      Byte           ' test value to write to LCD
```

```
tIn             VAR     Byte            ' test value to read from LCD
temp            VAR     Word            ' temp value for numeric display
width           VAR     Nib             ' width of number to display


' -------------------------------------------------------------------
' Initialization
' -------------------------------------------------------------------

Initialize:
  DirL = %11111101                      ' setup pins for LCD

LCD_Init:
  PAUSE 500                             ' let the LCD settle
  LCDbusOut = %0011                     ' 8-bit mode
  PULSOUT E, 1
  PAUSE 5
  PULSOUT E, 1
  PULSOUT E, 1
  LCDbusOut = %0010                     ' 4-bit mode
  PULSOUT E, 1
  char = %00001100                      ' disp on, crsr off, blink off
  GOSUB LCD_Command
  char = %00000110                      ' inc crsr, no disp shift
  GOSUB LCD_Command


' -------------------------------------------------------------------
' Program Code
' -------------------------------------------------------------------

Main:
  char = ClrLCD                         ' clear the LCD
  GOSUB LCD_Command

  FOR index = 0 TO 14                   ' create display
    LOOKUP index, ["ADDR=??  ???/???"], char
    GOSUB LCD_Write
  NEXT

Loop:
  RANDOM rVar                           ' generate random number
  addr = rVar.LowByte & $3F             ' create address (0 to 63)
  tOut = rVar.HighByte                  ' create test value (0 to 255)

  char = CGRam + addr                   ' set CGRAM pointer
  GOSUB LCD_Command
```

```
  char = tOut
  GOSUB LCD_Write                              ' move the value to CGRAM
  PAUSE 100                                    ' wait a bit, then go get it

  char = CGRam + addr                          ' set CGRAM pointer
  GOSUB LCD_Command
  GOSUB LCD_Read                               ' read value from LCD
  tIn = char

' display results

  char = DDRam + 5                             ' show address at position 5
  GOSUB LCD_Command
  temp = addr
  width = 2
  GOSUB Put_Val

  char = DDRam + 9                             ' show output at position 8
  GOSUB LCD_Command
  temp = tOut
  width = 3
  GOSUB Put_Val

  char = DDRam + 13                            ' show input at position 12
  GOSUB LCD_Command
  temp = tIn
  width = 3
  GOSUB Put_Val
  PAUSE 1000
  GOTO Loop                                    ' do it again

  END


' --------------------------------------------------------------------
' Subroutines
' --------------------------------------------------------------------

Put_Val:
  FOR index = (width - 1) TO 0                 ' display digits left to right
    char = (temp DIG index) + 48               ' convert digit to ASCII
    GOSUB LCD_Write                            ' put digit in display
  NEXT
  RETURN
```

```
LCD_Command:
  LOW RS                                    ' enter command mode

LCD_Write:
  LCDbusOut = char.HighNib                  ' output high nibble
  PULSOUT E, 1                              ' strobe the Enable line
  LCDbusOut = char.LowNib                   ' output low nibble
  PULSOUT E, 1
  HIGH RS                                   ' return to character mode
  RETURN


LCD_Read:
  HIGH RS                                   ' data command
  HIGH RW                                   ' read
  LCDdirs = %0000                           ' make data lines inputs
  HIGH E
  char.HighNib = LCDbusIn                   ' get high nibble
  LOW E
  HIGH E
  char.LowNib = LCDbusIn                    ' get low nibble
  LOW E
  LCDdirs = %1111                           ' return data lines to outputs
  LOW RW
  RETURN
```

Behind The Scenes

This program demonstrates the versatility of the BASIC Stamp's I/O lines and their ability to be reconfigured mid-program. Writing to the LCD was covered in the last two experiments. To read data back, the BASIC Stamp's I/O lines must be reconfigured as inputs. This is no problem for the BASIC Stamp. Aside from the I/O reconfiguration, reading from the LCD requires an additional control line: RW. In most programs this line can be tied low to allow writing to the LCD. For reading from the LCD the RW line is made high.

The program generates an address and data using the RANDOM function. The address is kept in the range of 0 to 63 by masking out the highest bits of the LowByte returned by the RANDOM function. The HighByte is used as the data to be written to and read back from the LCD.

The data is stored in the LCD's CGRAM area. This means -- in this program -- that the CGRAM memory cannot be used for custom characters. In programs that require less than eight custom characters the remaining bytes of CGRAM can be used as off-board memory.

Reading data from the LCD is identical to writing: the address is set and the data is retrieved. For this to take place, the LCD data lines must be reconfigured as inputs. Blipping the E (enable) line makes the data (one nibble at a time) available for the BASIC Stamp. Once again, HighNib and LowNib are used, this time to build a single byte from the two nibbles returned during the read operation.

When the retrieved data is ready, the address, output data and input data are written to the LCD for examination. As short subroutine, Put_Val, handles writing numerical values to the LCD. To use this routine, move the cursor to the desired location, put the value to be displayed in temp, the number of characters to display in width, then call Put_Val. The subroutine uses the DIG operator to extract a digit from temp and adds 48 to convert it to ASCII so that it can be displayed on the LCD.

 # Experiment #14:
Magic 8-Ball Game

This program demonstrates the 8x10 font capability of StampWorks LCD module. The 8x10 font allows descended letters (g, j, p, q and y) to be displayed properly.

New PBASIC elements/commands to know:

- LOOKDOWN

Building The Circuit

Add this pushbutton to the circuit in Experiment #11 (remember to reconnect LCD.RW to Vss).

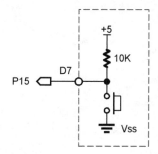

```
' =================================================================================
'
'   File...... Ex14 - LCD Magic 8-Ball.BS2
'   Purpose... Magic 8-Ball simulation
'   Author.... Parallax
'   E-mail.... stamptech@parallaxinc.com
'   Started...
'   Updated... 01 MAY 2002
'
'   {$STAMP BS2}
'
' =================================================================================
```

```
' -------------------------------------------------------------------------
' Program Description
' -------------------------------------------------------------------------

' This program simulates a Magic 8-Ball.  Ask a question, then press the
' button to get your answer.
'
' The program also demonstrates using a 2-Line display as a single-line display
' with the 5x10 font set.  When using the 5x10 font, true descended characters
' are available but must be remapped from the LCD ROM.
'
' The connections for this program conform to the BS2p LCDIN and LCDOUT
' commands.  Use this program for the BS2, BS2e or BS2sx.  There is a separate
' program for the BS2p.


' -------------------------------------------------------------------------
' I/O Definitions
' -------------------------------------------------------------------------

E               CON     0              ' LCD Enable pin  (1 = enabled)
RS              CON     3              ' Register Select (1 = char)
LCDbus          VAR     OutB           ' 4-bit LCD data out
AskButton       CON     15             ' Ask button input pin


' -------------------------------------------------------------------------
' Constants
' -------------------------------------------------------------------------

ClrLCD          CON     $01            ' clear the LCD
CrsrHm          CON     $02            ' move cursor to home position
CrsrLf          CON     $10            ' move cursor left
CrsrRt          CON     $14            ' move cursor right
DispLf          CON     $18            ' shift displayed chars left
DispRt          CON     $1C            ' shift displayed chars right
DDRam           CON     $80            ' Display Data RAM control
CGRam           CON     $40            ' Custom character RAM control

NumAnswers      CON     6              ' 6 possible answers

_g              CON     $E7            ' DDROM addresses of descenders
_j              CON     $EA
_p              CON     $F0
_q              CON     $F1
_y              CON     $F9
```

```
' ---------------------------------------------------------------------------
' Variables
' ---------------------------------------------------------------------------

char            VAR     Byte                    ' character sent to LCD
addr            VAR     Byte                    ' message address
swData          VAR     Byte                    ' workspace for BUTTON
answer          VAR     Nib                     ' answer pointer
clock           VAR     Nib                     ' animation clock
pntr            VAR     Nib                     ' pointer to animation character


' ---------------------------------------------------------------------------
' EEPROM Data
' ---------------------------------------------------------------------------

Prompt          DATA    "Ask a question", 0

Ans0            DATA    "Definitely YES", 0
Ans1            DATA    "Possible...", 0
Ans2            DATA    "Definitely NO", 0
Ans3            DATA    "Not likely...", 0
Ans4            DATA    "Answer uncertain", 0
Ans5            DATA    "Please ask again", 0


' ---------------------------------------------------------------------------
' Initialization
' ---------------------------------------------------------------------------

Initialize:
  DirL = %11111101                              ' setup pins for LCD

LCD_Init:
  PAUSE 500                                     ' let the LCD settle
  LCDbus = %0011                                ' 8-bit mode
  PULSOUT E, 1
  PAUSE 5
  PULSOUT E, 1
  PULSOUT E, 1
  LCDbus = %0010                                ' 4-bit mode
  PULSOUT E, 1
  char = %00100100                              ' select 5x10 font
  GOSUB LCD_Command
  char = %00001100                              ' disp on, crsr off, blink off
  GOSUB LCD_Command
```

```
  char = %00000110                              ' inc crsr, no disp shift
  GOSUB LCD_Command


' --------------------------------------------------------------------------
' Program Code
' --------------------------------------------------------------------------

Main:
  char = ClrLCD                                 ' clear the LCD
  GOSUB LCD_Command
  addr = Prompt
  GOSUB Show_Message                            ' print prompt

Rollem:
  GOSUB Shuffle                                 ' shuffle until button pressed
  PAUSE 5
  BUTTON AskButton, 0, 255, 10, swData, 1, Show_Answer
  GOTO Rollem

Show_Answer:
  ' get address of answer message
  LOOKUP answer, [Ans0, Ans1, Ans2, Ans3, Ans4, Ans5], addr

  char = ClrLCD
  GOSUB LCD_Command
  GOSUB Show_Message
  PAUSE 2000                                    ' give time to read answer
  GOTO Main                                     ' do it all over

  END


' --------------------------------------------------------------------------
' Subroutines
' --------------------------------------------------------------------------

LCD_Command:
  LOW RS                                        ' enter command mode

LCD_Write:
  LCDbus = char.HighNib                         ' output high nibble
  PULSOUT E,1                                   ' strobe the Enable line
  LCDbus = char.LowNib                          ' output low nibble
  PULSOUT E,1
  HIGH RS                                       ' return to character mode
  RETURN
```

```
Show_Message:
  READ addr,char                              ' read a character from EEPROM
  IF (char = 0) THEN Msg_Done                 ' if 0, message is complete
  GOSUB Translate                             ' fix letters with descenders
  GOSUB LCD_Write                             ' write the character
  addr = addr + 1                             ' point to next character
  GOTO Show_Message

Msg_Done:
  RETURN


' convert to descender font
' - does not change other characters

Translate:
  LOOKDOWN char, ["g", "j", "q", "p", "y"], char
  LOOKUP char, [_g, _j, _q, _p, _y], char
  RETURN


Shuffle:
  answer = (answer + 1) // NumAnswers         ' update answer pointer
  clock = (clock + 1) // 15                    ' update pointer clock
  IF (clock > 0) THEN Shuffle_Done             ' time to update animation?
  char = DDRam + 15                            ' yes, write at pos 15
  GOSUB LCD_Command
  LOOKUP pntr, ["-+|*"], char                  ' load animation character
  GOSUB LCD_Write                              ' write it
  pntr = (pntr + 1) // 4                        ' update animation char

Shuffle_Done:
  RETURN
```

Behind The Scenes

The standard 5x7 LCD font suffers aesthetically when it comes to descended letters, those letters with tails (g, j, p, q and y). The nature of the font map causes these letters to be "squashed" into the display. Many LCDs support a 5x10 character font and provide additional mapping for properly descended characters.

Using the 5x10 font is straightforward; it requires a single additional command in the initialization sequence. To display properly descended characters, however, is a bit trickier since these characters are not mapped at equal offsets to their ASCII counterparts. Thankfully, the BASIC Stamp has a couple of table-oriented commands that simplify the translation process.

After initialization, the screen is cleared and the user is prompted to think of a question. The Show_Message subroutine displays a message at the current cursor position. The message is stored in a DATA statement and passed to the subroutine by its EEPROM address. Show_Message reads characters from the EEPROM until it finds a zero, passing each character to the subroutine, Translate, which re-maps the ASCII value for descended letters. Translate uses a clever trick with LOOKUP and LOOKDOWN.

When a character is passed to Translate, it is compared to the list of known descended letters. If the character is in this list, it is converted to a value that will be used by the LOOKUP table to re-map the character to the descended version in the LCD font map. If the character is not in the descended list, it will pass through Translate unaffected.

The main loop of the program waits for you to press the button, creating a randomized answer by continuously calling the Shuffle subroutine. Shuffle updates the answer variable and creates an animated bug. The animation is created with standard characters and updated every 15 cycles through the Shuffle subroutine. When the button is finally pressed, the EEPROM address of the corresponding answer is loaded with LOOKUP and the "magic" answer is displayed.

Challenge

Create custom characters that use the 5x10 font mode. Note: 16 bytes must be used for each character, even though only ten will be displayed.

StampWorks   **Moving Forward**

The first three sections of this manual dealt specifically with output devices, because the choice of output to the user is often critical to the success of a project. By now, you should be very comfortable with LEDs, seven-segment displays and LCDs. From this point forward we will present a variety of experiments -- some simple, others complex which will round your education as a BASIC Stamp programmer and give you the confidence you need to develop your own BASIC Stamp-controlled applications.

Remember, the key to success here is to complete each experiment and to take on each challenge. Then, go further by challenging yourself. Each time you modify a program you will learn something. It's okay if your experiments don't work as expected, because you will still be learning.

Experiment #15: Debouncing Multiple Inputs

The experiment will teach you how to debounce multiple BASIC Stamp inputs. With modification, any number of inputs from two to 16 can be debounced with this code.

New PBASIC elements/commands to know:

- ~ (1's compliment operator)
- CLS (DEBUG modifier)
- IBIN, IBIN1 – IBIN16 (DEBUG modifier)

Building The Circuit

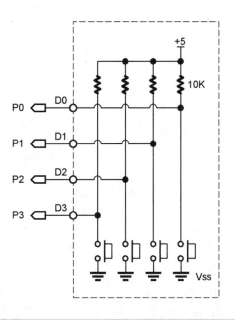

```
' =============================================================================
'
'   File...... Ex15 - Debounce.BS2
'   Purpose... Multi-input button debouncing
'   Author.... Parallax
'   E-mail.... stamptech@parallaxinc.com
```

```
'   Started...
'   Updated... 01 MAY 2002
'
'   {$STAMP BS2}
'
' =============================================================================


' ---------------------------------------------------------------------------
' Program Description
' ---------------------------------------------------------------------------

' This program demonstrates the simultaneous debouncing of multiple inputs. The
' input subroutine is easily adjusted to handle any number of inputs.


' ---------------------------------------------------------------------------
' I/O Definitions
' ---------------------------------------------------------------------------


SwInputs        VAR     InA                     ' four inputs, pins 0 - 3


' ---------------------------------------------------------------------------
' Variables
' ---------------------------------------------------------------------------

switches        VAR     Nib                     ' debounced inputs
x               VAR     Nib                     ' loop counter


' ---------------------------------------------------------------------------
' Program Code
' ---------------------------------------------------------------------------

Main:
  GOSUB Get_Switches                            ' get debounced inputs
  DEBUG Home, "Inputs = ", IBIN4 switches       ' display in binary mode
  PAUSE 50                                       ' a little time between readings
  GOTO Main                                      ' do it again

  END


' ---------------------------------------------------------------------------
' Subroutines
' ---------------------------------------------------------------------------
```

```
Get_Switches:
  switches = %1111                         ' enable all four inputs
  FOR x = 1 TO 10
    switches = switches & ~SwInputs        ' test inputs
    PAUSE 5                                 ' delay between tests
  NEXT
  RETURN
```

Behind The Scenes

When debouncing only one input, the BASIC Stamp's **BUTTON** function works perfectly and even adds a couple of useful features (like auto-repeat). To debounce two or more inputs, we need to create a bit of code. The workhorse of this experiment is the subroutine Get_Switches. As presented, it will accommodate four switch inputs. It can be modified for any number of inputs from two to 16.

The purpose of Get_Switches is to make sure that the inputs stay on solid for 50 milliseconds with no contact bouncing. Debounced inputs will be retuned in the variable, switches, with a valid input represented by a 1 in the switch position.

The Get_Switches routine starts by assuming that all switch inputs will be valid, so all the bits of switches are set to one. Then, using a FOR-NEXT loop, the inputs are scanned and compared to the previous state. Since the inputs are active low (zero when pressed), the one's compliment operator (~) inverts them. The And operator (&) is used to update the current state. For a switch to be valid, it must remain pressed through the entire FOR-NEXT loop.

Here's how the debouncing technique works: When a switch is pressed, the input to the BASIC Stamp will be zero. The one's compliment operator will invert zero to one. One "Anded" with one is still one, so that switch remains valid. If the switch is not pressed, the input to the BASIC Stamp will be one (because of the 10K pull-up to Vdd). One is inverted to zero. Zero "Anded" with any number is zero and will cause the switch to remain invalid through the entire debounce cycle.

The debounce switch inputs are displayed in a DEBUG window with the IBIN4 modifier so that the value of each switch input is clearly displayed.

Challenge

Modify the program to debounce and display eight switches.

StampWorks Experiment #16: Counting Events

This experiment demonstrates an events-based program delay.

Building The Circuit

```
              OUT ┌ ─ ─ ─ ─ ─ ─ ─ ─ ─ ─ ─ ─ ─ ─ ─ ─ ┐
  P15 ◁━━━━━○     │        PULSE GENERATOR          │
                  └ ─ ─ ─ ─ ─ ─ ─ ─ ─ ─ ─ ─ ─ ─ ─ ─ ┘
```

```
' ===============================================================================
'
'   File...... Ex16 - Counter.BS2
'   Purpose... Counts external events
'   Author.... Parallax
'   E-mail.... stamptech@parallaxinc.com
'   Started...
'   Updated... 01 MAY 2002
'
'   {$STAMP BS2}
'
' ===============================================================================


' -------------------------------------------------------------------------------
' Program Description
' -------------------------------------------------------------------------------

' Counts extenal events by wait for a low-to-high transition on the event
' input pin.


' -------------------------------------------------------------------------------
' Revision History
' -------------------------------------------------------------------------------


' -------------------------------------------------------------------------------
' I/O Definitions
' -------------------------------------------------------------------------------

EventIn         VAR     In15                            ' event input pin
```

```
' --------------------------------------------------------------
' Constants
' --------------------------------------------------------------

IsLow           CON     0
IsHigh          CON     1
Target          CON     1000                    ' target count


' --------------------------------------------------------------
' Variables
' --------------------------------------------------------------

eCount          VAR     Word                    ' event count


' --------------------------------------------------------------
' Initialization
' --------------------------------------------------------------

Init:
  PAUSE 250                                     ' let DEBUG window open
  DEBUG CLS, "Started... ", CR
  eCount = 0                                     ' clear counter


' --------------------------------------------------------------
' Program Code
' --------------------------------------------------------------

Main:
  GOSUB Wait_For_Count                          ' wait for 1000 pulses
  DEBUG "Count complete."

  END


' --------------------------------------------------------------
' Subroutines
' --------------------------------------------------------------

Wait_For_Count:
  IF (EventIn = IsLow) THEN Wait_For_Count      ' wait for input to go high
  eCount = eCount + 1                           ' increment event count
  DEBUG Home, 10, "Count = ", DEC eCount, CR
```

```
  IF (eCount = Target) THEN Wait_Done          ' check against target

Wait_Low:
  IF (EventIn = IsHigh) THEN Wait_Low          ' wait for input to go low
  GOTO Wait_For_Count

Wait_Done:
  RETURN
```

Behind The Scenes

The purpose of the `Wait_For_Count` subroutine is to cause the program to wait for a specified number of events. In an industrial setting, for example, a packaging system we might need to run a conveyor belt until 100 boxes pass.

When the program is passed to `Wait_For_Count`, the input pin is monitored for a low-to-high transition. When the line goes high, the counter is incremented and the program waits for the line to go low. When this happens, the code loops back for the next high input. When the target count is reached, the subroutine returns to the main program. The time spent in the subroutine is determined by the rate of incoming events.

Note that the subroutine expects a clean input. A noisy input could cause spurious counts, leading to early termination of the subroutine. One method of dealing with a noisy input – when the time between expected events is known – is to add a PAUSE statement after the start of an event. The idea is to PAUSE when the event starts and end the PAUSE after the event with a bit of lead-time before the next event is expected. The code that follows works when the events are about a half-second in length and the time between events is two seconds:

```
Wait_For_Count:
  IF (P_in = IsLow) THEN Wait_For_Count        ' wait for high pulse
  pCount = pCount + 1                           ' increment count
  DEBUG Home, 10, "Count = ", DEC eCount, CR
  IF (pCount = Target) THEN Wait_Done           ' check against target
  PAUSE 1500                                     ' clean-up noisy input

Wait_Low:
  IF (P_in = IsHigh) THEN Wait_Low             ' wait for pulse to go low
  GOTO Wait_For_Count

Wait_Done:
  RETURN
```

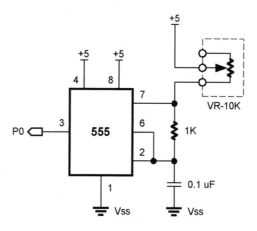

Experiment #17: Frequency Measurement

This experiment determines the frequency of an incoming pulse stream by using the BASIC Stamp's COUNT function.

New PBASIC elements/commands to know:

- COUNT

Building The Circuit (Note that schematic is NOT chip-centric)

```
' =============================================================================
'
'   File...... Ex17 - FreqIn1.BS2
'   Purpose... Frequency input
'   Author.... Parallax
'   E-mail.... stamptech@parallaxinc.com
'   Started...
'   Updated... 01 MAY 2002
'
'   {$STAMP BS2}
'
' =============================================================================
```

Experiment #17: Frequency Measurement

```
' -------------------------------------------------------------------
' Program Description
' -------------------------------------------------------------------

' This program monitors and displays the frequency of a signal on Pin 0.


' -------------------------------------------------------------------
' I/O Definitions
' -------------------------------------------------------------------

FreqPin         CON     0                       ' frequency input pin


' -------------------------------------------------------------------
' Constants
' -------------------------------------------------------------------

OneSec          CON     1000                    ' one second - BS2
' OneSec        CON     2500                    ' BS2sx
' OneSec        CON     3484                    ' BS2p


' -------------------------------------------------------------------
' Variables
' -------------------------------------------------------------------

freq            VAR     Word                    ' frequency


' -------------------------------------------------------------------
' Program Code
' -------------------------------------------------------------------

Main:
  COUNT FreqPin, OneSec, freq                   ' collect pulses for 1 second
  DEBUG CLS, "Frequency: ", DEC freq, " Hz"     ' display on DEBUG screen
  GOTO Main                                     ' do it again

  END
```

Behind The Scenes

In the previous experiment, several lines of code were used to count pulses on an input pin. That method works when counting to a specific number. Other programs will want to count the number of pulses that arrive during a specified time period. The BASIC Stamp's count function is designed for this purpose.

The frequency of an oscillating signal is defined as the number of cycles per second and is expressed in Hertz. The BASIC Stamp's count function monitors the specified pin for a given amount of time. To create a frequency meter, the specified time window is set to 1000 milliseconds (one second).

Challenge

Improve the responsiveness (make it update more frequently) of this program by changing the count period. What other adjustment has to be made? How does this change affect the ability to measure very low frequency signals?

StampWorks

Experiment #18:
Advanced Frequency Measurement

This experiment uses PULSIN to create a responsive frequency meter.

New PBASIC elements/commands to know:

- PULSIN

Building The Circuit

Use the same circuit as in Experiment #18.

```
' ===========================================================================
'
'   File...... Ex18 - FreqIn2.BS2
'   Purpose... Frequency Input
'   Author.... Parallax
'   E-mail.... stamptech@parallaxinc.com
'   Started...
'   Updated... 01 MAY 2002
'
'   {$STAMP BS2p}
'
' ===========================================================================


' ---------------------------------------------------------------------------
' Program Description
' ---------------------------------------------------------------------------

' This program monitors and displays the frequency of a signal on Pin 0.


' ---------------------------------------------------------------------------
' I/O Definitions
' ---------------------------------------------------------------------------

FreqPin         CON     0                       ' frequency input pin


' ---------------------------------------------------------------------------
' Constants
```

```
' --------------------------------------------------------------------------

Convert          CON       $0200                    ' input to uSeconds (BS2)
' Convert        CON       $00CC                    ' BS2sx
' Convert        CON       $00C0                    ' BS2p


' --------------------------------------------------------------------------
' Variables
' --------------------------------------------------------------------------

pHigh            VAR       Word                     ' high pulse width
pLow             VAR       Word                     ' low pulse width
period           VAR       Word                     ' cycle time (high + low)
freq             VAR       Word                     ' frequency


' --------------------------------------------------------------------------
' Program Code
' --------------------------------------------------------------------------

Main:
  PULSIN FreqPin, 0, pHigh                          ' get high portion of input
  PULSIN FreqPin, 1, pLow                           ' get low portion of input
  period = (pHigh + pLow) */ Convert                ' calculate cycle width in uSecs
  freq = 50000 / period * 20                        ' calculate frequency

  ' display on DEBUG screen

  DEBUG Home
  DEBUG "Period...... ", DEC period, " uS     ", CR
  DEBUG "Frequency... ", DEC freq, " Hz     "
  GOTO Main                                         ' do it again

  END
```

Behind The Scenes

In the last experiment, you learned that the frequency of a signal is defined as the number of cycles per second. You created a simple frequency meter by counting the number of pulses (cycles) in one second. This method works well, especially for low-frequency signals. There will be times, however, when project requirements will dictate a quicker response time for frequency measurement.

The frequency of a signal can be calculated from its period, or the time for one complete cycle.

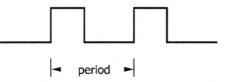

period

By measuring the period of an incoming signal, its frequency can be calculated with the equation (where the period is expressed in seconds):

frequency = 1 / period

The BASIC Stamp's PULSIN function is designed to measure the width of an incoming pulse. By using PULSIN to measure the high and low portions of an incoming signal, its period can be calculated and the frequency can be determined. The result of PULSIN is expressed in units of two microseconds. Thus, the formula for calculating frequency becomes:

frequency = 500,000 / period

This creates a problem for BASIC Stamp math though, as it can only deal with 16-bit numbers (maximum value is 65,535). To fix the formula, we convert 500,000 to 50,000 x 10 and rewrite the formula like this

frequency = 50,000 / period * 10

Run the program and adjust the 10K pot. Notice that the DEBUG screen is updated without delay and that there is no "hunting" as when using COUNT to determine frequency.

StampWorks

Experiment #19
A Light-Controlled Theremin

This experiment demonstrates FREQOUT by creating a light-controlled Theremin (the first electronic musical instrument ever produced).

Building The Circuit

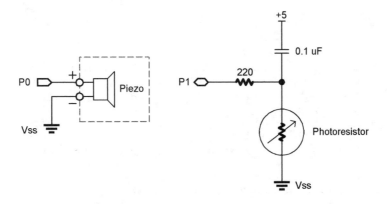

Note: Later versions of the StampWorks lab board come with a built-in audio amplifier. Attach an 8-ohm speaker to the output of the amplifier to get the best sound from this project.

```
' =============================================================================
'
'   File...... Ex19 - Theremin.BS2
'   Purpose... Simple Digital Theremin
'   Author.... Parallax
'   E-mail.... stamptech@parallaxinc.com
'   Started...
'   Updated... 01 MAY 2002
'
'   {$STAMP BS2}
'
' =============================================================================


' ---------------------------------------------------------------------------
' Program Description
' ---------------------------------------------------------------------------
```

```
' This program uses RCTIME with a photocell to create a light-controlled
' theremin.


' -----------------------------------------------------------------
' I/O Definitions
' -----------------------------------------------------------------

Speaker         CON     0                       ' piezo speaker output
PitchCtrl       CON     1                       ' pitch control (RCTIME) input


' -----------------------------------------------------------------
' Constants
' -----------------------------------------------------------------

Scale           CON     $0100                   ' divider for BS2/BS2e
'Scale          CON     $0066                   ' divider for BS2sx
'Scale          CON     $0073                   ' divider for BS2p

Threshold       CON     200                     ' cutoff frequency to play


' -----------------------------------------------------------------
' Variables
' -----------------------------------------------------------------

tone            VAR     Word                    ' frequency output


' -----------------------------------------------------------------
' Program Code
' -----------------------------------------------------------------

Main:
  HIGH PitchCtrl                                ' discharge cap
  PAUSE 1                                        ' for 1 ms
  RCTIME PitchCtrl, 1, tone                      ' read the light sensor
  tone = tone */ Scale                           ' scale input

  IF (tone < Threshold) THEN Main                ' skip for ambient light
  FREQOUT Speaker, 25, tone                       ' output the tone
  GOTO Main

  END
```

Behind The Scenes

A Theremin is an interesting musical device used to create those weird, haunting sounds often heard in old horror movies. This version uses the light falling onto a photocell to create the output tone.

Since the photocell is a resistive device, RCTIME can be used to read its value. FREQOUT is used to play the note. The constant, Threshold, is used to control the cutoff point of the Theremin. When the photocell reading falls below this value, no sound is played. This value should be adjusted to the point where the Theremin stops playing when the photocell is not covered in ambient light.

Challenge

Add a second RC circuit using a 10K pot instead of a photocell. Use this circuit to adjust the threshold value to varying light conditions.

Experiment #20
Sound Effects

This experiment uses FREQOUT and DTMFOUT to create a telephone sound effects machine.

New PBASIC elements/commands to know:

- DTMFOUT

Building The Circuit

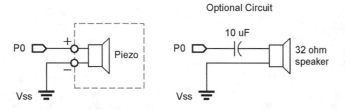

Note: Later versions of the StampWorks lab board come with a built-in audio amplifier. Attach an 8-ohm speaker to the output of the amplifier to get the best sound from this project.

```
' =============================================================================
'
'   File...... Ex20 - Sound FX.BS2
'   Purpose... Stamp-generated sounds
'   Author.... Parallax
'   E-mail.... stamptech@parallaxinc.com
'   Started...
'   Updated... 01 MAY 2002
'
'   {$STAMP BS2}
'
' =============================================================================


'   -----------------------------------------------------------------------------
'   Program Description
'   -----------------------------------------------------------------------------

'   This program demonstrates several realistic and interesting sound effects
'   that can be generated by the BASIC Stamp using FREQOUT and DTMFOUT.  This
```

```
' program works best when played through an amplifier.


' --------------------------------------------------------------------
' I/O Definitions
' --------------------------------------------------------------------

Speaker           CON      0                    ' speaker on pin 0


' --------------------------------------------------------------------
' Constants
' --------------------------------------------------------------------

R                 CON      0                    ' rest
C                 CON      33                   ' ideal is 32.703
Cs                CON      35                   ' ideal is 34.648
D                 CON      39                   ' ideal is 38.891
E                 CON      41                   ' ideal is 41.203
F                 CON      44                   ' ideal is 43.654
Fs                CON      46                   ' ideal is 46.249
G                 CON      49                   ' ideal is 48.999
Gs                CON      52                   ' ideal is 51.913
A                 CON      55                   ' ideal is 55.000
As                CON      58                   ' ideal is 58.270
B                 CON      62                   ' ideal is 61.735

N1                CON      500                  ' whole note duration
N2                CON      N1/2                 ' half note
N3                CON      N1/3                 ' third note
N4                CON      N1/4                 ' quarter note
N8                CON      N1/8                 ' eighth note

ScaleT            CON      $0100                ' time scale - BS2/BS2e
ScaleF            CON      $0100                ' frequency scale - BS2/BS2e

' ScaleT          CON      $0280                ' time scale - BS2sx
' ScaleF          CON      $0066                ' frequency scale - BS2sx

' ScaleT          CON      $03C6                ' time scale - BS2p
' ScaleF          CON      $0043                ' frequency scale - BS2p


' --------------------------------------------------------------------
' Variables
' --------------------------------------------------------------------
```

```
x               VAR     Word                        ' loop counter
note1           VAR     Word                        ' first tone for FREQOUT
note2           VAR     Word                        ' second tone for FREQOUT
onTime          VAR     Word                        ' duration for FREQOUT
offTime         VAR     Word
oct1            VAR     Nib                         ' octave for freq1 (1 - 8)
oct2            VAR     Nib                         ' octave for freq2 (1 - 8)
eePtr           VAR     Byte                        ' EEPROM pointer
digit           VAR     Byte                        ' DTMF digit
clickDly        VAR     Word                        ' delay betweens "clicks"


' -------------------------------------------------------------------------
' EEPROM Data
' -------------------------------------------------------------------------
'
Phone1          DATA    "972-555-1212", 0           ' a stored telephone number
Phone2          DATA    "916-624-8333", 0           ' another number


' -------------------------------------------------------------------------
' Program Code
' -------------------------------------------------------------------------

Main:
  PAUSE 250
  DEBUG CLS, "BASIC Stamp Sound FX Demo", CR, CR

Dial_Tone:
  DEBUG "Dial tone", CR
  onTime = 35 */ ScaleT
  note1 = 35 */ ScaleF
  FREQOUT Speaker, onTime, note1              ' "click"
  PAUSE 100
  onTime = 2000 */ ScaleT
  note1 = 350 */ ScaleF
  note2 = 440 */ ScaleF
  FREQOUT Speaker, onTime, note1, note2       ' combine 350 Hz & 440 Hz

Dial_Phone1:                                  ' dial phone from EE
  DEBUG "Dialing number: "
  eePtr = Phone1                              ' initialize eePtr pointer
  GOSUB Dial_Phone

Phone_Busy:
  PAUSE 1000
  DEBUG CR, " - busy...", CR
```

```
  onTime = 400 */ ScaleT
  note1 = 480 */ ScaleF
  note2 = 620 */ ScaleF
  FOR x = 1 TO 8
    FREQOUT Speaker, onTime, note1, note2          ' combine 480 Hz and 620 Hz
    PAUSE 620
  NEXT
  onTime = 35 */ ScaleT
  note1 = 35 */ ScaleF
  FREQOUT Speaker, onTime, note1                   ' "click"

Dial_Phone2:
  DEBUG "Calling Parallax: "
  eePtr = Phone2
  GOSUB Dial_Phone

Phone_Rings:
  PAUSE 1000
  DEBUG CR, " - ringing"
  onTime = 2000 */ ScaleT
  note1 = 440 */ ScaleF
  note2 = 480 */ ScaleF
  FREQOUT Speaker, onTime, note1, note2            ' combine 440 Hz and 480 Hz
  PAUSE 4000
  FREQOUT Speaker, onTime, note1, note2            ' combine 440 Hz and 480 Hz
  PAUSE 2000

Camptown_Song:
  DEBUG CR, "Play a Camptown song", CR
  FOR x = 0 TO 13
    LOOKUP x, [ G, G, E, G, A, G, E, R, E, D, R, E, D, R], note1
    LOOKUP x, [ 4, 4, 4, 4, 4, 4, 4, 1, 4, 4, 1, 4, 4, 1], oct1
    LOOKUP x, [N2, N2, N2, N2, N2, N2, N2, N2, N2, N1, N2, N2, N1, N8], onTime
    GOSUB Play_1_Note
  NEXT

Howler:
  DEBUG "Howler -- watch out!!!", CR
  FOR x = 1 TO 4
    onTime = 1000 */ ScaleT
    note1 = 1400 */ ScaleF
    note2 = 2060 */ ScaleF
    FREQOUT Speaker, onTime, note1, note2          ' combine 1400 Hz and 2060 Hz
    onTime = 1000 */ ScaleT
    note1 = 2450 */ ScaleF
    note2 = 2600 */ ScaleF
    FREQOUT Speaker, onTime, note1, note2          ' combine 2450 Hz and 2600 Hz
```

```
  NEXT

Roulette_Wheel:
  DEBUG "Roulette Wheel", CR
  onTime = 5 */ ScaleT                              ' onTime for "click"
  note1 = 35 */ ScaleF                              ' frequency for "click"
  clickDly = 250                                    ' starting delay between clicks
  FOR x = 1 TO 8                                    ' spin up wheel
    FREQOUT Speaker, onTime, note1                  ' click
    PAUSE clickDly
    clickDly = clickDly */ $00BF                    ' accelerate (speed * 0.75)
  NEXT
  FOR x = 1 TO 10                                   ' spin stable
    FREQOUT Speaker, onTime, note1
    PAUSE clickDly
  NEXT
  FOR x = 1 TO 20                                   ' slow down
    FREQOUT Speaker, onTime, note1
    PAUSE clickDly
    clickDly = clickDly */ $010C                    ' decelerate (speed * 1.05)
  NEXT
  FOR x = 1 TO 30                                   ' slow down and stop
    FREQOUT Speaker, onTime, note1
    PAUSE clickDly
    clickDly = clickDly */ $0119                    ' decelerate (speed * 1.10)
  NEXT

Computer_Beeps:                                     ' looks great with randmom LEDs
  DEBUG "50's Sci-Fi Computer", CR
  FOR x = 1 TO 50                                   ' run about 5 seconds
    onTime = 50 */ ScaleT
    RANDOM note1                                     ' create random note
    note1 = (note1 // 2500) */ ScaleF               ' don't let note go to high
    FREQOUT Speaker, onTime, note1                  ' play it
    PAUSE 100                                        ' short pause between notes
  NEXT

Space_Transporter:
  DEBUG "Space Transporter", CR
  onTime = 10 */ ScaleT
  FOR x = 5 TO 5000 STEP 5                          ' frequency sweep up
    note1 = x */ ScaleF
    FREQOUT Speaker, onTime, note1, note1 */ 323
  NEXT
  FOR x = 5000 TO 5 STEP 50                         ' frequency sweep down
    note1 = x */ ScaleF
    FREQOUT Speaker, onTime, note1, note1 */ 323
```

```
   NEXT

   DEBUG CR, "Sound demo complete."
   INPUT Speaker

   END


' --------------------------------------------------------------------
' Subroutines
' --------------------------------------------------------------------

Dial_Phone:
  READ eePtr, digit                         ' read a digit
  IF (digit = 0) THEN Dial_Exit             ' when 0, number is done
  DEBUG digit                               ' display digit
  IF (digit < "0") THEN Next_Digit          ' don't dial non-digits
  onTime = 150 */ ScaleT
  offTime = 75 */ ScaleT
  DTMFOUT Speaker, onTime, offTime, [digit - 48]

Next_Digit:
  eePtr = eePtr + 1                         ' update eePtr pointer
  GOTO Dial_Phone                           ' get another digit

Dial_Exit:
  RETURN


Play_1_Note:
  note1 = note1 << (oct1 - 1)               ' get frequency for note + octave
  onTime = onTime */ ScaleT
  note1 = note1 */ ScaleF
  FREQOUT Speaker, onTime, note1            ' play it
  RETURN


Play_2_Notes:
  note1 = note1 << (oct1 - 1)               ' get frequency for note + octave
  note2 = note2 << (oct2 - 1)               ' get frequency for note + octave
  onTime = onTime */ ScaleT
  note1 = note1 */ ScaleF
  note2 = note2 */ ScaleF
  FREQOUT Speaker, onTime, note1, note2     ' play both
  RETURN
```

Behind The Scenes

The a bit of programming creativity, the BASIC Stamp is able to create some very interesting sound effects. Since most of the sounds we hear on the telephone (other than voice) are generated with two tones, the BASIC Stamp's FREQOUT and DTMFOUT functions can be used to generate telephone sound effects.

DTMFOUT is actually a specialized version of FREQOUT. Its purpose is to play the dual-tones required to dial a telephone. Instead of passing a tone (or tones), the digit(s) to be dialed are passed as parameters. In actual dialing applications, the DTMF on-time and off-time can be specified to deal with telephone line quality.

This program also presents the BASIC Stamp's basic musical ability by playing a simple song. Constants for note frequency (in the first octave) and note timing simplify the operational code. The Play_1_Note subroutine adjusts note frequency for the specified octave. The musical quality can suffer a bit in the higher octaves because of rounding errors. Using the ideal values shown, the constants table can be expanded to create accurate musical notes. Keep in mind that each octave doubles the frequency of a note.

Octave 2 = Octave 1 * 2
Octave 3 = Octave 2 * 2
Octave 4 = Octave 3 * 2

And so on...

Challenge

Convert (a portion of) your favorite song to play on the BASIC Stamp.

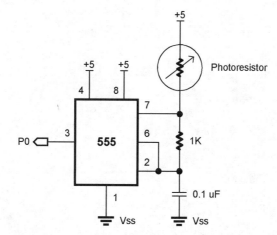

Experiment #21
Analog Input with PULSIN

The experiment reads a resistive component using PULSIN and a free-running oscillator.

Building The Circuit (Note that schematic is NOT chip-centric)

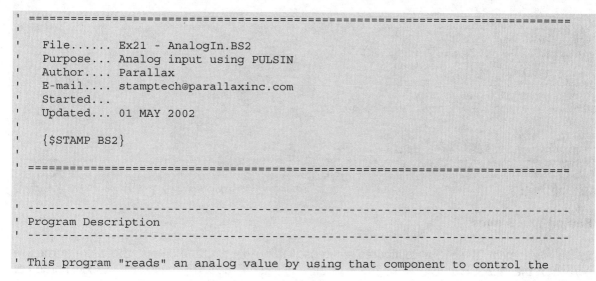

```
' =============================================================================
'
'
'   File...... Ex21 - AnalogIn.BS2
'   Purpose... Analog input using PULSIN
'   Author.... Parallax
'   E-mail.... stamptech@parallaxinc.com
'   Started...
'   Updated... 01 MAY 2002
'
'   {$STAMP BS2}
'
' =============================================================================
'
'
'
' ----------------------------------------------------------------------------
' Program Description
' ----------------------------------------------------------------------------
' This program "reads" an analog value by using that component to control the
```

```
' output frequency of a 555-based oscillator.  PULSIN is used to measure the
' high portion of the signal as it is controlled by the varialbe resistance.


' -------------------------------------------------------------------------
' I/O Definitions
' -------------------------------------------------------------------------

PulseInput        CON       0


' -------------------------------------------------------------------------
' Constants
' -------------------------------------------------------------------------

P75               CON       $00C0                   ' 0.75
P50               CON       $0080                   ' 0.50
P25               CON       $0040                   ' 0.25


' -------------------------------------------------------------------------
' Variables
' -------------------------------------------------------------------------

rValue            VAR       Word                    ' raw value
sValue            VAR       Word                    ' smoothed value


' -------------------------------------------------------------------------
' Program Code
' -------------------------------------------------------------------------

Main:
  PULSIN PulseInput, 1, rValue                      ' get high portion of input
  sValue = (rValue */ P25) + (sValue */ P75)

  DEBUG Home
  DEBUG "Raw value... ", DEC rValue, "      ", CR
  DEBUG "Filtered.... ", DEC sValue, "      "

  GOTO Main                                         ' do it again
```

Behind The Scenes

In this experiment, the 555 is configured as an oscillator. Analyzing the output, the width of the low portion of the output is controlled by the resistance of the photocell. By measuring the low portion of the 555's output signal with PULSIN, the BASIC Stamp is able to determine the relative value of the photocell.

Once the raw value is available, adding a portion of the raw value with a portion of the last filtered value digitally filters it. The ratio of raw-to-filtered readings in this equation will determine the responsiveness of the filter. The larger the raw portion, the faster the filter.

Challenge

Create a final output value that is scaled so that its range is between zero and 1000.

StampWorks

Experiment #22:
Analog Output with PWM

This program shows how create a variable voltage output with PWM.

New PBASIC elements/commands to know:

- PWM

Building The Circuit

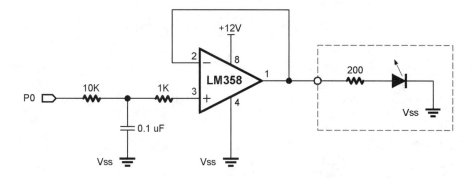

Note that this circuit requires 12V. The only place you can get 12V on the StampWorks lab board is from the +V screw terminal at the high-current driver location.

```
' =============================================================================
'
'   File...... Ex22 - Throb.BS2
'   Purpose... Output a variable voltage with PWM
'   Author.... Parallax
'   E-mail.... stamptech@parallaxinc.com
'   Started...
'   Updated... 01 MAY 2002
'
'   {$STAMP BS2}
'
' =============================================================================
```

```
' -----------------------------------------------------------------------
' Program Description
' -----------------------------------------------------------------------

' This program demonstrates how the PWM command can be used with an opamp
' buffer to create a variable voltage output.


' -----------------------------------------------------------------------
' I/O Definitions
' -----------------------------------------------------------------------

D2Aout          CON     0                       ' analog out pin


' -----------------------------------------------------------------------
' Constants
' -----------------------------------------------------------------------

OnTime          CON     10                      ' 10 milliseconds, BS2
'OnTime         CON     25                      ' BS2sx
'OnTime         CON     15                      ' BS2p


' -----------------------------------------------------------------------
' Variables
' -----------------------------------------------------------------------

level           VAR     Byte                    ' analog level


' -----------------------------------------------------------------------
' Program Code
' -----------------------------------------------------------------------

Main:
  FOR level = 0 TO 255                           ' increase voltage to LED
    PWM D2Aout, level, OnTime
  NEXT

  PAUSE 250

  FOR level = 255 TO 0                           ' decrease voltage to LED
    PWM D2Aout, level, OnTime
  NEXT

  GOTO Main                                      ' do it again
```

Behind The Scenes

While most BASIC Stamp applications will deal with digital signals, some will require analog output; a variable voltage between zero and some maximum voltage. The BASIC Stamp's PWM function is designed to generate analog voltages when combined with an R/C filter. The PWM function outputs a series of pulses which have a programmable on-time to off-time ratio (duty cycle). The greater the duty cycle, the greater voltage output. A duty cycle of 255 will charge the capacitor to five volts.

In this experiment, one half of the LM358 is used to provide a buffered voltage to the LED. The op-amp buffer prevents the capacitor from discharging too quickly under load. The LED brightness and dims because the changing voltage through its series resistor changes the current through the LED. Notice that the LED seems to snap on and get brighter, then dim to a level and snap off. This happens when the output of the LM358 crosses the forward voltage threshold (the minimum voltage for the LED to light) of the LED (about 1.8 volts).

Using the digital multimeter, monitor Pin 1 of the LM358.

Experiment #23:
Expanding Outputs

StampWorks

This experiment demonstrates the expansion of BASIC Stamp outputs with a simple shift register. Three lines are used to control eight LEDs with a 74x595 shift register.

New PBASIC elements/commands to know:

*   SHIFTOUT

Building The Circuit (Note that schematic is NOT chip-centric)

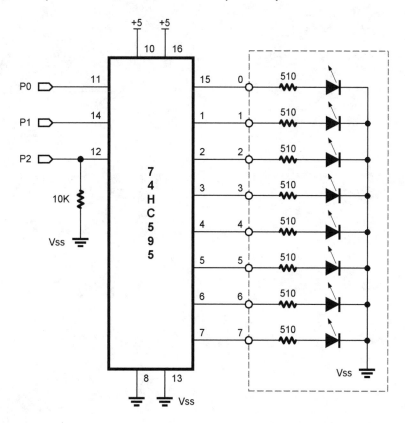

```
' ==============================================================================
'
'   File...... Ex23 - 74HC595.BS2
'   Purpose... Expanded outputs with 74HC595
'   Author.... Parallax
'   E-mail.... stamptech@parallaxinc.com
'   Started...
'   Updated... 01 MAY 2002
'
'   {$STAMP BS2}
'
' ==============================================================================


' ------------------------------------------------------------------------------
' Program Description
' ------------------------------------------------------------------------------

' This program demostrates a simple method of turning three Stamp lines into
' eight outputs with a 74HC595 shift register.


' ------------------------------------------------------------------------------
' I/O Definitions
' ------------------------------------------------------------------------------

Clock           CON     0                       ' shift clock (74HC595.11)
DataOut         CON     1                       ' serial data out (74HC595.14)
Latch           CON     2                       ' output latch (74HC595.12)


' ------------------------------------------------------------------------------
' Constants
' ------------------------------------------------------------------------------

DelayTime       CON     100


' ------------------------------------------------------------------------------
' Variables
' ------------------------------------------------------------------------------

pattern         VAR     Byte                    ' output pattern
```

```
' -------------------------------------------------------------------
' Initialization
' -------------------------------------------------------------------

Initialize:
  LOW Latch                                    ' make output and keep low
  pattern = %00000001


' -------------------------------------------------------------------
' Program Code
' -------------------------------------------------------------------

Go_Forward:
  GOSUB Out_595
  PAUSE DelayTime                              ' put pattern on 74x595
  pattern = pattern << 1                       ' shift pattern to the left
  IF (pattern = %10000000) THEN Go_Reverse     ' test for final position
  GOTO Go_Forward                              ' continue in this direction

Go_Reverse:
  GOSUB Out_595
  PAUSE DelayTime
  pattern = pattern >> 1
  IF (pattern = %00000001) THEN Go_Forward
  GOTO Go_Reverse


' -------------------------------------------------------------------
' Subroutines
' -------------------------------------------------------------------

Out_595:
  SHIFTOUT DataOut, Clock, MSBFirst, [pattern] ' send pattern to 74x595
  PULSOUT Latch, 5                             ' latch outputs
  RETURN
```

Behind The Scenes

The BASIC Stamp is extraordinarily flexible in its ability to redefine the direction (input or output) of its I/O pins, yet very few applications require this flexibility. For the most part, microcontroller applications will define pins as either inputs or outputs at initialization and the definitions will remain unchanged through the program.

We can use the fact that outputs are outputs and conserve valuable BASIC Stamp I/O lines at the same time by using a simple component called a serial-in, parallel-out shift register. In this experiment, the 74x595 is used. With just three BASIC Stamp lines, this program is able to control eight LEDs through the 74x595.

The 74x595 converts a synchronous serial data stream to eight parallel outputs. Synchronous serial data actually has two components: the serial data and a serial clock. The BASIC Stamp's SHIFTOUT command handles the details of the data and clock lines and writes data to a synchronous device, in this case, the 74x595. With the 74x595, the data must be latched to the outputs after the shift process. Latching is accomplished by briefly pulsing the Latch control line. This prevents the outputs from "rippling" as new data is being shifted in.

Being serial devices, shift registers can be cascaded. By cascading, the BASIC Stamp is able to control dozens of 74x595 outputs with the same three control lines. To connect cascaded 74x595s, the clock and latch lines are all tied together and the SQ output from one stage connects to the serial input of the next stage.

StampWorks

Experiment #23b: Expanding Outputs

This experiment demonstrates further expansion of BASIC Stamp outputs by cascading two 75x595 shift registers.

(Schematic on the next page)

Behind The Scenes

The 75x595 has a Serial Output pin (9) that allows the cascading of multiple devices for more outputs. In this configuration, the Clock and Latch pins are shared to keep all devices synchronized.

When cascading multiple shift registers, you must send the data for the device that is furthest down the chain first. Subsequent SHIFTOUT sequences will "push" the data through each register until the data is loaded into the correct device. Applying the latch pulse at that point causes the new data in all shift registers to appear at the outputs.

The demo program illustrates this point by independently displaying a binary counter and a ping-pong visual display using two 75x595 shift registers and eight LEDs for each. Note that the counter display is controlled by the 75x595 that is furthest from the BASIC Stamp, so its data is shifted out first.

Building The Circuit (Note that schematic is NOT chip-centric)

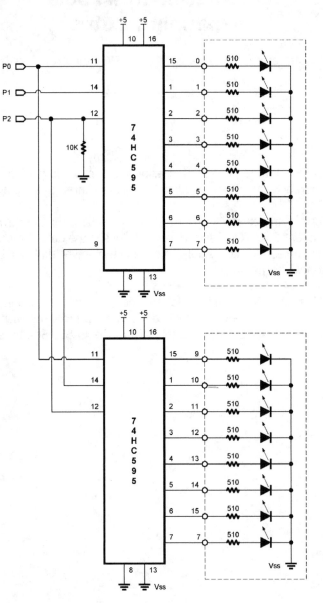

```
' ==============================================================================
'
'   File...... Ex23b - 74HC595 x 2.BS2
'   Purpose... Expanded outputs with 74HC595
'   Author.... Parallax
'   E-mail.... stamptech@parallaxinc.com
'   Started...
'   Updated... 01 MAY 2002
'
'   {$STAMP BS2}
'
' ==============================================================================


' ------------------------------------------------------------------------------
' Program Description
' ------------------------------------------------------------------------------

' This program demostrates a simple method of turning three Stamp lines into
' 16 outputs with two 74HC595 shift registers.  The data lines into the second
' 74HC595 is fed by the SQh output (pin 9) of the first.  The clock and latch
' pins of the second 74HC595 are connected to the same pins on the first.


' ------------------------------------------------------------------------------
' I/O Definitions
' ------------------------------------------------------------------------------

DataOut         CON     0                       ' serial data out (74HC595.14)
Clock           CON     1                       ' shift clock (74HC595.11)
Latch           CON     2                       ' output latch (74HC595.12)


' ------------------------------------------------------------------------------
' Constants
' ------------------------------------------------------------------------------

DelayTime       CON     100


' ------------------------------------------------------------------------------
' Variables
' ------------------------------------------------------------------------------

pattern         VAR     Byte                    ' output pattern
counter         VAR     Byte
```

Experiment #23b: Expanded Outputs

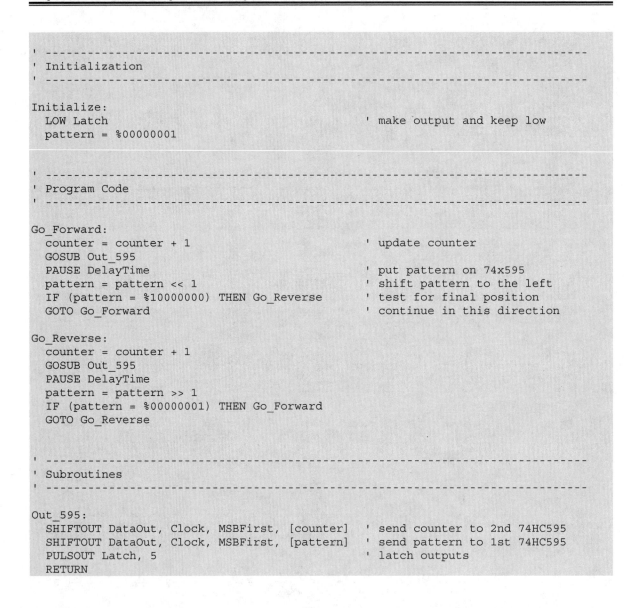

```
' -----------------------------------------------------------------
' Initialization
' -----------------------------------------------------------------

Initialize:
  LOW Latch                                 ' make output and keep low
  pattern = %00000001


' -----------------------------------------------------------------
' Program Code
' -----------------------------------------------------------------

Go_Forward:
  counter = counter + 1                     ' update counter
  GOSUB Out_595
  PAUSE DelayTime                           ' put pattern on 74x595
  pattern = pattern << 1                    ' shift pattern to the left
  IF (pattern = %10000000) THEN Go_Reverse  ' test for final position
  GOTO Go_Forward                           ' continue in this direction

Go_Reverse:
  counter = counter + 1
  GOSUB Out_595
  PAUSE DelayTime
  pattern = pattern >> 1
  IF (pattern = %00000001) THEN Go_Forward
  GOTO Go_Reverse


' -----------------------------------------------------------------
' Subroutines
' -----------------------------------------------------------------

Out_595:
  SHIFTOUT DataOut, Clock, MSBFirst, [counter] ' send counter to 2nd 74HC595
  SHIFTOUT DataOut, Clock, MSBFirst, [pattern] ' send pattern to 1st 74HC595
  PULSOUT Latch, 5                             ' latch outputs
  RETURN
```

Experiment #24: Expanding Inputs

This experiment demonstrates the expansion of BASIC Stamp inputs with a simple shift register. Three lines are used to read an eight-position DIP-switch.

New PBASIC elements/commands to know:

- SHIFTIN

Building The Circuit (Note that schematic is NOT chip-centric)

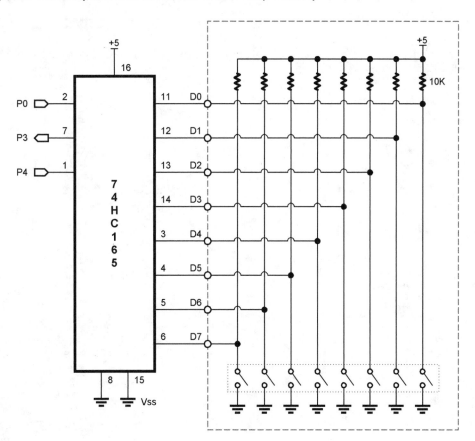

```
' ==============================================================================
'
'   File...... Ex24 - 74HC165.BS2
'   Purpose... Input expansion with 74HC165
'   Author.... Parallax
'   E-mail.... stamptech@parallaxinc.com
'   Started...
'   Updated... 01 MAY 2002
'
'   {$STAMP BS2}
'
' ==============================================================================


' ------------------------------------------------------------------------------
' Program Description
' ------------------------------------------------------------------------------

' This program shows how to read eight inputs with just three Stamp pins using
' a 74HC165 shift register.


' ------------------------------------------------------------------------------
' I/O Definitions
' ------------------------------------------------------------------------------

Clock           CON     0                       ' shift clock (74x165.2)
DataIn          CON     3                       ' shift data (74x165.7)
Load            CON     4                       ' input load (74x165.1)


' ------------------------------------------------------------------------------
' Variables
' ------------------------------------------------------------------------------

switches        VAR     Byte                    ' inputs switches


' ------------------------------------------------------------------------------
' Initialization
' ------------------------------------------------------------------------------

Initialize:
  HIGH Load                                     ' make output; initialize to 1
```

```
'   -------------------------------------------------------------------
'   Program Code
'   -------------------------------------------------------------------

Main:
  GOSUB Read_165                         ' read 8-pos dip switch
  DEBUG Home, "Switches = ", BIN8 switches   ' display binary mode
  PAUSE 100
  GOTO Main                              ' do it again


'   -------------------------------------------------------------------
'   Subroutines
'   -------------------------------------------------------------------

Read_165:
  PULSOUT Load, 5                        ' grab the switch inputs
  SHIFTIN DataIn, Clock, MSBPre, [switches]   ' shift them in
  RETURN
```

Behind The Scenes

The experiment demonstrates SHIFTIN, the complimentary function to SHIFTOUT. In this case, three BASIC Stamp I/O lines are used to read the state of eight input switches. To read the data from the 74x165, the parallel inputs are latched by briefly pulsing the Load line, then using SHIFTIN to move the data into the BASIC Stamp.

Note that the DIP-switches are pulled-up to Vdd, so setting them to "ON" creates a logic low input to the shift register. By using the Q\ (inverted) output from the 74x165, the data arrives at the BASIC Stamp with Bit 1 indicating a switch is on.

Experiment #24b: Expanding Inputs

StampWorks

This experiment demonstrates further expansion of BASIC Stamp inputs by cascading two shift registers.

(Schematic on next page)

Behind The Scenes

This program is very similar to 23b in that the Serial Output (pin 9) from one shift register is fed into the Serial input (pin 10) of the next device up the chain. Note that the non-inverted output is used on the second 74x165 because the inverted output of the deice connected directly to the BASIC Stamp will take care of the inversion.

In the program the **Read_165** subroutine has been updated to accommodate the second 74x165. The first **SHIFTIN** loads the data from the "buttons" shift register into the BASIC Stamp and transfers the contents from the "switches" shift register into the "buttons" shift register. The second **SHIFTIN** loads the "switches" data into the BASIC Stamp.

Building The Circuit (Note that schematic is NOT chip-centric)

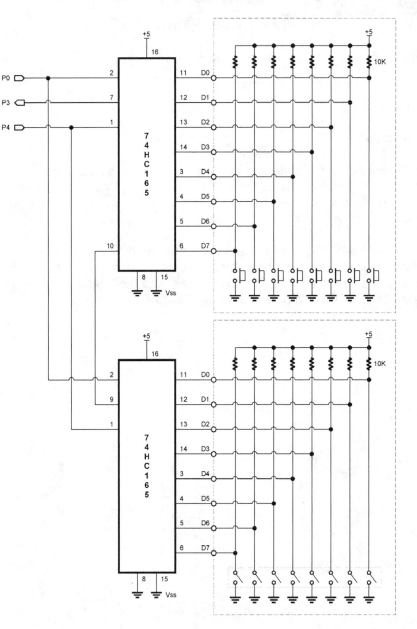

```
'  =============================================================================
'
'     File...... Ex24b - 74HC165 x 2.BS2
'     Purpose... Input expansion with 74HC165
'     Author.... Parallax
'     E-mail.... stamptech@parallaxinc.com
'     Started...
'     Updated... 01 MAY 2002
'
'     {$STAMP BS2}
'
'  =============================================================================


'  ----------------------------------------------------------------------------
'  Program Description
'  ----------------------------------------------------------------------------

'  This program shows how to read 16 inputs with just three Stamp pins using
'  two 74HC165 shift registers.  The serial output (pin 9) from one 74HC165
'  is fed into the serial input (pin 10) of the second.


'  ----------------------------------------------------------------------------
'  I/O Definitions
'  ----------------------------------------------------------------------------

Clock           CON     0                       ' shift clock (74x165.2)
DataIn          CON     3                       ' shift data (74x165.7)
Load            CON     4                       ' input load (74x165.1)


'  ----------------------------------------------------------------------------
'  Variables
'  ----------------------------------------------------------------------------

switches        VAR     Byte                    ' inputs switches
buttons         VAR     Byte                    ' push button inputs


'  ----------------------------------------------------------------------------
'  Initialization
'  ----------------------------------------------------------------------------

Initialize:
  HIGH Load                                     ' make output; initialize to 1
```

```
' -----------------------------------------------------------------------
' Program Code
' -----------------------------------------------------------------------

Main:
  GOSUB Read_165                                  ' read switches and buttons
  DEBUG Home
  DEBUG "Buttons = ", BIN8 buttons, CR            ' display binary mode
  DEBUG "Swithces =  ", BIN8 switches
  PAUSE 100
  GOTO Main                                       ' do it again


' -----------------------------------------------------------------------
' Subroutines
' -----------------------------------------------------------------------

Read_165:
  PULSOUT Load, 5                                 ' latch inputs
  SHIFTIN DataIn, Clock, MSBPre, [buttons]        ' get buttons
  SHIFTIN DataIn, Clock, MSBPre, [switches]       ' get switches
  RETURN
```

Experiment #25: Hobby Servo Control

This experiment demonstrates the control of a standard hobby servo. Hobby servos frequently are used in amateur robotics.

New PBASIC elements/commands to know:

- SDEC, SDEC1 – SDEC16 (DEBUG modifier)

Building The Circuit

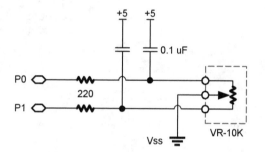

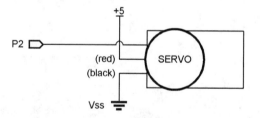

```
' =============================================================================
'
'   File...... Ex25 - Servo.BS2
'   Purpose... Hobby Servo Control
'   Author.... Parallax
'   E-mail.... stamptech@parallaxinc.com
'   Started...
'   Updated... 01 MAY 2002
'
'   {$STAMP BS2}
```

```
'
' ===========================================================================
'
'
' ---------------------------------------------------------------------------
' Program Description
' ---------------------------------------------------------------------------
'
' This program shows how to control a standard servo with the BASIC Stamp.
'
'
' ---------------------------------------------------------------------------
' I/O Definitions
' ---------------------------------------------------------------------------
'
PotCW           CON     0                       ' clockwise pot input
PotCCW          CON     1                       ' counter-clockwise pot input
Servo           CON     2                       ' servo control pin
'
'
' ---------------------------------------------------------------------------
' Constants
' ---------------------------------------------------------------------------
'
Scale           CON     $0068                   ' scale RCTIME to 0 - 250, BS2
' Scale         CON     $002C                   ' BS2sx
' Scale         CON     $002A                   ' BS2p
'
'
' ---------------------------------------------------------------------------
' Variables
' ---------------------------------------------------------------------------
'
rcRt            VAR     Word                    ' rc reading - right
rcLf            VAR     Word                    ' rc reading - left
diff            VAR     Word                    ' difference between readings
sPos            VAR     Word                    ' servo position
'
'
' ---------------------------------------------------------------------------
' Program Code
' ---------------------------------------------------------------------------
'
Main:
  HIGH PotCW                                    ' discharge caps
  HIGH PotCCW
  PAUSE 1
```

```
RCTIME PotCW, 1, rcRt                      ' read clockwise
RCTIME PotCCW, 1, rcLf                     ' read counter-clockwise

rcRt = (rcRt */ Scale) MAX 250             ' scale RCTIME to 0-250
rcLf = (rcLf */ Scale) MAX 250
sPos = rcRt - rcLf                         ' calculate position (-250 to 250)

PULSOUT Servo, (750 + sPos)                ' move the servo
PAUSE 20

GOTO Main
```

Behind The Scenes

Hobby servos are specialized electromechanical devices used most frequently to position the control surfaces of model aircraft. The position of the servo output shaft is determined by the width of an incoming control pulse. The control pulse is typically between one and two milliseconds wide. The servo will center when the control signal is 1.5 milliseconds. In order to maintain its position, the servo must constantly be updated. The typical update frequency is about 50 times per second.

The BASIC Stamp's PULSOUT command is ideal command for controlling hobby servos. In this experiment, two RCTIME circuits are constructed around the 10K potentiometer. This circuit and the project code can be used to determine the relative position of the potentiometer. The readings from each side of the potentiometer are scaled between 0 and 250 with the */ and MAX operators. By subtracting one side from the other, a servo position value between −250 and +250 is returned.

This value is added to the centering position of 750. Remember that PULSOUT works in two-microsecond units, so a PULSOUT value of 750 will create a pulse that is 1.5 milliseconds wide, causing the servo to center. When the servo position is −250, the PULSOUT value is 500, creating a 1.0-millisecond pulse. At an sPos value of +250, the PULSOUT value is 1000, creating a 2.0 millisecond control pulse.

This code demonstrates that the BASIC Stamp does, indeed, work with negative numbers. You can see the value of sPos by inserting this line after the calculation:

```
DEBUG Home, "Position: ", SDEC sPos, "    "
```

Negative numbers are stored in two's compliment format. The SDEC (signed decimal) modifier prints standard decimal with the appropriate sign.

Challenge

Replace the potentiometer with two photocells and update the code to cause the servo to center at the brightest light source.

Experiment #26:
Stepper Motor Control

This experiment demonstrates the control of a small 12-volt unipolar stepper motor. Stepper motors are used as precision positioning devices in robotics and industrial control applications.

New PBASIC elements/commands to know:

- ABS

Building The Circuit

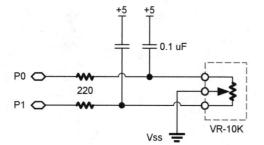

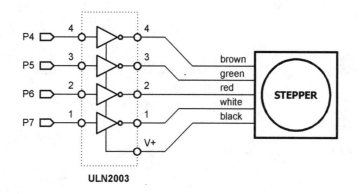

```
' ===============================================================================
'
'     File...... Ex26 - Stepper.BS2
'     Purpose... Stepper Motor Control
'     Author.... Parallax
'     E-mail.... stamptech@parallaxinc.com
'     Started...
'     Updated... 01 MAY 2002
'
'     {$STAMP BS2}
'
' ===============================================================================


' -------------------------------------------------------------------------------
' Program Description
' -------------------------------------------------------------------------------

' This program demonstrates unipolar stepper motor control.  The pot allows the
' program to control speed and direction of the motor.


' -------------------------------------------------------------------------------
' Revision History
' -------------------------------------------------------------------------------


' -------------------------------------------------------------------------------
' I/O Definitions
' -------------------------------------------------------------------------------

PotCW             CON     0                     ' clockwise pot input
PotCCW            CON     1                     ' counter-clockwise pot input
Coils             VAR     OutB                  ' output to stepper coils


' -------------------------------------------------------------------------------
' Constants
' -------------------------------------------------------------------------------

Scale             CON     $0100                 ' scale for BS2 (1.0)
' Scale           CON     $0080                 ' scale for BS2sx, BS2p (0.5)


' -------------------------------------------------------------------------------
' Variables
' -------------------------------------------------------------------------------
```

```
speed            VAR     Word                    ' delay between steps
x                VAR     Byte                    ' loop counter
sAddr            VAR     Byte                    ' EE address of step data
rcRt             VAR     Word                    ' rc reading - right
rcLf             VAR     Word                    ' rc reading - left
diff             VAR     Word                    ' difference between readings


' -----------------------------------------------------------------------
' EEPROM Data
' -----------------------------------------------------------------------
'
'                         ABAB
'                         -----
Step1            DATA    %1100                   ' A on   B on   A\ off  B\ off
Step2            DATA    %0110                   ' A off  B on   A\ on   B\ off
Step3            DATA    %0011                   ' A off  B off  A\ on   B\ on
Step4            DATA    %1001                   ' A on   B off  A\ off  B\ on


' -----------------------------------------------------------------------
' Initialization
' -----------------------------------------------------------------------

Initialize:
  DirB = %1111                                   ' make stepper pins outputs
  speed = 5                                      ' set starting speed


' -----------------------------------------------------------------------
' Program Code
' -----------------------------------------------------------------------

Main:
  FOR x = 1 TO 100                               ' 1 rev forward
    GOSUB Step_Fwd
  NEXT
  PAUSE 200

  FOR x = 1 TO 100                               ' 1 rev back
    GOSUB Step_Rev
  NEXT
  PAUSE 200

Step_Demo:
  HIGH PotCW                                     ' discharge caps
```

```
     HIGH PotCCW
     PAUSE 1
     RCTIME PotCW, 1, rcRt                           ' read clockwise
     RCTIME PotCCW, 1, rcLf                          ' read counter-clockwise

     rcRt = (rcRt */ Scale) MAX 600                  ' set speed limits
     rcLf = (rcLf */ Scale) MAX 600
     diff = ABS(rcRt - rcLf)                         ' get difference between readings

     IF (diff < 25) THEN Step_Demo                   ' allow dead band
     IF (rcLf > rcRt) THEN Step_CCW

Step_CW:
     speed = 60 - (rcRt / 10)                        ' calculate speed
     GOSUB Step_Fwd                                  ' do a step
     GOTO Step_Demo

Step_CCW:
     speed = 60 - (rcLf / 10)
     GOSUB Step_Rev
     GOTO Step_Demo


'    ----------------------------------------------------------------------
'    Subroutines
'    ----------------------------------------------------------------------

Step_Fwd:
     sAddr = sAddr + 1 // 4                          ' point to next step
     READ (Step1 + sAddr), Coils                     ' output step data
     PAUSE speed                                     ' pause between steps
     RETURN


Step_Rev:
     sAddr = sAddr + 3 // 4                          ' point to previous step
     READ (Step1 + sAddr), Coils
     PAUSE speed
     RETURN
```

Behind The Scenes

Stepper motors differ from standard DC motors in that they do not spin freely when power is applied. For a stepper motor to rotate, the power source must be continuously pulsed in specific patterns. The step sequence (pattern) determines the direction of the stepper's rotation. The time between sequence steps determines the rotational speed. Each step causes the stepper motor to rotate a fixed angular increment. The stepper motor supplied with the StampWorks kit rotates 3.6 degrees per step. This means that one full rotation (360 degrees) of the stepper requires 100 steps.

The step sequences for the motor are stored in DATA statements. The stepFwd subroutine will read the next sequence from the table to be applied to the coils. The stepRev subroutine is identical except that it will read the previous step. Note the trick with the modulus (//) operator used in stepRev. By adding the maximum value of the sequence to the current value and then applying the modulus operator, the sequence goes in reverse. Here's the math:

$$0 + 3 // 4 = 3$$
$$3 + 3 // 4 = 2$$
$$2 + 3 // 4 = 1$$
$$1 + 3 // 4 = 0$$

This experiment reads both sides of the 10K potentiometer to determine its relative position. The differential value between the two readings is kept positive by using the ABS function. The position is used to determine the rotational direction and the strength of the position is used to determine the rotational speed. Remember, the shorter the delay between steps, the faster the stepper will rotate. A dead-band check is used to cause the motor to stop rotating when the RCTIME readings are nearly equal.

Challenge

Rewrite the program to run the motor in 200 half steps. Here's the step sequence:

    Step1 = %1000
    Step2 = %1100
    Step3 = %0100
    Step4 = %0110
    Step5 = %0010
    Step6 = %0011
    Step7 = %0001
    Step8 = %1001

Experiment #27:
Voltage Measurement

This experiment demonstrates the use of an analog-to-digital converter to read a variable voltage input.

Building The Circuit (Note that schematic is NOT chip-centric)

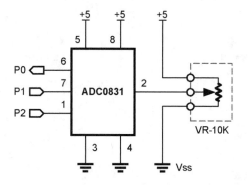

```
' =============================================================================
'
'   File...... Ex27 - ADC0831.BS2
'   Purpose... Analog to Digital conversion
'   Author.... Parallax
'   E-mail.... stamptech@parallaxinc.com
'   Started...
'   Updated... 01 MAY 2002
'
'   {$STAMP BS2}
'
' =============================================================================


' -----------------------------------------------------------------------------
' Program Description
' -----------------------------------------------------------------------------

' This program deomstrates reading a variable voltage with an ADC0831 analog-
' to-digital convertor chip.
```

```
' --------------------------------------------------------------------
' I/O Definitions
' --------------------------------------------------------------------

A2Ddata         CON     0                       ' A/D data line
A2Dclock        CON     1                       ' A/D clock
A2Dcs           CON     2                       ' A/D chip select (low true)


' --------------------------------------------------------------------
' Variables
' --------------------------------------------------------------------

result          VAR     Byte                    ' result of conversion
mVolts          VAR     Word                    ' convert to millivolts


' --------------------------------------------------------------------
' Initialization
' --------------------------------------------------------------------

Initialize:
  HIGH A2Dcs


' --------------------------------------------------------------------
' Program Code
' --------------------------------------------------------------------

Main:
  GOSUB Read_0831
  mVolts = result */ $139C                      ' x 19.6 (mv / unit)

  DEBUG Home
  DEBUG "ADC..... ", DEC result, "    ", CR
  DEBUG "volts... ", DEC mVolts DIG 3, ".", DEC3 mVolts

  PAUSE 100                                     ' delay between readings
  GOTO Main                                     ' do it again
```

```
'   --------------------------------------------------------------------
'   Subroutines
'   --------------------------------------------------------------------

Read_0831:
  LOW A2Dcs
  SHIFTIN A2Ddata, A2Dclock, MSBPost, [result\9]
  HIGH A2Dcs
  RETURN
```

Behind The Scenes

Previous projects have used RCTIME to read resistive components. This is a form of analog input, but isn't voltage measurement. For that, the BASIC Stamp needs help from an external device. The simplest way to measure a variable voltage is with an analog-to-digital converter.

In this experiment, the National Semiconductor ADC0831 is used to convert a voltage (0 – 5) to a synchronous serial signal that can be read by the BASIC Stamp with SHIFTIN. The nature of the ADC0831 requires nine bits to shift in the result. This is no problem for the BASIC Stamp as the SHIFTIN function allows the number of shifted bits to be specified.

The eight-bit result will be from zero (zero volts) to 255 (five volts). Dividing five (volts) by 255, we find that each bit in the result is equal to 19.6 millivolts. For display purposes, the result is converted to millivolts by multiplying by 19.6 (result */ $139C). A neat trick with DEBUG is used to display the variable, mVolts. The "DIG 3" operation prints the whole volts and the DEC3 modifier prints the fractional volts.

Challenge

Connect the output of Experiment 22 (Pin 1 of the LM358) to the input of the ADC0831. Write a program to create a voltage using **PWM** and read it back with the ADC0831.

Experiment #28:
Temperature Measurement

This experiment demonstrates the use of a digital temperature sensor. Temperature measurement is a necessary component of environmental control applications (heating and air conditioning).

Building The Circuit (Note that schematic is NOT chip-centric)

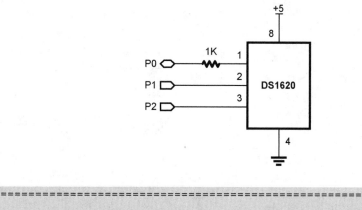

```
' =================================================================================
'
'   File...... Ex28 - DS1620.BS2
'   Purpose... Temperature measurement
'   Author.... Parallax
'   E-mail.... stamptech@parallaxinc.com
'   Started...
'   Updated... 01 MAY 2002
'
'   {$STAMP BS2}
'
' =================================================================================


'   -------------------------------------------------------------------------------
'   Program Description
'   -------------------------------------------------------------------------------

'   This program measures temperature using the Dallas Semiconductor DS1620
'   temperature sensor.
```

```
' -------------------------------------------------------------------
' I/O Definitions
' -------------------------------------------------------------------

DQ              CON     0                   ' DS1620.1 (data I/O)
Clock           CON     1                   ' DS1620.2
Reset           CON     2                   ' DS1620.3


' -------------------------------------------------------------------
' Constants
' -------------------------------------------------------------------

RdTmp           CON     $AA                 ' read temperature
WrHi            CON     $01                 ' write TH (high temp)
WrLo            CON     $02                 ' write TL (low temp)
RdHi            CON     $A1                 ' read TH
RdLo            CON     $A2                 ' read TL
StartC          CON     $EE                 ' start conversion
StopC           CON     $22                 ' stop conversion
WrCfg           CON     $0C                 ' write config register
RdCfg           CON     $AC                 ' read config register


' -------------------------------------------------------------------
' Variables
' -------------------------------------------------------------------

tempIn          VAR     Word                ' raw temperature
sign            VAR     tempIn.Bit8         ' 1 = negative temperature
tSign           VAR     Bit
tempC           VAR     Word                ' Celsius
tempF           VAR     Word                ' Fahrenheit


' -------------------------------------------------------------------
' Initialization
' -------------------------------------------------------------------

Initialize:
  HIGH Reset                                ' alert the DS1620
  SHIFTOUT DQ, Clock, LSBFirst, [WrCfg, %10] ' use with CPU; free-run
  LOW Reset
  PAUSE 10
  HIGH Reset
  SHIFTOUT DQ, Clock, LSBFirst, [StartC]            ' start conversions
  LOW Reset
```

```
' --------------------------------------------------------------
' Program Code
' --------------------------------------------------------------

Main:
  GOSUB Get_Temperature                        ' read the DS1620

  DEBUG Home
  DEBUG "DS1620", CR
  DEBUG "------", CR
  DEBUG SDEC tempC, " C     ", CR
  DEBUG SDEC tempF, " F     ", CR

  PAUSE 1000                                   ' pause between readings
  GOTO Main


' --------------------------------------------------------------
' Subroutines
' --------------------------------------------------------------

Get_Temperature:
  HIGH Reset                                   ' alert the DS1620
  SHIFTOUT DQ, Clock, LSBFIRST, [RdTmp]        ' give command to read temp
  SHIFTIN DQ, Clock, LSBPRE, [tempIn\9]        ' read it in
  LOW Reset                                    ' release the DS1620

  tSign = sign                                 ' save sign bit
  tempIn = tempIn / 2                          ' round to whole degrees
  IF (tSign = 0) THEN No_Neg1
  tempIn = tempIn | $FF00                      ' extend sign bits for negative

No_Neg1:
  tempC = tempIn                               ' save Celsius value
  tempIn = tempIn */ $01CC                     ' multiply by 1.8
  IF (tSign = 0) THEN No_Neg2                  ' if negative, extend sign bits
  tempIn = tempIn | $FF00

No_Neg2:
  tempIn = tempIn + 32                         ' finish C -> F conversion
  tempF = tempIn                               ' save Fahrenheit value
  RETURN
```

Behind The Scenes

The largest organ of the human body is the skin and it is most readily affected by temperature. Little wonder then that so much effort is put into environmental control systems (heating and air conditioning).

This experiment uses the Dallas Semiconductor DS1620 digital thermometer/thermostat chip. This chip measures temperature and makes it available to the BASIC Stamp through a synchronous serial interface. The DS1620 is an intelligent device and, once programmed, is capable of stand-alone operation using the T(com), T(hi) and T(lo) outputs.

The DS1620 requires initialization before use. In active applications like this, the DS1620 is configured for free running with a CPU. After the configuration data is sent to the DS1620, a delay of 10 milliseconds is required so that the configuration can be written to the DS1620's internal EEPROM. After the delay, the DS1620 is instructed to start continuous conversions. This will ensure a current temperature reading when the BASIC Stamp requests it.

To retrieve the current temperature, the Read Temperature ($AA) command byte is sent to the DS1620. Then the latest conversion value is read back. The data returned is nine bits wide. Bit8 indicates the sign of the temperature. If negative (sign bit is 1), the other eight bits hold the two's compliment value of the temperature. Whether negative or positive, each bit of the temperature is equal to 0.5 degrees Celsius.

The Celsius temperature is converted to whole degrees by dividing by two. If negative, the upper-byte bits are set to 1 so that the value will print properly with SDEC (signed numbers in the BASIC Stamp must be 16 bits in length). The temperature is converted to Fahrenheit using the standard formula:

$$F = (C * 1.8) + 32$$

Challenge

Rewrite the program to write the temperature values to the StampWorks LCD module.

Experiment #29: Advanced 7-Segment Multiplexing

This experiment demonstrates the use of seven-segment displays with an external multiplexing controller. Multi-digit seven-segment displays are frequently used on vending machines to display the amount of money entered.

Building The Circuit (Note that schematic is NOT chip-centric)

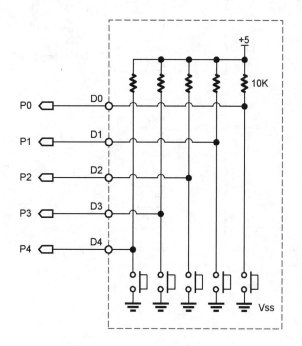

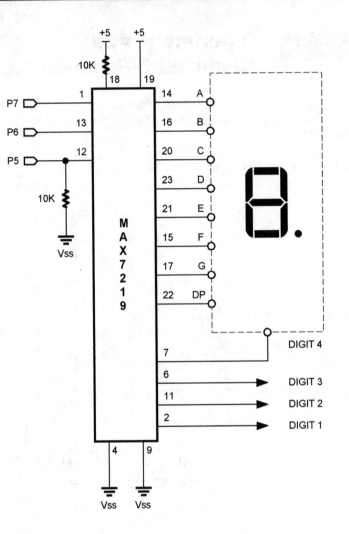

```
' ===========================================================================
'
'     File...... Ex29 - Change Counter.BS2
'     Purpose... Controlling 7-segment displays with MAX7219
'     Author.... Parallax
'     E-mail.... stamptech@parallaxinc.com
'     Started...
'     Updated... 01 MAY 2002
'
'     {$STAMP BS2}
'
' ===========================================================================


' ---------------------------------------------------------------------------
' Program Description
' ---------------------------------------------------------------------------

' This program is a coin counter -- it will count pennies, nickels, dimes and
' quarters using pushbutton inputs.  The "bank" is displayed on four 7-segment
' LED displays that are controlled with a MAX7219.


' ---------------------------------------------------------------------------
' Revision History
' ---------------------------------------------------------------------------


' ---------------------------------------------------------------------------
' I/O Definitions
' ---------------------------------------------------------------------------

DataPin         CON       7                      ' data pin (MAX7219.1)
Clock           CON       6                      ' clock pin (MAX7219.13)
Load            CON       5                      ' load pin (MAX7219.12)
Coins           VAR       InL                    ' coin count inputs


' ---------------------------------------------------------------------------
' Constants
' ---------------------------------------------------------------------------

Decode          CON       $09                    ' bcd decode register
Brite           CON       $0A                    ' intensity register
Scan            CON       $0B                    ' scan limit register
ShutDn          CON       $0C                    ' shutdown register (1 = on)
Test            CON       $0F                    ' display test mode
```

```
DecPnt          CON     %10000000
Blank           CON     %1111                          ' blank a digit

Yes             CON     1
No              CON     0


' ---------------------------------------------------------------------
' Variables
' ---------------------------------------------------------------------

money           VAR     Word                    ' current money count
deposit         VAR     Byte                    ' coins deposited
penny           VAR     deposit.Bit0            ' bit values of deposit
nickel          VAR     deposit.Bit1
dime            VAR     deposit.Bit2
quarter         VAR     deposit.Bit3
dollar          VAR     deposit.Bit4
digit           VAR     Nib                     ' display digit
d7219           VAR     Byte                    ' data for MAX7219
index           VAR     Nib                     ' loop counter
idxOdd          VAR     index.Bit0              ' is index odd? (1 = yes)


' ---------------------------------------------------------------------
' EEPROM Data
' ---------------------------------------------------------------------


' Segments              .abcdefg
'                       --------
Full            DATA    %01000111                       ' F
                DATA    %00111110                       ' U
                DATA    %00001110                       ' L
                DATA    %00001110                       ' L


' ---------------------------------------------------------------------
' Initialization
' ---------------------------------------------------------------------


Initialize:
  DirL = %11100000                              ' data, clock and load as outs
                                                '   coins as inputs


  FOR index = 0 TO 7
    LOOKUP index, [Scan, 3, Brite, 5, Decode, $0F, ShutDn, 1], d7219
    SHIFTOUT DataPin, Clock, MSBFirst, [d7219]
```

```
      IF (idxOdd = No) THEN No_Load
      PULSOUT Load, 5                                     ' load parameter

No_Load:
  NEXT

  GOSUB Show_The_Money



' ----------------------------------------------------------------------------
' Program Code
' ----------------------------------------------------------------------------

Main:
  GOSUB Get_Coins
  IF (deposit = 0) THEN Main                             ' wait for coins

  money = money + (penny * 1)                            ' add coins
  money = money + (nickel * 5)
  money = money + (dime * 10)
  money = money + (quarter * 25)
  money = money + (dollar * 100)

  GOSUB Show_The_Money                                   ' update the display
  PAUSE 100
  GOTO Main



' ----------------------------------------------------------------------------
' Subroutines
' ----------------------------------------------------------------------------

Get_Coins:
  deposit = %00011111                                    ' enable all coin inputs
  FOR index = 1 TO 10
    deposit = deposit & ~Coins                           ' test inputs
    PAUSE 5                                              ' delay between tests
  NEXT
  RETURN


Show_The_Money:
  IF (money >= 9999) THEN Show_Full
  FOR index = 4 TO 1
    d7219 = Blank
    IF ((index = 4) AND (money < 1000)) THEN Put_Digit
    d7219 = money DIG (index - 1)
```

```
        IF (index <> 3) THEN Put_Digit
        d7219 = d7219 | DecPnt                    ' decimal point on DIGIT 3

Put_Digit:
      SHIFTOUT DataPin, Clock, MSBFirst, [index, d7219]
      PULSOUT Load, 5
    NEXT
    RETURN


Show_Full:
    ' turn BCD decoding off
    SHIFTOUT DataPin, Clock, MSBFirst, [Decode, 0]
    PULSOUT Load, 5
    FOR index = 4 TO 1
      READ (4 - index + Full), d7219            ' read and send letter
      SHIFTOUT DataPin, Clock, MSBFirst, [index, d7219]
      PULSOUT Load, 5
    NEXT

    END
```

Behind The Scenes

Multiplexing multiple seven-segment displays requires a lot of effort that consumes most of the computational resources of the BASIC Stamp. Enter the MAXIM MAX7219 LED display driver. Using just three of the BASIC Stamp's I/O lines, the MAX7219 can be used to control up to eight, seven-segment displays or 64 discrete LEDs (four times the number of I/O pins available on the BASIC Stamp).

The MAX7219 connects to the LED displays in a straightforward way; pins SEG A through SEG G and SEG DP connect to segments A through G and the decimal point of all of the common-cathode displays. Pins DIGIT 0 through DIGIT 7 connect to the individual cathodes of each of the displays. If you use less than eight digits, omit the highest digit numbers. For example, this experiment uses four digits, numbered 0 through 3, not 4 through 7.

The MAX7219 has a scan-limit feature than limits display scanning to digits 0 through n, where n is the highest digit number. This feature ensures that the chip doesn't waste time and duty cycles (brightness) trying to scan digits that aren't there.

When the MAX7219 is used with seven-segment displays, it can be configured to automatically convert binary-coded decimal (BCD) values into appropriate patterns of segments. This makes the display of decimal numbers simple. The BCD decoding feature can be disabled to display custom patterns. This experiment does both.

From a software standpoint, driving the MAX7219 requires the controller to:

> Shift 16 data bits out to the device, MSB first.
> Pulse the Load line to transfer the data.

Each 16-bit data package consists of a register address followed by data to store to that register. For example, the 16-bit value $0407 (hex) writes a "7" to the fourth digit of the display. If BCD decoding is turned on for that digit, the numeral "7" will appear on that digit of the display. If decoding is not turned on, three LEDs will light, corresponding to segments G, F, and E.

In this experiment, the MAX7219 is initialized to:

> Scan = 3 (Display digits 0 – 3)
> Brightness = 5
> Decode = $0F (BCD decode digits 0 – 3)
> Shutdown = 1 (normal operation)

Initialization of the MAX7219 is handled by a loop. Each pass through the loop reads a register address or data value from a LOOKUP table. After each data value is shifted out, the address and data are latched into the MAX7219 by pulsing the Load line.

Most of the work takes place in the subroutine called Show_The_Money. When the money count is less than 9999, the value will be displayed on the seven-segment digits, otherwise the display will read "FULL." The routine scans through each digit of money and sends the digit position and value (from the DIG operator) to the MAX7219. Since the display shows dollars and cents, the decimal point on the third digit is enabled. When the position and digit have been shifted out, the display is updated by pulsing the Load line. To keep the display neat, the leading zero is blanked when the money value is less than 1000.

When the value of money reaches 9999, the display will change to "FULL." This is accomplished by disabling the BCD decoding of the MAX7219 and sending custom letter patterns to the MAX7219. These patterns are stored in DATA statements.

The main loop of the program is simple: it scans the switch inputs with `Get_Coins` and updates the money count for each switch pressed. This particular code is an excellent example of using variable aliases for readability.

Challenge

Modify the code in experiment 27 to display the input voltage on the seven-segment displays.

Experiment #30: Using a Real-Time Clock

This experiment demonstrates the BASIC Stamp's time-keeping functions through the use of an external real-time clock (RTC). RTC time capability is crucial to time-of-day applications and applications that require the measurement of elapsed time.

Building The Circuit (Note that schematic is NOT chip-centric)

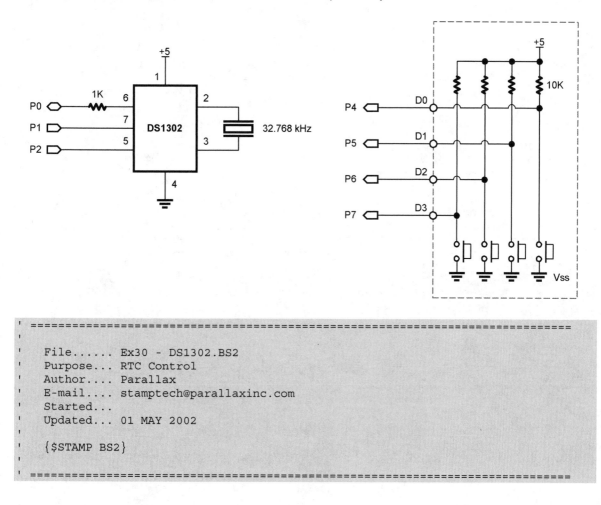

```
' =================================================================
'
'   File...... Ex30 - DS1302.BS2
'   Purpose... RTC Control
'   Author.... Parallax
'   E-mail.... stamptech@parallaxinc.com
'   Started...
'   Updated... 01 MAY 2002
'
'   {$STAMP BS2}
'
' =================================================================
```

```
' -------------------------------------------------------------------
' Program Description
' -------------------------------------------------------------------

' This program demonstrates the control and use of an external real-time clcok
' chip, the DS1302 from Dallas Semiconductor.


' -------------------------------------------------------------------
' I/O Definitions
' -------------------------------------------------------------------

DataIO          CON     0               ' DS1302.6
Clock           CON     1               ' DS1302.7
CS1302          CON     2               ' DS1302.5
BtnsIn          VAR     InB             ' button input


' -------------------------------------------------------------------
' Constants
' -------------------------------------------------------------------

WrSecs          CON     $80             ' write seconds
RdSecs          CON     $81             ' read seconds
WrMins          CON     $82             ' write minutes
RdMins          CON     $83             ' read minutes
WrHrs           CON     $84             ' write hours
RdHrs           CON     $85             ' read hours
CWPr            CON     $8E             ' write protect register
WPr1            CON     $80             ' set write protect
WPr0            CON     $00             ' clear write protect
WrBurst         CON     $BE             ' write burst of data
RdBurst         CON     $BF             ' read burst of data
WrRam           CON     $C0             ' RAM address control
RdRam           CON     $C1

Yes             CON     1
No              CON     0

Hr24            CON     0
Hr12            CON     1

ClockMode       CON     Hr12            ' use AM/PM mode
```

```
' -------------------------------------------------------------------------
' Variables
' -------------------------------------------------------------------------

index           VAR     Byte                    ' loop counter
reg             VAR     Byte                    ' DS1302 address to read/write
ioByte          VAR     Byte                    ' data to/from DS1302

secs            VAR     Byte                    ' seconds
secs01          VAR     secs.LowNib
secs10          VAR     secs.HighNib
mins            VAR     Byte                    ' minutes
mins01          VAR     mins.LowNib
mins10          VAR     mins.HighNib
hrs             VAR     Byte                    ' hours
hrs01           VAR     hrs.LowNib
hrs10           VAR     hrs.HighNib
day             VAR     Byte                    ' day

ampm            VAR     hrs.Bit5                ' 0 = AM, 1 = PM
tMode           VAR     hrs.Bit7                ' 0 = 24, 1 = 12

rawTime         VAR     Word                    ' raw storage of time values
work            VAR     Byte                    ' work variable for display output
oldSecs         VAR     Byte                    ' previous seconds value
apChar          VAR     Byte                    ' "A" or "P"

btns            VAR     Nib                     ' button inputs
btnMin          VAR     btns.Bit0               ' update minutes
btnHrs          VAR     btns.Bit1               ' update hours
btnDay          VAR     btns.Bit2               ' update day
btnBack         VAR     btns.Bit3               ' go backward


' -------------------------------------------------------------------------
' EEPROM Data
' -------------------------------------------------------------------------

Su              DATA    "Sunday", 0
Mo              DATA    "Monday", 0
Tu              DATA    "Tuesday", 0
We              DATA    "Wednesday", 0
Th              DATA    "Thursday", 0
Fr              DATA    "Friday", 0
Sa              DATA    "Saturday", 0
```

```
' ------------------------------------------------------------------
' Initialization
' ------------------------------------------------------------------

Initialize:
  DirL = %00000111                          ' switches are ins, others outs

  reg = CWPr                                ' clear write protect register
  ioByte = WPr0
  GOSUB RTC_Out

  oldSecs = $99                             ' set the display flag
  hrs = $06                                 ' preset time to 6:00 AM
  GOSUB Set_Time


' ------------------------------------------------------------------
' Program Code
' ------------------------------------------------------------------

Main1:
  GOSUB Get_Time                            ' read the DS1302
  IF (secs = oldSecs) THEN Check_Buttons    ' time for update?

Main2:
  GOSUB Show_Time                           ' yes, show it
  oldSecs = secs                            ' mark it

Check_Buttons:
  GOSUB Get_Buttons
  IF (btns = 0) THEN Do_Some_Task           ' let Stamp do other work
  IF (btnBack = Yes) THEN Go_Back           ' back button pressed?

Go_Forward:
  rawTime = rawTime + btnMin                ' add one minute
  rawTime = rawTime + (btnHrs * 60)         ' add one hour
  day = (day + btnDay) // 7                 ' next day
  GOTO Update_Clock

Go_Back:
  IF (btns <= %1000) THEN Do_Some_Task      ' no update button pressed
  rawTime = rawTime + (btnMin * 1439)       ' subtract one minute
  rawTime = rawTime + (btnHrs * 1380)       ' subtract one hour
  day = (day + (btnDay * 6)) // 7           ' previous day

Update_Clock:                               ' send updated value to DS1302
  rawTime = rawTime // 1440                 ' clean-up time mods
```

```
    GOSUB Set_Raw_Time                              ' set the clock with rawTime
    GOTO Main2

Do_Some_Task:                                       ' work when not setting clock

  ' other code here

    GOTO Main1


' -------------------------------------------------------------------------
' Subroutines
' -------------------------------------------------------------------------

Show_Time:
    DEBUG Home
    LOOKUP day,[Su,Mo,Tu,We,Th,Fr,Sa],work         ' get address of day string

Get_Day_Char:
    READ work, ioByte                               ' grab a character
    IF (ioByte = 0) THEN Check_Clock_Mode           ' if 0, string is complete
    DEBUG ioByte                                    ' print the character
    work = work + 1                                 ' point to next
    GOTO Get_Day_Char

Check_Clock_Mode:
    DEBUG "     ", CR                                ' clear day name debris
    IF (ClockMode = Hr24) THEN Show24

Show12:
    DEBUG DEC2 12 - (24 - (hrs10 * 10 + hrs01) // 12)
    DEBUG ":", HEX2 mins, ":", HEX2 secs
    apChar = "A"                                    ' assume AM
    IF (hrs < $12) THEN Show_AMPM                   ' check time
    apChar = "P"                                    ' hrs was >= $12

Show_AMPM:
    DEBUG " ", apChar, "M"                          ' print AM or PM
    GOTO Show_Time_Done

Show24:
    DEBUG HEX2 hrs, ":", HEX2 mins, ":", HEX2 secs

Show_Time_Done:
    RETURN


Get_Buttons:
```

```
  btns = %1111                                   ' enable all button inputs
  FOR index = 1 TO 10
    btns = btns & ~BtnsIn                         ' test inputs
    PAUSE 5                                             ' delay between tests
  NEXT
  PAUSE 200                                       ' slow held button(s)
  RETURN


RTC_Out:                                          ' send ioByte to reg in DS1302
  HIGH CS1302
  SHIFTOUT DataIO, Clock, LSBFirst, [reg, ioByte]
  LOW CS1302
  RETURN


RTC_In:                                           ' read ioByte from reg in DS1302
  HIGH CS1302
  SHIFTOUT DataIO, Clock, LSBFirst, [reg]
  SHIFTIN DataIO, Clock, LSBPre, [ioByte]
  LOW CS1302
  RETURN


Set_Raw_Time:                                     ' convert rawTime to BCD
  hrs10 = rawTime / 600
  hrs01 = (rawTime // 600) / 60
  mins10 = (rawTime // 60) / 10
  mins01 = rawTime // 10


Set_Time:                                         ' write data with burst mode
  HIGH CS1302
  SHIFTOUT DataIO, Clock, LSBFirst, [WrBurst]
  SHIFTOUT DataIO, Clock, LSBFirst, [secs, mins, hrs, 0, 0, day, 0, 0]
  LOW CS1302
  RETURN


Get_Time:                                         ' read data with burst mode
  HIGH CS1302
  SHIFTOUT DataIO, Clock, LSBFirst, [RdBurst]
  SHIFTIN DataIO, Clock, LSBPre, [secs, mins, hrs, day, day, day]
  LOW CS1302
  rawTime = ((hrs10 & %11) * 600) + (hrs01 * 60)
  rawTime = rawTime + (mins10 * 10) + mins01
  RETURN
```

Behind The Scenes

While it is possible to implement rudimentary timekeeping functions in code with PAUSE, problems arise when BASIC Stamp needs to handle other activities. This is especially true when an application needs to handle time, day and date. The cleanest solution is an external real-time clock. In this experiment, we'll use the Dallas Semiconductor DS1302. Like the DS1620, the DS1302 requires only three lines to communicate with the BASIC Stamp. Since these two devices are compatible with each other, the clock and data lines to can be shared giving the BASIC Stamp real-time clock and temperature measurement using only four I/O lines.

Once programmed the DS1302 runs by itself and accurately keeps track of seconds, minutes, hours (with an AM/PM indicator, if running in 12-hour mode), date of month, month, day of week and year with leap year compensation valid up to the year 2100. As a bonus, the DS1302 contains 31 bytes of RAM that we can use as we please. And for projects that use main's power, the DS1302 also contains a trickle-charging circuit that can charge a back-up battery.

The DS1302 is a register-based device, that is, each element of the time and date is stored in its own register (memory address). For convenience, two modes of reading and writing are available: register and burst. With register access, individual elements can be written or read. With burst access, all of the registers can be set at once and any number (starting with seconds) can be read back.

In order to keep our interface with the DS1302 simple, this experiment uses it in the 24-hour mode. In this mode, we don't have to fuss with the DS1302 AM/PM indicator bit. For a 12-hour display, we'll deduce AM/PM mathematically. In the code, time is handled as a single, word-sized variable (rawTime) that represents the number of minutes past midnight. This will make calculating durations and comparing alarm times with the current time very straightforward.

Another compelling reason to use a raw time format is that the DS1302 stores its registers in BCD (binary coded decimal). BCD is a method of storing a value between zero and 99 in a byte-sized variable. The ones digit occupies the lower nibble, the tens digit the upper. Neither nibble of a BCD byte is allowed to have a value greater than nine. Thankfully, the BASIC Stamp allows nibble-sized variables and, more importantly, it allows variables to be aliased.

This experiment demonstrates the DS1302 basics by setting the clock, then polling it for updates. Conversion to and from the DS1320 BCD register format is handled by the subroutines that set and retrieve information in burst mode.

Four pushbuttons are used to set the day, hours and minutes of the clock. Normally, the buttons cause each element to increment. By holding the fourth button, each element will roll back. When no button is pressed, the program passes to a routine called Do_Some_Task. This is where you would put additional code (reading a DS1620, for example).

Program output is sent to a DEBUG window. The Show_Time subroutine handles printing the day and time in the format specified by ClockMode.

Challenge (Advanced)

Add a DS1620 using the connections shown below. Write a program that tracks current, minimum and maximum temperature and will display (use DEBUG) the time and date on which the minimum and maximum temperature was measured.

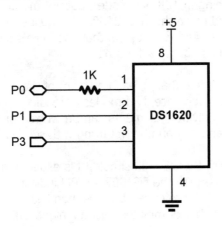

Experiment #31:
Serial Communications

This experiment demonstrates the BASIC Stamp's ability to communicate with other computers through any of its I/O pins. It also demonstrates the ability to store information in the BASIC Stamp's EEPROM space.

New PBASIC elements/commands to know:

- SERIN
- SEROUT
- WAIT (SERIN modifier)
- HEX (SERIN/SEROUT modifier)
- BIN (SERIN/SEROUT modifier)
- WRITE

Building The Circuit (Note that schematic is NOT chip-centric)

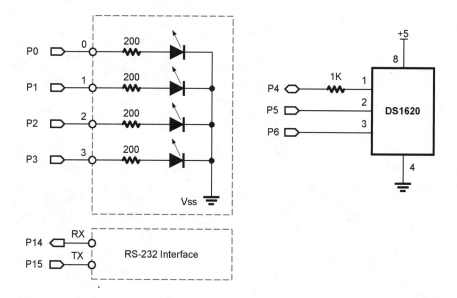

```
' ==============================================================================
'
'   File...... Ex31 - PollStamp.BS2
'   Purpose... Serial Communications
'   Author.... Parallax
'   E-mail.... stamptech@parallaxinc.com
'   Started...
'   Updated... 01 MAY 2002
'
'   {$STAMP BS2}
'
' ==============================================================================


' ------------------------------------------------------------------------------
' Program Description
' ------------------------------------------------------------------------------

' This program demonstrates serial communications through Stamp I/O pins.


' ------------------------------------------------------------------------------
' I/O Definitions
' ------------------------------------------------------------------------------

LEDs            VAR     OutA            ' LED outputs
DQ              CON     4               ' DS1620.1 (through 1K resistor)
Clock           CON     5               ' DS1620.2
Reset           CON     6               ' DS1620.3

RxD             CON     14              ' serial input - to INEX RxD
TxD             CON     15              ' serial output - to INEX TxD


' ------------------------------------------------------------------------------
' Constants
' ------------------------------------------------------------------------------

Baud96          CON     84              ' 9600-8-N-1, BS2/BS2e
' Baud96        CON     240             ' BS2sx/BS2p

CMenu           CON     $FF             ' show command menu
CID             CON     $F0             ' get string ID
CSet            CON     $F1             ' set string ID
CTmp            CON     $A0             ' get DS1620 - display raw count
CTmpC           CON     $A1             ' get DS1620 - display in C
CTmpF           CON     $A2             ' get DS1620 - display in F
```

```
CStat          CON      $B0                    ' get digital output status
CLEDs          CON      $B1                    ' set LED outputs

RTmp           CON      $AA                    ' read temperature
WTHi           CON      $01                    ' write TH (high temp register)
WTLo           CON      $02                    ' write TL (low temp register)
RTHi           CON      $A1                    ' read TH
RTLo           CON      $A2                    ' read TL
StartC         CON      $EE                    ' start conversion
StopC          CON      $22                    ' stop conversion
WrCfg          CON      $0C                    ' write configuration register
RdCfg          CON      $AC                    ' read configuration register


' --------------------------------------------------------------------------
' Variables
' --------------------------------------------------------------------------

cmd            VAR      Byte                   ' command from PC/terminal
eeAddr         VAR      Byte                   ' EE address pointer
eeData         VAR      Byte                   ' EE data
param          VAR      Word                   ' parameter from PC
char           VAR      param.LowByte          ' character from terminal
tmpIn          VAR      Word                   ' raw data from DS1620
halfBit        VAR      tmpIn.Bit0             ' 0.5 degree C indicator
sign           VAR      tmpIn.Bit8             ' 1 = negative temperature
tempC          VAR      Word                   ' degrees C in tenths
tempF          VAR      Word                   ' degrees F in tenths
potVal         VAR      Word                   ' reading from BSAC pot
buttons        VAR      Nib                    ' input buttons


' --------------------------------------------------------------------------
' EEPROM Data
' --------------------------------------------------------------------------

ID             DATA "StampWorks 1.2", CR       ' CR-terminated string


' --------------------------------------------------------------------------
' Initialization
' --------------------------------------------------------------------------

Initialize:
  DirA = %1111                                 ' LED pins are outputs

  HIGH Reset                                   ' alert the DS1620
```

```
  SHIFTOUT DQ, Clock, LSBFirst, [WrCfg, %10]     ' use with CPU; free-run
  LOW Reset
  PAUSE 10
  HIGH Reset
  SHIFTOUT DQ, Clock, LSBFirst, [StartC]         ' start conversions
  LOW Reset

  GOTO Show_Menu


' --------------------------------------------------------------------
' Program Code
' --------------------------------------------------------------------

Main:
  cmd = 0
  SERIN RxD, Baud96, [WAIT ("?"), HEX cmd]

  ' check for menu request
  IF (cmd = CMenu) THEN Show_Menu

  ' convert command for branching
  LOOKDOWN cmd, [CID, CSet, CTmp, CTmpC, CTmpF, CStat, CLEDs], cmd

  ' branch to requested routine
  BRANCH cmd, [Show_ID, Set_ID, Show_Temp, Show_Temp_C, Show_Temp_F]
  cmd = cmd - 5
  BRANCH cmd, [Show_Status, Set_LEDs]

BadCommand:
  SEROUT TxD, Baud96, ["Invalid Command: ", HEX2 cmd, CR]
  GOTO Main



' --------------------------------------------------------------------
' Subroutines
' --------------------------------------------------------------------

Show_Menu:
  SEROUT TxD, Baud96, [CLS]
  SEROUT TxD, Baud96, ["========================", CR]
  SEROUT TxD, Baud96, ["    StampWorks Monitor  ", CR]
  SEROUT TxD, Baud96, ["========================", CR]
  SEROUT TxD, Baud96, ["?FF - Show Menu", CR]
  SEROUT TxD, Baud96, ["?F0 - Display ID", CR]
  SEROUT TxD, Baud96, ["?F1 - Set ID", CR]
  SEROUT TxD, Baud96, ["?A0 - DS1620 (Raw count)", CR]
```

```
  SEROUT TxD, Baud96, ["?A1 - Temperature (C)", CR]
  SEROUT TxD, Baud96, ["?A2 - Temperature (F)", CR]
  SEROUT TxD, Baud96, ["?B0 - Display LED Status", CR]
  SEROUT TxD, Baud96, ["?B1 - Set LEDs", CR, CR]
  SEROUT TxD, Baud96, ["Please enter a command.", CR, CR]
  GOTO Main


Show_ID:
  SEROUT TxD, Baud96, ["ID="]                    ' label output
  eeAddr = ID                                    ' point to first character of ID

Get_EE:
  READ eeAddr, eeData                            ' read a character from EEPROM
  SEROUT TxD, Baud96, [eeData]                    ' print the character
  eeAddr = eeAddr + 1                            ' point to next character
  IF (eeData <> CR) THEN Get_EE                  ' if not CR, read another
  GOTO Main


Set_ID:
  eeAddr = ID                                    ' point to ID location

Get_Char:
  SERIN RxD, Baud96, [char]                      ' get character from PC
  WRITE eeAddr, char                             ' write character to EEPROM
  eeAddr = eeAddr + 1                            ' point to next location
  IF (char <> CR) THEN Get_Char                  ' if not CR, wait for another
  GOTO Show_ID                                   ' confirm new ID


Show_Temp:
  GOSUB Get_Temp
  ' send raw temp to PC
  SEROUT TxD, Baud96, ["DS1620=", DEC tmpIn, CR]
  GOTO Main


Show_Temp_C:
  GOSUB Get_Temp
  IF (sign = 0) THEN No_Neg_C
  tmpIn = 0                                      ' only temps above freezing

No_Neg_C:
  ' convert raw count to 10ths C
  tempC = tmpIn * 5
  SEROUT TxD, Baud96, ["TempC=", DEC (tempC/10), ".", DEC (tempC // 10), CR]
```

```
      GOTO Main


Show_Temp_F:
  GOSUB Get_Temp
  IF (sign = 0) THEN No_Neg_F
  tmpIn = 0

No_Neg_F:
  tempF = (tmpIn * 9) + 320                        ' convert raw count to 10ths F
  SEROUT TxD, Baud96, ["TempF=", DEC (tempF / 10), ".", DEC (tempF // 10), CR]
  GOTO Main


Show_Status:
  SEROUT TxD, Baud96, ["Status=", BIN4 LEDs, CR]
  GOTO Main


Set_LEDs:
  ' wait for output bits
  ' - as binary string
  '
  SERIN RxD, Baud96, [BIN param]
  LEDs = param.LowNib                              ' set the outputs
  GOTO Show_Status                                 ' confirm new outputs


Get_Temp:
  HIGH Reset                                       ' alert the DS1620
  SHIFTOUT DQ, Clock, LSBFirst, [RTmp]             ' read temperature
  SHIFTIN DQ, Clock, LSBPre, [tmpIn\9]             ' get the temperature
  LOW Reset
  RETURN
```

Behind The Scenes

Without asynchronous serial communications the world would not be what it is today. Businesses would be hard pressed to exchange information with each other. There would be no ATMs for checking our bank accounts and withdrawing funds. There would be no Internet.

Previous experiments have used synchronous serial communications. In that scheme, two lines are required: clock and data. The benefit is the automatic synchronization of sender and receiver. The downside is that it requires at least two wires to send a message.

Asynchronous serial communications requires only a single wire to transmit a message. What is necessary to allow this scheme is that both the sender and receiver must agree on the communications speed before the transmission can be received. Some "smart" systems can detect the communications speed (baud rate), the BASIC Stamp cannot.

In this experiment we'll use SEROUT to send information to a terminal program and SERIN to take data in. The input will usually be a command and sometimes the command will be accompanied with new data.

After initializing the LED outputs and the DS1620, the program enters the main loop and waits for input from the terminal program. First, SERIN waits for the "?" character to arrive, ignoring everything else until that happens. The question mark, then, is what signifies the start of a query. Once a question mark arrives, the HEX modifier causes the BASIC Stamp to look for valid hex characters (0 - 9, A - F). The arrival of any non-hex character (usually a carriage return [Enter] when using a terminal) tells the BASIC Stamp to stop accepting input (to the variable called param in our case) and continue on.

What actually has happened is that the BASIC Stamp has used the SERIN function to do a text-to-numeric conversion. Now that a command is available, the program uses LOOKDOWN to decode the command and BRANCH to jump to the requested subroutine if the command was valid. If the command isn't valid, a message and the offending input is displayed.

The BASIC Stamp responds to a request sending a text string using SEROUT set to 9600 baud (so we can use the BASIC Stamp's DEBUG terminal as the host). Each of the response strings consists of a label, the equal sign, the value of that particular parameter and finally, a carriage return. When using a terminal program, the output is easily readable. Something like this:

    ID=Parallax BS2

The carriage return at the end of the output gives us a new line when using a terminal program and serves as an "end of input" when we process the input with our own program (similar to BASIC Stamp Plot Lite). The equal sign can be used as a delimiter when another computer program communicates with the BASIC Stamp. We'll use it to distinguish the label from its value.

Most of the queries are requests for information. Two of them, however, can modify information that is stored in the BASIC Stamp.

The first one is "?F1" which will allow us to write a string value to the BASIC Stamp's EEPROM (in a location called ID). When F1 is received as a command value, the program jumps to the subroutine called set_ID. On entry to set_ID, the EE pointer called addr is initialized, then the BASIC Stamp waits for a character to arrive. Notice that no modifier is used here. Since terminal programs and the BASIC Stamp represent characters using ASCII codes, we don't have to do anything special. When a character does arrive, WRITE is used to put the character into EEPROM and the address pointer is incremented. If the last character was a carriage return (13), the program outputs the new string (using the code at show_ID), otherwise it loops back and waits for another character.

The second modifying query is "?B1" which allows us to set the status of four LEDs. Take a look at the subroutine called set_LEDs. This time, the BIN modifier of SERIN is used so that we can easily define individual bits we wish to control. By using the BIN modifier, our input will be a string of ones and zeros (any other character will terminate the binary input). In this program, a "1" will cause the LED to turn on and a "0" will cause the LED to turn off. Here's an example of using the B1 query.

> ?B1 0011 <CR>

The figure below shows an actual on-line session using the BASIC Stamp's DEBUG terminal. To run the experiment, follow these steps:

1. Remove components from previous experiment.
2. Enter and download the program
3. Remove power from StampWorks lab board and build the circuit
4. Move the programming cable to the RS-232 Interfacing port
5. Open a DEBUG window by clicking on the DEBUG icon
6. Set the StampWorks lab board power switch to on.

Challenge (for PC programmers)

Write a PC program that interfaces with this experiment.

Experiment #32: I²C Communications

This experiment demonstrates the BASIC Stamp's ability to communicate with other devices through the use of the popular Philips I²C protocol. The experiment uses this protocol to write and read data to a serial EEPROM and the low-level I²C routines can be used to communicate with any I²C device.

Building The Circuit

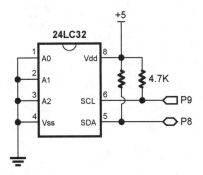

```
'    ==============================================================================
'
'
'    File...... Ex32 - 24LC32.BS2
'    Purpose... 24LC32 control via I2C
'    Author.... Parallax
'    E-mail.... stamptech@parallaxinc.com
'    Started...
'    Updated... 01 MAY 2002
'
'    {$STAMP BS2}
'
'    ==============================================================================
'
'
'    ------------------------------------------------------------------------------
'    Program Description
'    ------------------------------------------------------------------------------
'
'    This program demonstrates essential I2C routines and communication with the
'    Microchip 24LC32 serial EEPROM.
'
'    The connections for this program conform to the BS2p I2CIN and I2COUT
```

```
' commands.  Use this program for the BS2, BS2e or BS2sx.  There is a separate
' program for the BS2p.


' --------------------------------------------------------------------------
' I/O Definitions
' --------------------------------------------------------------------------
'
SDA             CON     8                       ' I2C serial data line
SCL             CON     9                       ' I2C serial clock line


' --------------------------------------------------------------------------
' Constants
' --------------------------------------------------------------------------

DevType         CON     %1010 << 4              ' device type
DevAddr         CON     %000 << 1               ' address = %000 -> %111
Wr2432          CON     DevType | DevAddr | 0   ' write to 24LC32
Rd2432          CON     DevType | DevAddr | 1   ' read from 24LC32

ACK             CON     0                       ' acknowledge bit
NAK             CON     1                       ' no ack bit

CrsrXY          CON     2                       ' DEBUG Position Control


' --------------------------------------------------------------------------
' Variables
' --------------------------------------------------------------------------

i2cSDA          VAR     Nib                     ' I2C serial data pin
i2cData         VAR     Byte                    ' data to/from device
i2cWork         VAR     Byte                    ' work byte for TX routine
i2cAck          VAR     Bit                     ' ACK bit from device

eeAddr          VAR     Word                    ' address: 0 - 4095
test            VAR     Nib
outVal          VAR     Byte                    ' output to EEPROM
inVal           VAR     Byte                    ' input from EEPROM


' --------------------------------------------------------------------------
' Initialization
' --------------------------------------------------------------------------

Initialize:
```

```
  PAUSE 250                                         ' let DEBUG open
  DEBUG CLS, "24LC32 Demo", CR, CR                  ' setup output screen
  DEBUG "Address... ", CR
  DEBUG "Output.... ", CR
  DEBUG "Input..... ", CR

  i2cSDA = SDA                                      ' define SDA pin



' ------------------------------------------------------------------------
' Program Code
' ------------------------------------------------------------------------

Main:
  FOR eeAddr = 0 TO 4095                            ' test all locations
    DEBUG CrsrXY, 11, 2, DEC eeAddr, "    "
    FOR test = 0 TO 3                               ' use four patterns
      LOOKUP test, [$FF, $AA, $55, $00], outVal
      DEBUG CrsrXY, 11, 3, IHEX2 outVal
      i2cData = outVal
      GOSUB Write_Byte
      PAUSE 10
      GOSUB Read_Byte
      inVal = i2cData
      DEBUG CrsrXY, 11, 4, IHEX2 inVal, "  "
      IF (inVal <> outVal) THEN Bad_Addr
      DEBUG "Pass "
      GOTO Next_Addr

Bad_Addr:
      DEBUG "Fail "

Next_Addr:
      PAUSE 50
    NEXT
  NEXT

  DEBUG CR, CR, "Done!"
  END



' ------------------------------------------------------------------------
' Subroutines
' ------------------------------------------------------------------------

' Byte to be written is passed in i2cData
' -- address passed in eeAddr
```

```
Write_Byte:
  GOSUB I2C_Start                              ' send Start
  i2cWork = Wr2432                             ' send write command
  GOSUB I2C_TX_Byte
  IF (i2cAck = NAK) THEN Write_Byte            ' wait until not busy
  i2cWork = eeAddr / 256                       ' send word address (1)
  GOSUB I2C_TX_Byte
  i2cWork = eeAddr // 256                       ' send word address (0)
  GOSUB I2C_TX_Byte
  i2cWork = i2cData                            ' send data
  GOSUB I2C_TX_Byte
  GOSUB I2C_Stop
  RETURN


' Byte read is returned in i2cData
' -- address passed in eeAddr

Read_Byte:
  GOSUB I2C_Start                              ' send Start
  i2cWork = Wr2432                             ' send write command
  GOSUB I2C_TX_Byte
  IF (i2cAck = NAK) THEN Write_Byte            ' wait until not busy
  i2cWork = eeAddr / 256                       ' send word address (1)
  GOSUB I2C_TX_Byte
  i2cWork = eeAddr // 256                       ' send word address (0)
  GOSUB I2C_TX_Byte
  GOSUB I2C_Start
  i2cWork = Rd2432                             ' send read command
  GOSUB I2C_TX_Byte
  GOSUB I2C_RX_Byte_Nak
  GOSUB I2C_Stop
  i2cData = i2cWork
  RETURN



' --------------------------------------------------------------------
' Low Level I2C Subroutines
' --------------------------------------------------------------------


' --- Start ---

I2C_Start:                                     ' I2C start bit sequence
  INPUT i2cSDA
  INPUT SCL
  LOW i2cSDA                                   ' SDA -> low while SCL high
```

```
Clock_Hold:
  IF (Ins.LowBit(SCL) = 0) THEN Clock_Hold      ' device ready?
  RETURN


' --- Transmit ---

I2C_TX_Byte:
  SHIFTOUT i2cSDA, SCL, MSBFIRST, [i2cWork\8]   ' send byte to device
  SHIFTIN i2cSDA, SCL, MSBPRE, [i2cAck\1]       ' get acknowledge bit
  RETURN


' --- Receive ---

I2C_RX_Byte_Nak:
  i2cAck = NAK                                   ' no ACK = high
  GOTO I2C_RX

I2C_RX_Byte:
  i2cAck = ACK                                   ' ACK = low

I2C_RX:
  SHIFTIN i2cSDA, SCL, MSBPRE, [i2cWork\8]       ' get byte from device
  SHIFTOUT i2cSDA, SCL, LSBFIRST, [i2cAck\1]     ' send ack or nak
  RETURN


' --- Stop ---

I2C_Stop:                                        ' I2C stop bit sequence
  LOW i2cSDA
  INPUT SCL
  INPUT i2cSDA                                   ' SDA --> high while SCL high
  RETURN
```

Behind the Scenes

The I²C-bus is a two-wire, synchronous bus that uses a Master-Slave relationship between components. The Master initiates communication with the Slave and is responsible for generating the clock signal. If requested to do so, the Slave can send data back to the Master. This means the data pin (SDA) is bi-directional and the clock pin (SCL) is [usually] controlled only by the Master.

The transfer of data between the Master and Slave works like this:

Master sending data
- Master initiates transfer
- Master addresses Slave
- Master sends data to Slave
- Master terminates transfer

Master receiving data
- Master initiates transfer
- Master addresses Slave
- Master receives data from Slave
- Master terminates transfer

The I²C specification actually allows for multiple Masters to exist on a common bus and provides a method for arbitrating between them. That's a bit beyond the scope of what we need to do so we're going to keep things simple. In our setup, the BS2 (or BS2e or BS2sx) will be the Master and anything connected to it will be a Slave.

You'll notice in I²C schematics that the SDA and SCL lines are pulled up to Vdd (usually through 4.7K). The specification calls for device bus pins to be open drain. To put a high on either line, the associated bus pin is made an input (floats) and the pull-up takes the line to Vdd. To make a line low, the bus pin pulls it to Vss (ground).

This scheme is designed to protect devices on the bus from a short to ground. Since neither line is driven high, there is no danger. We're going to cheat a bit. Instead of writing code to pull a line low or release it (certainly possible – I did it), we're going to use **SHIFTOUT** and **SHIFTIN** to move data back and forth. Using **SHIFTOUT** and **SHIFTIN** is faster and saves precious code space. If you're concerned about a bus short damaging the Stamp's SDA or SCL pins during **SHIFTOUT** and **SHIFTIN**, you can protect each of them with a 220 ohm resistor. I've been careful with my wiring and code and haven't found this necessary.

Low Level I²C Code

At its lowest level, the I²C Master needs to do four things:

- Generate a Start condition
- Transmit 8-bit data to the Slave
- Receive 8-bit data from Slave – with or without Acknowledge
- Generate Stop condition

A Start condition is defined as a HIGH to LOW transition on the SDA line while the SCL line is HIGH. All transmissions begin with a Start condition. A Stop condition is defined as a LOW to HIGH transition of the SDA line while the clock line is HIGH. A Stop condition terminates a transfer and can be used to abort it as well.

There is a brief period when the Slave can take control of the SCL line. If a Slave is not ready to transmit or receive data, it can hold the SCL line low after the Start condition. The Master can monitor this to wait for the Slave to be ready. At the speed of the BS2, monitoring the clock line usually isn't necessary but I've built the clock-hold test into the I2C_Start subroutine just to be safe.

Data is transferred eight bits at a time, sending the MSB first. After each byte, the I²C specification calls for the receiving device to acknowledge the transmission by bringing the bus low for the ninth clock. The exception to this is when the Master is the receiver and is receiving the final byte from the Slave. In this case, there is no Acknowledge bit sent from Master to Slave.

Sending and receiving data from a specific slave always requires a Start condition, sending the Slave address and finally, the Stop condition. What happens between the Slave address and the Stop are dependent on the device and what we're doing.

What you'll need to do is get the data sheet for the I²C device you want to connect to. I have found, without exception, that data sheets for I²C-compatible parts have very clear protocol definitions – usually in graphic form – that makes implementing our low-level I²C routines very simple.

The experiment uses the low-level I²C routines to implement the **Write_Byte** and **Read_Byte** routines. The sequence for these routines was lifted right from the 24LC32 data sheet. Notice that each routine begins with an I²C Start condition and is terminated with the Stop condition. The code in between sends the device command/type code, the address to deal with and then actually deals with (writes or reads) the data. While this takes a few lines of code, it is actually very straightforward.

Most I²C routines follow a very similar structure; varying only in the internal address and for a few devices, the way the device code is transmitted (there are a few devices that carry an address setting in the device code byte).

Challenge

From the hundreds of I²C devices available, pick one that will be most useful for your projects and write the high-level code necessary to communicate with it.

StampWorks   **Striking Out on Your Own**

Congratulations, you're a BASIC Stamp programmer! So what's next? Well, that's up to you. Many new programmers get stuck when it comes to developing their own projects. Don't worry, this is natural – and there are ways out of being stuck. The following tips will help you succeed in moving your ideas to reality.

Plan Your Work, Work Your Plan

You've heard it a million times: plan, plan, and plan. Nothing gets a programmer into more trouble than bad or inadequate planning. This is particularly true with the BASIC Stamp as resources are so limited. Most of the programs we've fixed were "broken" due to bad planning and poor formatting which lead to errors.

Talk It Out

Talk yourself through the program. Don't just think it through, *talk it through*. Talk to yourself–out loud–as if you were explaining the operation of the program to a fellow programmer. Often, just hearing our own voice is what makes the difference. Better yet, talk it out as if the person you're talking to *isn't* a programmer. This will force you to explain details. Many times we take things for granted when we're talking to ourselves or others of similar ability.

Write It Out

Design the details of your program on a white (dry erase) board before you sit down at your computer. And use a lot of colors. You'll find working through a design visually will offer new insights, and the use of this medium allows you to write code snippets within your functional diagrams.

Design With "Sticky Notes"

Get out a pad of small "sticky notes". Write module names or concise code fragments on individual notes and then stick them up on the wall. Now stand back and take a look. Then move them around. Add notes, take some away; just do what feels right to you. This exercise works particularly well with groups. How do you know when you're done? When the sticky notes stop moving! It's a good idea to record the final outcome before starting your editor. Another tip: this trick works even better when combined with trick #2. You can draw lines between and around notes to indicate program flow or logical groupings. If it's not quite right, just erase the lines or move some notes. Try this trick; it really does work.

Going Beyond The Box

By now, your appetite for BASIC Stamp projects has probably grown well beyond what you ever expected. So where do you turn now? Don't worry, there are many BASIC Stamp and related resources available, both in print and on the Internet. Here's a list to get you started:

Books & Magazines

- *Microcontroller Application Cookbook* By Matt Gilliland
- *Microcontroller Projects with BASIC Stamps* By Al Williams
- *Programming and Customizing the BASIC Stamp Computer* By Scott Edwards
- *BASIC Stamp* By Claus Kühnel and Klaus Zahnert
- *Getting Started In Electronics* By Forrest Mims
- *Engineer's Notebook* By Forrest Mims
- *Nuts & Volts* Magazine "Stamp Applications" column

Internet Sites

www.parallaxinc.com	Parallax main site
www.stampsinclass.com	Parallax educational site
www.al-williams.com/awce/index.htm	Al Williams web site
www.seetron.com	Scott Edwards Electronics web site
www.hth.com/losa	List of Stamp Applications – great idea source
www.emesystems.com/BS2index.htm	Tracy Allen's Stamp resources – very technical

StampWorks

Appendix A:
BASIC Stamp II Manual Version 2.0c

Pages 198-344 of the BASIC Stamp Manual are included in this appendix. The entire manual (and future updates) is available for purchase or download from www.parallaxinc.com.

BASIC Stamp ® Programming Manual
Version 2.0b

Warranty

Parallax warrants its products against defects in materials and workmanship for a period of 90 days. If you discover a defect, Parallax will, at its option, repair, replace, or refund the purchase price. Simply call our sales department for an RMA number, write it on the label and return the product with a description of the problem. We will return your product, or its replacement, using the same shipping method used to ship the product to Parallax (for instance, if you ship your product via overnight express, we will do the same).

This warranty does not apply if the product has been modified or damaged by accident, abuse, or misuse.

14-Day Money-Back Guarantee

If, within 14 days of having received your product, you find that it does not suit your needs, you may return it for a refund. Parallax will refund the purchase price of the product, excluding shipping/handling costs. This does not apply if the product has been altered or damaged.

Copyrights and Trademarks

Copyright © 2000 by Parallax, Inc. All rights reserved. PBASIC is a trademark and BASIC Stamp is a registered trademark or Parallax, Inc. PIC is a registered trademark of Microchip Technology, Inc. Windows is a registered trademark of Microsoft Corporation. 1-wire is a registered trademark of Dallas Semiconductor. Other brand and product names are trademarks or registered trademarks of their respective holders.

Disclaimer of Liability

Parallax, Inc. is not responsible for special, incidental, or consequential damages resulting from any breach of warranty, or under any legal theory, including lost profits, downtime, goodwill, damage to or replacement of equipment or property, and any costs of recovering, reprogramming, or reproducing any data stored in or used with Parallax products.

Internet Access

We maintain Internet systems for your convenience. These may be used to obtain software, communicate with members of Parallax, and communicate with other customers. Access information is shown below:

Web:	http://www.parallaxinc.com
	http://www.stampsinclass.com
General e-mail:	info@parallaxinc.com
Tech. e-mail:	stamptech@parallaxinc.com

Internet BASIC Stamp Discussion List

We maintain a BASIC Stamp discussion list for people interested in BASIC Stamps. Many people subscribe to the list, and all questions and answers to the list are distributed to all subscribers. It's a fun, fast, and free way to discuss BASIC Stamp issues. To subscribe to the BASIC Stamps list, visit the Tech Support section of the Parallax, Inc website.

This manual is valid with the following software and firmware versions:

BASIC Stamp 1:
STAMP.EXE software version 2.1
Firmware version 1.4

BASIC Stamp 2:
STAMP2.EXE software version 1.1
STAMPW.EXE software version 1.096
Firmware version 1.0

BASIC Stamp 2e:
STAMP2E.EXE software version 1.0
STAMPW.EXE software version 1.096
Firmware version 1.0

BASIC Stamp 2sx:
STAMP2SX.EXE software version 1.0
STAMPW.EXE software version 1.096
Firmware version 1.0

BASIC Stamp 2p:
STAMP2P.EXE software version 1.6
STAMPW.EXE software version 1.098
Firmware version 1.1

The information herein will usually apply to newer versions but may not apply to older versions. New software can be obtained free on our ftp and web site (ftp.parallaxinc.com, www.parallaxinc.com). If you have any questions about what you need to upgrade your product, please contact Parallax.

Contents

Contents

Contents

Contents

Thank you for purchasing the Parallax BASIC Stamp development system. We have done our best to produce a full-featured, yet easy to use development system for the BASIC Stamp microcontrollers. We hope you will find this system as enjoyable to use as we do.

This manual is written for the latest available BASIC Stamp modules and software as of November 2000. As the product-line evolves new information may become available. It is always recommended to visit the Parallax, Inc. web site, www.parallaxinc.com, for the latest information.

This manual is intended to be a complete reference manual to the architecture and command structure of the BASIC Stamps. This manual is not meant to teach programming or electrical design; though a person can learn a lot by paying close attention to the details in this book. If you have never programmed in the BASIC language or are unfamiliar with electronics, it would be best to locate one or more of the following books for further information:

1. Programming and Customizing the BASIC Stamp Computer
   Scott Edwards, TAB Books ISBN: 0-07-913684-2
2. Microcontroller Projects with BASIC Stamps
   Al Williams, R&D Books ISBN: 0-87930-587-8
3. The Microcontroller Application Cookbook
   Matt Gilliland, Woodglen Press ISBN: 0-615-11552-7
4. What's A Microcontroller
   Free on Parallax CD (Documentation -> Educational Curriculum section) and web site (Downloads section), or for purchase in print
5. BASIC Analog and Digital
   Free on Parallax CD (Documentation -> Educational Curriculum section) and web site (Downloads section), or for purchase in print
6. Earth Measurements
   Free on Parallax CD (Documentation -> Educational Curriculum section) and web site (Downloads section), or for purchase in print
7. Robotics
   Free on Parallax CD (Documentation -> Educational Curriculum section) and web site (Downloads section), or for purchase in print

In addition, there are hundreds of great examples available on the Parallax CD and web site (www.parallaxinc.com). Also, Nut & Volts Magazine (www.nutsvolts.com / 1-800-783-4624) is a national electronic hobbyist's magazine that features monthly articles featuring the BASIC Stamps. This is an excellent resource for beginners and experts alike! For a sample of the BASIC Stamp articles, visit their web site.

Packing List

The BASIC Stamps are available in many different forms. You may have received them in a Starter Kit in a special limited-time package or individually. The packing list below describes the general list of items that would be included in a BASIC Stamp Starter Kit at the time of this writing:

BASIC Stamp Starter Kit

- (1) BASIC Stamp Module (Rev. D, BS1-IC, OEMBS1, BS2-IC, OEMBS2, BS2e-IC, BS2sx-IC or BS2p-IC)
- (1) BASIC Stamp development software (on CD in Software section)
- (1) BASIC Stamp manual (this manual)
- (1) BASIC Stamp development board (Stamp 1 Carrier Board, Stamp 2 Carrier Board, Super Carrier Board, BASIC Stamp Activity Board or Board or Education)
- (1) Set of jumper wires (only included with Board of Education)
- (1) 9-pin serial cable

If any items are missing, please let us know.

Welcome to the wonderful world of BASIC Stamp microntrollers. BASIC Stamp microcontrollers have been in use by engineers and hobbyists since we first introduced them in 1992. As of July 2000, Parallax customers have put more than 200,000 BASIC Stamp modules into use. Over this eight-year period, the BASIC Stamp line of controllers has evolved into five models and many physical package types, explained below.

General Operation Theory

BASIC Stamps are microcontrollers (tiny computers) that are designed for use in a wide array of applications. Many projects that require an embedded system with some level of intelligence can use a BASIC Stamp module as the controller.

Each BASIC Stamp comes with a BASIC Interpreter chip, internal memory (RAM and EEPROM), a 5-volt regulator, a number of general-purpose I/O pins (TTL-level, 0-5 volts), and a set of built-in commands for math and I/O pin operations. BASIC Stamps are capable of running a few thousand instructions per second and are programmed with a simplified, but customized form of the BASIC programming language, called PBASIC.

PBASIC Language

We developed PBASIC specifically for the BASIC Stamps as a simple, easy to learn language that is also well suited for this architecture. It includes many of the instructions featured in other forms of BASIC (GOTO, FOR...NEXT, IF...THEN) as well as some specialized instructions (SERIN, PWM, BUTTON, COUNT and DTMFOUT). This manual includes an extensive section devoted to each of the available instructions.

Hardware

At the time of this writing, there are currently five models of the BASIC Stamp; the BASIC Stamp 1, BASIC Stamp 2, BASIC Stamp 2e, BASIC Stamp 2sx and BASIC Stamp 2p. The diagrams below detail the various package types and part numbers of these modules.

BASIC Stamp 1

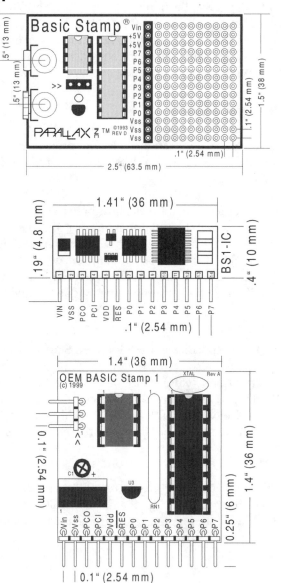

Figure 1.1: BASIC Stamp 1 Rev. D (27100)

Figure 1.2: BASIC Stamp 1 (Rev. B) (BS1-IC)

Figure 1.3: OEM BASIC Stamp 1 (Rev. A) (27295 or 27296)

The BASIC Stamp 1 is available in the above three physical packages. The BASIC Stamp 1 Rev. D (simply called the Rev. D), see Figure 1.1, includes prototyping area suitable for soldering electronic components. The BS1-IC (Figure 1.2) uses surface mount components to fit in a small 14-pin SIP package. The OEMBS1 (Figure 1.3) features an easier-to-trace layout meant to aid customers who wish to integrate the BASIC Stamp 1 circuit directly into their design (as a lower-cost solution). The OEMBS1 is available in either an assembled form or a kit form. All three packages are functionally equivalent with the exception that the Rev. D does not have an available reset pin.

Table 1.1: BASIC Stamp 1 Pin Descriptions.

Pin	Name	Description
1	VIN	Unregulated power in: accepts 5.5 - 15 VDC (6-40 VDC on BS1-IC rev. b), which is then internally regulated to 5 volts. May be left unconnected if 5 volts is applied to the VDD (+5V) pin.
2	VSS	System ground: connects to PC parallel port pin 25 (GND) for programming.
3	PCO	PC Out: connects to PC parallel port pin 11 (BUSY) for programming.
4	PCI	PC In: connects to PC parallel port pin 2 (D0) for programming.
5	VDD	5-volt DC input/output: (Also called +5V) if an unregulated voltage is applied to the VIN pin, then this pin will output 5 volts. If no voltage is applied to the VIN pin, then a regulated voltage between 4.5V and 5.5V should be applied to this pin.
6	RES	Reset input/output: goes low when power supply is less than approximately 4.2 volts, causing the BASIC Stamp to reset. Can be driven low to force a reset. This pin is internally pulled high and may be left disconnected if not needed. Do not drive high.
7-14	P0-P7	General-purpose I/O pins: each can sink 25 mA and source 20 mA. However, the total of all pins should not exceed 50 mA (sink) and 40 mA (source).

See the "BASIC Stamp Programming Connections" section, below, for more information on the required programming connections between the PC and the BASIC Stamp.

BASIC Stamp 2

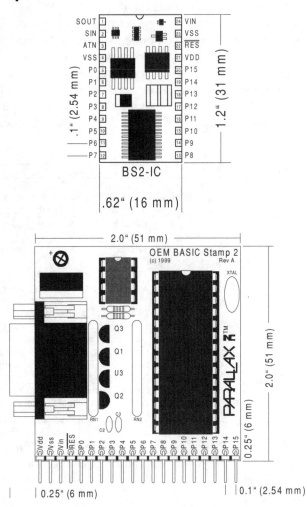

Figure 1.4: BASIC Stamp 2 (Rev. E) (BS2-IC)

Figure 1.5: OEM BASIC Stamp 2 (Rev. A) (27290 or 27291)

The BASIC Stamp 2 is available in the above two physical packages. The BS2-IC (Figure 1.4) uses surface mount components to fit in a small 24-pin DIP package. The OEMBS2 (Figure 1.5) features an easier-to-trace layout meant to aid customers who wish to integrate the BASIC Stamp 2 circuit directly into their design (as a lower-cost solution). The OEMBS2 is available in either an assembled form or a kit form. Both packages are functionally equivalent.

Table 1.2: BASIC Stamp 2 Pin Descriptions.

Pin	Name	Description
1	SOUT	Serial Out: connects to PC serial port RX pin (DB9 pin 2 / DB25 pin 3) for programming.
2	SIN	Serial In: connects to PC serial port TX pin (DB9 pin 3 / DB25 pin 2) for programming.
3	ATN	Attention: connects to PC serial port DTR pin (DB9 pin 4 / DB25 pin 20) for programming.
4	VSS	System ground: (same as pin 23) connects to PC serial port GND pin (DB9 pin 5 / DB25 pin 7) for programming.
5-20	P0-P15	General-purpose I/O pins: each can sink 25 mA and source 20 mA. However, the total of all pins should not exceed 50 mA (sink) and 40 mA (source) if using the internal 5-volt regulator. The total per 8-pin groups (P0 – P7 or P8 – 15) should not exceed 50 mA (sink) and 40 mA (source) if using an external 5-volt regulator.
21	VDD	5-volt DC input/output: if an unregulated voltage is applied to the VIN pin, then this pin will output 5 volts. If no voltage is applied to the VIN pin, then a regulated voltage between 4.5V and 5.5V should be applied to this pin.
22	RES	Reset input/output: goes low when power supply is less than approximately 4.2 volts, causing the BASIC Stamp to reset. Can be driven low to force a reset. This pin is internally pulled high and may be left disconnected if not needed. Do not drive high.
23	VSS	System ground: (same as pin 4) connects to power supply's ground (GND) terminal.
24	VIN	Unregulated power in: accepts 5.5 - 15 VDC (6-40 VDC on BS2-IC rev. e), which is then internally regulated to 5 volts. May be left unconnected if 5 volts is applied to the VDD (+5V) pin.

See the "BASIC Stamp Programming Connections" section, below, for more information on the required programming connections between the PC and the BASIC Stamp.

BASIC Stamp 2e

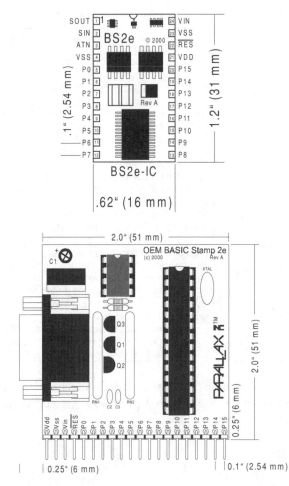

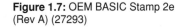

Figure 1.6: BASIC Stamp 2e
(Rev. A) (BS2e-IC)

Figure 1.7: OEM BASIC Stamp 2e
(Rev A) (27293)

The BASIC Stamp 2e is available in the above two physical packages. The BS2e-IC (Figure 1.6) uses surface mount components to fit in a small 24-pin DIP package. The OEMBS2e (Figure 1.7) features an easier-to-trace layout meant to aid customers who wish to integrate the BASIC Stamp 2e circuit directly into their design (as a lower-cost solution). The OEMBS2e is available in assembled form only.

Table 1.3: BASIC Stamp 2e Pin Descriptions.

Pin	Name	Description
1	SOUT	Serial Out: connects to PC serial port RX pin (DB9 pin 2 / DB25 pin 3) for programming.
2	SIN	Serial In: connects to PC serial port TX pin (DB9 pin 3 / DB25 pin 2) for programming.
3	ATN	Attention: connects to PC serial port DTR pin (DB9 pin 4 / DB25 pin 20) for programming.
4	VSS	System ground: (same as pin 23) connects to PC serial port GND pin (DB9 pin 5 / DB25 pin 7) for programming.
5-20	P0-P15	General-purpose I/O pins: each can source and sink 30 mA. However, the total of all pins should not exceed 75 mA (source or sink) if using the internal 5-volt regulator. The total per 8-pin groups (P0 – P7 or P8 – 15) should not exceed 100 mA (source or sink) if using an external 5-volt regulator.
21	VDD	5-volt DC input/output: if an unregulated voltage is applied to the VIN pin, then this pin will output 5 volts. If no voltage is applied to the VIN pin, then a regulated voltage between 4.5V and 5.5V should be applied to this pin.
22	RES	Reset input/output: goes low when power supply is less than approximately 4.2 volts, causing the BASIC Stamp to reset. Can be driven low to force a reset. This pin is internally pulled high and may be left disconnected if not needed. Do not drive high.
23	VSS	System ground: (same as pin 4) connects to power supply's ground (GND) terminal.
24	VIN	Unregulated power in: accepts 5.5 - 12 VDC (7.5 recommended), which is then internally regulated to 5 volts. May be left unconnected if 5 volts is applied to the VDD (+5V) pin.

See the "BASIC Stamp Programming Connections" section, below, for more information on the required programming connections between the PC and the BASIC Stamp.

Introduction to the BASIC Stamps

BASIC Stamp 2sx

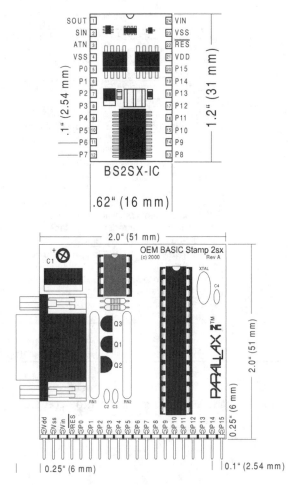

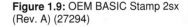

Figure 1.8: BASIC Stamp 2sx (Rev. B) (BS2sx-IC)

Figure 1.9: OEM BASIC Stamp 2sx (Rev. A) (27294)

The BASIC Stamp 2sx is available in the above two physical packages. The BS2sx-IC (Figure 1.8) uses surface mount components to fit in a small 24-pin DIP package. The OEMBS2sx (Figure 1.9) features an easier-to-trace layout meant to aid customers who wish to integrate the BASIC Stamp 2sx circuit directly into their design (as a lower-cost solution). The OEMBS2sx is available in assembled form only.

Table 1.4: BASIC Stamp 2sx Pin Descriptions.

Pin	Name	Description
1	SOUT	Serial Out: connects to PC serial port RX pin (DB9 pin 2 / DB25 pin 3) for programming.
2	SIN	Serial In: connects to PC serial port TX pin (DB9 pin 3 / DB25 pin 2) for programming.
3	ATN	Attention: connects to PC serial port DTR pin (DB9 pin 4 / DB25 pin 20) for programming.
4	VSS	System ground: (same as pin 23) connects to PC serial port GND pin (DB9 pin 5 / DB25 pin 7) for programming.
5-20	P0-P15	General-purpose I/O pins: each can source and sink 30 mA. However, the total of all pins should not exceed 75 mA (source or sink) if using the internal 5-volt regulator. The total per 8-pin groups (P0 – P7 or P8 – 15) should not exceed 100 mA (source or sink) if using an external 5-volt regulator.
21	VDD	5-volt DC input/output: if an unregulated voltage is applied to the VIN pin, then this pin will output 5 volts. If no voltage is applied to the VIN pin, then a regulated voltage between 4.5V and 5.5V should be applied to this pin.
22	RES	Reset input/output: goes low when power supply is less than approximately 4.2 volts, causing the BASIC Stamp to reset. Can be driven low to force a reset. This pin is internally pulled high and may be left disconnected if not needed. Do not drive high.
23	VSS	System ground: (same as pin 4) connects to power supply's ground (GND) terminal.
24	VIN	Unregulated power in: accepts 5.5 - 12 VDC (7.5 recommended), which is then internally regulated to 5 volts. May be left unconnected if 5 volts is applied to the VDD (+5V) pin.

See the "BASIC Stamp Programming Connections" section, below, for more information on the required programming connections between the PC and the BASIC Stamp.

Introduction to the BASIC Stamps

BASIC Stamp 2p

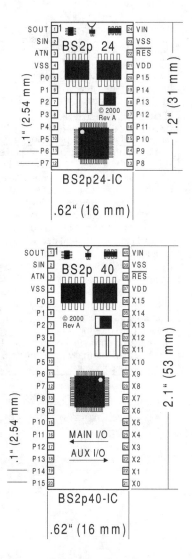

Figure 1.10: BASIC Stamp 2p24 (Rev A) (BS2p24-IC) This module is identical in function to the BS2p40-IC, except that it has 16 I/O pins.

Figure 1.11: BASIC Stamp 2p40 (Rev A) (BS2p40-IC) This module is identical in function to the BS2p24-IC, except that it has 32 I/O pins.

The BASIC Stamp 2p is available in the above two physical packages. Both packages use surface mount components to fit in a small package. The BS2p24-IC (Figure 1.10) is a 24-pin DIP package. The BS2p40-IC (Figure 1.11) is a 40-pin DIP package. Both packages are functionally equivalent accept that the BS2p40 has 32 I/O pins instead of 16.

Table 1.5: BASIC Stamp 2p Pin Descriptions.

Pin	Name	Description
1	SOUT	Serial Out: connects to PC serial port RX pin (DB9 pin 2 / DB25 pin 3) for programming.
2	SIN	Serial In: connects to PC serial port TX pin (DB9 pin 3 / DB25 pin 2) for programming.
3	ATN	Attention: connects to PC serial port DTR pin (DB9 pin 4 / DB25 pin 20) for programming.
4	VSS	System ground: (same as pin 23 on BS2p24, or pin 39 on BS2p40) connects to PC serial port GND pin (DB9 pin 5 / DB25 pin 7) for programming.
5-20	P0-P15	General-purpose I/O pins: each can source and sink 30 mA. However, the total of all pins (including X0-X15, if using the BS2p40) should not exceed 75 mA (source or sink) if using the internal 5-volt regulator. The total per 8-pin groups (P0 – P7, P8 – 15, X0 – X7 or X8 – X15) should not exceed 100 mA (source or sink) if using an external 5-volt regulator.
{21-36}	X0-X15	(BS2p40 Only!) Auxiliary Bank of General-purpose I/O pins: each can source and sink 30 mA. However, the total of all pins (including P0 – P15) should not exceed 75 mA (source or sink) if using the internal 5-volt regulator. The total per 8-pin groups (P0 – P7, P8 – 15, X0 – X7 or X8 – X15) should not exceed 100 mA (source or sink) if using an external 5-volt regulator.
21 {37}	VDD	5-volt DC input/output: if an unregulated voltage is applied to the VIN pin, then this pin will output 5 volts. If no voltage is applied to the VIN pin, then a regulated voltage between 4.5V and 5.5V should be applied to this pin.
22 {38}	RES	Reset input/output: goes low when power supply is less than approximately 4.2 volts, causing the BASIC Stamp to reset. Can be driven low to force a reset. This pin is internally pulled high and may be left disconnected if not needed. Do not drive high.
23 {39}	VSS	System ground: (same as pin 4) connects to power supply's ground (GND) terminal.
24 {40}	VIN	Unregulated power in: accepts 5.5 - 12 VDC (7.5 recommended), which is then internally regulated to 5 volts. May be left unconnected if 5 volts is applied to the VDD (+5V) pin.

NOTE: Pin numbers in braces {} are BS2p40 pin numbers.

See the "BASIC Stamp Programming Connections" section, below, for more information on the required programming connections between the PC and the BASIC Stamp.

Development Boards

We provide a number of development boards to make using the BASIC Stamps more convenient. Below is a short description of the boards and their intended use. Please refer to the development board's documentation (if any) for more details.

BASIC Stamp 1 Carrier Board (Rev. E)

The BASIC Stamp 1 Carrier Board (also called the BS1 Carrier Board) is designed to accommodate the BS1-IC module. The BASIC Stamp 1 Carrier Board provides nearly the same form factor and prototyping space as with the BASIC Stamp 1 Rev. D, but with the added feature of the reset button. Figure 1.12 shows the BASIC Stamp 1 Carrier Board with the BS1-IC properly inserted into the socket. This board features a 3-pin programming header and 9-volt battery clips to connect a power source. A male, 14-pin 0.1" header (to the left of the through-hole array) allows access to all the BS1's pins. The first two columns of solder pads (closest to the header) are connected to the respective header pin. All other solder pads are isolated from each other. The entire through-hole array is provided for permanent or semi-permanent circuit design.

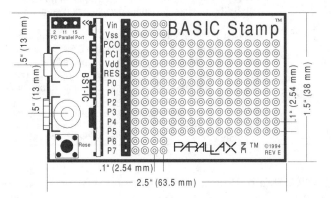

Figure 1.12: BASIC Stamp 1 Carrier Board (Rev. E) (shown with BS1-IC properly inserted) (27110)

BASIC Stamp 2 Carrier Board (Rev. B)

The BASIC Stamp 2 Carrier Board (also called the BS2 Carrier Board) is designed to accommodate the BS2-IC, BS2e-IC and BS2sx-IC modules. The BASIC Stamp 2 Carrier Board provides ample prototyping space for simple or moderate circuits. Figure 1.13 shows the BASIC Stamp 2 Carrier Board with the BS2-IC properly inserted into the socket. This board features a DB9 programming connector, reset button, and 9-volt battery clips. Two male, 12-pin 0.1" headers (to the left and right of the chip socket) allows access to all the modules's pins. The first two columns of solder pads (closest to the headers) are connected to the respective header pin. All other solder pads are isolated from each other. The entire through-hole array is provided for permanent or semi-permanent circuit design.

Figure 1.13: BASIC Stamp 2 Carrier Board (Rev. B) (shown with BS2-IC properly inserted) (27120)

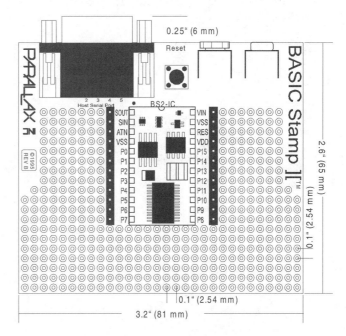

Introduction to the BASIC Stamps

BASIC Stamp Super Carrier (Rev. A)

The BASIC Stamp Super Carrier board is designed to accommodate the BS1-IC, BS2-IC, BS2e-IC and BS2sx-IC modules. This board provides ample prototyping space for simple or moderate circuits. Figures 1.14 and 1.15 show the board with the BS1-IC or BS2-IC properly inserted into the sockets. **NOTE: Do not power-up the board with a BS1-IC and a BS2-IC, BS2e-IC or BS2sx-IC inserted at the same time.** This board features a 3-pin programming connector (Stamp 1), DB9 programming connector (Stamp 2, 2e, 2sx), reset button, 9-volt battery clips, barrel connector, separate 5-volt regulator, and power LED. A female, 20-pin 0.1" socket allows access to all the module's pins. Many of the solder pads (see Figure 1.16) are connected to each other in a fashion that allows breadboard-like assembly of circuits (examine the through-hole array carefully before soldering). **Note: the barrel jack is designed for a center positive, 2.1 mm (pin) x 5.5 mm (barrel) plug.**

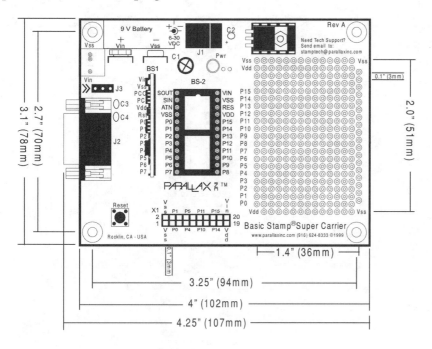

Figure 1.14: BASIC Stamp Super Carrier Board (Rev. A) (shown with BS1-IC properly inserted) (27130)

Figure 1.15: BASIC Stamp Super Carrier Board (Rev. A) (shown with BS2-IC properly inserted) (27130)

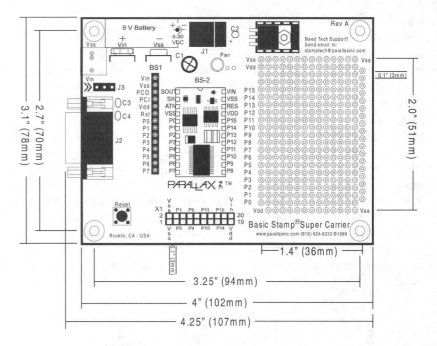

In the prototype area, upper and lower rows as well as two inner columns of solder pads are connected to Vdd and Vss to provide easy access to power. IC's measuring from 0.3" to 0.7" in width can straddle the center power rails similar to a breadboard. The right-most column of solder pads is offset to accommodate components like RJ-11 and DB9 connectors.

Figure 1.16: Prototype area of the BASIC Stamp Super Carrier Board (Rev. A) (black lines indicate interconnected solder pads)

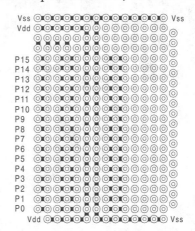

Board of Education (Rev. B)

The Board of Education is designed to accommodate the BS2-IC, BS2e-IC and BS2sx-IC modules. This board provides a small breadboard for quickly prototyping simple or moderate circuits. Figure 1.17 shows the board with the BS2-IC properly inserted into the socket. This board features a, DB9 programming connector, reset button, 9-volt battery clips, barrel connector, separate 5-volt regulator, power LED, 4 servo connectors and a breadboard. Three female 0.1" sockets allow for access to all the module's pins plus Vdd, Vin and Vss. Vdd is +5 volts and Vin is 6 – 9 volts (depending on your power supply). **NOTE: the Vdd pin on the 20-pin socket comes from the Vdd of the Stamp module (pin 21) while the 5 Vdd sockets above the breadboard come from the Board of Education's 5-volt regulator. Use the 5 Vdd sockets for anything requiring more current than what the Stamp can provide. Also, the pins in the "red" row of the servo connectors are connected to Vin. Also note: the barrel jack is designed for a center positive, 2.1 mm (pin) x 5.5 mm (barrel) plug.**

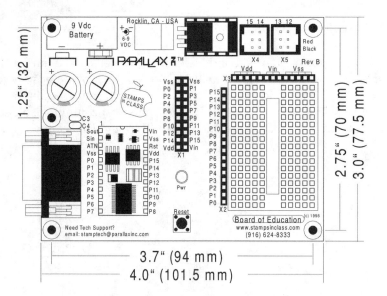

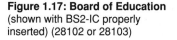

Figure 1.17: Board of Education (shown with BS2-IC properly inserted) (28102 or 28103)

BASIC Stamp Activity Board (Rev. C)

The BASIC Stamp Activity Board (sometimes called BSAC) is designed to accommodate the BS1-IC, BS2-IC, BS2e-IC, BS2sx-IC and BS2p24-IC modules. This board provides a number of prewired components for quick prototyping of common, simple circuits. Figure 1.18 shows the board with the BS1-IC properly inserted into the socket. Figure 1.19 show the board with the BS2-IC properly inserted into the socket. This board features a, DB9 programming connector, reset button, barrel connector for power, power LED, 4 push-buttons, 4 LEDs, a piezo speaker a 10K potentiometer, an RJ-11 jack (for interfacing to an X10 powerline interface), an analog output pin and two 8-pin sockets for EEPROM and ADC chips. One female 0.1" socket allows for access to all the module's pins plus Vdd, Vin and Vss. Vdd is +5 volts and Vin is 6 – 9 volts (depending on your power supply). **Also note: the barrel jack is designed for a center positive, 2.1 mm (pin) x 5.5 mm (barrel) plug.**

Figure 1.18: BASIC Stamp Activity Board (shown with BS1-IC properly inserted) (27905 or 27906)

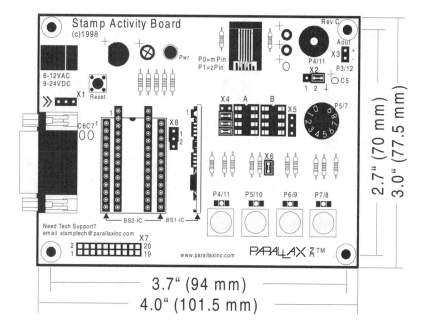

The BASIC Stamp Activity Board is excellent for projects requiring buttons, LEDs, a speaker, etc. All the components are prewired and have labels next to them to indicate the I/O pin they are connected to. You can find additional information on the board and source code for the BS1 and BS2 on the Parallax CD.

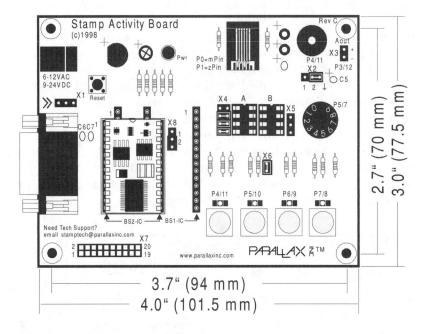

Figure 1.19: BASIC Stamp Activity Board (shown with BS2-IC properly inserted) (27905 or 27906)

Other Boards

Other development boards for the BASIC Stamps may now be available at this time. Please refer to any documentation available for those products for specific information.

Guidelines and Precautions

When using the BASIC Stamp, or any IC chip, please follow the guidelines below.

1. **Be alert to static sensitive devices and static-prone situations.**
   a. The BASIC Stamp, like other IC's, can be damaged by static discharge that commonly occurs touching grounded surfaces or other conductors. Environmental conditions (humidity changes, wind, static prone surfaces, etc) play a major role in the presence of random static charges. It is always recommended to use grounding straps and anti-static or static dissipative mats when handling devices like the BASIC Stamp. If the items above are not available, be sure to touch a grounded surface after you have approached the work area and before you handle static sensitive devices.

2. **Verify that all power is off before connecting/disconnecting.**
   a. If power is connected to the BASIC Stamp or any device it is connected to while inserting or removing it from a circuit, damage to the BASIC Stamp or circuit could result.

3. **Verify BASIC Stamp orientation before connection to development boards and other circuits.**
   a. Like other IC's, the BASIC Stamp should be inserted in a specific orientation in relation to the development board or circuit. Powering the circuit with an IC connected backwards will likely damage the IC and/or other components in the circuit. Most IC's have some form of a "pin 1 indicator" as do most IC sockets. This indicator usually takes the form of a dot, a half-circle, or the number 1 placed at or near pin 1 of the device.

   The BS1-IC has a "1" and a half-circle indicator on the backside of the module. Additionally, Figure 1.2 above indicates the pin numbering and labels.

   The 24-pin modules (BS2, BS2e, etc) have a half-circle indicator on the topside of the module (see Figure 1.20). This indicates (when holding the module with the half-circle facing up, or north) that pin number one is the first pin on the upper left of the device. The socket that accepts this 24-pin module also has a half-circle or notch on one end, indicating the correct orientation. See Figure 1.21 for other examples.

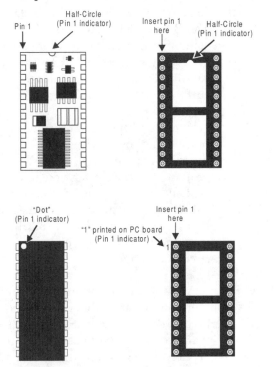

Figure 1.20: Pin 1 Indicators BS2-IC shown in the correct orientation in relation to a 24-pin socket.

Figure 1.21: Additional Examples of Pin 1 Indicators (chip and socket shown in the correct orientation in relation to each other)

BASIC Stamp Programming Connections:

Parallax, Inc. suggests using the cables provided in the BASIC Stamp Starter Kit for programming the BASIC Stamps. When those cables are not available, you may create your own by duplicating the following diagrams in your cables and circuits.

Be very careful to follow these diagrams closely; it is quite common for programming problems with the BASIC Stamps to be a result of a poorly made custom cable or programming connections on your applications board. With the BS2, BS2e, BS2sx and BS2p programming connections, it is possible to reverse a couple of wires and still get positive results using some of the "connection" tests our Tech. Support team tries and yet you still will not be able to communicate with the BASIC Stamp. It is vital that you check your connections with a meter and verify the pin numbering to avoid problems like this.

Figure 1.22: BS1 Programming Connections. Note: Though it is not shown, power must be connected to the BS1 to program it.

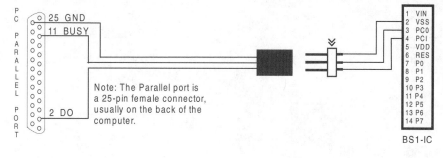

Note: The Parallel port is a 25-pin female connector, usually on the back of the computer.

Figure 1.23: BS2, BS2e, BS2sx and BS2p Programming Connections. Note: Though it is not shown, power must be connected to the BASIC Stamp to program it. Also, the programming connections are the same for the BS2p40.

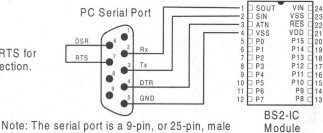

Connect DSR and RTS for automatic port detection.

Note: The serial port is a 9-pin, or 25-pin, male connector, usually on the back of the computer. Use a 25-pin to 9-pin adapter when trying to interface to a 9-pin cable.

Quick Start Introduction

This chapter is a quick start guide to connecting the BASIC Stamp to the PC and programming it. Without even knowing how the BASIC Stamp functions, you should be able to complete the exercise below. This exercise assumes you have a BASIC Stamp and one of the development boards shown in Chapter **1**.

Connecting and Downloading

1) If the BASIC Stamp isn't already plugged into your development board, insert it into the appropriate socket as indicated in the "Development Boards" section of Chapter **1**. Be careful to insert it in the correct orientation. NOTE: The BASIC Stamp 1 Rev. D is built into its own development board.

2) If using a BASIC Stamp 1, connect the 25-pin side of your programming cable to an available parallel port on your computer. Then connect the 3-pin side to the 3-pin programming header on the development board. See Figure 2.1 for an example. The 3-pin connector must be connected so that the arrows on one side of the plug line up with the arrows "<<" printed on the board.

Figure 2.1: BS1-IC and BASIC Stamp 1 Carrier Board being properly connected for programming. The BS1-IC must be powered and the 3-pin cable must be connected in the correct orientation, as shown.

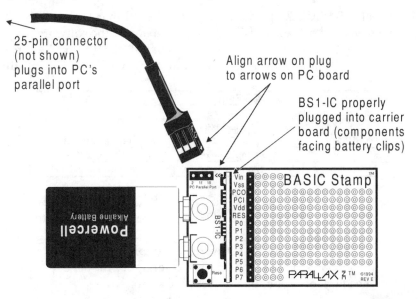

25-pin connector (not shown) plugs into PC's parallel port

Align arrow on plug to arrows on PC board

BS1-IC properly plugged into carrier board (components facing battery clips)

Quick Start Guide

3) If using a BASIC Stamp 2, 2e, 2sx or 2p, connect the 9-pin female side of a serial cable to an available serial port on your computer. Note: the serial cable should we a "straight-though" cable, not a null-modem cable. Connect the 9-pin male side of the cable to the DB9 connector on the development board. See Figure 2.2 for an example.

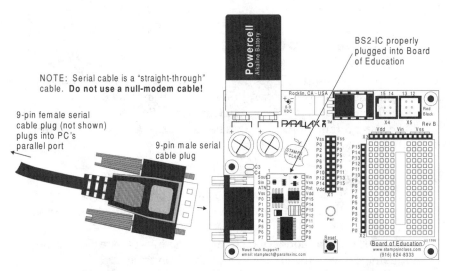

NOTE: Serial cable is a "straight-through" cable. **Do not use a null-modem cable!**

9-pin female serial cable plug (not shown) plugs into PC's parallel port

9-pin male serial cable plug

Figure 2.2: BS2-IC and Board of Education being properly connected for programming. The BS2-IC must be powered and the "straight-through" serial cable must be connected, as shown.

4) Run the BASIC Stamp editor software. Refer Table 2.1 for software versions and names. If using the DOS version of the software, try running it though DOS mode only; running it though Windows may cause it to malfunction when communicating with the BASIC Stamp.

	DOS Software	Windows Software
BS1	Stamp.exe	N/A
BS2	Stamp2.exe	Stampw.exe
BS2e	Stamp2e.exe	Stampw.exe (v1.096+)
BS2sx	Stamp2sx.exe	Stampw.exe (v1.091+)
BS2p	Stamp2p.exe	Stampw.exe (v1.1+)

Table 2.1: BASIC Stamp Editors for DOS and Windows.

a) If using the Parallax CD, go to the Software -> BASIC Stamp -> Windows section (or the DOS section) to locate and run the software).

b) If using the Windows software, it may prompt you with a list of serial ports. Follow the prompt to configure the serial port list (if needed) for proper operation of the editor.

5) Enter the following two lines of PBASIC code in the editor window (change the "BS2" to the proper name of your module, as indicated below):

```
' { $STAMP BS2 }
DEBUG  "Hello World!"
```

   a) Note: The above code is written for a BASIC Stamp 2. Change the "BS2" in the first line to BS1, BS2e, BS2sx or BS2p depending on the model of the BASIC Stamp you are using. Failure to do this may cause the editor to fail to recognize your BASIC Stamp during the next step.

6) Download the program you just typed in to the BASIC Stamp. If using the DOS software, press ALT-R to download. If using the Windows software, press CTRL-R to download.

   a) If the program is typed in correctly (and the BASIC Stamp is connected properly) a progress bar window should appear (perhaps very briefly) showing the download progress. Afterwards a debug window should appear and display "Hello World!"

   b) If there is a syntax error in the program, the editor will highlight the text in question and display an error message. Review the error, fix the code and then try downloading again.

   c) If the error reported a connection problem with the BASIC Stamp, make sure the first line of code indicates the proper module name and verify the programming cable connections, module orientation (in the socket) and that it is properly powered, then try downloading again.

7) Congratulations! You've just written and downloaded your first BASIC Stamp program! The "Hello World!" text that appeared on the screen was sent from the BASIC Stamp, back up the programming cable, to the PC.

The BASIC Stamp Editor software is available for Windows and DOS operating systems. The following system requirements are a minimum for using the BASIC Stamp Editor:

SYSTEM REQUIREMENTS FOR THE
BASIC STAMP EDITOR SOFTWARE.

- 80486 (80286 for DOS) (or higher) IBM or compatible PC;
- Windows 95/98/NT4/2000 operating system (DOS 5.0 or higher for DOS versions);
- 16 Mb of RAM (1 Mb for DOS);
- 1 Mb of available hard drive space;
- CD-ROM drive;
- 1 available serial port (1 available parallel port for BS1).

(Note: though it is suggested that the BASIC Stamp Editor be installed on your hard drive, it is not required. The software may be run right off the Parallax CD).

INSTALLING THE SOFTWARE.

To install the BASIC Stamp Editor:

1. Insert the Parallax CD into the CD-ROM drive. The CD should auto-start (unless that feature has been disabled on your computer). If using DOS, explore it with the CD (change directory) and DIR (directory list) commands.
2. Select the Software -> BASIC Stamp section.
3. Select the DOS or Windows version you wish to use and click the Install button. If exploring the CD through DOS, use the COPY command to copy it to a desired directory on your hard drive.
4. Close the CD and run the BASIC Stamp Editor program from the directory it was copied to. You may also create a shortcut to it (if using Windows).

Table 3.1 lists the available BASIC Stamp editors, their names, versions, operating system and BASIC Stamp model they support.

Table 3.1: BASIC Stamp Editors for DOS and Windows.

	DOS Software	Windows Software
BS1	Stamp.exe	N/A
BS2	Stamp2.exe	Stampw.exe
BS2e	Stamp2e.exe	Stampw.exe (v1.096+)
BS2sx	Stamp2sx.exe	Stampw.exe (v1.091+)
BS2p	Stamp2p.exe	Stampw.exe (v1.1+)

Using the BASIC Stamp Editor

Software Interface (Windows)

This section describes the Windows version of the BASIC Stamp Editor. See the "Software Interface (DOS)" section for information on using the DOS version. The Windows version supports multiple BASIC Stamp modules and is recommended for most tasks.

The BASIC Stamp Windows Editor, shown in Figure 3.1 was designed to be easy to use and mostly intuitive. Those that are familiar with standard Windows software should feel comfortable using the BASIC Stamp Windows Editor.

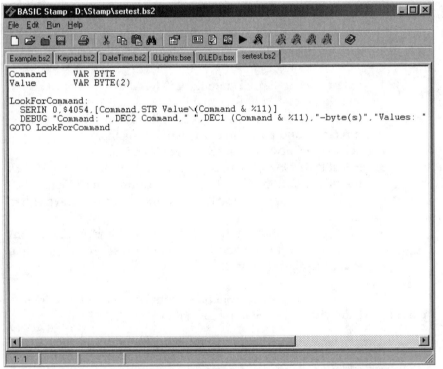

Figure 3.1: BASIC Stamp Windows Editor. Shown here with 6 separate source code files open.

The editor consists of one main editor window that can be used to view and modify up to 16 different source code files at once. Each source code file that is loaded into the editor will have its own tab at the top of the page labeled with the name of the file (see Figure 3.2). Source code that

THE EDITOR WINDOW.

has never been saved to disk will default to "Untitled#"; where # is an automatically generated number. A user can switch between source code files by simply pointing and clicking on a file's tab.

Figure 3.2: Example Editor tabs. Shown with 5 separate files open.

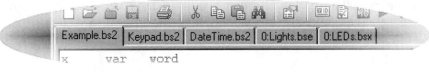

The status of the active source code page is indicated in a status bar below it and the full path to the source code (if it has been loaded from or saved to disk) will appear in the title bar of the BASIC Stamp Editor. The status bar (see Figure 3.3) contains information such as cursor position, file save status, download status and syntax error/download messages.

Figure 3.3: Example Status Bar.

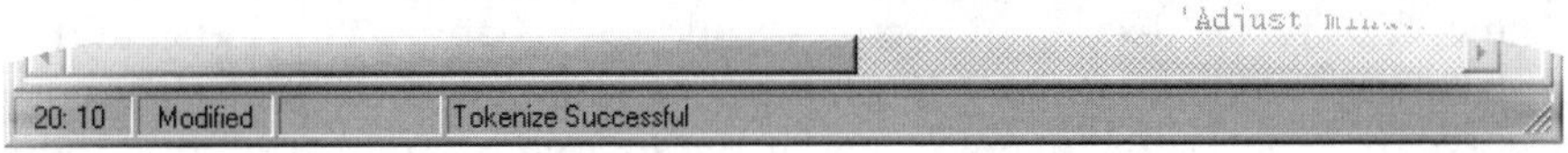

After entering the desired source code in the editor window, selecting Run -> Run (or pressing Ctrl-R) will tokenize and download the code to the BASIC Stamp (assuming the code is correct and the BASIC Stamp is properly connected).

SUPPORTING MULTIPLE BASIC STAMP MODELS – USING THE STAMP DIRECTIVE.

Because the Windows editor supports more than one model of the BASIC Stamp, it is necessary to tell the editor which model you are trying to program.

There are three methods the editor uses to determine the model of the BASIC Stamp you are programming for. They are: 1) the STAMP directive, 2) the extension on the file name of the source code and 3) the Default Stamp Mode (as set by preferences). Whenever a file is loaded, tokenized, downloaded or viewed in the Memory Map, the BASIC Stamp looks for the STAMP directive first. If it cannot find the STAMP directive in the source code, it looks at the extension on the file name (for a .bs2, .bse, .bsx or .bsp). If it doesn't understand the extension, then it uses the Default Stamp Mode, as defined by preferences.

The best way to force the editor to recognize the intended model of the BASIC Stamp is to use the STAMP directive, since the STAMP directive will override all other settings. If you forget to enter the STAMP directive in your code, the editor may try to program another model of the BASIC Stamp, which may lead to some confusing error messages.

The STAMP directive is a special command that should be included (usually near the top) in a program to indicate the model of BASIC Stamp targeted. The line below is an example of the STAMP directive (in this case, it indicates that the program is intended for a BASIC Stamp 2):

FORMAT OF THE **STAMP** DIRECTIVE.

`'{ $STAMP  BS2 }`

This line should be entered into your code, usually near the top, on a line by itself. Note that the directive appears on a comment line (the apostrophe (') indicates this) for compatibility with the DOS versions of the editor.

The 'BS2' in the example above should be changed to indicate the appropriate model of the BASIC Stamp you are using. For example, to use the BS2e, BS2sx or BS2p, enter one of the following lines into your code, respectively.

INDICATING DIFFERENT BASIC STAMP MODELS.

```
'{ $STAMP  BS2e }          'This indicates to use the BASIC Stamp 2e

'{ $STAMP  BS2sx }         'This indicates to use the BASIC Stamp 2sx

'{ $STAMP  BS2p }          'This indicates to use the BASIC Stamp 2p
```

The directive itself must be enclosed in brackets, {…}. There should not be any spaces between the dollar sign, $, and the word STAMP, however, the directive may contain additional spaces in certain other areas. For example:

EXTRA SPACES ARE ALLOWED IN CERTAIN AREAS.

'   { $STAMP   BS2   }

-- or --

'{$STAMP   BS2}

-- and --

'{$STAMP   BS2   }

are all acceptable variations, however:

'{$ STAMP   BS2}

-- and --

'{$STAMPBS2}

are not acceptable and will be ignored. If one of the above two lines were entered into the source code, the editor would ignore it and, instead, rely on the extension of the filename or the Default Stamp Mode to determine the appropriate model.

The STAMP directive is read and acted upon by the BASIC Stamp Windows Editor any time a source code file is loaded, tokenized, downloaded (run) or viewed in the Memory Map.

INTRODUCTION TO BASIC STAMP PROJECTS.

For BS2e, BS2sx and BS2p programs, each editor page can be a separate project, or part of a single project. A project is a set of up to eight files that should all be downloaded to the BASIC Stamp for a single application. Each of the files within the project is downloaded into a separate "program slot". Only the BASIC Stamp 2e, 2sx and 2p modules support projects (multiple program slots).

USING THE STAMP DIRECTIVE TO DEFINE MULTI-FILE PROJECTS.

For BASIC Stamp projects (consisting of multiple programs), the STAMP directive has an option to specify additional filenames. The syntax below demonstrates this form of the STAMP directive:

```
'  { $STAMP  BS2e, file2, file3, …, file8 }
```

Use this form of the STAMP directive if a project, consisting of multiple files, is desired. This directive must be entered into the first program (to be downloaded into program slot 0) and not in any of the other files in the project. The *file2*, *file3*, etc. items should be the actual name (and optionally the path) of the other files in the project. *File2* refers to the program that should be downloaded into program slot 1, *file3* is the program that should be downloaded into program slot 2, etc. If no path is given, the path of program 0 (the program in which the STAMP directive is entered) is used.

Up to seven filenames can be included, bringing the total to eight files in the project all together. Upon tokenizing, running or viewing program 0 in the Memory Map, the editor will read the STAMP directive, determine if the indicated files exist, will load them if necessary and change their captions to indicate the project they belong to and their associated program number. After the directive is tokenized properly, and all associated files are labeled properly, tokenizing, running or viewing any program in the Memory Map will result in that program's entire project being tokenized, downloaded or viewed.

When a file that is part of a BS2SX project is closed, the entire project (all the associated files) will be closed as well. When program #0 of a project is opened from diskette, the entire project will be loaded as well.

To create a project consisting of multiple files, follow these steps:

EASY STEPS FOR CREATING A MULTI-FILE PROJECT.

1. Create the first file in the editor and save it (we'll call it Sample.bsx). This will be the program that is downloaded into program slot 0.
2. Create at least one other file in the editor and save it also (we'll call it NextProgram.bsx).

Note: At this point the editor tabs will be:

> 0:Sample.bsx   and   0:NextProgram.bsx.

indicating that there are two unrelated files open "Sample.bsx" and "NextProgram.bsx" and each will be downloaded into program slot 0.

3. Go back to the first program and enter the STAMP directive using the project format. Use "NextProgram" as the *File2* argument. For example:

    ```
    ' { $STAMP BS2sx, NextProgram.bsx }
    ```

4. Then tokenize the code by pressing F7 or selecting Check Syntax from the RUN menu.

Note: At this point, the BASIC Stamp Editor will see the STAMP directive and realize that this file (Sample.bsx) is the first file in a project and that the second file should be NextProgram.bsx. It will then search for the file on the hard drive (to verify it's path is correct), will see that it is already loaded, and then will change the editor tabs to indicate the project relationship. At this point the editor tabs will be:

    0:Sample.bsx   and   [Sample] 1:NextProgram.bsx.

indicating that there are two related files open; "Sample.bsx" and "NextProgram.bsx". NextProgram.bsx belongs to the "Sample" project and it will be downloaded into program slot 1 and Sample.bsx will be downloaded into program slot 0.

PROJECT DOWNLOAD MODES.

The editor has the ability to treat projects as one logical unit and can download each of the associated source code files to the BS2e, BS2sx or BS2p at once. In order to minimize download time for large projects a Project Download Mode is available in the Preferences window. The available modes are: "Modified" (the default), "All" or "Current" and are explained below. This item only affects download operations for the BS2e, BS2sx and BS2p. See Table 3.2.

Download Mode	Function
Modified (default)	This mode will cause only the source code files that were modified since the last download to be downloaded next time. If no files have been modified since the last download, or the entire project has just been loaded into the editor, all the files will be downloaded next time. This mode decreases the delay during downloading projects and should help speed development and testing.
All	This mode will cause all the source code files to be downloaded each time. This will be noticeably slow with large projects.
Current	This mode will cause only the current source code file to be downloaded, ignoring all the others.

Table 3.2: Project Download Modes.

Regardless of the download mode selected, the programs will be downloaded into the program slot indicated in their tab.

The BASIC Stamp Windows Editor also features a Memory Map (not shown) that displays the layout of the current PBASIC program, DATA usage and RAM register usage. Type CTRL+M, or press F7, to activate this window.

MEMORY MAP FUNCTION.

When you activate the Memory Map, the editor will check your program for syntax errors and, if the program's syntax is OK, will present you with a color-coded map of the RAM and EEPROM. You'll be able to tell at a glance how much memory you have used and how much remains. Two important points to remember about this map are: 1) it only indicates how your program will be downloaded to the BASIC Stamp; it does not "read" the BASIC Stamp's memory, and 2) fixed variables like B3 and W1 and any aliases do not show up on the memory map as memory used. The editor ignores fixed variables when it arranges automatically allocated variables in memory. Remember, fixed and allocated variables can overlap.

Another useful feature is the Identify function, CTRL+I. This will cause the editor to try to connect to the BASIC Stamp to determine its firmware version number. Use the Identify function to quickly determine if the BASIC Stamp is correctly connected to the PC for programming.

IDENTIFY FUNCTION.

The following tables list the available keyboard shortcuts within the BASIC Stamp Windows Editor.

Table 3.3: Shortcut Keys for File Functions (Windows editor).

File Functions	
Shortcut Key	**Function**
Ctrl+O	Open a source code file into the Editor window.
Ctrl+S	Save current source code file to disk.
Ctrl+P	Print current source code.

Table 3.4: Shortcut Keys for Editing Functions (Windows editor).

Editing Functions	
Shortcut Key	**Function**
Ctrl+Z	Undo last action.
Ctrl+X	Cut selected text to the clipboard.
Ctrl+C	Copy selected text to the clipboard.
Ctrl+V	Paste text from clipboard to selected area.
Ctrl+A	Select all text in current source code.
Ctrl+F	Find or Replace text.
F3	Find text again.
F5	Open Preferences window.

Table 3.5: Shortcut Keys for Coding Functions (Windows editor).

Coding Functions	
Shortcut Key(s)	**Function**
F6 or Ctrl+I	Identify BASIC Stamp firmware.
F7 or Ctrl+T	Perform a syntax check on the code and display any error messages.
F8 or Ctrl+M	Open Memory Map window.
F9 or Ctrl+R	Tokenize code, download to the BASIC Stamp and open Debug window if necessary.
F11 or Ctrl+D	Open a new Debug window.
F12	Switch to next window (Editor, Debug #1, Debug #2, Debug #3 or Debug #4)
Ctrl+1, Ctrl+2, Ctrl+3, Ctrl+4	Switch to Debug Terminal #1, Debug Terminal #2, etc. if that Terminal window is open.
Ctrl+`	Switch to Editor window.
ESC	Close current window.

Software Interface (DOS)

This section describes the DOS versions of the BASIC Stamp Editor. See the "Software Interface (Windows)" section for information on using the Windows version. The DOS versions support only one BASIC Stamp module; a separate DOS editor is available for each model of the BASIC Stamp.

Using the BASIC Stamp Editor

The BASIC Stamp DOS Editor, shown in Figure 3.4 was designed to be very simple and to provide only the necessary functionality needed for developing with a BASIC Stamp. Those that are familiar with standard DOS software should feel comfortable using the BASIC Stamp DOS Editor.

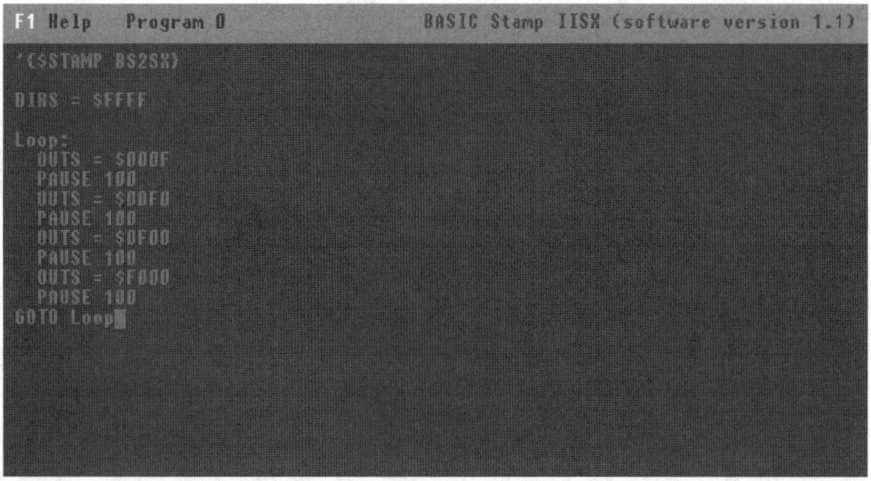

Figure 3.4: BASIC Stamp DOS Editor. Shown here with the program ID (slot #) set to 0.

You must run the version of the DOS editor that is intended for the model of the BASIC Stamp you are using. There is a different version for each model. Refer to Table 3.1 for a list of the editors, versions and the BASIC Stamp models they support.

THE DOS EDITOR ONLY SUPPORTS ONE BASIC STAMP MODEL.

The BASIC Stamp DOS Editor can only load and edit one source code file at a time. Source code can be loaded into the editor by pressing ALT-L and selecting a file from the menu. NOTE: That the browse menu only shows files in the current directory; the directory that the BASIC Stamp DOS Editor is run from.

THE EDITOR WINDOW.

BS2e, BS2sx and BS2p models support up to eight programs to be downloaded into separate program slots. From here on, any application for these models of the BASIC Stamp will be called a project. A project is a set of up to eight files that should all be downloaded to the BASIC Stamp for a single application. Each of the files within the project must be downloaded into a separate "program slot". Only the BASIC Stamp 2e, 2sx and 2p modules support projects (multiple program slots).

INTRODUCTION TO BASIC STAMP PROJECTS.

For BASIC Stamp projects (consisting of multiple programs), the BASIC Stamp DOS Editor must be used to individually load and download each of the files into the appropriate slot. Keep in mind that the DOS editor can only load up one source code file at a time. NOTE: The Windows version does not have this limitation.

Pressing ALT+# (where # is a number from 0 to 7) will change the ID (shown on the title bar; see Figure 3.5) of the currently visible source code in the editor. This ID is not saved with the program and must be set and verified manually each time it is loaded from disk and before each download.

Figure 3.5: Example Editor Title Bar. Shown with the program ID (slot #) set to 0

```
F1  Help    Program 0              BASIC Stamp IISX (software version 1.1)
```

The sequence of keystrokes to load and download two programs into two separate program slots would consist of the following:

1. ALT+L loads a program into the editor.
2. ALT+0 sets the editor to program ID 0.
3. ALT+R downloads this program into program slot 0 of the BASIC Stamp's EEPROM.
4. ALT+L loads another program into the editor.
5. ALT+1 sets the editor to program ID 1.
6. ALT+R downloads this program into program slot 1 of the BASIC Stamp's EEPROM.

The shortcut key ALT+R downloads only one program at a time. Note that you must load each program separately.

MEMORY MAP FUNCTION.

The BASIC Stamp DOS Editors for the BS2, BS2e, BS2sx and BS2p, also feature a Memory Map (not shown) that displays the layout of the current PBASIC program, DATA usage and RAM register usage. Type ALT+M to activate this window.

When you activate the Memory Map, the editor will check your program for syntax errors and, if the program's syntax is OK, will present you with a color-coded map of the RAM. You'll be able to tell at a glance how much memory you have used and how much remains. (You may also press the space bar to cycle through similar maps of EEPROM program memory.)

Two important points to remember about this map are, 1) it only indicates how your program will be downloaded to the BASIC Stamp; it does not "read" the BASIC Stamp's memory, and 2) fixed variables like B3 and W1 and any aliases do not show up on the memory map as memory used. The editor ignores fixed variables when it arranges automatically allocated variables in memory. Remember, fixed and allocated variables can overlap.

The following tables list the available keyboard shortcuts within the BASIC Stamp Windows Editor.

File Functions	
Shortcut Key	**Function**
Alt+L	Open a source code file into the Editor window.
Alt+S	Save current source code file to disk.
Alt+Q	Close the editor.

Table 3.6: Shortcut Keys for File Functions (DOS editor).

Editing Functions	
Shortcut Key	**Function**
Alt+X	Cut selected text to the clipboard.
Alt+C	Copy selected text to the clipboard.
Alt+V	Paste text from clipboard to selected area.
Alt+F	Find or Replace text.
Alt+N	Find text again.

Table 3.7: Shortcut Keys for Editing Functions (DOS editor).

Coding Functions	
Shortcut Key(s)	**Function**
Alt+0..7	Set Program Slot # to download to. (not supported on the BS1 or BS 2)
Alt+I	Identify BASIC Stamp firmware. (not supported on the BS1)
Alt+M	Open Memory Map window. (not supported on the BS1)
Alt+R	Tokenize code, download to the BASIC Stamp and open Debug window if necessary.
Alt+P	Open the potentiometer calibration window. (only supported on the BS1)

Table 3.8: Shortcut Keys for Coding Functions (DOS editor).

This chapter provides detail on the architecture (RAM usage) and math functions of the BS1, BS2, BS2e, BS2sx and BS2p.

The following icons will appear to indicate where there are differences between versions of the BASIC Stamp:

⌗1⌗ ⌗2⌗ ⌗2e⌗ ⌗2sx⌗ ⌗2p⌗ One or more of these icons indicates the item applies only to the BS1, BS2, BS2e, BS2sx or BS2p, respectively.

MEMORY ORGANIZATION

The BASIC Stamp has two kinds of memory; RAM (for variables used by your program) and EEPROM (for storing the program itself). EEPROM may also be used to store long-term data in much the same way that desktop computers use a hard drive to hold both programs and files.

An important distinction between RAM and EEPROM is this:

- RAM loses its contents when the BASIC Stamp loses power; when power returns, all RAM locations are cleared to 0s.
- EEPROM retains the contents of memory, with or without power, until it is overwritten (such as during the program-downloading process or with a WRITE instruction.)

RAM ORGANIZATION (BS1)

⌗1⌗ The BS1 has 16 bytes (8 words) of RAM space arranged as shown in Table 4.1. The first word, called PORT, is used for I/O pin control. It consists of two bytes, PINS and DIRS. The bits within PINS correspond to each of the eight I/O pins on the BS1. Reading PINS effectively reads the I/O pins directly, returning an 8-bit set of 1's and 0's corresponding to the high and low state of the respective I/O pin at that moment. Writing to PINS will store a high or low value on the respective I/O pins (though only on pins that are set to outputs).

THE INPUT/OUTPUT VARIABLES.

The second byte of PORT, DIRS, controls the direction of the I/O pins. Each bit within DIRS corresponds to an I/O pin's direction. A high bit (1) sets the corresponding I/O pin to an output direction and a low bit (0) sets the corresponding I/O pin to an input direction.

The remaining words (W0 – W6) are available for general-purpose use. Each word consists of separately addressable bytes and the first two bytes (B0 and B1) are bit addressable as well.

You may assign other names (symbols) to these RAM registers as shown in section "Defining and Using Variables", below.

When the BS1 is powered up, or reset, all memory locations are cleared to 0, so all pins are inputs (DIRS = %00000000). Also, if the PBASIC program sets all the I/O pins to outputs (DIRS = %11111111), then they will initially output low, since the output latch (PINS) is cleared to all zeros upon power-up or reset, as well.

Word Name	Byte Names	Bit Names	Special Notes
PORT	PINS	PIN0 – PIN7	I/O pins; bit addressable.
	DIRS	DIR0 – DIR7	I/O pins directions; bit addressable.
W0	B0	BIT0 – BIT7	Bit addressable.
	B1	BIT8 – BIT15	Bit addressable.
W1	B2		
	B3		
W2	B4		
	B5		
W3	B6		
	B7		
W4	B8		
	B9		
W5	B10		
	B11		
W6	B12		Used by GOSUB instruction.
	B13		Used by GOSUB instruction.

Table 4.1: BS1 RAM Organization. Note: There are eight words, consisting of two bytes each for a total of 16 bytes. The bits within the upper two words are individually addressable.

The BS2, BS2e, BS2sx and BS2p have 32 bytes of Variable RAM space arranged as shown in Table 4.2. Of these, the first six bytes are reserved for input, output, and direction control of the I/O pins. The remaining 26 bytes are available for general-purpose use as variables.

RAM ORGANIZATION (BS2, BS2E, BS2SX, BS2P).

The word variable INS is unique in that it is read-only. The 16 bits of INS reflect the state of I/O pins P0 through P15. It may only be read, not written. OUTS contains the states of the 16 output latches. DIRS controls the direction (input or output) of each of the 16 I/O pins.

THE INPUT/OUTPUT VARIABLES.

A 0 in a particular DIRS bit makes the corresponding pin an input and a 1 makes the corresponding pin an output. So if bit 5 of DIRS is 0 and bit 6 of DIRS is 1, then I/O pin 5 (P5) is an input and I/O pin 6 (P6) is an output. A pin that is an input is at the mercy of circuitry outside the BASIC Stamp;

the BASIC Stamp cannot change its state. A pin that is an output is set to the state indicated by the corresponding bit of the OUTS register.

When the BASIC Stamp is powered up, or reset, all memory locations are cleared to 0, so all pins are inputs (DIRS = %0000000000000000). Also, if the PBASIC program sets all the I/O pins to outputs (DIRS = %1111111111111111), then they will initially output low, since the output latch (OUTS) is cleared to all zeros upon power-up or reset, as well.

Table 4.2: BS2, BS2e, BS2sx and BS2p RAM Organization. Note: There are 16 words, consisting of two bytes each for a total of 32 bytes. All bits are individually addressable through modifiers and the bits within the upper three words are also individually addressable though the pre-defined names shown.

Word Name	Byte Names	Nibble Names	Bit Names	Special Notes
INS	INL INH	INA, INB INC, IND	IN0 – IN7 IN8 – IN15	Input pins
OUTS	OUTL OUTH	OUTA, OUTB OUTC, OUTD	OUT0 – OUT7 OUT8 – OUT15	Output pins
DIRS	DIRL DIRH	DIRA, DIRB DIRC, DIRD	DIR0 – DIR7 DIR8 – DIR15	I/O pin direction control
W0	B0 B1			
W1	B2 B3			
W2	B4 B5			
W3	B6 B7			
W4	B8 B9			
W5	B10 B11			
W6	B12 B13			
W7	B14 B15			
W8	B16 B17			
W9	B18 B19			
W10	B20 B21			
W11	B22 B23			
W12	B24 B25			

Note: All registers are word, byte, nibble and bit addressable

The INS variable always shows the state of the I/O pins themselves, regardless of the direction of each I/O pin. We call this, "reading the pins". If a pin was set to an input mode (within DIRS) and an external circuit connected the I/O pin to ground, the corresponding bit of INS would be low. If a pin was set to an output mode and the pin's state was set to a high level (within OUTS), the corresponding bit of INS would be high. If, however, that same pin was externally connected directly to ground, the corresponding bit of INS would be low; since we're reading the state of the pin itself and the BASIC Stamp cannot override a pin that is driven to ground or 5 volts externally. Note: The last example is an error, is a direct short and can cause damage to the BASIC Stamp! Do not intentionally connect output pins directly to an external power source or you risk destroying your BASIC Stamp.

To summarize: DIRS determines whether a pin's state is set by external circuitry (input, 0) or by the state of OUTS (output, 1). INS always matches the actual states of the I/O pins, whether they are inputs or outputs. OUTS holds bits that will only appear on pins whose DIRS bits are set to output.

SUMMARY OF THE FUNCTION OF DIRS, INS AND OUTS.

In programming the BASIC Stamp, it's often more convenient to deal with individual bytes, nibbles or bits of INS, OUTS and DIRS rather than the entire 16-bit words. PBASIC has built-in names for these elements, shown in Table 4.2.

Here's an example of what is described in Table 4.2. The INS register is 16-bits (corresponding to I/O pins 0 though 15). The INS register consists of two bytes, called INL (the Low byte) and INH (the High byte). INL corresponds to I/O pins 0 through 7 and INH corresponds to I/O pins 8 though 15. INS can also be though of as containing four nibbles, INA, INB, INC and IND. INA is I/O pins 0 though 3, INB is I/O pins 4 though 7, etc. In addition, each of the bits of INS can be accessed directly using the names IN0, IN1, IN2... IN5.

The same naming scheme holds true for the OUTS and DIRS variables as well.

As Table 4.2 shows, the BASIC Stamp's memory is organized into 16 words of 16 bits each. The first three words are used for I/O. The remaining 13 words are available for use as general-purpose variables.

PREDEFINED "FIXED" VARIABLES.

Just like the I/O variables, the general-purpose variables have predefined names: W0 through W12 and B0 through B25. B0 is the low byte of W0; B1 is the high byte of W0; and so on through W12 (B24=low byte, B25=high byte). Unlike I/O variables, there's no reason that your program variables have to be stuck in a specific position in the BASIC Stamp's physical memory. A byte is a byte regardless of its location. And if a program uses a mixture of variables of different sizes, it can be a pain in the neck to logically dole them out or allocate storage.

More importantly, mixing fixed variables with automatically allocated variables (discussed in the next section) is an invitation to bugs. A fixed variable can overlap an allocated variable, causing data meant for one variable to show up in another! The fixed variable names (of the general-purpose variables) are only provided for power users who require absolute access to a specific location in RAM.

We recommend that you avoid using the fixed variables in most situations. Instead, let PBASIC allocate variables as described in the next section. The editor software will organize your storage requirements to make optimal use of the available memory.

DEFINING AND USING VARIABLES.

Before you can use a variable in a PBASIC program you must declare it. "Declare" means letting the BASIC Stamp know that you plan to use a variable, what you want to call it, and how big it is. Although PBASIC does have predefined variables that you can use without declaring them first (see previous sections), the preferred way to set up variables is to use the directive SYMBOL (for the BS1) or VAR (for all other BASIC Stamps). Here is the syntax for a variable declaration:

SYMBOL   Name = RegisterName

-- OR --

Name   VAR   Size

where *Name* is the name by which you will refer to the variable, *RegisterName* is the "fixed" name for the register and *Size* indicates the number of bits of storage for the variable. NOTE: The top example is for the BS1 and the bottom example is for all other BASIC Stamps.

THE RULES OF SYMBOL NAMES.

There are certain rules regarding symbol names. Symbols must start with a letter, can contain a mixture of letters, numbers, and underscore (_) characters, and must not be the same as PBASIC keywords or labels used in your program. Additionally, symbols can be up to 32 characters long.

See Appendix B for a list of PBASIC keywords. PBASIC does not distinguish between upper and lower case, so the names MYVARIABLE, myVariable, and MyVaRiAbLe are all equivalent.

For the BS1, the RegisterName is one of the predefined "fixed" variable names, such as W0, W1, B0, B1, etc. Here are a few examples of variable declarations on the BS1:

```
SYMBOL    Temporary = W0          ' value can be 0 to 65535
SYMBOL    Counter   = B1          ' value can be 0 to 255
SYMBOL    Result    = B2          ' value can be 0 to 255
```

The above example will create a variable called *Temporary* whose contents will be stored in the RAM location called W0. Also, the variable *Counter* will be located at RAM location B1 and *Result* at location B2. *Temporary* is a word-sized variable (because that's what size W0 is) while the other two are both byte-sized variables. Throughout the rest of the program, we can use the names *Temporary*, *Counter*, and *Result* instead of W0, B1 and B2, respectively. This makes the code much more readable; it's easier to determine what *Counter* is used for than it would be to figure out what the name B1 means. Please note, that *Counter* resides at location B1, and B1 happens to be the high byte of W0. This means than changing *Counter* will also change *Temporary* since they overlap. A situation like this usually is a mistake and results in strange behavior, but is also a powerful feature if used carefully.

For the BS2, BS2e, BS2sx and BS2p, the *Size* argument has four choices: 1) BIT (1 bit), 2) NIB (nibble; 4 bits), 3) BYTE (8 bits), and 4) WORD (16 bits). Here are some examples of variable declarations on the BS2, BS2e, BS2sx or BS2p:

```
Mouse     VAR  BIT       ' Value can be 0 or 1.
Cat       VAR  NIB       ' Value can be 0 to 15.
Dog       VAR  BYTE      ' Value can be 0 to 255.
Rhino     VAR  WORD      ' Value can be 0 to 65535.
```

The above example will create a bit-sized variable called *Mouse*, and nibble-sized variable called *Cat*, a byte-size variable called *Dog* and a word-sized variable called *Rhino*. Unlike in the BS1, these variable declarations don't point to a specific location in RAM. Instead, we only specified the desired size for each variable; the BASIC Stamp will arrange them in RAM as it sees fit. Throughout the rest of the program, we can use the names *Mouse, Cat, Dog and Rhino* to set or retrieve the contents of these variables.

A variable should be given the smallest size that will hold the largest value that will ever be stored in it. If you need a variable to hold the on/off status (1 or 0) of switch, use a bit. If you need a counter for a FOR…NEXT loop that will count from 1 to 100, use a byte. And so on.

If you assign a value to a variable that exceeds its size, the excess bits will be lost. For example, suppose you use the nibble variable *Dog*, from the example above, and write Dog = 260 (%100000100 binary). What will *Dog* contain? It will hold only the lowest 8 bits of 260: %00000100 (4 decimal).

DEFINING ARRAYS.

On the BS2, BS2e, BS2sx and BS2p, you can also define multipart variables called arrays. An array is a group of variables of the same size, and sharing a single name, but broken up into numbered cells, called elements. You can define an array using the following syntax:

```
Name    VAR    Size(n)
```

where *Name* and *Size* are the same as described earlier. The new argument, (n), tells PBASIC how many elements you want the array to have. For example:

```
MyList    VAR    BYTE(10)                ' Create a 10-byte array.
```

Once an array is defined, you can access its elements by number. Numbering starts at 0 and ends at n–1. For example:

```
MyList(3)  =  57
DEBUG  ?  MyList(3)
```

This code will display "MyList(3) = 57" on the PC screen. The real power of arrays is that the index value can be a variable itself. For example:

```
MyBytes    VAR   BYTE(10)        ' Define 10-byte array.
Index      VAR   NIB             ' Define normal nibble variable.

FOR Index = 0 TO 9              ' Repeat with Index= 0,1,2...9
  MyBytes(Index) = Index * 13    ' Write index*13 to each cell of array.
NEXT

FOR Index = 0 TO 9              ' Repeat with Index= 0,1,2...9
  DEBUG ? MyBytes(Index)         ' Show contents of each cell.
NEXT
STOP
```

If you run this program, DEBUG will display each of the 10 values stored in the elements of the array: MyBytes(0) = 0*13 = 0, MyBytes(0) = 1*13 = 13, MyBytes(2) = 2*13 = 26 ... MyBytes(9) = 9*13 = 117.

A word of caution about arrays: If you're familiar with other BASICs and have used their arrays, you have probably run into the "subscript out of range" error. Subscript is another term for the index value. It is out-of-range when it exceeds the maximum value for the size of the array. For instance, in the example above, MyBytes is a 10-cell array. Allowable index numbers are 0 through 9. If your program exceeds this range, PBASIC will not respond with an error message. Instead, it will access the next RAM location past the end of the array. If you are not careful about this, it can cause all sorts of bugs.

If accessing an out-of-range location is bad, why does PBASIC allow it? Unlike a desktop computer, the BASIC Stamp doesn't always have a display device connected to it for displaying error messages. So it just continues the best way it knows how. It's up to the programmer (you!) to prevent bugs.

Another unique property of PBASIC arrays is this: You can refer to the 0th cell of the array by using just the array's name without an index value. For example:

```
MyBytes    VAR   BYTE(10)        ' Define 10-byte array.
MyBytes(0) = 17                  ' Store 17 to 0th cell.

DEBUG ? MyBytes(0)               ' Display contents of 0th cell.
DEBUG ? MyBytes                  ' Also displays contents of 0th cell.
```

This feature is how the "string" capabilities of the DEBUG and SEROUT command expect to work. A string is simply a byte array used to store text. See the "Displaying Strings (Byte Arrays)" section in the DEBUG command description for more information.

ALIASES AND VARIABLE MODIFIERS. An alias is an alternative name for an existing variable. For example:

```
1  SYMBOL   Cat      = B0        ' Create a byte-sized variable.
   SYMBOL   Tabby    = Cat       ' Create another name for the same variable.

   -- OR --

2 2e 2sx 2p  Cat    VAR   BYTE   ' Create a byte-sized variable
             Tabby  VAR   Cat    ' Create another name for the same variable.
```

In this example, *Tabby* is an alias to the variable *Cat*. Anything stored in *Cat* shows up in *Tabby* and vice versa. Both names refer to the same physical piece of RAM. This kind of alias can be useful when you want to reuse a temporary variable in different places in your program, but also want the variable's name to reflect its function in each place. Use caution, because it is easy to forget about the aliases; during debugging, you might end up asking 'how did that value get here?!' The answer is that it was stored in the variable's alias.

2 2e 2sx 2p On the BS2, BS2e, BS2sx and BS2p, an alias can also serve as a window into a portion of another variable. This is done using "modifiers." Here the alias is assigned with a modifier that specifies what part:

```
Rhino   VAR   WORD            ' A 16-bit variable.
Head    VAR   Rhino.HIGHBYTE  ' Highest 8 bits of Rhino.
Tail    VAR   Rhino.LOWBYTE   ' Lowest 8 bits of Rhino.
```

Given that example, if you write the value %1011000011111101 to *Rhino*, then *Head* would contain %10110000 and *Tail* would contain %11111101.

Table 4.3 lists all the variable modifiers. PBASIC2 lets you apply these modifiers to any variable name and to combine them in any fashion that makes sense. For example, it will allow:

```
Rhino   VAR   WORD                       ' A 16-bit variable.
Eye     VAR   Rhino.HIGHBYTE.LOWNIB.BIT1 ' A bit.
```

Symbol	Definition
LOWBYTE	low byte of a word
HIGHBYTE	high byte of a word
BYTE0	byte 0 (low byte) of a word
BYTE1	byte 1 (high byte) of a word
LOWNIB	low nibble of a word or byte
HIGHNIB	high nibble of a word or byte
NIB0	nib 0 of a word or byte
NIB1	nib 1 of a word or byte
NIB2	nib 2 of a word
NIB3	nib 3 of a word
LOWBIT	low bit of a word, byte, or nibble
HIGHBIT	high bit of a word, byte, or nibble
BIT0	bit 0 of a word, byte, or nibble
BIT1	bit 1 of a word, byte, or nibble
BIT2	bit 2 of a word, byte, or nibble
BIT3	bit 3 of a word, byte, or nibble
BIT4 … BIT7	bits 4 though 7 of a word or byte
BIT8 … Bit15	bits 8 through 15 of a word

Table 4.3: BS2, BS2e, BS2sx and BS2p Variable Modifiers.

The commonsense rule for combining modifiers is that they must get progressively smaller from left to right. It would make no sense to specify, for instance, the low byte of a nibble, because a nibble is smaller than a byte! And just because you can stack up modifiers doesn't mean that you should unless it is the clearest way to express the location of the part you want get at. The example above might be improved:

```
Rhino      VAR    WORD            ' A 16-bit variable.
Eye        VAR    Rhino.BIT9      ' A bit.
```

Although we've only discussed variable modifiers in terms of creating alias variables, you can also use them within program instructions:

```
Rhino      VAR    WORD            ' A 16-bit variable.
Head       VAR    Rhino.HIGHBYTE  ' Highest 8 bits of rhino.

Rhino = 13567
DEBUG ? Head                      ' Show the value of alias variable Head.
DEBUG ? Rhino.HIGHBYTE            ' Rhino.HIGHBYTE works too.
STOP
```

Modifiers also work with arrays. For example:

```
MyBytes    VAR    BYTE(10)        ' Define 10-byte array.
MyBytes(0) = $AB                  ' Hex $AB into 0th byte
DEBUG HEX ? MyBytes.LOWNIB(0)     ' Show low nib ($B)
DEBUG HEX ? MyBytes.LOWNIB(1)     ' Show high nib ($A)
```

4: BASIC Stamp Architecture – Aliases and Modifiers

If you looked closely at that example, you probably thought it was a misprint. Shouldn't MyBytes.LOWNIB(1) give you the low nibble of byte 1 of the array rather than the high nibble of byte 0? Well, it doesn't. The modifier changes the meaning of the index value to match its own size. In the example above, when MyBytes() is addressed as a byte array, it has 10 byte-sized cells numbered 0 through 9. When it is addressed as a nibble array, using MyBytes.LOWNIB(), it has 20 nibble-sized cells numbered 0 through 19. You could also address it as individual bits using MyBytes.LOWBIT(), in which case it would have 80 bit-sized cells numbered 0 through 79.

What if you use something other than a "low" modifier, say MyBytes.HIGHNIB()? That will work, but its effect will be to start the nibble array with the high nibble of MyBytes(0). The nibbles you address with this nib array will all be contiguous, one right after the other, as in the previous example.

```
MyBytes    VAR    BYTE(10)              ' Define 10-byte array.

MyBytes(0) = $AB                        ' Hex $AB into 0th byte
MyBytes(1) = $CD                        ' Hex $CD into next byte
DEBUG  HEX ?  MyBytes.highnib(0)        ' Show high nib of cell 0 ($A)
DEBUG  HEX ?  MyBytes.highnib(1)        ' Show next nib ($D)
```

This property of modified arrays makes the names a little confusing. If you prefer, you can use the less-descriptive versions of the modifier names; BIT0 instead of LOWBIT, NIB0 instead of LOWNIB, and BYTE0 instead of LOWBYTE. These have exactly the same effect, but may be less likely to be misconstrued.

You may also use modifiers with the 0th cell of an array by referring to just the array name without the index value in parentheses. It's fair game for aliases and modifiers, both in VAR directives and in instructions.

THE MEMORY MAP

On the BS2, BS2e, BS2sx and BS2p, if you're working on a program and wondering how much variable space you have left, you can use the memory map feature of the editor (ALT-M in the DOS editor and CTRL-M in the Windows editor). See the "Memory Map" section of the "Using the BASIC Stamp Editor" chapter for more information.

The BS2e, BS2sx and BS2p have some additional RAM called Scratch Pad RAM. The BS2e and BS2sx have are 64 bytes of Scratch Pad RAM (0 – 63) and the BS2p has 128 bytes of Scratch Pad RAM (0 – 127). Scratch Pad RAM can only be accessed with the GET and PUT commands (see the GET and PUT command descriptions for more information) and cannot have variable names assigned to it.

SCRATCH PAD RAM.

The highest location in Scratch Pad RAM (location 63 on the BS2e and BS2sx, location 127 on the BS2p) is read-only, and always contains the number of the currently running program slot. This can be handy for programs that need to know which program slot they exist in.

Suppose you're working on a program called "Three Cheers" that flashes LEDs, makes hooting sounds, and activates a motor that crashes cymbals together, all in sets of three. A portion of your PBASIC program might contain something like:

CONSTANTS AND COMPILE-TIME EXPRESSIONS.

```
FOR  Counter = 1  TO  3
   GOSUB MakeCheers
NEXT
...
FOR  Counter = 1  TO  3
   GOSUB BlinkLEDs
NEXT
...
FOR  Counter = 1  TO  3
   GOSUB CrashCymbals
NEXT
```

The numbers 1 and 3 in the code above are called constants. They are constants because, while the program is running, nothing can happen to change those numbers. This distinguishes constants from variables, which can change while the program is running.

PBASIC allows you to use several numbering systems. By default, it assumes that numbers are in decimal (base 10), our everyday system of numbers. But you can also use binary and hexadecimal (hex) numbers by identifying them with prefixes. And PBASIC will automatically convert quoted text into the corresponding ASCII code(s). For example:

99	decimal
%1010	binary
$FE	hex
"A"	ASCII code for A (65)

You can assign names to constants in a similar fashion to how variables are declared. On a BS1, it is identical to variable declarations and on the other BASIC Stamps you use the CON directive. Here is the syntax:

[1] SYMBOL   Name =   ConstantValue

-- OR --

[2] [2] [2] [2] Name   CON   ConstantValue

Once created, named constants may be used in place of the numbers they represent. For example:

[1] SYMBOL   Cheers   =   3   ' Number of cheers.

```
FOR  Counter = 1  TO  Cheers
  GOSUB  MakeCheers
NEXT
...
```

-- or --

[2] [2] [2] [2] Cheers   CON   3   ' Number of cheers.

```
FOR  Counter = 1  TO  Cheers
  GOSUB  MakeCheers
NEXT
...
```

That code would work exactly the same as the previous FOR...NEXT loops. The editor software would substitute the number 3 for the constant named *Cheers* throughout your program. Like variable names, labels and instructions, constant names are not case sensitive; CHEERS, and ChEErs would all be processed as identical to *Cheers*.

Using named constants does not increase the amount of code downloaded to the BASIC Stamp, and it often improves the clarity of the program. Weeks after a program is written, you may not remember what a particular number was supposed to represent—using a name may jog your memory (or simplify the detective work needed to figure it out).

Named constants also have another benefit. Suppose the "Three Cheers" program had to be upgraded to "Five Cheers." In the original example you would have to change all of the 3s to 5s. Search and replace would help, but you might accidentally change some 3s that weren't numbers of cheers, too. However, if you made smart use of a named constant, all you would have to do is change 3 to 5 in one place, the constant's declaration:

```
SYMBOL    Cheers    =    5              ' Number of cheers.
```

-- or --

```
Cheers    CON  5                        ' Number of cheers.
```

Now, assuming that you used the constant cheers wherever your program needed 'the number of cheers,' your upgrade would be done.

On the BS2, BS2e, BS2sx and BS2p, you can take this idea a step further by defining constants with expressions; groups of math and/or logic operations that the editor software solves (evaluates) at compile time (the time right after you start the download and before the BASIC Stamp starts running your program). For example, suppose the "Cheers" program also controls a pump to fill glasses with champagne. Perhaps the number of glasses to fill is always twice the number of cheers, minus 1 (another constant):

```
Cheers    CON  5                        ' # of cheers.
Glasses   CON  Cheers*2-1               ' # of glasses.
```

As you can see, one constant can be defined in terms of another. That is, the number glasses depends on the number cheers.

The expressions used to define constants must be kept fairly simple. The editor software solves them from left to right, and doesn't allow you to use parentheses to change the order of evaluation. The operators that are allowed in constant expressions are shown in Table 4.4.

Operator Symbol	Description
+	Add
-	Subtract
*	Multiply
/	Divide
<<	Shift Left
>>	Shift Right
&	Logical AND
|	Logical OR
^	Logical XOR

Table 4.4: BS2, BS2e, BS2sx and BS2p operators allowed in constant expressions.

RUNTIME MATH AND LOGIC.

The BASIC Stamp, like any computer, excels at math and logic. However, being designed for control applications, the BASIC Stamp does math a little differently than a calculator or spreadsheet program. This section will help you understand BASIC Stamp numbers, math, and logic.

NUMBER REPRESENTATIONS.

In your programs, you may express a number in various ways, depending on how the number will be used and what makes sense to you. By default, the BASIC Stamp recognizes numbers like 0, 99 or 62145 as being in our everyday decimal (base-10) system. However, you may also use hexadecimal (base-16; also called hex) or binary (base-2).

Since the symbols used in decimal, hex and binary numbers overlap (e.g., 1 and 0 are used by all; 0 through 9 apply to both decimal and hex) the editor software needs prefixes to tell the numbering systems apart, as shown below:

```
99        Decimal (no prefix)
$1A6      Hex
%1101     Binary
```

The BASIC Stamp also automatically converts quoted text into ASCII codes, and allows you to apply names (symbols) to constants from any of the numbering systems. For example:

```
SYMBOL    LetterA   =   "A"           ' ASCII code for A (65).
SYMBOL    Cheers    =   3
SYMBOL    Hex128    =   $80
SYMBOL    FewBits   =   %1101
```

-- or --

```
LetterA   CON   "A"     ' ASCII code for A (65).
Cheers    CON   3
Hex128    CON   $80
FewBits   CON   %1101
```

For more information on constants, see the section "Constants and Compile-Time Expressions", above.

On the BS2, BS2e, BS2sx and BS2p, not all of the math or logic operations in a program are solved by the BASIC Stamp. The editor software solves operations that define constants before the program is downloaded to the BASIC Stamp. The preprocessing that takes place before the program is downloaded is referred to as "compile time."

After the download is complete, the BASIC Stamp starts executing your program; this is referred to as "runtime." At runtime the BASIC Stamp processes math and logic operations involving variables, or any combination of variables and constants.

Because compile-time and runtime expressions appear similar, it can be hard to tell them apart. A few examples will help:

```
Result      VAR   BYTE                'Compile time assignment

Cheers      CON   3                   ' Compile time.
Glasses     CON   Cheers * 2 - 1      ' Compile time.
OneNinety   CON   100 + 90            ' Compile time.
NoWorkee    CON   3 * Result          ' ERROR: Variables not allowed here

Result = Glasses                      ' Runtime.
Result = 99 + Glasses                 ' Runtime.
Result = OneNinety + 1                ' "100 + 90" solved at compile-time,
                                      ' OneNinety + 1 solved at runtime.
Result = 100 + 90                     ' 100 + 90 solved at runtime.
```

Notice that the last example is solved at runtime, even though the math performed could have been solved at compile time since it involves two constants. If you find something like this in your own programs, you can save some EEPROM space by converting the run-time expression 100+90 into a compile-time expression like OneNinety CON 100+90.

To sum up: compile-time expressions are those that involve only constants; once a variable is involved, the expression must be solved at runtime. That's why the line "NoWorkee CON 3 * Result" would generate an error message. The CON directive works only at compile time, so variables are not allowed.

Let's talk about the basic four operations of arithmetic: addition (+), subtraction (-), multiplication (*), and division (/).

You may recall that the order in which you do a series of additions and subtractions doesn't affect the result. The expression 12+7-3+22 works out the same as 22-3+12+7. However, when multiplication or division are involved, it's a different story; 12+3*2/4 is not the same as 2*12/4+3. In fact, you may have the urge to put parentheses around portions of those equations to clear things up.

The BASIC Stamp solves math problems in the order they are written; from left to right. The result of each operation is fed into the next operation. So to compute 12+3*2/4, the BASIC Stamp goes through a sequence like this:

$$12 + 3 = 15$$
$$15 * 2 = 30$$
$$30 / 4 = 7$$

Note that since the BASIC Stamp performs integer math (whole numbers only) 30 / 4 results in 7, not 7.5. We'll talk more about integers in the next section.

Some other dialects of BASIC would compute that same expression based on their precedence of operators, which requires that multiplication and division be done before addition. So the result would be:

$$3 * 2 = 6$$
$$6 / 4 = 1$$
$$12 + 1 = 13$$

Once again, because of integer math, the fractional portion of 6 / 4 is dropped, so we get 1 instead of 1.5.

The BS1 does not allow parenthesis in expressions. Unfortunately, all expressions have to be written so that they evaluate as intended strictly from left to right.

The BS2, BS2e, BS2sx and BS2p, however, allow parenthesis to be used to change the order of evaluation. Enclosing a math operation in parentheses gives it priority over other operations. To make the BASIC Stamp compute the previous expression in the conventional way, you would write it as 12 + (3*2/4). Within the parentheses, the BASIC Stamp works from left to right. If you wanted to be even more specific, you could write 12 + ((3*2)/4). When there are parentheses within parentheses, the BASIC Stamp works from the innermost parentheses outward. Parentheses placed within parentheses are called nested parentheses.

The BASIC Stamp performs all math operations by the rules of positive integer math. That is, it handles only whole numbers, and drops any fractional portions from the results of computations. The BASIC Stamp handles negative numbers using two's complement rules.

INTEGER MATH.

The BS2, BS2e, BS2sx and BS2p can interpret two's complement negative numbers correctly in DEBUG and SEROUT instructions using modifiers like SDEC (for signed decimal). In calculations, however, it assumes that all values are positive. This yields correct results with two's complement negative numbers for addition, subtraction, and multiplication, but not for division.

The standard operators we just discussed: +, - ,* and / all work on two values; as in 1 + 3 or 26 * 144. The values that operators process are referred to as arguments. So we say that the add, subtract, multiply and divide operators take two arguments.

UNARY AND BINARY OPERATORS.

Operators that take one argument are called unary operators and those that take two are called binary operators. Please note that the term "binary operator" has nothing to do with binary numbers; it's just an inconvenient coincidence that the same word, meaning 'involving two things' is used in both cases.

The minus sign (-) is a bit of a hybrid, it can be used as a unary operator as well: as in -4.

In classifying the BASIC Stamp's math and logic operators, we divide them into two types: unary and binary. Unary operators take precedence over binary; the unary operation is always performed first. For example, on the BS2, BS2e, BS2sx and BS2p, SQR is the unary operator for square root. In the expression 10 - SQR 16, the BASIC Stamp first takes the square root of 16, then subtracts it from 10.

Most of the descriptions that follow say something like 'computes (some function) of a 16-bit value.' This does not mean that the operator does not

NOTES ABOUT THE 16-BIT WORKSPACE.

work on smaller byte or nibble values. It just means that the computation is done in a 16-bit workspace. If the value is smaller than 16 bits, the BASIC Stamp pads it with leading 0s to make a 16-bit value. If the 16-bit result of a calculation is to be packed into a smaller variable, the higher-order bits are discarded (truncated).

Keep this in mind, especially when you are working with two's complement negative numbers, or moving values from a larger variable to a smaller one. For example, look at what happens when you move a two's complement negative number into a byte (rather than a word):

```
Value          VAR   BYTE
Value = - 99
DEBUG  SDEC  ?  Value                        ' Show signed decimal result (157).
```

How did -99 become 157? Let's look at the bits: 99 is %01100011 binary. When the BASIC Stamp negates 99, it converts the number to 16 bits %0000000001100011, and then takes the two's complement, %1111111110011101. Since we've asked for the result to be placed in an 8-bit (byte) variable, the upper eight bits are truncated and the lower eight bits stored in the byte: %10011101.

Now for the second half of the story. DEBUG's SDEC modifier (on the BS2, BS2e, BS2sx and BS2p) expects a 16-bit, two's complement value, but we've only given it a byte to work with. As usual, it creates a 16-bit value by padding the leading eight bits with 0s: %0000000010011101. And what's that in signed decimal? 157.

UNARY OPERATORS.

Table 4.5 lists the available Unary Operators. Note: the BS1 only supports negative (-).

Table 4.5: Unary Operators. Note: the BS1 only supports the negative (-) unary operator.

Operator	Description	Supported By:
ABS	Returns absolute value	All except BS1
COS	Returns cosine in two's compliment binary radians	All except BS1
DCD	2^n-power decoder	All except BS1
~	Inverse	All except BS1
-	Negative	All
NCD	Priority encoder of a 16-bit value	All except BS1
SIN	Returns sine in two's compliment binary radians	All except BS1
SQR	Returns square root of value	All except BS1

The Absolute Value operator (ABS) converts a signed (two's complement) 16-bit number to its absolute value. The absolute value of a number is a positive number representing the difference between that number and 0. For example, the absolute value of -99 is 99. The absolute value of 99 is also 99. ABS works on two's complement negative numbers. Examples of ABS at work:

ABSOLUTE VALUE: ABS

```
Result      VAR   WORD
Result = -99                      ' Put -99 (2's complement format) into Result.
DEBUG SDEC ? Result               ' Display it on the screen as a signed #.
DEBUG SDEC ? ABS Result           ' Display it on the screen as a signed #.
```

The Cosine operator (COS) returns the two's complement, 16-bit cosine of an angle specified as an 8-bit (0 to 255) angle. See the explanation of the SIN operator, below. COS is the same in all respects, except that the cosine function returns the x distance instead of the y distance. To demonstrate the COS operator, use the example program from SIN, below, but substitute COS for SIN.

COSINE: COS

The Decoder operator (DCD) is a 2^n-power decoder of a four-bit value. DCD accepts a value from 0 to 15, and returns a 16-bit number with the bit, described by value, set to 1. For example:

DECODER: DCD

```
Result      VAR   WORD
Result = DCD 12          ' Set bit 12.
DEBUG BIN ? Result       ' Display result (%0001000000000000)
```

The Inverse operator (~) complements (inverts) the bits of a number. Each bit that contains a 1 is changed to 0 and each bit containing 0 is changed to 1. This process is also known as a "bitwise NOT" and one's compliment. For example:

INVERSE: ~

```
Result      VAR   BYTE
Result = %11110001                ' Store bits in byte Result.
DEBUG BIN ? Result                ' Display in binary (%11110001).
Result = ~ Result                 ' Complement Result.
DEBUG BIN ? Result                ' Display in binary (%00001110).
```

The Negative operator (-) negates a 16-bit number (converts to its two's complement).

NEGATIVE: -

```
SYMBOL Result    =  W1
Result = -99                      ' Put -99 (2's complement format) into Result.
Result = Result + 100             ' Add 100 to it.
DEBUG Result                      ' Display Result (1)
```

-- or --

Result VAR WORD	
Result = 99	' Put -99 (2's complement format) into Result.
DEBUG SDEC ? Result	' Display it on the screen as a signed #.
Result = - Result	' Negate the value
DEBUG SDEC ? Result	' Display it on the screen as a signed #.

ENCODER: NCD

The Encoder operator (NCD) is a "priority" encoder of a 16-bit value. NCD takes a 16-bit value, finds the highest bit containing a 1 and returns the bit position plus one (1 through 16). If no bit is set (the input value is 0) NCD returns 0. NCD is a fast way to get an answer to the question "what is the largest power of two that this value is greater than or equal to?" The answer NCD returns will be that power, plus one. Example:

```
Result     VAR    WORD
Result = %1101          ' Highest bit set is bit 3.
DEBUG ? NCD Result      ' Show the NCD of Result (4).
```

SINE: SIN

The Sine operator (SIN) returns the two's complement, 16-bit sine of an angle specified as an 8-bit (0 to 255) angle. To understand the SIN operator more completely, let's look at a typical sine function. By definition: given a circle with a radius of 1 unit (known as a unit circle), the sine is the y-coordinate distance from the center of the circle to its edge at a given angle. Angles are measured relative to the 3-o'clock position on the circle, increasing as you go around the circle counterclockwise.

At the origin point (0 degrees) the sine is 0, because that point has the same y (vertical) coordinate as the circle center. At 45 degrees the sine is 0.707. At 90 degrees, sine is 1. At 180 degrees, sine is 0 again. At 270 degrees, sine is -1.

The BASIC Stamp SIN operator breaks the circle into 0 to 255 units instead of 0 to 359 degrees. Some textbooks call this unit a binary radian or brad. Each brad is equivalent to 1.406 degrees. And instead of a unit circle, which results in fractional sine values between 0 and 1, BASIC Stamp SIN is based on a 127-unit circle. Results are given in two's complement form in order to accommodate negative values. So, at the origin, SIN is 0. At 45 degrees (32 brads), sine is 90. At 90 degrees (64 brads), sine is 127. At 180 degrees (128 brads), sine is 0. At 270 degrees (192 brads), sine is -127.

To convert brads to degrees, multiply by 180 then divide by 128. To convert degrees to brads, multiply by 128, then divide by 180. Here's a small program that demonstrates the SIN operator:

```
Degr        VAR   WORD                         ' Define variables.
Sine        VAR   WORD
FOR  Degr = 0  TO  359  STEP  45               ' Use degrees.
  Sine = SIN (Degr * 128 / 180)                ' Convert to brads, do SIN.
    DEBUG  "Angle: ", DEC  Degr, TAB, "Sine: ", SDEC  Sine, CR    ' Display.
NEXT
```

The Square Root operator (SQR) computes the integer square root of an unsigned 16-bit number. (The number must be unsigned since the square root of a negative number is an 'imaginary' number.) Remember that most square roots have a fractional part that the BASIC Stamp discards when doing its integer-only math. So it computes the square root of 100 as 10 (correct), but the square root of 99 as 9 (the actual is close to 9.95). Example:

SQUARE ROOT: SQR

```
DEBUG  SQR  100          ' Display square root of 100 (10).
DEBUG  SQR  99           ' Display of square root of 99 (9 due to truncation)
```

Table 4.6 lists the available Binary (two-argument) Operators.

BINARY OPERATORS.

Operator	Description	Supported By:
+	Addition	All
-	Subtraction	All
*	Multiplication	All
**	Multiplication (returns upper 16-bits)	All
*/	Multiply by 8-bit integer, 8-bit fraction	All except BS1
/	Division	All
//	Modulus (Remainder of division)	All
MIN	Limits a value to a specified low	All
MAX	Limits a value to a specified high	All
DIG	Returns specified digit of number	All except BS1
<<	Shift bits left by specified amount	All except BS1
>>	Shift bits right by specified amount	All except BS1
REV	Reverse specified number of bits	All except BS1
&	Bitwise AND	All
|	Bitwise OR	All
^	Bitwise XOR	All
&/	Logical AND NOT	Only BS1
|/	Logical OR NOT	Only BS1
^/	Logical XOR NOT	Only BS1

Table 4.6: Binary Operators. Note: some binary operators are not supported by all BASIC Stamps.

ADD: +

The Addition operator (+) adds variables and/or constants, returning a 16-bit result. Works exactly as you would expect with unsigned integers from 0 to 65535. If the result of addition is larger than 65535, the carry bit will be lost. If the values added are signed 16-bit numbers and the destination is a 16-bit variable, the result of the addition will be correct in both sign and value. For example:

```
SYMBOL    Value1 = W0
SYMBOL    Value2 = W1
Value1= - 99
Value2= 100
Value1= Value1 + Value2          ' Add the numbers.
DEBUG  Value1                    ' Show the result (1).
```

-- OR --

```
Value1    VAR    WORD
Value2    VAR    WORD
Value1= - 1575
Value2= 976
Value1= Value1 + Value2          ' Add the numbers.
DEBUG  SDEC  ?  Value1           ' Show the result (-599).
```

SUBTRACT: -

The Subtraction operator (-) subtracts variables and/or constants, returning a 16-bit result. Works exactly as you would expect with unsigned integers from 0 to 65535. If the result is negative, it will be correctly expressed as a signed 16-bit number. For example:

```
SYMBOL    Value1 = W0
SYMBOL    Value2 = W1
Value1= 199
Value2= 100
Value1= Value1 - Value2          ' Subtract the numbers.
DEBUG  Value1                    ' Show the result (99).
```

-- OR --

```
Value1    VAR    WORD
Value2    VAR    WORD
Value1= 1000
Value2= 1999
Value1= Value1 - Value2          ' Subtract the numbers.
DEBUG  SDEC  ?  Value1           ' Show the result (-999).
```

MULTIPLY: *

The Multiply operator (*) multiplies variables and/or constants, returning the low 16 bits of the result. Works exactly as you would expect with unsigned integers from 0 to 65535. If the result of multiplication is larger than 65535, the excess bits will be lost. Multiplication of signed variables will be correct in both number and sign, provided that the result is in the range -32767 to +32767.

```
SYMBOL    Value1 =  W0
SYMBOL    Value2 =  W1
Value1= 1000
Value2= 19
Value1= Value1 * Value2          ' Multiply Value1 by Value2.
DEBUG  Value1                     ' Show the result (19000).
```

-- or --

```
Value1    VAR    WORD
Value2    VAR    WORD
Value1= 1000
Value2= - 19
Value1= Value1 * Value2          ' Multiply Value1 by Value2.
DEBUG SDEC ? Value1               ' Show the result (-19000).
```

The Multiply High operator (**) multiplies variables and/or constants, returning the high 16 bits of the result. When you multiply two 16-bit values, the result can be as large as 32 bits. Since the largest variable supported by PBASIC is 16 bits, the highest 16 bits of a 32-bit multiplication result are normally lost. The ** (double-star) instruction gives you these upper 16 bits. For example, suppose you multiply 65000 ($FDE8) by itself. The result is 4,225,000,000 or $FBD46240. The * (star, or normal multiplication) instruction would return the lower 16 bits, $6240. The ** instruction returns $FBD4.

MULTIPLY HIGH: **

```
SYMBOL    Value1 =  W0
SYMBOL    Value2 =  W1
Value1= $FDE8
Value2= Value1 ** Value1         ' Multiply $FDE8 by itself
DEBUG $Value2                     ' Return high 16 bits.
```

-- or --

```
Value1    VAR    WORD
Value2    VAR    WORD
Value1= $FDE8
Value2= Value1 ** Value1         ' Multiply $FDE8 by itself
DEBUG HEX ? Value2                ' Return high 16 bits.
```

The Multiply Middle operator (*/) multiplies variables and/or constants, returning the middle 16 bits of the 32-bit result. This has the effect of multiplying a value by a whole number and a fraction. The whole number

MULTIPLY MIDDLE: */

is the upper byte of the multiplier (0 to 255 whole units) and the fraction is the lower byte of the multiplier (0 to 255 units of 1/256 each). The */ (starslash) instruction gives you an excellent workaround for the BASIC Stamp's integer-only math. Suppose you want to multiply a value by 1.5. The whole number, and therefore the upper byte of the multiplier, would be 1, and the lower byte (fractional part) would be 128, since 128/256 = 0.5. It may be clearer to express the */ multiplier in hex—as $0180—since hex keeps the contents of the upper and lower bytes separate. Here's an example:

```
Value1      VAR    WORD
Value1= 100
Value1= Value1*/ $0180         ' Multiply by 1.5 [1 + (128/256)]
debug ? Value1                 ' Show result (150).
```

To calculate constants for use with the */ instruction, put the whole number portion in the upper byte, then use the following formula for the value of the lower byte: Hint: INT(fraction * 256). For instance, take Pi (π, 3.14159). The upper byte would be $03 (the whole number), and the lower would be INT(0.14159 * 256) = 36 ($24). So the constant Pi for use with */ would be $0324. This isn't a perfect match for Pi, but the error is only about 0.1%.

DIVIDE: /

The Divide operator (/) divides variables and/or constants, returning a 16-bit result. Works exactly as you would expect with unsigned integers from 0 to 65535. Use / only with positive values; signed values do not provide correct results. Here's an example of unsigned division:

```
SYMBOL    Value1 = W0
SYMBOL    Value2 = W1
Value1= 1000
Value2= 5
Value1= Value1 / Value2         ' Divide the numbers.
DEBUG  Value1                   ' Show the result (200).
```

-- OR --

```
Value1      VAR    WORD
Value2      VAR    WORD
Value1= 1000
Value2= 5
Value1= Value1 / Value2         ' Divide the numbers.
DEBUG DEC ? Value1              ' Show the result (200).
```

A workaround to the inability to divide signed numbers is to have your program divide absolute values, then negate the result if one (and only one) of the operands was negative. All values must lie within the range of -32767 to +32767. Here is an example:

```
Sign      VAR    BIT                      ' Bit to hold the sign.
Value1    VAR    WORD
Value2    VAR    WORD
Value1 = 100
Value2 = - 3200

Sign = Value1.BIT15 ^ Value2.BIT15       ' Sign = (Value1 sign) XOR (Value1 sign).
Value2 = ABS Value2 / ABS Value1         ' Divide absolute values.
IF  Sign = 0  THEN  Skip0      ' Negate result if one of the
  Value2 = - Value2            ' argument was negative.
Skip0:
DEBUG SDEC ? Value2      ' Show the result (-32)
```

The Modulus operator (//) returns the remainder left after dividing one value by another. Some division problems don't have a whole-number result; they return a whole number and a fraction. For example, 1000/6 = 166.667. Integer math doesn't allow the fractional portion of the result, so 1000/6 = 166. However, 166 is an approximate answer, because 166*6 = 996. The division operation left a remainder of 4. The // (double-slash) returns the remainder of a given division operation. Naturally, numbers that divide evenly, such as 1000/5, produce a remainder of 0. Example:

MODULUS: //

```
SYMBOL    Value1 =   W0
SYMBOL    Value2 =   W1
Value1= 1000
Value2= 6
Value1= Value1 // Value2      ' Get remainder of Value1 / Value2.
DEBUG  Value1                 ' Show the result (4).
```

-- or --

```
Value1    VAR   WORD
Value2    VAR   WORD
Value1= 1000
Value2= 6
Value1= Value1 // Value2      ' Get remainder of Value1 / Value2.
DEBUG DEC ? Value1            ' Show the result (4).
```

The Minimum operator (MIN) limits a value to a specified 16-bit positive minimum. The syntax of MIN is:

MINIMUM: MIN

Value MIN Limit

Where *Value* is a constant or variable value to perform the MIN function upon and *Limit* is the minimum value that *Value* is allowed to be. Its logic is, 'if *Value* is less than *Limit*, then make result = *Limit*; if *Value* is greater than or equal to *Limit*, make result = *Value*.' MIN works in positive math only; its comparisons are not valid when used on two's complement negative numbers, since the positive-integer representation of a number like -1 ($FFFF or 65535 in unsigned decimal) is larger than that of a number like 10 ($000A or 10 decimal). Use MIN only with unsigned integers. Because of the way fixed-size integers work, you should be careful when using an expression involving MIN 0. For example, 0-1 MIN 0 will result in 65535 because of the way fixed-size integers wrap around.

```
SYMBOL    Value1 = W0
SYMBOL    Value2 = W1
FOR Value1= 100 TO 0 STEP -10      ' Walk value of Value1 from 100 to 0.
  Value2 = Value1 MIN 50           ' Use MIN to clamp at 50.
  DEBUG Value2                     ' Show "clamped" value
NEXT
```

-- or --

```
Value1      VAR    WORD
FOR Value1= 100 TO 0 STEP 10       ' Walk value of Value1 from 100 to 0.
  DEBUG ? Value1 MIN 50            ' Show Value1, but use MIN to clamp at 50.
NEXT
```

MAXIMUM: MAX

The Maximum operator (MAX) limits a value to a specified 16-bit positive maximum. The syntax of MAX is:

Value MAX Limit

Where *Value* is a constant or variable value to perform the MAX function upon and *Limit* is the maximum value that *Value* is allowed to be. Its logic is, 'if *Value* is greater than *Limit*, then make result = *Limit*; if *Value* is less than or equal to *Limit*, make result = *Value*.' MAX works in positive math only; its comparisons are not valid when used on two's complement negative numbers, since the positive-integer representation of a number like -1 ($FFFF or 65535 in unsigned decimal) is larger than that of a number like 10 ($000A or 10 decimal). Use MAX only with unsigned integers. Because of the way fixed-size integers work, you should be careful when using an expression involving MAX 65535. For example,

65535+1 MAX 65535 will result in 0 because of the way fixed-size integers wrap around.

```
SYMBOL    Value1 = W0
SYMBOL    Value2 = W1
FOR Value1= 0 TO 100 STEP 10      ' Walk value of Value1 from 0 to 100.
  Value2 = Value1 MAX 50          ' Use MAX to clamp at 50.
  DEBUG Value2                    ' Show "clamped" value
NEXT
```

-- or --

```
Value1    VAR   WORD
FOR Value1= 0 TO 100 STEP 10      ' Walk value of Value1 from 0 to 100.
  DEBUG ? Value1 MAX 50           ' Show Value1, but use MAX to clamp at 50.
NEXT
```

The Digit operator (DIG) returns the specified decimal digit of a 16-bit positive value. Digits are numbered from 0 (the rightmost digit) to 4 (the leftmost digit of a 16-bit number; 0 to 65535). Example:

DIGIT: DIG

```
Value     VAR   WORD
Idx       VAR   BYTE
Value = 9742
DEBUG ? Value DIG 2               ' Show digit 2 (7)

FOR Idx = 0 TO 4
  DEBUG ? Value DIG Idx           ' Show digits 0 through 4 of 9742.
NEXT
```

The Shift Left operator (<<) shifts the bits of a value to the left a specified number of places. Bits shifted off the left end of a number are lost; bits shifted into the right end of the number are 0s. Shifting the bits of a value left n number of times has the same effect as multiplying that number by 2 to the nth power. For instance 100 << 3 (shift the bits of the decimal number 100 left three places) is equivalent to $100 * 2^3$. Here's an example:

SHIFT LEFT: <<

```
Value     VAR   WORD
Idx       VAR   BYTE
Value = %1111111111111111
FOR Idx = 1 TO 16                 ' Repeat with Idx = 1 to 16.
  DEBUG BIN ? Value << Idx        ' Shift Value left Idx places.
NEXT
```

The Shift Right operator (>>) shifts the bits of a variable to the right a specified number of places. Bits shifted off the right end of a number are lost; bits shifted into the left end of the number are 0s. Shifting the bits of a

SHIFT RIGHT: >>

value right *n* number of times has the same effect as dividing that number by 2 to the nth power. For instance 100 >> 3 (shift the bits of the decimal number 100 right three places) is equivalent to $100 / 2^3$. Here's an example:

```
Value       VAR    WORD
Idx         VAR    BYTE
Value = %1111111111111111
FOR  Idx = 1  TO  16                  ' Repeat with Idx = 1 to 16.
  DEBUG  BIN ?  Value >> Idx          ' Shift Value right Idx places.
NEXT
```

REVERSE: REV

The Reverse operator (REV) returns a reversed (mirrored) copy of a specified number of bits of a value, starting with the rightmost bit (lsb). For instance, %10101101 REV 4 would return %1011, a mirror image of the first four bits of the value. Example:

```
DEBUG  BIN ?  %11001011 REV 4         ' Mirror 1st 4 bits (%1101)
```

AND: &

The And operator (&) returns the bitwise AND of two values. Each bit of the values is subject to the following logic:

$$0 \text{ AND } 0 = 0$$
$$0 \text{ AND } 1 = 0$$
$$1 \text{ AND } 0 = 0$$
$$1 \text{ AND } 1 = 1$$

The result returned by & will contain 1s in only those bit positions in which both input values contain 1s. Example:

```
SYMBOL    Value1 = B0
SYMBOL    Value2 = B1
SYMBOL    Result = B2
Value1 = %00001111
Value2 = %10101101
Result = Value1 & Value2
DEBUG %Result                         ' Show AND result (%00001101)
```

-- or --

```
DEBUG  BIN ?  %00001111 & %10101101   ' Show AND result (%00001101)
```

OR: |

The OR operator (|) returns the bitwise OR of two values. Each bit of the values is subject to the following logic:

```
0 OR 0 = 0
0 OR 1 = 1
1 OR 0 = 1
1 OR 1 = 1
```

The result returned by | will contain 1s in any bit positions in which one or the other (or both) input values contain 1s. Example:

```
SYMBOL    Value1 = B0
SYMBOL    Value2 = B1
SYMBOL    Result = B2
Value1 = %00001111
Value2 = %10101001
Result = Value1 | Value2
DEBUG %Result                    ' Show OR result (%10101111)
```

-- or --

```
DEBUG BIN ? %00001111 | %10101001     ' Show OR result (%10101111)
```

The Xor operator (^) returns the bitwise XOR of two values. Each bit of the values is subject to the following logic:

```
0 XOR 0 = 0
0 XOR 1 = 1
1 XOR 0 = 1
1 XOR 1 = 0
```

The result returned by ^ will contain 1s in any bit positions in which one or the other (but not both) input values contain 1s. Example:

```
SYMBOL    Value1 = B0
SYMBOL    Value2 = B1
SYMBOL    Result = B2
Value1 = %00001111
Value2 = %10101001
Result = Value1 ^ Value2
DEBUG %Result                    ' Show OR result (%10100110)
```

-- or --

```
DEBUG BIN ? %00001111 ^ %10101001     ' Show XOR result (%10100110)
```

AND NOT: &/

The And Not operator (&/) returns the bitwise AND NOT of two values. Each bit of the values is subject to the following logic:

    0 AND NOT 0 = 0
    0 AND NOT 1 = 0
    1 AND NOT 0 = 1
    1 AND NOT 1 = 0

The result returned by &/ will contain 1s in any bit positions in which the first value is 1 and the second value is 0. Example:

```
SYMBOL    Value1 = B0
SYMBOL    Value2 = B1
SYMBOL    Result = B2
Value1 = %00001111
Value2 = %10101001
Result = Value1 &/ Value2
DEBUG  %Result                    ' Show AND NOT result (%00000110)
```

OR NOT: |/

The Or Not operator (| /) returns the bitwise OR NOT of two values. Each bit of the values is subject to the following logic:

    0 OR NOT 0 = 1
    0 OR NOT 1 = 0
    1 OR NOT 0 = 1
    1 OR NOT 1 = 1

The result returned by | / will contain 1s in any bit positions in which the first value is 1 or the second value is 0. Example:

```
SYMBOL    Value1 = B0
SYMBOL    Value2 = B1
SYMBOL    Result = B2
Value1 = %00001111
Value2 = %10101001
Result = Value1 |/ Value2
DEBUG  %Result                    ' Show OR NOT result (%01011111)
```

XOR NOT: ^/

The Xor Not operator (^/) returns the bitwise XOR NOT of two values. Each bit of the values is subject to the following logic:

0 XOR NOT 0 = 1
0 XOR NOT 1 = 0
1 XOR NOT 0 = 0
1 XOR NOT 1 = 1

The result returned by ^/ will contain 1s in any bit positions in which the
first value and second values are equal. Example:

```
SYMBOL     Value1 = B0
SYMBOL     Value2 = B1
SYMBOL     Result = B2
Value1 = %00001111
Value2 = %10101001
Result = Value1 ^/ Value2
DEBUG %Result                    ' Show OR NOT result (%01011001)
```

This chapter provides detail on all the available PBASIC instructions for the BS1, BS2, BS2e, BS2sx and BS2p. The following icons will appear to indicate where there are differences between versions of the BASIC Stamp:

⌁1⌁ ⌁2⌁ ⌁2⌁ₑ ⌁2⌁ₛₓ ⌁2⌁ₚ   One or more of these icons indicates the item applies only to the BS1, BS2, BS2e, BS2sx or BS2p, respectively.

All instructions listed below exist on all versions of the BASIC Stamp, except where noted.

BRANCHING

	IF...THEN	Compare and conditionally branch.
	BRANCH	Branch to address specified by offset.
	GOTO	Branch to address.
	GOSUB	Branch to subroutine at address.
	RETURN	Return from subroutine.
⌁2⌁ₑ⌁2⌁ₛₓ⌁2⌁ₚ	RUN	Switch execution to another program page.
⌁2⌁ₚ	POLLRUN	Switch execution to another program page upon the occurrence of a polled interrupt.

LOOPING

	FOR...NEXT	Establish a FOR-NEXT loop.

EEPROM ACCESS

⌁1⌁	EEPROM	Store data in EEPROM before downloading PBASIC program.
⌁2⌁⌁2⌁ₑ⌁2⌁ₛₓ⌁2⌁ₚ	DATA	Store data in EEPROM before downloading PBASIC program.
	READ	Read EEPROM byte into variable.
	WRITE	Write byte into EEPROM.
⌁2⌁ₚ	STORE	Switch READ/WRITE access to different program slot.

BASIC Stamp Command Reference

RAM ACCESS

GET   Read Scratch Pad RAM byte into variable.

PUT   Write byte into Scratch Pad RAM.

NUMERICS

LET   Optional instruction to perform variable manipulation, such as A=5, B=A+2, etc. This instruction is not required and only exists on the BASIC Stamp 1.

LOOKUP   Lookup data specified by offset and store in variable. This instruction provides a means to make a lookup table.

LOOKDOWN   Find target's match number (0-N) and store in variable.

RANDOM   Generate a pseudo-random number.

DIGITAL I/O

INPUT   Make pin an input.

OUTPUT   Make pin an output.

REVERSE   Reverse direction of a pin. If pin is an output, make it an input. If pin is an input, make it an output.

LOW   Make pin output low.

HIGH   Make pin output high.

TOGGLE   Make pin an output and toggle state.

PULSIN   Measure an input pulse.

PULSOUT   Output a timed pulse by inverting a pin for some time.

BUTTON   Debounce button, perform auto-repeat, and branch to address if button is in target state.

COUNT   Count cycles on a pin for a given amount of time.

XOUT   Generate X-10 power line control codes. For use with TW523 or TW513 power line interface module.

AUXIO   Activates auxiliary I/O pins in place of main I/O.

MAINIO   Activates main I/O pins in place of auxiliary I/O.

IOTERM   Activates specified I/O pin group.

POLLIN   Specify pin and state for a polled-interrupt.

POLLOUT   Specify pin and state for output upon a polled-interrupt.

POLLMODE Specifies the polled-interrupt mode.

ASYNCHRONOUS SERIAL I/O

SERIN   Input data in an asynchronous serial stream.

SEROUT   Output data in an asynchronous serial stream.

OWIN   Input data from a 1-wire device.

OWOUT   Output data to a 1-wire device.

SYNCHRONOUS SERIAL I/O

SHIFTIN   Shift data in from synchronous serial device.

SHIFTOUT Shift data out to synchronous serial device.

I2CIN   Input data in from I2C serial device.

I2COUT   Output data out to I2C serial device.

PARALLEL I/O

LCDCMD   Writes a command to an LCD.

LCDIN   Reads data from an LCD.

LCDOUT   Writes data to an LCD.

ANALOG I/O

PWM   Output PWM, then return pin to input. This can be used to output analog voltages (0-5V) using a capacitor and resistor.

POT   Read a 5K - 50K ohm potentiometer and scale result.

RCTIME   Measure an RC charge/discharge time. Can be used to measure potentiometers.

TIME

PAUSE   Pause execution for 0–65535 milliseconds.

POLLWAIT Pause until a polled-interrupt occurs.

SOUND

1️⃣ SOUND		Generate tones or white noise.
2️⃣ 2️⃣ 2️⃣sx 2️⃣p FREQOUT		Generate one or two sine waves of specified frequencies.
2️⃣ 2️⃣ 2️⃣sx 2️⃣p DTMFOUT		Generate DTMF telephone tones.

POWER CONTROL

NAP   Nap for a short period. Power consumption is reduced.

SLEEP   Sleep for 1-65535 seconds. Power consumption is reduced.

END   Sleep until the power cycles or the PC connects. Power consumption is reduced.

PROGRAM DEBUGGING

DEBUG   Send information to the PC for viewing.

AUXIO

| BS1 | BS2 | BS2e | BS2sx | **BS2p** |

AUXIO

Function

Switch from control of main I/O pins to auxiliary I/O pins (on the BS2p40 only).

Quick Facts

Table 5.1: AUXIO Quick Facts.

	BS2p
I/O pin IDs	0 – 15 (just like main I/O, but after AUXIO command, all references affect physical pins 21 – 36).
Special notes	Both the BS2p24 and the BS2p40 accept this command, however, only the BS2p40 gives access to the auxiliary I/O pins.

Explanation

The BS2p is available in two module styles, 1) a 24-pin module (called the BS2p24) that is pin compatible with the BS2, BS2e and BS2sx and 2) a 40-pin module (called the BS2p40) that has an additional 16 I/O pins (for a total of 32). The BS2p40's extra, or auxiliary, I/O pins can be accessed in the same manner as the main I/O pins (by using the IDs 0 to 15) but only after issuing an AUXIO or IOTERM command. The AUXIO command causes the BASIC Stamp to affect the auxiliary I/O pins instead of the main I/O pins in all further code until the MAINIO command is reached, or the BASIC Stamp is reset or power-cycled.

A SIMPLE AUXIO EXAMPLE.

The following example illustrates this:

```
HIGH  0
AUXIO
LOW  0
```

The first line of the above example will set I/O pin 0 of the main I/O pins (physical pin 5) high. Afterward, the AUXIO command tells the BASIC Stamp that all commands following it should affect the auxiliary I/O pins. The following LOW command will set I/O pin 0 of the auxiliary I/O pins (physical pin 21) low.

MAIN I/O AND AUXILIARY I/O PINS ARE INDEPENDENT AND UNAFFECTED BY CHANGES IN THE OPPOSITE GROUP.

Note that the main I/O and auxiliary I/O pins are independent of each other; the states of the main I/O pins remain unchanged while the program affects the auxiliary I/O pins, and vice versa.

Other commands that affect I/O group access are MAINIO and IOTERM.

Demo Program (AUX_MAIN_TERM.bsp)

' This program demonstrates the use of the AUXIO, MAINIO and IOTERM commands to
' affect I/O pins in the auxiliary and main I/O groups.

```
'{$STAMP BS2p}                          'STAMP directive (specifies a BS2p)

Port  VAR    BIT

Loop:
  MAINIO                    'Switch to main I/O pins
  TOGGLE  0                 'Toggle state of I/O pin 0 (physical pin 5)
  PWM  1, 100, 40           'Generate PWM on I/O pin 1 (physical pin 6)

  AUXIO                     'Switch to auxiliary I/O pins
  TOGGLE  0                 'Toggle state of I/O pin 0 (physical pin 21)
  PULSOUT  1, 1000          'Generate a pulse on I/O pin 1 (physical pin 22)
  PWM  2, 100, 40           'Generate PWM on I/O pin 2 (physical pin 23)

  IOTERM  Port              'Switch to main or aux I/Os (depending on Port)
  TOGGLE  3                 'Toggle state of I/O pin 3 (on main and aux, alternately)
  Port = ~Port             'Invert port (switch between 0 and 1)
  PAUSE  1000
GOTO Loop
```

NOTE: This is written for the BS2p but its effects can only be seen on the 40-pin version: the BS2p40.

BRANCH

BS1	BS2	BS2e	BS2sx	BS2p

1 BRANCH *Offset, (Address0, Address1, ...AddressN)*

2 2e 2sx 2p BRANCH *Offset, [Address0, Address1, ...AddressN]*

1
NOTE: Expressions are not allowed as arguments on the BS1.

Function

Go to the address specified by offset (if in range).

- *Offset* is a variable/constant/expression $(0 - 255)$ that specifies the index of the address, in the list, to branch to $(0 - N)$.

- *Addresses* are labels that specify where to go. BRANCH will ignore any list entries beyond offset 255.

Quick Facts

Table 5.2: BRANCH Quick Facts.

	BS1	BS2, BS2e, BS2sx and BS2p
Limit of *Address* entries	Limited only by memory	256

Explanation

The BRANCH instruction is useful when you want to write something like this:

```
IF value = 0 THEN case_0    ' value =0: go to label "case_0"
IF value = 1 THEN case_1    ' value =1: go to label "case_1"
IF value = 2 THEN case_2    ' value =2: go to label "case_2"
```

You can use BRANCH to organize this into a single statement:

```
BRANCH value, [case_0, case_1, case_2]
```

1
BS1 syntax not shown here.

This works exactly the same as the previous IF...THEN example. If the value isn't in range (in this case if *value* is greater than 2), BRANCH does nothing and the program continues with the next instruction after BRANCH.

BRANCH can be teamed with the LOOKDOWN instruction to create a simplified SELECT CASE statement. See LOOKDOWN for an example.

Demo Program (BRANCH.bas)

This program shows how the value of *Idx* controls the destination of the BRANCH instruction.

```
'{$STAMP BS1}                          'STAMP directive (specifies a BS1)
SYMBOL   Idx    =  B0

Start:
FOR Idx = 0 to 3
    DEBUG "Idx: ", #Idx
    BRANCH Idx, (Case0, Case1, Case2)   'If Idx = 0..2 branch to specified label
GOTO Start        'If Idx>2 then Start.

Case0:
    DEBUG "Branched to Case0",cr
GOTO Start

Case1:
    DEBUG "Branched to Case1",cr
GOTO Start

Case2:
    DEBUG "Branched to Case2",cr
GOTO Start
```

Demo Program (BRANCH.bs2)

This program shows how the value of *Idx* controls the destination of the BRANCH instruction.

```
'{$STAMP BS2}                          'STAMP directive (specifies a BS2)
Idx          VAR    BYTE

Start:
FOR Idx = 0 to 3
    DEBUG "Idx: ", DEC Idx
    BRANCH Idx, [Case0, Case1, Case2]   'If Idx = 0..2 branch to specified label
GOTO Start          'If Idx>2 then Start.

Case0:
    DEBUG "Branched to Case0",cr
GOTO Start

Case1:
    DEBUG "Branched to Case1",cr
GOTO Start

Case2:
    DEBUG "Branched to Case2",cr
GOTO Start
```

NOTE: This is written for the BS2 but can be used for the BS2e, BS2sx and BS2p also. Locate the proper source code file or modify the STAMP directive before downloading to the BS2e, BS2sx or BS2p.

BUTTON | BS1 | BS2 | BS2e | BS2sx | BS2p

BUTTON *Pin, DownState, Delay, Rate, Workspace, TargetState, Address*

Function

Debounce button input, perform auto-repeat, and branch to address if button is in target state. Button circuits may be active-low or active-high.

NOTE: Expressions are not allowed as arguments on the BS1. The range of the *Pin* argument on the BS1 is 0 – 7.

- *Pin* is a variable/constant/expression (0–15) that specifies the I/O pin to use. This pin will be set to input mode.

- *DownState* is a variable/constant/expression (0 or 1) that specifies which logical state occurs when the button is pressed.

- *Delay* is a variable/constant/expression (0 – 255) that specifies how long the button must be pressed before auto-repeat starts. The delay is measured in cycles of the Button routine. Delay has two special settings: 0 and 255. If Delay is 0, Button performs no debounce or auto-repeat. If Delay is 255, Button performs debounce, but no auto-repeat.

- *Rate* is a variable/constant/expression (0 – 255) that specifies the number of cycles between auto-repeats. The rate is expressed in cycles of the BUTTON routine.

- *Workspace* is a byte variable used by BUTTON for workspace. It must be cleared to 0 before being used by BUTTON for the first time and should not be adjusted outside of the BUTTON command. **NOTE: All RAM is cleared to 0 by default upon power-up or reset of the BASIC Stamp.**

- *TargetState* is a variable/constant/expression (0 or 1) that specifies which state the button should be in for a branch to occur. (0=not pressed, 1=pressed)

- *Address* is a label that specifies where to branch if the button is in the target state.

Explanation

When you press a button or flip a switch, the contacts make or break a connection. A brief (1 to 20-ms) burst of noise occurs as the contacts scrape and bounce against each other. BUTTON's debounce feature prevents this noise from being interpreted as more than one switch action. (For a demonstration of switch bounce, see the demo program for the Count instruction.)

BUTTON also lets PBASIC react to a button press the way your computer keyboard does to a key press. When you press a key, a character immediately appears on the screen. If you hold the key down, there's a delay, then a rapid-fire stream of characters appears on the screen. BUTTON's auto-repeat function can be set up to work much the same way.

BUTTON is designed for use inside a program loop. Each time through the loop, BUTTON checks the state of the specified pin. When it first matches *DownState*, BUTTON debounces the switch. Then, in accordance with *TargetState*, it either branches to *address* (TargetState = 1) or doesn't (TargetState = 0).

If the switch stays in *DownState*, BUTTON counts the number of program loops that execute. When this count equals *Delay*, BUTTON once again triggers the action specified by *TargetState* and *address*. Hereafter, if the switch remains in *DownState*, BUTTON waits *Rate* number of cycles between actions. The *Workspace* variable is used by BUTTON to keep track of how many cycles have occurred since the *pin* switched to *TargetState* or since the last auto-repeat.

BUTTON does not stop program execution. In order for its delay and auto repeat functions to work properly, BUTTON must be executed from within a program loop.

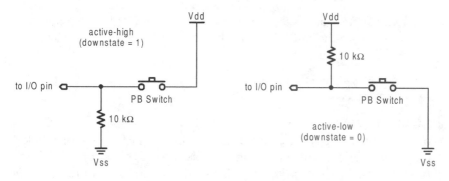

Figure 5.1: Sample BUTTON circuits. Active-high (left) and active-low (right).

ogram (BUTTON.bas)

e active-low circuit shown in Figure 5.1 to pin P0 of the BS1. When you press the
Debug screen will display an asterisk (*). Feel free to modify the program to see
of your changes on the way BUTTON responds.

```
BS1}                                    'STAMP directive (specifies a BS1)
    BtnWrk=   B0                        ' Workspace for BUTTON instruction.


ging the Delay value (255) in BUTTON to see the effect of
uto-repeat (one action per button press).
,0,255,250,BtnWk,0,NoPress             ' Go to NoPress unless P0 = 0.

 GOTO Loop                             ' Repeat endlessly.
```

NOTE: This is written for the BS2
but can be used for the BS2e,
BS2sx and BS2p also. Locate the
proper source code file or modify
the STAMP directive before
downloading to the BS2e, BS2sx or
BS2p.

Demo Program (BUTTON.bs2)

Connect the active-low circuit shown in Figure 5.1 to pin P0 of the BS2. When you press the
button, the Debug screen will display an asterisk (*). Feel free to modify the program to see
the effects of your changes on the way BUTTON responds.

```
'{$STAMP  BS2}                          'STAMP directive (specifies a BS2)
BtnWrk    VAR    BYTE                   ' Workspace for BUTTON instruction.

Loop:
 ' Try changing the Delay value (255) in BUTTON to see the effect of
 ' its modes: 0=no debounce; 1-254=varying delays before auto-repeat;
 ' 255=no auto-repeat (one action per button press).
  BUTTON 0,0,255,250,BtnWk,0,NoPress        ' Go to NoPress unless P0 = 0.
  debug "* "
NoPress:
 GOTO Loop
```

COUNT

| BS1 | BS2 | BS2e | BS2sx | BS2p |

COUNT *Pin, Period, Variable*

Function

Count the number of cycles (0-1-0 or 1-0-1) on the specified pin during the *Period* time frame and store that number in *Variable*.

- **Pin** is a variable/constant/expression (0 – 15) that specifies the I/O pin to use. This pin will be set to input mode.

- **Period** is a variable/constant/expression (1 – 65535) specifying the time during which to count. The unit of time for *Period* is described in Table 5.3.

- **Variable** is a variable (usually a word) in which the count will be stored.

Quick Facts

Table 5.3: COUNT Quick Facts. **NOTE: All timing values are approximate.**

	BS2	BS2e	BS2sx	BS2p
Units in *Period*	1 ms	1 ms	400 µs	287 µs
Period range	1 ms to 65.535 s	1 ms to 65.535 s	400 µs to 26.214 s	287 µs to 18.809 s
Minimum pulse width	4.16 µs	4.16 µs	1.66 µs	1.20 µs
Maximum frequency (square wave)	120,000 Hz	120,000 Hz	300,000 Hz	416,700 Hz

Explanation

The COUNT instruction makes the *Pin* an input, then for the specified period of time, counts cycles on that pin and stores the total in a variable. A cycle is a change in state from 1 to 0 to 1, or from 0 to 1 to 0.

According to Table 5.3, COUNT on the BS2 can respond to transitions (pulse widths) as small as 4.16 microseconds (µs). A cycle consists of two transitions (e.g., 0 to 1, then 1 to 0), so COUNT (on the BS2) can respond to square waves with periods as short as 8.32 µs; up to 120 kilohertz (kHz) in frequency. For non-square waves (those whose high time and low time are unequal), the shorter of the high and low times must be at least 4.16 µs in width (on the BS2). Refer to Table 5.3 for data on other BASIC Stamps.

If you use COUNT on slowly changing analog waveforms like sine waves, you may find that the value returned is higher than expected. This is because the waveform may pass through the BASIC Stamp's 1.4-volt logic threshold slowly enough that noise causes false counts. You can fix this by passing the signal through a Schmitt Trigger, like one of the inverters of a 74HCT14.

Demo Program (COUNT.bs2)

Connect the active-low circuit shown in Figure 5.1 (BUTTON instruction) to pin P0 of the BS2. The Debug screen will prompt you to press the button as quickly as possible for a 1-second count. When the count is done, the screen will display your "score," the total number of cycles registered by COUNT. Note that this score will almost always be greater than the actual number of presses because of switch bounce.

NOTE: This is written for the BS2 but can be used for the BS2e, BS2sx and BS2p also (with modifications). Locate the proper source code file or modify the STAMP directive and the *period* of the COUNT command before downloading to the BS2e, BS2sx or BS2p.

```
'{$STAMP BS2}                            'STAMP directive (specifies a BS2)
Cycles      var      word               ' Variable to store counted cycles.

Loop:
  DEBUG cls,"How many times can you press the button in 1 second?",cr
  PAUSE 1000
  DEBUG "Ready, set... "
  PAUSE 500
  DEBUG "GO!",cr
  COUNT 0,1000,Cycles
  DEBUG cr,"Your score: ", DEC Cycles,cr
  PAUSE 3000
  DEBUG "Press button to go again."
Hold:
  IF IN0 = 1 THEN Hold
GOTO Loop
```

DATA

| BS1 | BS2 | BS2e | BS2sx | BS2p |

1 (See EEPROM)

2 2e 2sx 2p {*Symbol*} DATA *DataItem* {, *DataItem*...}

Function

Write data to the EEPROM during program download.

- **Symbol** is an optional, unique symbol name that will be automatically defined as a constant equal to the location number of the first data item.

- **DataItem** is a constant/expression (0 – 65535) indicating a value or how to store a value.

Explanation

When you download a program into the BASIC Stamp, it is stored in the EEPROM starting at the highest address (2047) and working towards the lowest address. Most programs don't use the entire EEPROM, so the lower portion is available for other uses. The DATA directive allows you to define a set of data to store in the available EEPROM locations. It is called a "directive" rather than a "command" because it performs an activity at compile-time rather than at run-time (ie: the DATA directive is not downloaded to the BASIC Stamp, but the data it contains is downloaded).

WRITING SIMPLE, SEQUENTIAL DATA.

The simplest form of the DATA directive is something like the following:

```
DATA      100, 200, 52, 45
```

This example, when downloaded, will cause the values 100, 200, 52 and 45 to be written to EEPROM locations 0, 1, 2 and 3, respectively. You can then use the READ and WRITE commands in your code to access these locations and the data you've stored there.

THE DATA POINTER (COUNTER).

DATA uses a counter, called a pointer, to keep track of available EEPROM addresses. The value of the pointer is initially 0. When a program is downloaded, the DATA directive stores the first byte value at the current pointer address, then increments (adds 1 to) the pointer. If the program contains more than one DATA directive, subsequent DATAs start with the pointer value left by the previous DATA. For example, if the program contains:

```
DATA      72, 69, 76, 76, 79
DATA      104, 101, 108, 108, 111
```

The first DATA directive will start at location 0 and increment the pointer for each data value it stores (1, 2, 3, 4 and 5). The second DATA directive will start with the pointer value of 5 and work upward from there. As a result, the first 10 bytes of EEPROM will look like the following:

	EEPROM Location (address)									
	0	**1**	**2**	**3**	**4**	**5**	**6**	**7**	**8**	**9**
Contents	72	69	76	76	79	104	101	108	108	111

Table 5.4: Example EEPROM storage.

What if you don't want to store values starting at location 0? Fortunately, the DATA directive has an option to specify the next location to use. You can specify the next location number (to set the pointer to) by inserting a *DataItem* in the form @x ;where x is the location number. The following code writes the same data in Table 5.4 to locations 100 through 109:

WRITING DATA TO OTHER LOCATIONS.

```
DATA    @100, 72, 69, 76, 76, 79, 104, 101, 108, 108, 111
```

In this example, the first *DataItem* is @100. This tells the DATA directive to store the following *DataItem(s)* starting at location 100. All the *DataItems* to the right of the @100 are stored in their respective locations (100, 101, 102... 109).

In addition, the DATA directive allows you to specify new starting locations at any time within the *DataItem* list. If, for example, you wanted to store 56 at location 100 and 47 at location 150 (while leaving every other location intact), you could type the following:

```
DATA    @100, 56, @150, 47
```

If you have multiple DATA directives in your program, it may be difficult to remember exactly what locations contain the desired data. For this reason, the DATA directive can optionally be prefixed with a unique symbol name. This symbol becomes a constant that is set equal to the location number of the first byte of data within the directive. For example,

AUTOMATIC CONSTANTS FOR DEFINED DATA.

```
MyNumbers       DATA    @100, 72, 73
```

This would store the values 72 and 73 starting with location 100 and will create a constant, called *MyNumbers*, which is set equal to 100. Your program can then use the *MyNumbers* constant as a reference to the start of the data within a READ or WRITE command. Each DATA directive can have a unique symbol preceding it, allowing you to reference the data defined at different locations.

RESERVING EEPROM LOCATIONS.

There may be a time when you wish to reserve a section of EEPROM for use by your BASIC code, but not necessarily store data there to begin with. To do this, simply specify a *DataItem* within parentheses, as in:

DATA   @100, (20)

The above DATA directive will reserve 20 bytes of EEPROM, starting with location 100. It doesn't store any values there, rather it simply leaves the data as it is and increments DATA's location pointer by 20. A good reason to do this is when you have a program already downloaded into the BASIC Stamp that has created or manipulated some data in EEPROM. To protect that section of EEPROM from being overwritten by your next program (perhaps a new version of the same program) you can reserve the space as shown above. The EEPROM's contents from locations 100 to 119 will remain intact. NOTE: This only "reserves" the space for the program you are currently downloading; the BASIC Stamp does not know to "reserve" the space for future programs. In other words, make sure use this feature of the DATA directive in every program you download if you don't want to risk overwriting valuable EEPROM data.

IMPORTANT CONCEPT: HOW DATA AND PROGRAMS ARE DOWNLOADED INTO EEPROM.

It is important to realize that EEPROM is not overwritten during programming unless it is needed for program storage, or is filled by a DATA directive specifying data to be written. **During downloading, EEPROM is always written in 16-byte sections if, and only if, any location within that section needs writing.**

WRITING A BLOCK OF THE SAME VALUE.

DATA can also store the same number in a block of consecutive locations. This is similar to reserving a block of EEPROM, above, but with a value added before the first parenthesis. For example,

DATA   @100, 0 (20)

This statement writes the value 0 in all the EEPROM locations from 100 to 119.

DATA - BASIC Stamp Command Reference

A common use for DATA is to store strings; sequences of bytes representing text. PBASIC converts quoted text like "A" into the corresponding ASCII character code (65 in this case). To make data entry easier, you can place quotes around a whole chunk of text used in a DATA directive, and PBASIC will understand it to mean a series of bytes (see the last line of code below). The following three DATA directives are equivalent:

```
DATA      72, 69, 76, 76, 79
DATA      "H", "E", "L", "L", "O"
DATA      "HELLO"
```

All three lines of code, above, will result in the numbers 72, 69, 76, 76, and 79 being stored into EEPROM upon downloading. These numbers are simply the ASCII character codes for "H", "E", "L", "L", and "O", respectively. See the Demo Program, below, for an example of storing and reading multiple text strings.

The EEPROM is organized as a sequential set of byte-sized memory locations. By default, the DATA directive stores bytes into EEPROM. If you try to store a word-size value (ex: DATA 1125) only the lower byte of the value will be stored. This does not mean that you can't store word-sized values, however. A word consists of two bytes, called a low-byte and a high-byte. If you wanted to store the value 1125 using the DATA directive, simply insert the prefix "word" before the number, as in:

```
DATA      word 1125
```

The directive above will automatically break the word-size value into two bytes and store them into two sequential EEPROM locations (the low-byte first, followed by the high-byte). In this case, the low-byte is 101 and the high byte is 4 and they will be stored in locations 0 and 1, respectively. If you have multiple word-size values, you must prefix each value with "word", as in:

```
DATA      word 1125, word 2000
```

To retrieve a word-size value, you'll need to use two READ commands and a word-size variable (along with some handy modifiers). For example,

```
Result      VAR   WORD
DATA        word  1125

READ        0, Result.LOWBYTE
READ        1, Result.HIGHBYTE
DEBUG       DEC Result
```

This code would write the low-byte and high-byte of the number 1125 into locations 0 and 1 during download. When the program runs, the two READ commands will read the low-byte and high-byte out of EEPROM (reconstructing it in a word-size variable) and then display the value on the screen. See the READ and WRITE commands for more information.

NOTE: This is written for the BS2 but can be used for the BS2e, BS2sx and BS2p also. Locate the proper source code file or modify the STAMP directive before downloading to the BS2e, BS2sx or BS2p.

Demo Program (DATA.bs2)

This program stores a number of large text strings into EEPROM with the DATA directive and then sends them, one character at a time via the DEBUG command. This is a good demonstration of how to save program space by storing large amounts of data in EEPROM directly, rather than embedding the data into DEBUG commands.

```
'{$STAMP BS2}                                    'STAMP directive (specifies a BS2)
'-----Define variables-----
Index       VAR   WORD    'Holds current location number
PhraseNum   VAR   NIB     'Holds current phrase number
Character   VAR   BYTE    'Holds current character to print

'-----Define all text phrases (out of order, just for fun!)-----
Text1       DATA  "Here is the first part of a large chunk of textual data", CR
            DATA  "that needs to be transmitted.  There's a 12 second delay", CR
            DATA  "between text paragraphs.", CR, 255

Text3       DATA  "The alternative (having multiple DEBUGs or SEROUTs, each", CR
            DATA  "with their own line of text) consumes MUCH more EEPROM", CR
            DATA  "(program) space; up to 854 more bytes, in this case!", CR, CR, 255

Text6       DATA  "The 255 is used by this program to indicate we've reached the", CR
            DATA  "End of Text.  The Main routine pauses in between each block of", CR
            DATA  "text, and then uses a LOOKUP command to retrieve the location", CR
            DATA  "of the next desired block of text to print.", 255

Text4       DATA  CLS, "This program also demonstrates retrieving data out of order", CR
            DATA  "in relation to the way it is stored in EEPROM.  Additionally", CR
            DATA  "control codes (like carriage-returns, clear-screens, etc) can", CR
            DATA  "be embedded right in the data, as it is here.", CR, CR, 255

Text2       DATA  "This is an example of a good way to save space in your", CR
            DATA  "BASIC Stamp's program by storing data into EEPROM and", CR
            DATA  "retrieving it, one byte at a time, and transmitting it", CR
            DATA  "with just a single DEBUG (or SEROUT) command.", CR, CR, 255

Text5       DATA  "The PrintIt routine simply takes the Index variable, retrieves", CR
```

```
           DATA  "the character at the EEPROM location pointed to by it, and", CR
           DATA  "prints it to the screen until if finds a byte with a value", CR
           DATA  "of 255.", CR, CR, 255


'-----Main Routine-----
Main:
  FOR PhraseNum = 1 TO 6                 'For all text blocks, print them one by one
    LOOKUP PhraseNum-1,[Text1, Text2, Text3, Text4, Text5, Text6], Index
    GOSUB PrintIt
    PAUSE 12000                          'Pause for 12 seconds in between text blocks
  NEXT
STOP


'-----PrintIt Subroutine-----
PrintIt:
  READ Index, Character                  'Get next character
  IF Character = 255 THEN Done           'If it is 255, we're done with this block
  DEBUG Character                        'Otherwise, transmit it
  Index = Index + 1                      'Increment Index to the next EEPROM
location
GOTO PrintIt                             'Loop again

Done:
  RETURN                                 'Return to the main routine
```

DEBUG

BS1	BS2	BS2e	BS2sx	BS2p

DEBUG *OutputData* {, *OutputData*}

Function

Display information on the PC screen within the BASIC Stamp editor program. This command can be used to display text or numbers in various formats on the PC screen in order to follow program flow (called debugging) or as part of the functionality of the BASIC Stamp application.

NOTE: Expressions are not allowed as arguments on the BS1. The only constant allowed for the BS1 DEBUG command is a text string.

- **OutputData** is a variable/constant/expression (0 – 65535) that specifies the information to output. Valid data can be ASCII characters (text strings and control characters), decimal numbers (0 - 65535), hexadecimal numbers ($0000 - $FFFF) or binary numbers (up to %1111111111111111). Data can be modified with special formatters as explained below.

Explanation

DEBUG provides a convenient way for your BASIC Stamp to send messages to the PC screen while running. The name "debug" suggests its most popular use; debugging programs by showing you the value of a variable or expression, or by indicating what portion of a program is currently executing. DEBUG is also a great way to rehearse programming techniques. Throughout this manual, we use DEBUG to give you immediate feedback on the effects of instructions. The following example demonstrates using the DEBUG command to send the text string message "Hello World!".

```
DEBUG "Hello World!"                    ' Test message.
```

After you download this one-line program, the BASIC Stamp Editor will open a Debug Terminal on your PC screen and wait for a response from the BASIC Stamp. A moment later, the phrase "Hello World!" will appear. Note that if you close the Debug Terminal, your program keeps executing, but you can't see the DEBUG data anymore.

Multiple pieces of data can be sent with one DEBUG command by separating the data with commas (,). The following example produces exactly the same results as the example above.

```
DEBUG "Hello ", "World!"                'Test message
```

DEBUG - BASIC Stamp Command Reference

DEBUG can also print and format numbers (values) from both constants and variables. The formatting methods for DEBUG are very different for the BS1, than for any other BASIC Stamp. Please read the appropriate sections, below, carefully.

BASIC Stamp 1 Formatting

On the BS1, the DEBUG command, by default, displays numbers in the format "symbol = value" (followed by a carriage return), using the decimal number system. For example,

```
SYMBOL   X = B0
X = 75
DEBUG X
```

displays "X = 75" on the screen. To display the value, in decimal, without the "X =" text, use the decimal formatter (#) before the variable name. For example, the following code displays "75" on the screen.

```
SYMBOL   X = B0
X = 75
DEBUG #X
```

To display numbers in hexadecimal or binary form, use the $ or % formatter, respectively. The code below displays the same number in its hexadecimal and binary forms.

```
SYMBOL   X = B0
X = 75
DEBUG $X, %X
```

After running the above code, "X = $4B" and "X = %01001011" should appear on the screen. **The hexadecimal ($) and binary (%) formatters always display the number using the format "symbol = value" (followed by a carriage return). There is no built-in way to display hexadecimal or binary numbers in any other form when using the BS1's DEBUG command.**

To display a number as its ASCII character equivalent, use the ASCII formatter (@). Typing DEBUG @X (in place of the DEBUG statement in the code above) would display "X = 'K'" on the screen.

USING CR AND CLS (BS1).

Two pre-defined symbols, CR and CLS, can be used to send a carriage-return or clear-screen command to the Debug Terminal. The CR symbol will cause the Debug Terminal to start a new line and the CLS symbol will cause the Debug Terminal to clear itself and place the cursor at the top-left corner of the screen. The following code demonstrates this.

```
DEBUG "You can not see this.", CLS, "Here is line 1", CR, "Here is line 2"
```

When the above is run, the final result is "Here is line 1" on the first line of the screen and "Here is line 2" on the second line. You may or may not have seen "You can not see this." appear first. This is because it was immediately followed by a clear-screen symbol, CLS, which caused the display to clear the screen before displaying the rest of the information.

NOTE: The rest of this discussion does not apply to the BASIC Stamp 1.

BASIC Stamp 2, 2e, 2sx and 2p Formatting

DISPLAYING ASCII CHARACTERS.

On the all BASIC Stamps except the BS1, the DEBUG command, by default, displays everything as ASCII characters. What if you want to display a number? You might think the following example would do this:

```
x    VAR    BYTE
x = 65
DEBUG x                          ' Try to show decimal value of x.
```

DISPLAYING DECIMAL NUMBERS.

Since we set X equal to 65 (in line 2), you might expect the DEBUG line to display "65" on the screen. Instead of "65", however, you'll see the letter "A" if you run this example. The problem is that we never told the BASIC Stamp how to output X, and it defaults to ASCII (the ASCII character at position 65 is "A"). Instead, we need to tell it to display the "decimal form" of the number in X. We can do this by using the decimal formatter (DEC) before the variable. The example below will display "65" on the screen.

```
x    VAR    BYTE
x = 65
DEBUG DEC x                      ' Show decimal value of x.
```

DISPLAYING HEXADECIMAL AND BINARY NUMBERS.

In addition to decimal (DEC), DEBUG can display numbers in hexadecimal (HEX) and binary (BIN). See Table 6.3 for a complete list of formatters.

DEBUG - BASIC Stamp Command Reference

Expressions are allowed within the DEBUG command arguments as well. In the above code, DEBUG DEC x+25 would yield "95" and DEBUG DEC x*10/2-3 would yield "322".

EXPRESSIONS IN DEBUG COMMANDS.

Table 5.5: DEBUG Formatters.

Formatter	Description
?	Displays "symbol = x" + carriage return; where x is a number. Default format is decimal, but may be combined with number formatters below (ex: bin ? x to display "x = binary_number").
ASC ?	Displays "symbol = 'x'" + carriage return; where x is an ASCII character.
DEC{1..5}	Decimal text, optionally fixed for 1 to 5 digits.
SDEC{1..5}	Signed decimal text, optionally fixed for 1 to 5 digits.
HEX{1..4}	Hexadecimal text, optionally fixed for 1 to 4 digits.
SHEX{1..4}	Signed hex text, optionally fixed for 1 to 4 digits.
IHEX{1..4}	Indicated hex text ($ prefix; ex.: $7A3), optionally fixed for 1 to 4 digits.
ISHEX{1..4}	Indicated, signed hex text, optionally fixed for 1 to 4 digits.
BIN{1..16}	Binary text, optionally fixed for 1 to 16 digits.
SBIN{1..16}	Signed binary text, optionally fixed for 1 to 16 digits.
IBIN{1..16}	Indicated binary text (% prefix; ex.: %1001), optionally fixed for 1 to 16 digits.
ISBIN{1..16}	Indicated, signed binary text, optionally fixed for 1 to 16 digits.
STR bytearray	ASCII string from bytearray until byte = 0.
STR bytearray\n	ASCII string consisting of n bytes from bytearray.
REP byte\n	Display ASCII character n times.

As seen in Table 6.3, special versions of the DEC, HEX and BIN formatters allow for the display of indicated, signed and fixed-width numbers. The term "indicated" simply means that a special symbol is displayed, before the number, indicating what number system it belongs to. For example,

DISPLAYING "INDICATED" NUMBERS.

```
x    VAR   BYTE
x = 65
DEBUG HEX x                          ' Show hexadecimal value of x.
```

displays "41" (65, in decimal, is 41, in hexadecimal). You might see a problem here... unless you knew the number was supposed to be hexadecimal, you might think it was 41, in decimal... a totally different number. To help avoid this, use the IHEX formatter (the "I" stands for indicated). Changing the DEBUG line to read: DEBUG IHEX x would print "$41" on the screen. A similar formatter for binary also exists, IBIN, which prints a "%" before the number.

Signed numbers are preceded with a space ( ) or a minus sign (-) to indicate a positive or negative number, respectively. Normally, any number displayed by the BASIC Stamp is shown in its unsigned (positive) form without any indicator. The signed formatters allow you to display the number as a signed (rather than unsigned) value. **NOTE: Only Word-sized variables can be used for signed number display.** The code below demonstrates the difference in all three numbering schemes.

```
x    VAR    WORD
x = -65
DEBUG "Signed: ", SDEC x, " ", ISHEX x, " ", ISBIN x, CR
DEBUG "Unsigned: ", DEC x, " ", IHEX x, " ", IBIN x
```

This code will generate the display shown below:

```
Signed: -65   -$41   -%1000001
Unsigned: 65471   $FFBF   %1111111110111111
```

The signed form of the number –65 is shown in decimal, hexadecimal and then in binary on the top line. The unsigned form, in all three number systems, is shown on the bottom line. If the unsigned form looks strange to you, it's because negative numbers are stored in twos-compliment format within the BASIC Stamp.

Suppose that your program contained several DEBUG instructions showing the contents of different variables. You would want some way to tell them apart. One possible way is to do the following:

```
x    VAR    BYTE
y    VAR    BYTE
x = 100
y = 250
DEBUG "X = ", DEC x, CR            ' Show decimal value of x
DEBUG "Y = ", DEC y, CR            ' Show decimal value of y
```

but typing the name of the variables in quotes (for the display) can get a little tedious. A special formatter, the question mark (?), can save you a lot of time. The code below does exactly the same thing (with less typing):

```
x    VAR    BYTE
y    VAR    BYTE
x = 100
y = 250
DEBUG DEC ? x                        ' Show decimal value of x
DEBUG DEC ? y                        ' Show decimal value of y
```

The display would look something like this:

```
x = 100
y = 250
```

The ? formatter always displays data in the form "symbol = value" (followed by a carriage return). In addition, it defaults to displaying in decimal, so we really only needed to type: DEBUG ? x for the above code. You can, of course, use any of the three number systems. For example: DEBUG HEX ? x or DEBUG BIN ? y.

It's important to note that the "symbol" it displays is taken directly from what appears to the right of the ?. If you were to use an expression, for example: DEBUG ? x*10/2+3 in the above code, the display would show: "x*10/2+3 = 503".

A special formatter, ASC, is also available for use only with the ? formatter to display ASCII characters, as in: DEBUG ASC ? x.

What if you need to display a table of data; multiple rows and columns? The Signed/Unsigned code (above) approaches this but, if you notice, the columns don't line up. The number formatters (DEC, HEX and BIN) have some useful variations to make the display fixed-width (see Table 6.3). Up to 5 digits can be displayed for decimal numbers. To fix the value to a specific number of decimal digits, you can use DEC1, DEC2, DEC3, DEC4 or DEC5. For example:

DISPLAYING FIXED-WIDTH NUMBERS.

```
x    VAR    BYTE
x = 165
DEBUG DEC5 x                        ' Show decimal value of x in 5 digits.
```

displays "00165". Notice that leading zeros? The display is "fixed" to 5 digits, no more and no less. Any unused digits will be filled with zeros.

Using DEC4 in the same code would display "0165". DEC3 would display "165". What would happen if we used DEC2? Regardless of the number, the BASIC Stamp will ensure that it is always the exact number of digits you specified. In this case, it would truncate the "1" and only display "65".

Using the fixed-width version of the formatters in the Signed/Unsigned code above, may result in the following code:

```
x   VAR   WORD
x = -65
DEBUG "Signed: ", SDEC5 x, " ", ISHEX4 x, " ", ISBIN16 x, CR
DEBUG "Unsigned: ", DEC5 x, " ", IHEX4 x, " ", IBIN16 x
```

and displays:

```
Signed:   -00065   -$0041   -%0000000001000001
Unsigned: 65471    $FFBF    %1111111110111111
```

Note: The columns don't line up exactly (due to the extra "sign" characters in the first row), but it certainly looks better than the alternative.

DISPLAYING STRINGS (BYTE ARRAYS).

VARIABLE-WIDTH STRINGS.

If you have a string of characters to display (a byte array), you can use the STR formatter to do so. The STR formatter has two forms (as shown in Table 6.3) for variable-width and fixed-width data. The example below is the variable-width form.

```
x   VAR   BYTE(5)
x(0) = "A"
x(1) = "B"
x(2) = "C"
x(3) = "D"
x(4) = 0
DEBUG STR x
```

This code displays "ABCD" on the screen. In this form, the STR formatter displays each character contained in the byte array until it finds a character that is equal to 0 (value 0, not "0"). This is convenient for use with the SERIN command's STR formatter, which appends 0's to the end of variable-width character string inputs. NOTE: If your byte array doesn't end with 0, the BASIC Stamp will read and output all RAM register contents until it finds a 0 or until it cycles through all RAM locations.

To specify a fixed-width format for the STR formatter, use the form STR x\n; where x is the byte array and n is the number of characters to print. Changing the DEBUG line in the example above to: DEBUG STR x\2 would display "AB" on the screen.

If you need to display the same ASCII character multiple times, the REP (repeat) formatter can help. REP takes the form: REP x\n ;where x is the character and n is the number of times to repeat it. For example:

DEBUG REP "-"\10

would display 10 hyphens on the screen, "----------".

Since individual DEBUG instructions can grow to be fairly complicated, and since a program can contain many DEBUGS, you'll probably want to control the character positioning of the Debug Terminal screen. DEBUG supports a number of different control characters, some with pre-defined symbols (see Table 6.4). The Debug Terminal in the Windows version of the editor supports all the control characters in Table 6.4, while the DOS version only supports a few of them.

Some of the control characters have pre-defined symbols associated with them. In your DEBUG commands, you can use those symbols, for example: DEBUG "Hello", CR displays "Hello" followed by a carriage return. You can always use the ASCII value for any of the control characters, however. For example: DEBUG "Hello", 13 is exactly the same as the code above.

The Move To control character is perhaps the most unique of the set. If the Debug Terminal receives this character, it expects to see an x and y position value to follow (in the next two characters received). The following line moves the cursor to column number 4 in row number 5 and displays "Hello":

DEBUG 2, 4, 5, "Hello"

The upper-left cursor position is 0,0 (that is column 0, row 0). The right-most cursor positions depend on the size of the Debug Terminal window (which is user adjustable). If a character position that is out of range is received, the Debug Terminal wraps back around to the opposite side of the screen.

The Clear Right control character clears the characters that appear to the right of, and on, the cursor's current position. The cursor is not moved by this action.

The Clear Down control character clears the characters that appear below, and on, the cursor's current line. The cursor is not moved by this action.

Table 5.6: Special Control Characters.

Name	Symbol	ASCII Value	Description
Clear Screen	CLS	0	Clear the screen and place cursor at home position.
Home	HOME	1	Place cursor at home in upper-left corner of the screen.
Move To (x,y)*		2	Move cursor to specified location. Must be followed by two values (x and then y)
Cursor Left*		3	Move cursor one character to left.
Cursor Right*		4	Move cursor one character to right.
Cursor Up*		5	Move cursor one character up.
Cursor Down*		6	Move cursor one character down.
Bell	BELL	7	Beep the PC speaker.
Backspace	BKSP	8	Back up cursor to left one space.
Tab	TAB	9	Tab to the next column.
Line Feed*		10	Move cursor down one line.
Clear Right*		11	Clear line contents to the right of cursor.
Clear Down*		12	Clear screen contents below cursor.
Carriage Return	CR	13	Move cursor to the first column of the next line (shift any data on the right down to that line as well)

* This control character only works with the Windows version of the editor software.

TECHNICAL BACKGROUND

DEBUG is actually a special case of the SEROUT instruction. It is set for inverted (RS-232-compatible) serial output through the programming connector (the SOUT pin) at 9600 baud, no parity, 8 data bits, and 1 stop bit. For example,

DEBUG "Hello"

is exactly like:

 SEROUT 16, $4054, ["Hello"]

in terms of function (on a BS2). The DEBUG line actually takes less program space, and is obviously easier to type.

You may view DEBUG's output using a terminal program set to the above parameters, but you may have to modify either your carrier board or the serial cable to temporarily disconnect pin 3 of the BASIC Stamp (pin 4 of the DB-9 connector). See the SEROUT command for more detail.

DTMFOUT | BS1 | BS2 | BS2e | BS2sx | BS2p |

DTMFOUT *Pin, {OnTime, OffTime,} [Tone {, Tone...}]*

Function

Generate dual-tone, multifrequency tones (DTMF, i.e., telephone "touch" tones).

- **Pin** is a variable/constant/expression (0 – 15) that specifies the I/O pin to use. This pin will be set to output mode during generation of tones and set to input mode aftwerwards.

- **OnTime** is an optional variable/constant/expression (0 – 65535) specifying a duration of the tone. The unit of time and the default time for *OnTime* is described in Table 5.7.

- **OffTime** is an optional variable/constant/expression (0 – 65535) specifying the length of silent pause after a tone (or between tones, if multiple tones are specified). The unit of time and the default time for *OffTime* is described in Table 5.7.

- **Tone** is a variable/constant/expression (0 – 15) specifying the DTMF tone to generate. Tones 0 through 11 correspond to the standard layout of the telephone keypad, while 12 through 15 are the fourth-column tones used by phone test equipment and in ham-radio applications.

Quick Facts

Table 5.7: DTMFOUT Quick Facts.

	BS2, BS2e	BS2sx	BS2p
Default *OnTime*	200 ms	80 ms	55 ms
Default *OffTime*	50 ms	50 ms	50 ms
Units in *OnTime* and *OffTime*	1 ms	0.4 ms	0.265 ms

Explanation

DTMF tones are used to dial the phone or remotely control certain radio equipment. The BASIC Stamp can generate these tones digitally using the DTMFOUT instruction. Figure 5.2 shows how to connect a speaker or audio amplifier to hear these tones and Figure 5.3 shows how to connect the BASIC Stamp to the phone line.

The following DTMFOUT instruction will generate DTMF tones on I/O pin 0:

DTMFOUT 0, [6, 2, 4, 8, 3, 3, 3]   ' Call Parallax.

If the BASIC Stamp is connected to the phone line properly, the above command would be equivalent to dialing 624-8333 from a phone keypad. If you wanted to slow the pace of the dialing to accommodate a noisy phone line or radio link, you could use the optional *OnTime* and *OffTime* values:

DTMFOUT 0, 500, 100, [6, 2, 4, 8, 3, 3, 3]   ' Call Parallax, slowly.

In this example, on a BS2 the *OnTime* is set to 500 ms (1/2 second) and *OffTime* to 100 ms (1/10th second).

Tone Value	Corresponding Telephone Key
0 – 9	Digits 0 through 9
10	Star (*)
11	Pound (#)
12 – 15	Fourth column tones A through D

Table 5.8: DTMF Tones and Corresponding Telephone Keys.

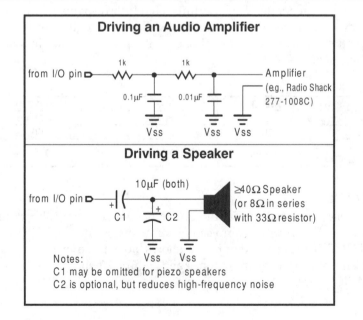

Figure 5.2: Example RC Filter Circuits for Driving an Audio Amplifier or a Speaker.

TECHNICAL BACKGROUND.

The BASIC Stamp controller is a purely digital device. DTMF tones are analog waveforms, consisting of a mixture of two sine waves at different audio frequencies. So how does a digital device generate analog output? The BASIC Stamp creates and mixes the sine waves mathematically, then uses the resulting stream of numbers to control the duty cycle of a very fast pulse-width modulation (PWM) routine. So what's actually coming out of the I/O pin is a rapid stream of pulses. The purpose of the filtering arrangements shown in Figures 5.2 and 5.3 is to smooth out the high-frequency PWM, leaving only the lower frequency audio behind.

Keep this in mind if you want to interface BASIC Stamp's DTMF output to radios and other equipment that could be adversely affected by the presence of high-frequency noise on the input. Make sure to filter the DTMF output thoroughly. The circuits in Figure 5.2 are only a starting point; you may want to use an active low-pass filter with a roll-off point around 2 kHz.

Figure 5.3: Example DAA Circuit to Interface to a Standard Telephone Line.

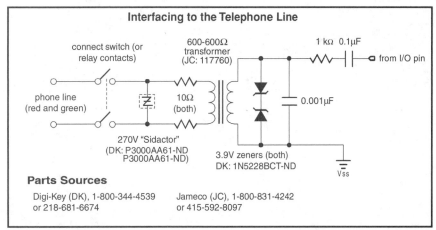

Interfacing to the Telephone Line

Parts Sources

Digi-Key (DK), 1-800-344-4539 or 218-681-6674

Jameco (JC), 1-800-831-4242 or 415-592-8097

NOTE: This is written for the BS2 but can be used for the BS2e, BS2sx and BS2p also. Locate the proper source code file or modify the STAMP directive before downloading to the BS2e, BS2sx or BS2p.

Demo Program (DTMFOUT.bs2)

This demo program is a rudimentary memory dialer. Since DTMF digits fit within a nibble (four bits), the program below packs two DTMF digits into each byte of three EEPROM data tables. The end of a phone number is marked by the nibble $F, since this is not a valid phone-dialing digit.

```
'{$STAMP BS2}                            'STAMP directive (specifies a BS2)
'-----Define variables-----
EEloc      VAR    BYTE                   ' EEPROM address of stored number.
EEByte     VAR    BYTE                   ' Byte containing two DTMF digits.
```

```
DTdigit      VAR    EEBYTE.highNIB        ' Digit to dial.
Phone        VAR    NIB                   ' Pick a phone #.
HiLo         VAR    BIT                   ' Bit to select upper and lower nibble.

'-----Define data-----
Parallax     DATA   $19,$16,$62,$48,$33,$3F  ' Phone: 1-916-624-8333
ParallaxFax  DATA   $19,$16,$62,$48,$00,$3F  ' Phone: 1-916-624-8003
Information  DATA   $15,$20,$55,$51,$21,$2F  ' Phone: 1-520-555-1212

'-----Main Routine-----
FOR Phone = 0 TO 2                       ' For each phone #, get location of # in
EEPROM.
  LOOKUP Phone,[Parallax,ParallaxFax,Information],EEloc

Dial:
  READ EEloc,EEByte                      ' Retrieve byte from EEPROM.
    FOR HiLo = 0 to 1                    ' Dial upper and lower digits.
      IF DTdigit = $F THEN Done          ' Hex $F is end-of-number flag
      DTMFout 11,[DTdigit]               ' Dial digit.
      EEBYTE = EEBYTE << 4               ' Shift in next digit.
    NEXT
  EEloc = EEloc + 1                      ' next pair of digits.
GOTO dial                                ' Keep dialing until done ($F in DTdigit).

  done:                                  ' This number is done.
   PAUSE 2000                            ' Wait a couple of seconds.
  NEXT
                                         ' Dial next phone number.
STOP
```

EEPROM

BS1	BS2	BS2e	BS2sx	BS2p

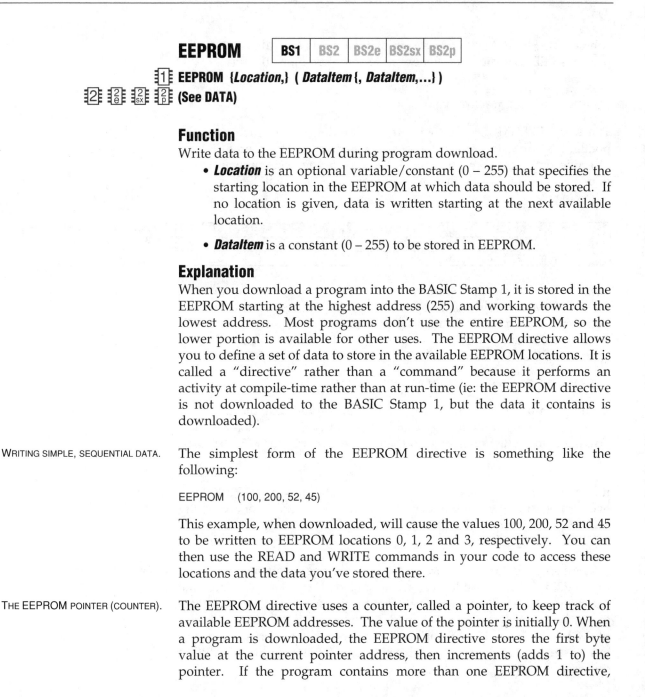

1 EEPROM {*Location,*} (*DataItem* {, *DataItem,...*})

2 2e 2sx 2p (See DATA)

Function

Write data to the EEPROM during program download.

- **Location** is an optional variable/constant (0 – 255) that specifies the starting location in the EEPROM at which data should be stored. If no location is given, data is written starting at the next available location.

- **DataItem** is a constant (0 – 255) to be stored in EEPROM.

Explanation

When you download a program into the BASIC Stamp 1, it is stored in the EEPROM starting at the highest address (255) and working towards the lowest address. Most programs don't use the entire EEPROM, so the lower portion is available for other uses. The EEPROM directive allows you to define a set of data to store in the available EEPROM locations. It is called a "directive" rather than a "command" because it performs an activity at compile-time rather than at run-time (ie: the EEPROM directive is not downloaded to the BASIC Stamp 1, but the data it contains is downloaded).

WRITING SIMPLE, SEQUENTIAL DATA.

The simplest form of the EEPROM directive is something like the following:

EEPROM   (100, 200, 52, 45)

This example, when downloaded, will cause the values 100, 200, 52 and 45 to be written to EEPROM locations 0, 1, 2 and 3, respectively. You can then use the READ and WRITE commands in your code to access these locations and the data you've stored there.

THE EEPROM POINTER (COUNTER).

The EEPROM directive uses a counter, called a pointer, to keep track of available EEPROM addresses. The value of the pointer is initially 0. When a program is downloaded, the EEPROM directive stores the first byte value at the current pointer address, then increments (adds 1 to) the pointer. If the program contains more than one EEPROM directive, subsequent EEPROM directives start with the pointer value left by the previous EEPROM directive. For example, if the program contains:

```
EEPROM    (72, 69, 76, 76, 79)
EEPROM    (104, 101, 108, 108, 111)
```

The first EEPROM directive will start at location 0 and increment the pointer for each data value it stores (1, 2, 3, 4 and 5). The second EEPROM directive will start with the pointer value of 5 and work upward from there. As a result, the first 10 bytes of EEPROM will look like the following:

	EEPROM Location (address)									
	0	1	2	3	4	5	6	7	8	9
Contents	72	69	76	76	79	104	101	108	108	111

Table 5.9: Example EEPROM storage.

What if you don't want to store values starting at location 0? Fortunately, the EEPROM directive has an option to specify the next location to use. You can specify the next location number (to set the pointer to) by using the optional Location argument before the list of Dataitems. The following code writes the same data in Table 5.9 to locations 50 through 59:

WRITING DATA TO OTHER LOCATIONS.

```
DATA      50, (72, 69, 76, 76, 79, 104, 101, 108, 108, 111)
```

In this example, the Location argument is given and tells the EEPROM directive to store the following DataItem(s) starting at location 50. The DataItems in the list are stored in their respective locations (50, 51, 52... 59).

It is important to realize that the entire BASIC Stamp 1 EEPROM is overwritten during programming. Any EEPROM location not containing a PBASIC program or DataItems from an EEPROM directive is written with a 0.

IMPORTANT CONCEPT: HOW DATA AND PROGRAMS ARE DOWNLOADED INTO EEPROM.

A common use for EEPROM is to store strings; sequences of bytes representing text. PBASIC converts quoted text like "A" into the corresponding ASCII character code (65 in this case). To make data entry easier, you can place quotes around a whole chunk of text used in a EEPROM directive, and PBASIC will understand it to mean a series of bytes (see the last line of code below). The following three EEPROM directives are equivalent:

WRITING TEXT STRINGS.

```
EEPROM    (72, 69, 76, 76, 79)
EEPROM    ("H", "E", "L", "L", "O")
EEPROM    ("HELLO")
```

All three lines of code, above, will result in the numbers 72, 69, 76, 76, and 79 being stored into EEPROM upon downloading. These numbers are simply the ASCII character codes for "H", "E", "L", "L", and "O", respectively. See the Demo Program, below, for an example of storing and reading multiple text strings.

WRITING WORD VALUES VS. BYTE VALUES.

The EEPROM is organized as a sequential set of byte-sized memory locations. The EEPROM directive only stores bytes into EEPROM. If you try to store a word-size value, for example: EEPROM (1125), only the lower byte of the value will be stored (in this case, 101). This does not mean that you can't store word-sized values, however. A word consists of two bytes, called a low-byte and a high-byte. If you wanted to store the value 1125 using the EEPROM directive you'll have to calculate the low-byte and the high-byte and insert them in the list in the proper order, as in:

```
EEPROM    (101, 4)
```

The directive above will store the two bytes into two sequential EEPROM locations (the low-byte first, followed by the high-byte). We calculated this in the following manner: 1) high-byte is INT(value / 256) and 2) low-byte is value – (high-byte * 256).

To retrieve a word-size value, you'll need to use two READ commands and a word-size variable. For example,

```
SYMBOL    Result       = W0        'The full word-sized variable
SYMBOL    Result_Low   = B0        'B0 happens to be the low-byte of W0
SYMBOL    Result_High  = B1        'B1 happens to be the high-byte of W0
EEPROM    (101, 4)

READ      0, Result_Low
READ      1, Result_High
DEBUG     #Result
```

This code would write the low-byte and high-byte of the number 1125 into locations 0 and 1 during download. When the program runs, the two READ commands will read the low-byte and high-byte out of EEPROM (reconstructing it in a word-size variable) and then display the value on the screen. See the READ and WRITE commands for more information.

Demo Program (EEPROM.bas)

This program stores a couple of text strings into EEPROM with the EEPROM directive and then sends them, one character at a time via the SEROUT command. This is a good demonstration of how to save program space by storing large amounts of data in EEPROM directly, rather than embedding the data into SEROUT commands.

```
'{$STAMP BS1}                                'STAMP directive (specifies a BS1)
'-----Define variables-----
SYMBOL     Index     = B0  'Holds current location number
SYMBOL     Phrase    = B1
SYMBOL     Character = B2  'Holds current character to print

'-----Define all text phrases -----
EEPROM    ("Here is a long message that needs to be transmitted.", 255)
EEPROM    ("Here is some more text to be transmitted.", 255)

'-----Main Routine-----
Main:
  Index = 0
  FOR Phrase = 1 TO 2
    GOSUB PrintIt
    PAUSE 12000                              'Pause for 12 seconds in between text blocks
  NEXT
END

'-----PrintIt Subroutine-----
PrintIt:
  READ Index, Character                      'Get next character
  IF Character = 255 THEN Done                'If it is 255, we're done with this block
  SEROUT 0,N2400,(Character)                  'Otherwise, transmit it
  Index = Index + 1        'Increment Index to the next EEPROM location
GOTO PrintIt                     'Loop again

Done:
  RETURN                                      'Return to the main routine
```

END

| BS1 | BS2 | BS2e | BS2sx | BS2p |

⟦1⟧ ⟦2⟧ ⟦2e⟧ ⟦2sx⟧ ⟦2p⟧ **END**

Function

End the program, placing the BASIC Stamp into low-power mode indefinitely. This is equivalent to having a program that does not loop continuously; once the BASIC Stamp reaches the end of the PBASIC program, it enters low-power mode indefinitely. The END command is optional and is rarely used.

Quick Facts

Table 5.10: END Quick Facts. Note: Current Consumption is approximate and assumes no loads.

	BS1	BS2	BS2e	BS2sx	BS2p
Apx. current draw @ 5 vdc during run*	2 mA	8 mA	25 mA	60 mA	40 mA
Apx. current draw @ 5 vdc during end*	20 µA	40 µA	60 µA	60 µA	60 µA

* This is an approximate value, not including loads on the I/O pins.

Explanation

END puts the BASIC Stamp into its inactive, low-power mode. In this mode the Stamp's current draw (excluding loads driven by the I/O pins) is reduced to the amount shown in Table 5.10. END keeps the BASIC Stamp inactive until the reset line is activated, the power is cycled off and back on or the PC downloads another program.

Just as with the SLEEP command, pins will retain their input or output settings after the BASIC Stamp is deactivated by END. For example, if the BASIC Stamp is powering an LED when END executes, the LED will stay lit after END, but every 2.3 seconds, there will be a visible wink of the LED as the output pin switches to the input direction for 18 ms. (See the SLEEP command for more information).

FOR...NEXT | BS1 | BS2 | BS2e | BS2sx | BS2p |

[1] FOR *Counter* = *StartValue* **TO** *EndValue* {**STEP** {-} *StepValue*} ... **NEXT** {*Counter*}

[2] [2e] [2sx] [2p] FOR *Counter* = *StartValue* **TO** *EndValue* {**STEP** *StepValue*} ... **NEXT**

Function

Create a repeating loop that executes the program lines between FOR and NEXT, incrementing or decrementing *Counter* according to *StepValue* until the value of the *Counter* variable passes the *EndValue*.

- **[1]**

  NOTE: Expressions are not allowed as arguments on the BS1.

- • **Counter** is a variable (usually a byte or a word) used as a counter.

- • **StartValue** is a variable/constant/expression (0 – 65535) that specifies the initial value of the variable (*Counter*).

- • **EndValue** is a variable/constant/expression (0 – 65535) that specifies the end value of the variable (*Counter*). When the value of *Counter* is outside of the range *StartValue* to *EndValue*, the FOR...NEXT loop stops executing and the program goes on to the instruction after NEXT.

[1]

NOTE: Use a minus sign to indicate negative *StepValues* on the BS1.

- • **StepValue** is an optional variable/constant/expression (0 – 65535) by which the *Counter* increases or decreases with each iteration through the FOR...NEXT loop. On the BS1, use a minus sign (-) in front of the *StepValue* to indicate a negative step. On all other BASIC Stamps, if *StartValue* is larger than *EndValue*, PBASIC understands *StepValue* to be negative, even though no minus sign is used.

Quick Facts

Table 5.11: FOR...NEXT Quick Facts.

	BS1	BS2, BS2e, BS2sx and BS2p
Max. nested commands	8	16
To decrement counter variable	Set StartValue > EndValue and enter negative StepValue*	Set StartValue > EndValue
Counter comparison	Exit loop if Counter exceeds EndValue	Exit loop if Counter outside of range set by StartValue to EndValue

* Direction (ie: increment/decrement) cannot be changed at runtime.

FOR...NEXT - BASIC Stamp Command Reference

Explanation

FOR...NEXT loops let your program execute a series of instructions for a specified number of repetitions (called iterations). By default, each time through the loop, the counter variable is incremented by 1. It will continue to loop until the result of the counter is outside of the range set by *StartValue* and *EndValue*. Also, FOR...NEXT loops always execute at least once. The simplest form is shown here:

SIMPLEST FORM OF FOR...NEXT.

NOTE: On the BS1, the loop will continue until *Counter* has gone past *EndValue*.

```
Reps        VAR   NIB          ' Counter for the FOR/NEXT loop.
FOR Reps = 1 TO 3              ' Repeat with Reps = 1, 2, 3.
  DEBUG "*"                    ' Each repetition, put one * on the screen.
NEXT
```

NOTE: Replace the first line with **SYMBOL Reps = B0** on the BS1.

In the above code, the FOR command sets *Reps* = 1. Then the DEBUG line (within the FOR...NEXT loop) is executed; printing an asterisk (*) on the screen. When the BASIC Stamp sees the NEXT command, it goes back to the previous FOR command, adds 1 to *Reps* and compares the result to the range set by *StartValue* and *EndValue*. If *Reps* is still within range, it executes the code in the loop again. Each time the FOR...NEXT loop executes, the value of *Reps* is updated (incremented by 1) and the code within the loop (the DEBUG line) is executed; printing another asterisk on the screen. This code will run through the loop three times; setting *Reps* to 1, 2 and 3, and printing three asterisks on the screen. After the third loop, again the BASIC Stamp goes back up to the FOR command, adds 1 to *Reps* and compares the result (4 in this case) to the range. Since the range is 1 to 3 and the value is 4 (outside the range) the FOR...NEXT loop is done and the BASIC Stamp will jump down to the first line of code following the NEXT command.

PROCESSING A FOR...NEXT LOOP.

You can view the changing values of *Reps* by including the *Reps* variable in a DEBUG command within the loop:

```
Reps        VAR   NIB          ' Counter for the FOR/NEXT loop.
FOR Reps = 1 TO 3              ' Repeat with Reps = 1, 2, 3.
  DEBUG DEC Reps, CR           ' Each repetition, put the number of the
NEXT                           ' repetition on the screen.
```

NOTE: Change the first line as noted above and replace line 3 with **DEBUG #Reps, CR** on the BS1.

Running this example should display "1" , "2", and "3" on the screen.

FOR...NEXT can also be made to decrement (rather than increment) the counter variable. The BS1 does this when you specify a negative *StepValue* (as well as a *StartValue* that is greater than the *EndValue*). All other BASIC

DECREMENTING THE COUNTER INSTEAD OF INCREMENTING IT.

Stamps do this automatically when the *StartValue* is greater than the *EndValue*. Examples of both are shown below:

```
 1  SYMBOL   Reps  =  B0            ' Counter for the FOR/NEXT loop.
    FOR Reps = 3 TO 1  STEP -1      ' Repeat with Reps = 3, 2, 1.
      DEBUG #Reps, CR               ' Each repetition, put the number of the
    NEXT                            ' repetition on the screen.
```

-- or --

```
 2  2  2  2  Reps      VAR   NIB    ' Counter for the FOR/NEXT loop.
    e  sx  p  FOR Reps = 3 TO 1     ' Repeat with Reps = 3, 2, 1.
      DEBUG DEC Reps, CR            ' Each repetition, put the number of the
    NEXT                            ' repetition on the screen.
```

Note that the code for the BS2, BS2e, BS2sx and BS2p did not use the optional STEP argument. This is because we wanted to decrement by positive 1 anyway (the default unit) and the BASIC Stamp realizes it needs to decrement because the *StartValue* is greater than the *EndValue*. A negative *StepValue* on the BS2, BS2e, BS2sx and BS2p would be treated as its positive, two's compliment counterpart. For example, –1 in two's complement is 65535. So the following code executes only once:

```
    Reps      VAR   NIB            ' Counter for the FOR/NEXT loop.
    FOR Reps = 3 TO 1 STEP -1      ' This will try to decrement 3 by 65535.
      DEBUG DEC Reps, CR           ' Each repetition, put the number of the
    NEXT                           ' repetition on the screen.
```

The above code would run through the loop once with *Reps* set to 3. The second time around, it would decrement *Reps* by 65535 (-1 is 65535 in two's compliment) effectively making the number –65532 (4 in two's compliment) which is outside the range of the loop.

USING VARIABLES AS ARGUMENTS.

All the arguments in the FOR...NEXT command can be constants, variables or expressions (on the BS2, BS2e, BS2sx and BS2p). This leads to some interesting uses. For example, if you make the *StartValue* and *EndValue* a variable, and change their values within the loop, you'll change the behavior of the loop itself. Try the following:

```
Reps        VAR    BYTE              ' Counter for the FOR/NEXT loop.
StartVal    VAR    BYTE
EndVal      VAR    BYTE

StartVal = 1                         ' Initialize StartVal to 1
EndVal = 3                           ' Initialize EndVal to 3
FOR  Reps = StartVal  TO  EndVal     ' Repeat until Reps is not in range 1 to 3.
  DEBUG  DEC Reps,CR
  IF Reps <> 3 THEN Done             ' If Reps <> 3 then continue as normal
    StartVal = 3                     ' otherwise, swap StartVal and EndVal
    EndVal = 1
Done:
NEXT
```

NOTE: The increment/decrement direction of the FOR...NEXT loop cannot be changed on the BS1.

Here the loop starts with a range of 1 to 3. First, the DEBUG line prints the value of *Reps*. Then the IF...THEN line makes a decision; if *Reps* is not equal to 3, jump to the label "Done." If, however, *Reps* is equal to 3, the two lines following IF...THEN swap the order of *StartVal* and *EndVal*, making the range 3 to 1. The next time through the loop, *Reps* will be decremented instead of incremented because *StartVal* is greater than *EndVal*. The result is a display on the screen of the numbers 1, 2, 3, 2, 1.

The following example uses the value of *Reps* as the *StepValue*. This creates a display of power's of 2 (1, 2, 4, 8, 16, 32, 64, etc):

```
Reps       VAR   WORD               ' Counter for the loop.
FOR  Reps = 1  TO  256 STEP Reps    ' Each loop add current value of Reps
  DEBUG  DEC ? Reps                 ' Show reps in debug window.
NEXT
```

NOTE: For BS1's, change line 1 to
SYMBOL Reps = W0
and line 3 to
DEBUG Reps

There is a potential bug that you should be careful to avoid. The BASIC Stamp uses unsigned 16-bit integer math for any math operation it performs, regardless of the size of values or variables. The maximum value the BASIC Stamp can internally calculate is 65535 (the largest 16-bit number). If you add 1 to 65535, you get 0 as the 16-bit register rolls over (like a car's odometer does when you exceed the maximum mileage it can display). Similarly, if you subtract 1 from 0, you'll get 65535 as the 16-bit register rolls under (a rollover in the opposite direction).

WATCH OUT FOR 16-BIT ROLLOVER, OR VARIABLE RANGE, ERRORS.

If you write a FOR...NEXT loop who's *StepValue* would cause the counter variable to go past 65535, this rollover may cause the loop to execute more times than you expect. Try the following example:

NOTE: For BS1's, change line 1 to
SYMBOL Reps = W0
and line 3 to
DEBUG Reps

```
Reps        VAR   WORD             ' Counter for the loop.
FOR Reps = 0  TO  65535  STEP 3000  ' Each loop add 3000.
  DEBUG DEC ? Reps                  ' Show reps in debug window.
NEXT
```

The value of reps increases by 3000 each trip through the loop. As it approaches the *EndValue*, an interesting thing happens; *Reps* is: 57000, 60000, 63000, 464, 3464... It passes the *EndValue*, rolls over and keeps going. That's because the result of the calculation 63000 + 3000 exceeds the maximum capacity of a 16-bit number and then rolls over to 464. When the result of 464 is tested against the range ("Is Reps > 0 and is Reps < 65500?") it passes the test and the loop continues.

A similar symptom can be seen in a program who's *EndValue* is mistakenly set higher than what the counter variable can hold. The example below uses a byte-sized variable, but the *EndValue* is set to a number greater than what will fit in a byte:

```
SYMBOL   Reps  =  B0              ' Counter for the loop.
FOR Reps = 0  TO  300            ' Each loop add 1.
  DEBUG  Reps                     ' Show reps in debug window.
NEXT
```

-- or --

```
Reps        VAR   BYTE            ' Counter for the loop.
FOR Reps = 0  TO  300            ' Each loop add 1.
  DEBUG  DEC ? Reps               ' Show reps in debug window.
NEXT
```

Here, *Reps* is a byte variable; which can only hold the number range 0 to 255. The *EndValue* is set to 300, however; greater than 255. This code will loop endlessly because when *Reps* is 255 and the FOR...NEXT loop adds 1, *Reps* becomes 0 (bytes will rollover after 255 just like words will rollover after 65535). The result, 0, is compared against the range (0 – 255) and it is found to be within the range, so the FOR...NEXT loop continues.

NOTE: On the BS1, the loop will continue until *Counter* has gone past *EndValue*. The rollover error will still occur if the BS1 cannot determine if *Counter* went past *EndValue*.

It's important to realize that on the BS2, BS2e, BS2sx and BS2p, the test is against the entire range, not just the *EndValue*. The code below is a slight modification of the previous example (the *StartValue* is 10 instead of 0) and will not loop endlessly.

```
Reps        VAR   BYTE        ' Counter for the loop.
FOR Reps = 10 to 300          ' Each loop add 1.
  DEBUG DEC ? Reps            ' Show reps in debug window.
NEXT
```

Reps still rolls over to 0, as before, however, this time it is outside the range of 10 to 255. The loop stops, leaving *Reps* at 0. Note that this code is still in error since *Reps* will never reach 300 until it is declared as a WORD.

Demo Program (FORNEXT.bas)

```
' This example uses a FOR...NEXT loop to churn out a series of sequential squares
' (numbers 1, 2, 3, 4... raised to the second power) by using a variable to set the
' FOR...NEXT StepValue, and incrementing StepValue within the loop. Sir Isaac Newton
' is generally credited with the discovery of this technique.

'{$STAMP BS1}                      'STAMP directive (specifies a BS1)
SYMBOL    Square    = B0          ' FOR/NEXT counter and series of squares.
SYMBOL    StepSize  = B1          ' Step size, which will increase by 2 each
loop.

StepSize = 1
Square = 1
FOR Square = 1 TO 250 STEP StepSize    ' Show squares up to 250.
  DEBUG Square                         ' Display on screen.
  StepSize = StepSize + 2              ' Add 2 to StepSize
NEXT                                   ' Loop til square > 250.
```

Demo Program (FORNEXT.bs2)

```
' This example uses a FOR...NEXT loop to churn out a series of sequential squares
' (numbers 1, 2, 3, 4... raised to the second power) by using a variable to set the
' FOR...NEXT StepValue, and incrementing StepValue within the loop. Sir Isaac Newton
' is generally credited with the discovery of this technique.

'{$STAMP BS2}                      'STAMP directive (specifies a BS2)
Square    VAR   BYTE              ' FOR/NEXT counter and series of squares.
StepSize  VAR   BYTE             ' Step size, which will increase by 2 each
loop.

StepSize = 1
Square = 1
FOR Square = 1 TO 250 STEP StepSize    ' Show squares up to 250.
  DEBUG DEC ? Square                    ' Display on screen.
  StepSize = StepSize + 2              ' Add 2 to StepSize
NEXT                                    ' Loop til square > 250.
```

NOTE: This is written for the BS2 but can be used for the BS2e, BS2sx and BS2p also. Locate the proper source code file or modify the STAMP directive before downloading to the BS2e, BS2sx or BS2p.

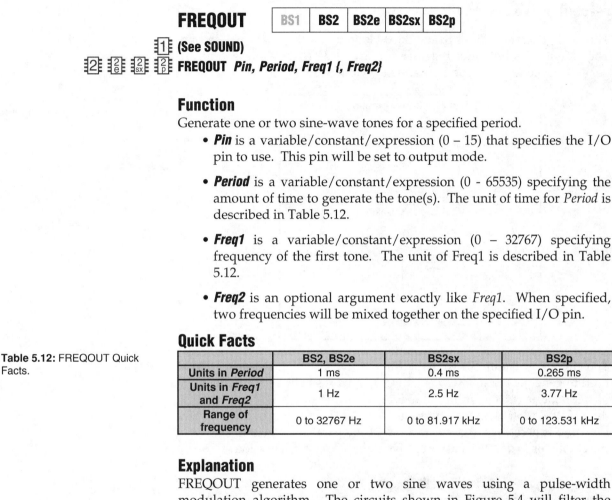

FREQOUT | BS1 | BS2 | BS2e | BS2sx | BS2p

⚏1 (See SOUND)

⚏2 ⚏2e ⚏2sx ⚏2p FREQOUT *Pin, Period, Freq1 {, Freq2}*

Function

Generate one or two sine-wave tones for a specified period.

- **Pin** is a variable/constant/expression (0 – 15) that specifies the I/O pin to use. This pin will be set to output mode.

- **Period** is a variable/constant/expression (0 - 65535) specifying the amount of time to generate the tone(s). The unit of time for *Period* is described in Table 5.12.

- **Freq1** is a variable/constant/expression (0 – 32767) specifying frequency of the first tone. The unit of Freq1 is described in Table 5.12.

- **Freq2** is an optional argument exactly like *Freq1*. When specified, two frequencies will be mixed together on the specified I/O pin.

Quick Facts

Table 5.12: FREQOUT Quick Facts.

	BS2, BS2e	BS2sx	BS2p
Units in *Period*	1 ms	0.4 ms	0.265 ms
Units in *Freq1* and *Freq2*	1 Hz	2.5 Hz	3.77 Hz
Range of frequency	0 to 32767 Hz	0 to 81.917 kHz	0 to 123.531 kHz

Explanation

FREQOUT generates one or two sine waves using a pulse-width modulation algorithm. The circuits shown in Figure 5.4 will filter the signal in order to play the tones through a speaker or audio amplifier. Here's a simple FREQOUT command:

SIMPLEST FORM OF FREQOUT.

FREQOUT 2, 1000, 2500

On the BS2, this command generates a 2500 Hz tone for 1 second (1000 ms) on I/O pin 2. See Table 5.12 for timing data on other BASIC Stamps.

GENERATING TWO TONES AT ONCE.

To play two tones on the same I/O pin at once:

FREQOUT 2, 1000, 2500, 3000

This will generate a 2500 Hz and 3000 Hz tone (on the BS2) for 1 second. The frequencies will mix together for a chord- or bell-like sound. To generate a silent pause, specify frequency value(s) of 0.

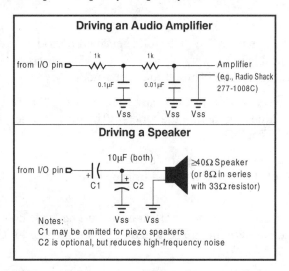

Figure 5.4: Example RC filter circuits for driving an audio amplifier or a speaker.

The circuits in Figure 5.4 work by filtering out the high-frequency PWM used to generate the sine waves. FREQOUT works over a very wide range of frequencies (as shown in Table 5.12) so at the upper end of its range, those PWM filters will also filter out most of the desired frequency. You may find it necessary to reduce values of the parallel capacitors shown in the circuit, or to devise a custom active filter for your application.

FREQUENCY CONSIDERATIONS.

Demo Program (FREQOUT.bs2)

```
' This program plays "Mary Had a Little Lamb" by reading the notes from a LOOKUP table.
' It was designed to sound good on the piezo speaker that comes with the BASIC Stamp
' Activity Board.  To demonstrate the effect of mixing sine waves, the first frequency
' is the musical note itself, while the second is 8 Hz lower. The difference creates a
' quiver (vibrato) on each note. Subtracting 8 from the note frequency poses a problem
' when the frequency is 0, because the BASIC Stamp's positive-integer math wraps around
' to 65528. FREQOUT would ignore the highest bit of this value and generate a frequency
' of 32760 Hz rather than a truly silent pause. Although humans can't hear 32762 Hz,
' slight imperfections in filtering will cause an audible noise in the speaker. To clean
' this up, we use the expression "(f-8) max 32768," which changes 65528 to 32768.
FREQOUT
' discards the highest bit of 32768, which results in 0, the desired silent pause.
```

NOTE: This is written for the BS2 but can be used for the BS2e, BS2sx and BS2p also. Locate the proper source code file or modify the STAMP directive before downloading to the BS2e, BS2sx or BS2p.

```
'{$STAMP BS2}                              'STAMP directive (specifies a BS2)

i    VAR    BYTE      ' Counter for position in tune.
f    VAR    WORD      ' Frequency of note for FREQOUT.
C    CON    2092      ' C note
D    CON    2348      ' D note
E    CON    2636      ' E note
G    CON    3136      ' G note
R    CON    8         ' Silent pause (rest).

FOR i = 0 TO 28       ' Play the 29 notes of the LOOKUP table.
  LOOKUP i,[E,D,C,D,E,E,E,R,D,D,D,R,E,G,G,R,E,D,C,D,E,E,E,E,D,D,E,D,C],f
  FREQOUT 11,225,f,(f-8) MAX 32768
NEXT
STOP
```

GET

| BS1 | BS2 | BS2e | BS2sx | BS2p |

GET *Location, Variable*

Function

Read value from Scratch Pad RAM *Location* and store in *Variable*.

- **Location** is a variable/constant/expression (0 – 63 for Bs2e and BS2sx and 0 – 127 for BS2p) that specifies the Scratch Pad RAM location to read from.

- **Variable** is a variable (usually a byte) to store the value into.

Quick Facts

Table 5.13: GET Quick Facts.

	BS2e, BS2sx	BS2p
Scratch Pad RAM size and organization	64 bytes (0 – 63). Organized as bytes only.	128 bytes (0 – 127). Organized as bytes only.
ieneral purpos locations	0 - 62	0 – 126
Special use location	Current program slot number in read-only location 63.	Current program slot number in lowest nibble of read-only location 127. Current read/write slot number in highest nibble of location 127.

Explanation

The GET command reads a byte-sized value from the specified Scratch Pad RAM location and stores it into *Variable*. All values in all locations can be retrieved from within any of the 8 program slots.

USES FOR SCRATCH PAD RAM.

Scratch Pad RAM is useful for passing data to programs in other program slots and for additional workspace. It is different than regular RAM in that symbol names cannot be assigned directly to locations and each location is always configured as a byte only. The following code will read the value at location 25, store it in a variable called Temp and display it:

```
Temp     VAR   BYTE
GET  25, Temp
DEBUG  DEC  Temp
```

SCRATCH PAD RAM LOCATIONS AND THEIR PURPOSE.

Scratch Pad RAM locations 0 though 62 are available for general use. The highest location (63 for BS2e and BS2sx and 127 for the BS2p) is a special, read-only, location that always contains the number of the currently running program slot. On the BS2p, the upper nibble of location 127 also contains the current program slot that will be used for the READ and WRITE commands. See the demo program below for an example of use.

Demo Program (GETPUT1.bsx)

```
' This example demonstrates the use of the GET and PUT commands.  First, location 63
' is read using GET to display the currently running program number.  Then a set of
' values are written (PUT) into locations 0 to 9.  Afterwards, program number 1 is run.
' This program is a BS2sx project consisting of GETPUT1.bsx and GETPUT2.bsx.  See the
' BASIC Stamp Project section in the manual for more information.

'{$STAMP  BS2sx, GETPUT2.BSX}            'STAMP directive (specifies a BS2sx and
                                         'a second program, GETPUT2.BSX)


Value       VAR   BYTE
Index       VAR   BYTE

GET 63, Value
DEBUG "Program #",DEC Value, CR

FOR Index = 0 TO 9
  Value = (Index + 3) * 8
  PUT Index, Value
  DEBUG "  Writing: ", DEC2 Value, " to location: ", DEC2 Index, CR
NEXT

RUN 1
```

NOTE: This is written for the BS2sx but can be used for the BS2e, and BS2p also. Locate the proper source code file or modify the STAMP directive before downloading to the BS2e, or BS2p.

Demo Program (GETPUT2.bsx)

```
' This example demonstrates the use of the GET and PUT commands.  First, location 63
' is read using GET to display the currently running program number.  Then a set of
' values are read (GET) from locations 0 to 9 and displayed on the screen for verification.
' This program is a BS2sx project consisting of GETPUT1.bsx and GETPUT2.bsx.  See the
' BASIC Stamp Project section in the manual for more information.

'{$STAMP  BS2sx}                         'STAMP directive (specifies a BS2sx)

Value       VAR   BYTE
Index       VAR   BYTE

GET 63, Value
DEBUG CR, "Program #",DEC Value, CR

FOR Index = 0 TO 9
  GET Index, Value
  DEBUG "  Reading: ", DEC2 Value, " from location: ", DEC2 Index, CR
NEXT

STOP
```

NOTE: This is written for the BS2sx but can be used for the BS2e, and BS2p also. Locate the proper source code file or modify the STAMP directive before downloading to the BS2e, or BS2p.

GOSUB

BS1	BS2	BS2e	BS2sx	BS2p

GOSUB *Address*

Function

Store the address of the next instruction after GOSUB, then go to the point in the program specified by *Address*; with the intention of returning to the stored address.

• **Address** is a label that specifies where to go.

Quick Facts

Table 5.14: GOSUB Quick Facts.

	BS1	BS2, BS2e, BS2sx and BS2p
Max. GOSUBs per program	16	255
Max. nested GOSUBs	4	4

Explanation

GOSUB is a close relative of GOTO, in fact, its name means, "GO to a SUBroutine". When a PBASIC program reaches a GOSUB, the program executes the code beginning at the specified address label. Unlike GOTO, GOSUB also stores the address of the instruction immediately following itself. When the program encounters a RETURN command, it interprets it to mean, "go to the instruction that follows the most recent GOSUB." In other words, a GOSUB makes the BASIC Stamp do a similar operation as you do when you see a table or figure reference in this manual; 1) you remember where you are, 2) you go to the table or figure and read the information there, and 3) when you've reached the end of it, you "return" to the place you were reading originally.

GOSUB CAN SAVE EEPROM (PROGRAM) SPACE.

GOSUB is mainly used to execute the same piece of code from multiple locations. If you have, for example, a block of three lines of code that need to be run from 10 different locations in your entire program you could simple copy and paste those three lines to each of those 10 locations. This would amount to a total of 30 lines of repetitive code (and extra space wasted in the program memory). A better solution is to place those three lines in a separate routine, complete with it's own label and followed by a RETURN command, then just use a GOSUB command at each of the 10 locations to access it. This technique can save a lot of program space.

Try the example below:

```
GOSUB  Hello
DEBUG "How are you?"
END

Hello:
 DEBUG "Hello my friend.", CR
RETURN
```

The above code will start out by GOSUB'ing to the section of code beginning with the label *Hello*. It will print "Hello my friend." on the screen then RETURN to the line after the GOSUB... which prints "How are you?" and ENDs.

WATCH OUT FOR SUBROUTINES THAT YOUR PROGRAM CAN "FALL INTO."

There's another interesting lesson here; what would happen if we removed the END command from this example? Since the BASIC Stamp reads the code from left to right / top to bottom (like the English language) once it had returned to and run the "How are you?" line, it would naturally "fall into" the *Hello* routine again. Additionally, at the end of the *Hello* routine, it would see the RETURN again (although it didn't GOSUB to that routine this time) and because there wasn't a previous place to return to, the BASIC Stamp will start the entire program over again. This would cause an endless loop. The important thing to remember here is to always make sure your program doesn't allow itself to "fall into" a subroutine.

🔢1

NOTE: On the BS1, a RETURN without a GOSUB will return the program to the last GOSUB (or will end the program if no GOSUB was executed).

GOSUB LIMITATIONS.

Only a limited number of GOSUBs are allowed per program (as shown in Table 5.14), but they may be nested only four levels deep. In other words, the subroutine that's the destination of a GOSUB can contain a GOSUB to another subroutine, and so on, to a maximum depth (total number of GOSUBS before the first RETURN) of four. Any deeper, and the program will "forget" its way back to the starting point (the instruction following the very first GOSUB).

When GOSUBS are nested, each RETURN takes the program back to the instruction after the most-recent GOSUB. As is mentioned above, if the BASIC Stamp encounters a RETURN without a previous GOSUB, the entire program starts over from the beginning. Take care to avoid these phenomena.

[1] Demo Program (GOSUB.bas)

```
' This program is a guessing game that generates a random number in a subroutine called
' PickANumber. It is written to stop after three guesses. To see a common bug associated
' with GOSUB, delete or comment out the line beginning with STOP after the FOR/NEXT
' loop. This means that after the loop is finished, the program will wander into the
' PickANumber subroutine. When the RETURN at the end executes, the program will go back
' to the beginning of the program. This will cause the program to execute endlessly. Make
' sure that your programs can't accidentally execute subroutines!

'{$STAMP BS1}                                'STAMP directive (specifies a BS1)
SYMBOL    Rounds    = B2                      ' Number of reps.
SYMBOL    NumGen    = W0                      ' Random number holder (must be 16 bits).
SYMBOL    MyNum     = B3                      ' Random number, 1-10.

NumGen = 11500                               ' Initialize random "seed"

FOR Rounds = 1 TO 3                          ' Go three rounds.
  DEBUG CLS,"Pick a number from 1 to 10", CR
  GOSUB PickANumber                          ' Get a random number, 1-10.
  PAUSE 2000                                 ' Dramatic pause.
  DEBUG "My number was: ", #MyNum            ' Show the number.
  PAUSE 2000                                 ' Another pause.
NEXT
END                                          ' When done, stop execution here.

' Random-number subroutine. A subroutine is just a piece of code with the RETURN
' instruction at the end. Always make sure your program enters subroutines with a GOSUB.
' If you don't, the RETURN won't have the correct address, and your program will have a bug!
PickANumber:
  RANDOM NumGen                              ' Stir up the bits of NumGen.
  DEBUG NumGen
  MyNum = NumGen / 6550 MIN 1                ' Scale to fit 1-10 range.
RETURN                                       ' Go back to the 1st instruction
                                             ' after the GOSUB that got us here.
```

[2] [2e] [2sx] [2p] Demo Program (GOSUB.bs2)

NOTE: This is written for the BS2 but can be used for the BS2e, BS2sx and BS2p also. Locate the proper source code file or modify the STAMP directive before downloading to the BS2e, BS2sx or BS2p.

```
' This program is a guessing game that generates a random number in a subroutine called
' PickANumber. It is written to stop after three guesses. To see a common bug associated
' with GOSUB, delete or comment out the line beginning with STOP after the FOR/NEXT
' loop. This means that after the loop is finished, the program will wander into the
' PickANumber subroutine. When the RETURN at the end executes, the program will go back
' to the beginning of the program. This will cause the program to execute endlessly. Make
' sure that your programs can't accidentally execute subroutines!

'{$STAMP BS2}                                'STAMP directive (specifies a BS2)
Rounds    VAR    NIB                          ' Number of reps.
NumGen    VAR    WORD                         ' Random-number holder (must be 16 bits).
MyNum     VAR    NIB                          ' Random number, 1-10.
```

```
FOR Rounds = 1 TO 3                     ' Go three rounds.
  DEBUG CLS,"Pick a number from 1 to 10", CR
  GOSUB PickANumber                     ' Get a random number, 1-10.
  PAUSE 2000                            ' Dramatic pause.
  DEBUG "My number was: ", DEC MyNum    ' Show the number.
  PAUSE 2000                            ' Another pause.
NEXT
STOP                                    ' When done, stop execution here.


' Random-number subroutine. A subroutine is just a piece of code with the RETURN
' instruction at the end. Always make sure your program enters subroutines with a GOSUB.
' If you don't, the RETURN won't have the correct address, and your program will have a bug!
PickANumber:
  RANDOM NumGen                         ' Stir up the bits of NumGen.
  MyNum = NumGen / 6550 MIN 1           ' Scale to fit 1-10 range.
RETURN                                  ' Go back to the 1st instruction
                                        ' after the GOSUB that got us here.
```

GOTO

| BS1 | BS2 | BS2e | BS2sx | BS2p |

GOTO *Address*

Function

Go to the point in the program specified by *Address*.
- **Address** is a label that specifies where to go.

Quick Facts

Table 5.15: GOTO Quick Facts.

	BS1, BS2, BS2e, BS2sx and BS2p
Max. GOTOs per program	Unlimited, but good programming practices suggest using the least amount possible.

Explanation

The GOTO command makes the BASIC Stamp execute the code that starts at the specified *Address* location. The BASIC Stamp reads PBASIC code from left to right / top to bottom, just like in the English language. The GOTO command forces the BASIC Stamp to jump to another section of code.

A common use for GOTO is to create endless loops; programs that repeat a group of instructions over and over. For example:

```
Loop:
 DEBUG "Hi", CR
GOTO Loop
```

The above code will print "Hi" on the screen, over and over again. The GOTO Loop line simply tells it to go back to the code that begins with the label *Loop*.

NOTE: This is written for the BS2 but can be used for the BS1, BS2e, BS2sx and BS2p also. Locate the proper source code file or modify the STAMP directive before downloading to the BS1, BS2e, BS2sx or BS2p.

Demo Program (GOTO.bs2)

```
' This program is not very practical, but demonstrates the use of GOTO to jump around
' the code. This code jumps between three different routines, each of which print
' something different on the screen. The routines are out of order for this example.

'{$STAMP BS2}                                'STAMP directive (specifies a BS2)

GOTO Routine1

Routine2:
 DEBUG "We're in routine #2",CR
 PAUSE 1000
```

```
GOTO Routine3

Routine1:
  DEBUG "We're in routine #1",CR
  PAUSE 1000
GOTO Routine2

Routine3:
  DEBUG "We're in routine #3",CR
  PAUSE 1000
GOTO Routine1
```

HIGH

BS1	BS2	BS2e	BS2sx	BS2p

HIGH *Pin*

NOTE: Expressions are not allowed as arguments on the BS1. The range of the *Pin* argument on the BS1 is 0 – 7.

Function
Make the specified pin output high.

- **Pin** is a variable/constant/expression (0 – 15) that specifies which I/O pin to set high. This pin will be placed into output mode.

Explanation
The HIGH command sets the specified pin to 1 (a +5 volt level) and then sets its mode to output. For example,

HIGH 6

does exactly the same thing as:

OUT6 = 1
DIR6 = 1

Using the HIGH command is faster, in this case.

Connect an LED and a resister as shown in Figure 5.5 for the demo program below.

Figure 5.5: Example LED Circuit.

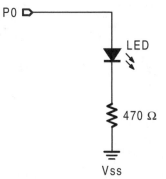

Demo Program (HIGH.bs2)

```
' This simple program sets I/O pin 0 high for 1/2 second and low for 1/2 second
' in an endless loop.
'{$STAMP BS2}                              'STAMP directive (specifies a BS2)

Loop:
  HIGH 0
  PAUSE 500
  LOW 0
  PAUSE 500
GOTO Loop
```

NOTE: This is written for the BS2 but can be used for the BS1, BS2e, BS2sx and BS2p also. Locate the proper source code file or modify the STAMP directive before downloading to the BS1, BS2e, BS2sx or BS2p.

I2CIN

I2CIN *Pin, SlaveID, Address {\LowAddress}, [InputData]*

Function

Receive data from a device using the I²C protocol.

- **Pin** is a variable/constant/expression (0 or 8) that specifies which I/O pins to use. I²C devices require two I/O pins to communicate. The *Pin* argument serves a double purpose; specifying the first pin (for connection to the chip's SDA pin) and, indirectly, the other required pin (for connection to the chip's SCL pin). See explanation below. Both I/O pins will be toggled between output and input mode during the I2CIN command and both will be set to input mode by the end of the I2CIN command.
- **SlaveID** is a variable/constant/expression (0 – 255) indicating the unique ID of the I²C chip.
- **Address** is a variable/constant/expression (0 – 255) indicating the desired address within the I²C chip to receive data from. The *Address* argument may be used with the optional *LowAddress* argument to indicate a word-sized address value.
- **LowAddress** is a variable/constant/expression (0 – 255) indicating the low-byte of the word-sized address within the I²C chip to receive data from. This argument must be used along with the *Address* argument.
- **InputData** is a list of variables and modifiers that tells I2CIN what to do with incoming data. I2CIN can store data in a variable or array, interpret numeric text (decimal, binary, or hex) and store the corresponding value in a variable, wait for a fixed or variable sequence of bytes, or ignore a specified number of bytes. These actions can be combined in any order in the *InputData* list.

Quick Facts

Table 5.16: I2CIN Quick Facts.

	BS2p
Values for *Pin*	0 or 8
I/O pin arrangement	When *Pin* is 0: 0: Serial Data (SDA) pin 1: Serial Clock (SCL) pin When *Pin* is 8: 8: Serial Data (SDA) pin 9: Serial Clock (SCL) pin
Transmission Rate	Approximately 81 kbits/sec (not including overhead).
Special notes	Both the SDA and SCL pins must have 4.7 KΩ pull-up resisters. The I2CIN command does not allow for multiple masters. The BASIC Stamp cannot operate as an I²C slave device.

I2CIN - BASIC Stamp Command Reference

Explanation

The I²C protocol is a form of synchronous serial communication developed by Phillips Semiconductors. It only requires two I/O pins and both pins can be shared between multiple I²C devices. The I2CIN command allows the BASIC Stamp to receive data from an I²C device.

The following is an example of the I2CIN command:

A SIMPLE I2CIN EXAMPLE.

```
Result    VAR   BYTE
I2CIN 0, $A1, 0, [Result]
```

This code will transmit a "read" command to an I²C device (connected to I/O pins 0 and 1) and then will receive one byte and store it in the variable *Result*. Though it may seem strange, the I2CIN command first transmits some data and then receives data. It must first transmit information (ID, read/write and address) in order to tell the I²C device what information it would like to receive. The exact information transmitted ($A1, 0) depends on the I²C device that is being used.

The above example will read a byte of data from location 0 of a 24LC16B EEPROM from Microchip. Figure 5.6 shows the proper wiring for this example to work. The *SlaveID* argument ($A1) is both the ID of the chip and the command to read from the chip; the 1 means read. The *Address* argument (0) is the EEPROM location to read from.

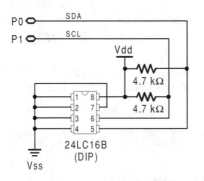

Figure 5.6: Example Circuit for the I2CIN command and a 24LC16B EEPROM. **Note: The 4.7 KΩ resisters are required for the I2CIN command to function properly.**

The I2CIN command's *InputData* argument is similar to the SERIN command's *InputData* argument. This means data can be received as ASCII character values, decimal, hexadecimal and binary translations and string data as in the examples below. (Assume the 24LC16B EEPROM is used and it has the string, "Value: 3A:101" stored, starting at location 0).

RECEIVING FORMATTED DATA.

```
Value           VAR   BYTE(13)
I2CIN  0, $A1, 0, [Value]              'receive the ASCII value for "V"
I2CIN  0, $A1, 0, [DEC  Value]         'receive the number 3.
I2CIN  0, $A1, 0, [HEX  Value]         'receive the number $3A.
I2CIN  0, $A1, 0, [BIN  Value]         'receive the number %101.
I2CIN  0, $A1, 0, [STR Value\13]       'receive the string "Value: 3A:101"
```

Tables 5.17 and 5.18 list all the available conversion formatters and special formatters available to the I2CIN command. See the SERIN command for additional information and examples of their use.

Table 5.17: I2CIN Conversion Formatters.

Conversion Formatter	Type of Number	Numeric Characters Accepted	Notes
DEC{1..5}	Decimal, optionally limited to 1 – 5 digits	0 through 9	1
SDEC{1..5}	Signed decimal, optionally limited to 1 – 5 digits	-, 0 through 9	1,2
HEX{1..4}	Hexadecimal, optionally limited to 1 – 4 digits	0 through 9, A through F	1,3
SHEX{1..4}	Signed hexadecimal, optionally limited to 1 – 4 digits	-, 0 through 9, A through F	1,2,3
IHEX{1..4}	Indicated hexadecimal, optionally limited to 1 – 4 digits	$, 0 through 9, A through F	1,3,4
ISHEX{1..4}	Signed, indicated hexadecimal, optionally limited to 1 – 4 digits	-, $, 0 through 9, A through F	1,2,3,4
BIN{1..16}	Binary, optionally limited to 1 – 16 digits	0, 1	1
SBIN{1..16}	Signed binary, optionally limited to 1 – 16 digits	-, 0, 1	1,2
IBIN{1..16}	Indicated binary, optionally limited to 1 – 16 digits	%, 0, 1	1,4
ISBIN{1..16}	Signed, indicated binary, optionally limited to 1 – 16 digits	-, %, 0, 1	1,2,4

1 All numeric conversions will continue to accept new data until receiving either the specified number of digits (ex: three digits for DEC3) or a non-numeric character.
2 To be recognized as part of a number, the minus sign (-) must immediately precede a numeric character. The minus sign character occurring in non-numeric text is ignored and any character (including a space) between a minus and a number causes the minus to be ignored.
3 The hexadecimal formatters are not case-sensitive; "a" through "f" means the same as "A" through "F".
4 Indicated hexadecimal and binary formatters ignore all characters, even valid numerics, until they receive the appropriate prefix ($ for hexadecimal, % for binary). The indicated formatters can differentiate between text and hexadecimal (ex: ABC would be interpreted by HEX as a number but IHEX would ignore it unless expressed as $ABC). Likewise, the binary version can distinguish the decimal number 10 from the binary number %10. A prefix occurring in non-numeric text is ignored, and any character (including a space) between a prefix and a number causes the prefix to be ignored. Indicated, signed formatters require that the minus sign come before the prefix, as in -$1B45.

Special Formatter	Action
STR *ByteArray* \L {\E}	Input a character string of length L into an array. If specified, an end character E causes the string input to end before reaching length L. Remaining bytes are filled with 0s (zeros).
WAITSTR *ByteArray* {\L}	Wait for a sequence of bytes matching a string stored in an array variable, optionally limited to L characters. If the optional L argument is left off, the end of the array-string must be marked by a byte containing a zero (0).
SKIP *Length*	Ignore *Length* bytes of characters.

Table 5.18: I2CIN Special Formatters.

The I²C protocol has a well-defined standard for the information passed at the start of each transmission. First of all, any information sent must be transmitted in units of 1 byte (8-bits). The first byte, we call the *SlaveID*, is an 8-bit pattern whose upper 7-bits contain the unique ID of the device you wish to communicate with. The lowest bit indicates whether this is a write operation (0) or a read operation (1). Figure 5.7 shows this format. THE I²C PROTOCOL FORMAT.

7	6	5	4	3	2	1	0
A_6	A_5	A_4	A_3	A_2	A_1	A_0	R/W

Figure 5.7: SlaveID Format.

The second byte, immediately following the *SlaveID*, is the *Address*. It indicates the 8-bit address (within the device) containing the data you would like to receive.

Some devices require more than 8 bits of address. For this case, the optional *LowAddress* argument can be used for the low-byte of the required address. When using the *LowAddress* argument, the *Address* argument is effectively the high-byte of the address value. For example, if the entire address value is 2050, use 8 for the *Address* argument and 2 for the *LowAddress* argument (8 * 256 + 2 = 2050). USING LONG ADDRESSES.

Following the last address byte is the first byte of data. This data byte may be transmitted or received by the BASIC Stamp. In the case of the I2CIN command, this data byte is transmitted by the device and received by the BASIC Stamp. Additionally, multiple data bytes can follow the address, depending on the I²C device. Note that every device has different limitations regarding how may contiguous bytes they can receive or transmit in one session. Be aware of these device limitations and program accordingly.

START AND STOP CONDITIONS AND ACKNOWLEDGMENTS.

Every I²C transmission session begins with a Start Condition and ends with a Stop Condition. Additionally, immediately after every byte is transmitted, an extra clock cycle is used to send or receive an acknowledgment signal (ACK). All of these operations are automatically taken care of by the I2CIN command so that you need not be concerned with them. The general I²C transmission format is shown in Figure 5.8.

Figure 5.8: I²C Transmission Format.

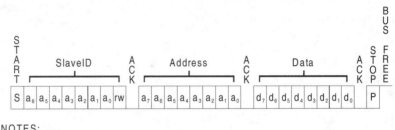

NOTES:
S = Start Condition
P = Stop Condition
a = id or address bit
d = data bit (transmitted by the BASIC Stamp or the I²C device)
ACK = Acknowledge signal. (Most acknowledge signals are generated by the I²C device)

SPECIAL NOTE ABOUT I2CIN INPLIMENTATION.

Since the I2CIN command is intended for input only, it actually overrides the "R/W" bit (bit 0) in the *SlaveID* argument. This is done so that it can use the I²C protocol's "Combined Format" for receiving data. Put simply, this means a command such as: I2CIN 0, $A1, 10, [Result] actually transmits $A0, then 10, then $A1 and then it reads the data back from the device. The $A0 means "write", the 10 is the address to write to and, finally, the $A1 indicates a change of direction; to "read" the location, instead. Even though the I2CIN command really doesn't care what the value of the *SlaveID*'s LSB is, it is suggested that you still set it appropriately for clarity.

Also note that the I2CIN command does not support multiple I²C masters and the BASIC Stamp cannot operate as an I²C slave device.

Demo Program (I2C.bsp)

```
' This program demonstrates writing and reading every location in the 24LC16B EEPROM
' using the BS2p's I2C commands. Connect the BS2p to the 24LC16B DIP EEPROM as
' shown in the diagram in the I2CIN or I2COUT command description.

'{$STAMP BS2p}                'STAMP directive (specifies a BS2p)
```

```
Idx          VAR    WORD                    'Index variable for address
Check        VAR    NIB                     'Index for checking returned values
Result       VAR    BYTE(16)                '16-byte array for returned value

WriteToEEPROM:
 DEBUG  "Writing...", CR
 PAUSE  2000
 FOR  Idx = 0  TO  2047  STEP  16           'For all 2K locations,
   I2COUT  0, $A0+((Idx>>8)*2), Idx, [REP  Idx>>4\16]  'Write 16 bytes at once
   PAUSE  5
   DEBUG  "Addr: ", DEC4  Idx, "-", DEC4  Idx+15, " Value: ", DEC3  Idx>>4 & $FF, CR
 NEXT
 PAUSE  2000

ReadFromEEPROM:
 DEBUG  CR, "Reading...", CR
 PAUSE  2000
 FOR  Idx = 0  TO  2047  STEP  16           'For all 2K locations,
   I2CIN  0, $A1+((Idx>>8)*2), Idx, [STR  Result\16]   'Read 16 bytes at once
   FOR  Check = 0  TO  15                   'Check all 16 for
    IF  Result(Check) <> Idx>>4 & $FF  THEN  Error  'accuracy, stop if error
   NEXT
   DEBUG  "Addr: ", DEC4  Idx, "-", DEC4  Idx+15, " Value: ", DEC3  Result, CR
 NEXT
 PAUSE  1000
 DEBUG  CR, "   All Locations PASSED!"
STOP

Error:
 DEBUG  "Error at location: ", DEC4  Idx+Check, CR
 DEBUG  "Found: ", DEC3  Result(Check), " Expected: ", DEC3  Idx>>4 & $FF
STOP
```

I2COUT

I2COUT *Pin, SlaveID, Address {\LowAddress}, [OutputData]*

Function

Send data to a device using the I²C protocol.

- **Pin** is a variable/constant/expression (0 or 8) that specifies which I/O pins to use. I²C devices require two I/O pins to communicate. The *Pin* argument serves a double purpose; specifying the first pin (for connection to the chip's SDA pin) and, indirectly, the other required pin (for connection to the chip's SCL pin). See explanation below. Both I/O pins will be toggled between output and input mode during the I2COUT command and both will be set to input mode by the end of the I2COUT command.
- **SlaveID** is a variable/constant/expression (0 – 255) indicating the unique ID of the I²C chip.
- **Address** is a variable/constant/expression (0 – 255) indicating the desired address within the I²C chip to send data to. The *Address* argument may be used with the optional *LowAddress* argument to indicate a word-sized address value.
- **LowAddress** is a variable/constant/expression (0 – 255) indicating the low-byte of the word-sized address within the I²C chip to receive data from. This argument must be used along with the *Address* argument.
- **OutputData** is a list of variables, constants, expressions and formatters that tells I2COUT how to format outgoing data. I2COUT can transmit individual or repeating bytes, convert values into decimal, hexadecimal or binary text representations, or transmit strings of bytes from variable arrays. These actions can be combined in any order in the *OutputData* list.

Quick Facts

Table 5.19: I2COUT Quick Facts.

	BS2p	
Values for *Pin*	0 or 8	
I/O pin arrangement	When *Pin* is 0: 0: Serial Data (SDA) pin 1: Serial Clock (SCL) pin	When *Pin* is 8: 8: Serial Data (SDA) pin 9: Serial Clock (SCL) pin
Transmission Rate	Approximately 81 kbits/sec (not including overhead).	
Special notes	Both the SDA and SCL pins must have 4.7 KΩ pull-up resisters. The I2COUT command does not allow for multiple masters. The BASIC Stamp cannot operate as an I²C slave device.	

Explanation

The I²C protocol is a form of synchronous serial communication developed by Phillips Semiconductors. It only requires two I/O pins and both pins can be shared between multiple I²C devices. The I2COUT command allows the BASIC Stamp to send data to an I²C device.

The following is an example of the I2COUT command:

A SIMPLE I2COUT EXAMPLE.

I2COUT 0, $A0, 5, [100]

This code will transmit a "write" command to an I²C device (connected to I/O pins 0 and 1), followed by an address of 5 and finally will transmit the number 100.

The above example will write a byte of data to location 5 of a 24LC16B EEPROM from Microchip. Figure 5.9 shows the proper wiring for this example to work. The *SlaveID* argument ($A0) is both the ID of the chip and the command to write to the chip; the 0 means write. The *Address* argument (5) is the EEPROM location to write to.

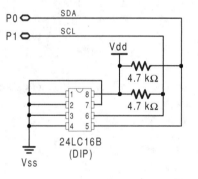

Figure 5.9: Example Circuit for the I2COUT command and a 24LC16B EEPROM. **Note: The 4.7 KΩ resisters are required for the I2COUT command to function properly.**

The I2COUT command's *OutputData* argument is similar to the DEBUG and SEROUT command's *OutputData* argument. This means data can be sent as literal text, ASCII character values, repetitive values, decimal, hexadecimal and binary translations and string data as in the examples below. (Assume the 24LC16B EEPROM is being used).

SENDING AND FORMATTING DATA.

```
Value        VAR    BYTE
Value = 65
I2COUT  0, $A0, 0, [Value]         'send the ASCII value for "A"
I2COUT  0, $A0, 0, [REP  Value\5]  'send the ASCII value for "A" five times, ie: "AAAAA"
I2COUT  0, $A0, 0, [DEC  Value]    'send two characters, "6" and "5"
I2COUT  0, $A0, 0, [HEX  Value]    'send two characters, "4" and "1"
I2COUT  0, $A0, 0, [BIN  Value]    'send seven characters, "1000001"
```

Tables 5.20 and 5.21 list all the available conversion formatters and special formatters available to the I2COUT command. See the DEBUG and SEROUT commands for additional information and examples of their use.

Table 5.20: I2COUT Conversion Formatters.

Conversion Formatter	Type of Number	Notes
DEC{1..5}	Decimal, optionally fixed to 1 – 5 digits	1
SDEC{1..5}	Signed decimal, optionally fixed to 1 – 5 digits	1,2
HEX{1..4}	Hexadecimal, optionally fixed to 1 – 4 digits	1
SHEX{1..4}	Signed hexadecimal, optionally fixed to 1 – 4 digits	1,2
IHEX{1..4}	Indicated hexadecimal, optionally fixed to 1 – 4 digits ($ prefix)	1
ISHEX{1..4}	Signed, indicated hexadecimal, optionally fixed to 1 – 4 digits ($ prefix)	1,2
BIN{1..16}	Binary, optionally fixed to 1 – 16 digits	1
SBIN{1..16}	Signed binary, optionally fixed to 1 – 16 digits	1,2
IBIN{1..16}	Indicated binary, optionally fixed to 1 – 16 digits (% prefix)	1
ISBIN{1..16}	Signed, indicated binary, optionally fixed to 1 – 16 digits (% prefix)	1,2

1 Fixed-digit formatters like DEC4 will pad the number with leading 0s if necessary; ex: DEC4 65 sends 0065. If a number is larger than the specified number of digits, the leading digits will be dropped; ex: DEC4 56422 sends 6422.
2 Signed modifiers work under two's complement rules.

Table 5.21: I2COUT Special Formatters.

Special Formatter	Action
?	Displays "symbol = x' + carriage return; where x is a number. Default format is decimal, but may be combined with conversion formatters (ex: BIN ? x to display "x = binary_number").
ASC ?	Displays "symbol = 'x'" + carriage return; where x is an ASCII character.
STR ByteArray {\L}	Send character string from an array. The optional \L argument can be used to limit the output to L characters, otherwise, characters will be sent up to the first byte equal to 0 or the end of RAM space is reached.
REP Byte \L	Send a string consisting of Byte repeated L times (ex: REP "X"\10 sends "XXXXXXXXXX").

THE I²C PROTOCOL FORMAT.

The I²C protocol has a well-defined standard for the information passed at the start of each transmission. First of all, any information sent must be transmitted in units of 1 byte (8-bits). The first byte, we call the *SlaveID*, is an 8-bit pattern whose upper 7-bits contain the unique ID of the device you wish to communicate with. The lowest bit indicates whether this is a write operation (0) or a read operation (1). Figure 5.10 shows this format.

7	6	5	4	3	2	1	0
A_6	A_5	A_4	A_3	A_2	A_1	A_0	R/W

Figure 5.10: SlaveID Format.

The second byte, immediately following the *SlaveID*, is the *Address*. It indicates the 8-bit address (within the device) you would like to send data to.

Some devices require more than 8 bits of address. For this case, the optional *LowAddress* argument can be used for the low-byte of the required address. When using the *LowAddress* argument, the *Address* argument is effectively the high-byte of the address value. For example, if the entire address value is 2050, use 8 for the *Address* argument and 2 for the *LowAddress* argument (8 * 256 + 2 = 2050).

USING LONG ADDRESSES.

Following the last address byte is the first byte of data. This data byte may be transmitted or received by the BASIC Stamp. In the case of the I2COUT command, this data byte is transmitted by the BASIC Stamp and received by the device. Additionally, multiple data bytes can follow the address, depending on the I^2C device. Note that every device has different limitations regarding how may contiguous bytes they can receive or transmit in one session. Be aware of these device limitations and program accordingly.

START AND STOP CONDITIONS AND ACKNOWLEDGMENTS.

Every I²C transmission session begins with a Start Condition and ends with a Stop Condition. Additionally, immediately after every byte is transmitted, an extra clock cycle is used to send or receive an acknowledgment signal (ACK). All of these operations are automatically taken care of by the I2CIN command so that you need not be concerned with them. The general I²C transmission format is shown in Figure 5.11.

Figure 5.11: I²C Transmission Format.

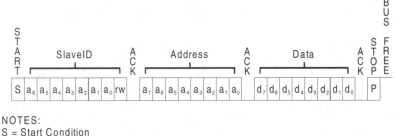

```
NOTES:
S = Start Condition
P = Stop Condition
a = id or address bit
d = data bit (transmitted by the BASIC Stamp or the I²C device)
ACK = Acknowledge signal. (Most acknowledge signals are generated by the I²C device)
```

SPECIAL NOTE ABOUT I2COUT INPLIMENTATION.

Since the I2COUT command is intended for output only, it actually overrides the "R/W" bit (bit 0) in the *SlaveID* argument. This is done to avoid device conflicts should the value be mistyped. Put simply, this means commands such as: I2COUT 0, $A0, 10, [0] and I2COUT 0, $A1, 10, [0] both transmit the same thing ($A0, then 10, then the data). Even though the I2COUT command really doesn't care what the value of the *SlaveID*'s LSB is, it is suggested that you still set it appropriately for clarity.

Also note that the I2COUT command does not support multiple I²C masters and the BASIC Stamp cannot operate as an I²C slave device.

Demo Program (I2C.bsp)

```
' This program demonstrates writing and reading every location in the 24LC16B EEPROM
' using the BS2p's I2C commands. Connect the BS2p to the 24LC16B DIP EEPROM as
' shown in the diagram in the I2CIN or I2COUT command description.

'{$STAMP BS2p}                    'STAMP directive (specifies a BS2p)

Idx        VAR    WORD            'Index variable for address
Check      VAR    NIB             'Index for checking returned values
Result     VAR    BYTE(16)        '16-byte array for returned value

WriteToEEPROM:
```

```
 DEBUG  "Writing...", CR
 PAUSE  2000
 FOR  Idx = 0  TO  2047  STEP  16                    'For all 2K locations,
   I2COUT  0, $A0+((Idx>>8)*2), Idx, [REP  Idx>>4\16]  'Write 16 bytes at once
   PAUSE  5
   DEBUG  "Addr: ", DEC4  Idx, "-", DEC4  Idx+15, " Value: ", DEC3  Idx>>4 & $FF, CR
 NEXT
 PAUSE  2000

ReadFromEEPROM:
 DEBUG  CR, "Reading...", CR
 PAUSE  2000
 FOR  Idx = 0  TO  2047  STEP  16                    'For all 2K locations,
   I2CIN  0, $A1+((Idx>>8)*2), Idx, [STR  Result\16]   'Read 16 bytes at once
   FOR  Check = 0  TO  15                            'Check all 16 for
     IF  Result(Check) <> Idx>>4 & $FF  THEN  Error  'accuracy, stop if error
   NEXT
   DEBUG  "Addr: ", DEC4  Idx, "-", DEC4  Idx+15, " Value: ", DEC3  Result, CR
 NEXT
 PAUSE  1000
 DEBUG  CR, "  All Locations PASSED!"
 STOP

Error:
 DEBUG  "Error at location: ", DEC4  Idx+Check, CR
 DEBUG  "Found: ", DEC3  Result(Check), " Expected: ", DEC3  Idx>>4 & $FF
 STOP
```

IF...THEN | BS1 | BS2 | BS2e | BS2sx | BS2p

⌦1 ⌦2 ⌦2e ⌦2sx ⌦2p **IF** *Condition* **THEN** *Address*

Function

Evaluate *Condition* and, if it is true, go to the point in the program marked by *Address*.

- **Condition** is a statement, such as "x = 7" that can be evaluated as true or false. The *Condition* can be a very simple or very complex relationship, as described below.

- **Address** is a label that specifies where to go in the event that *Condition* is true.

Quick Facts

Table 5.22: IF...THEN Quick Facts.

	BS1	BS2, BS2e, BS2sx and BS2p
Comparison operators	=, <>, >, <, >=, <=	=, <>, >, <, >=, <=
Conditional logic operators	AND, OR	NOT, AND, OR, XOR
Format of condition	Variable Comparison Value ;where Value is a variable or constant	Value1 Comparison Value2 ;where Value1 and Value2 can by any of variable, constant or expression
Parentheses	Not Allowed	Allowed

Explanation

IF...THEN is PBASIC's decision maker. It tests a condition and, if that condition is true, goes to a point in the program specified by an address label. The condition that IF...THEN tests is written as a mixture of comparison and logic operators. The available comparison operators are:

Table 5.23: IF...THEN Comparison Operators.

Comparison Operator Symbol	Definition
=	Equal
<>	Not Equal
>	Greater Than
<	Less Than
>=	Greater Than or Equal To
<=	Less Than or Equal To

NOTE: On the BS1, expressions are not allowed as arguments. Also, the Value1 (to the left of comparison) must be a variable.

Comparisons are always written in the form: Value1 Comparison Value2. The values to be compared can be any combination of variables (any size), constants, or expressions. The following example is an IF...THEN command with a simple condition:

```
IF 10 < 200 THEN Loop
```

A SIMPLE FORM OF IF...THEN

This code will compare the number 10 to the number 200. If 10 is less than 200, the condition is true. In this case, 10 is less than 200 (and always will be), so the program will jump (or GOTO) the label called *Loop*. Of course, this is a silly example (10 is always less than 200 so this line will always cause a jump to *Loop*). Most of the time, you'll use at least one variable in your condition:

```
Value        VAR    WORD
Loop:
 PULSIN 0, Value
 DEBUG DEC Value, CR
 IF Value < 4000 THEN Loop
 DEBUG "Value was greater than 4000!"
```

NOTE: For BS1's, change line 1 to
SYMBOL Value = W0
and line 4 to
DEBUG #Value, CR

Here, the BASIC Stamp will look for and measure a pulse on I/O pin 0, then compare the result, *Value*, against 4000. If *Value* is less than (<) 4000, it will jump back to *Loop*. Each time through the loop, it displays the measured value and once it is greater than or equal to 4000, it displays, "Value was greater than 4000!"

On the BS2, BS2e, BS2sx and BS2p, the values can be expressions as well. This leads to very flexible and sophisticated comparisons. The IF...THEN statement below is functionally the same as the one in the program above:

```
IF Value < 45 * 100 – ( 25 * 20 ) THEN Loop
```

Here the BASIC Stamp evaluates the expression: 45 * 100 = 4500, 25 * 20 = 500, and 4500 – 500 = 4000. Then the BAISC Stamp performs the comparison: is Value < 4000? Another example that is functionally the same:

```
IF Value / 100 < 40 THEN Loop
```

It's important to realize that all comparisons are performed using unsigned, 16-bit math. This can lead to strange results if you mix signed and unsigned numbers in IF...THEN conditions. Watch what happens here when we include a signed number (–99):

WATCH OUT FOR UNSIGNED MATH COMPARISON ERRORS

```
IF  -99  <  100  THEN  IsLess
DEBUG  "Greater than or equal to 100"
END

IsLess:
DEBUG  "Less than 100"
END
```

Although –99 is obviously less than 100, the program will say it is greater. The problem is that –99 is internally represented as the two's complement value 65437, which (using unsigned math) is greater than 100. This phenomena will occur whether or not the negative value is a constant, variable or expression.

LOGICAL OPERATORS (NOT, AND, OR AND XOR).

IF...THEN supports the conditional logic operators NOT, AND, OR, and XOR. See Table 5.24 for a list of the operators and their effects.

NOTE: The NOT operator is not available on the BS1.

The NOT operator inverts the outcome of a condition, changing false to true, and true to false. The following IF...THENs are equivalent:

```
IF  x  <>  100  THEN  NotEqual          ' Goto NotEqual if x is not 100.
IF  NOT  x = 100  THEN  NotEqual        ' Goto NotEqual if x is not 100.
```

NOTE: The XOR operator is not available on the BS1.

The operators AND, OR, and XOR can be used to join the results of two conditions to produce a single true/false result. AND and OR work the same as they do in everyday speech. Run the example below once with AND (as shown) and again, substituting OR for AND:

NOTE: For BS1's, change line 1 and 2 to:
SYMBOL Value1 = B0
SYMBOL Value2 = B1

```
Value1      VAR    BYTE
Value2      VAR    BYTE
Value1  =  5
Value2  =  9
IF Value1 = 5 AND Value2 = 10 THEN  True  ' Change AND to OR and see
DEBUG  "Statement was false."            ' what happens.
END

True:
DEBUG "Statement was true."
```

The condition "Value1 = 5 AND Value2 = 10" is not true. Although *Value1* is 5, *Value2* is not 10. The AND operator works just as it does in English; both conditions must be true for the statement to be true. The OR operator also works in a familiar way; if one or the other or both conditions are true, then the statement is true. The XOR operator (short for exclusive-OR) may not be familiar, but it does have an English

NOTE: The XOR operator is not available on the BS1.

counterpart: If one condition or the other (but not both) is true, then the statement is true.

Table 5.24 below summarizes the effects of the conditional logic operators. As with math, you can alter the order in which comparisons and logical operations are performed by using parentheses. Operations are normally evaluated left-to-right. Putting parentheses around an operation forces PBASIC2 to evaluate it before operations not in parentheses.

NOTE: On the BS1, parentheses are not allowed within arguments.

Condition A	NOT A
False	True
True	False

Table 5.24: Conditional Logic Operator's Truth-Table.

NOTE: The NOT operator is not available on the BS1.

Condition A	Condition B	A AND B
False	False	False
False	True	False
True	False	False
True	True	True

Condition A	Condition B	A OR B
False	False	True
False	True	True
True	False	True
True	True	False

Condition A	Condition B	A XOR B
False	False	False
False	True	True
True	False	True
True	True	False

NOTE: The XOR operator is not available on the BS1.

Unlike the IF...THEN commands in other BASIC's, PBASIC's IF...THEN can only go to a label as the result of a decision. It cannot conditionally perform some instruction, as in "IF x < 20 THEN y = y + 1." To achieve this in PBASIC, you have to invert the logic using NOT and skip over the conditional instruction unless the condition is met:

IF...THEN CAN ONLY JUMP TO A LABEL IF THE CONDITION IS TRUE.

```
IF NOT x < 20 THEN NoInc      ' Don't increment y unless x < 20.
  y = y + 1                   ' Increment y if x < 20.
NoInc:                        ' Program continues.
```

You can also code a conditional GOSUB, as in "IF x = 100 THEN GOSUB Centennial." In PBASIC:

MAKING A CONDITIONAL GOSUB.

```
IF NOT x = 100 then NoCent
  GOSUB Centennial                          ' IF x = 100 THEN GOSUB Centennial.
NoCent:                                      ' Program continues.
```

INTERNAL REPRESENTATION OF BOOLEAN VALUES (TRUE VS. FALSE).

Internally, the BASIC Stamp defines "false" as 0 and "true" as any value other than 0. Consider the following instructions:

```
Flag          VAR   BIT
Flag = 1

IF  Flag  THEN  IsTrue
DEBUG  "false"
END

IsTrue:
DEBUG  "true"
END
```

Since *Flag* is 1, IF...THEN would evaluate it as true and print the message "true" on the screen. Suppose you changed the IF...THEN command to read "IF NOT Flag THEN IsTrue." That would also evaluate as true. Whoa! Isn't NOT 1 the same thing as 0? No, at least not in the 16-bit world of the BASIC Stamp.

Internally, the BASIC Stamp sees a bit variable containing 1 as the 16-bit number %0000000000000001. So it sees the NOT of that as %1111111111111110. Since any non-zero number is regarded as true, NOT 1 is true. Strange but true.

AVOIDING ERRORS WITH BOOLEAN RESULTS.

The easiest way to avoid the kinds of problems this might cause is to always use a conditional operator with IF...THEN. Change the example above to read IF Flag = 1 THEN IsTrue. The result of the comparison will follow IF...THEN rules. Also, the logical operators will work as they should; IF NOT Flag = 1 THEN IsTrue will correctly evaluate to false when *Flag* contains 1.

This also means that you should only use the "named" conditional logic operators NOT, AND, OR, and XOR with IF...THEN. The conditional logic operators format their results correctly for IF...THEN instructions. The other logical operators, represented by symbols ~ & | and ^ do not; they are binary logic operators.

Demo Program (IFTHEN.bas)

```
' The program below generates a series of 16-bit random numbers and tests each to
' determine whether they're evenly divisible by 3. If a number is evenly divisible
' by 3, then it is printed, otherwise, the program generates another random number.
' The program counts how many numbers it prints, and quits when this number reaches 10.

'{$STAMP BS1}                            'STAMP directive (specifies a BS1)

SYMBOL    Sample    =    W0              ' Random number to be tested.
SYMBOL    Samps     =    B2              ' Number of samples taken.
SYMBOL    Temp      =    B3              ' Temporary workspace

Sample = 11500
Mul3:
  RANDOM Sample                          ' Put a random number into sample.
  Temp = Sample // 3
  IF Temp <> 0 THEN Mul3                 ' Not multiple of 3? Try again.
    DEBUG #Sample," is divisible by 3.", CR   ' Print message.
    Samps = Samps + 1                    ' Count multiples of 3.
    IF Samps = 10 THEN DONE              ' Quit with 10 samples.
GOTO Mul3

Done:
DEBUG CR, "All done."
END
```

Demo Program (IFTHEN.bs2)

NOTE: This is written for the BS2 but can be used for the BS2e, BS2sx and BS2p also. Locate the proper source code file or modify the STAMP directive before downloading to the BS2e, BS2sx or BS2p.

```
' The program below generates a series of 16-bit random numbers and tests each to
' determine whether they're evenly divisible by 3. If a number is evenly divisible
' by 3, then it is printed, otherwise, the program generates another random number.
' The program counts how many numbers it prints, and quits when this number reaches 10.

'{$STAMP BS2}                            'STAMP directive (specifies a BS2)

Sample    VAR    WORD                    ' Random number to be tested.
Samps     VAR    NIB                     ' Number of samples taken.

Mul3:
  RANDOM Sample                          ' Put a random number into sample.
  IF NOT Sample // 3 = 0 THEN Mul3       ' Not multiple of 3? Try again.
    DEBUG DEC Sample," is divisible by 3.",CR   ' Print message.
    Samps = Samps + 1                    ' Count multiples of 3.
    IF Samps = 10 THEN DONE              ' Quit with 10 samples.
GOTO Mul3

Done:
DEBUG CR,"All done."
STOP
```

INPUT

BS1	BS2	BS2e	BS2sx	BS2p

INPUT *Pin*

Function

Make the specified pin an input.

- **Pin** is a variable/constant/expression (0 – 15) that specifies which I/O pin to set to input mode.

NOTE: Expressions are not allowed as arguments on the BS1. The range of the *Pin* argument on the BS1 is 0 – 7.

Explanation

There are several ways to make a pin an input. When a program begins, all of the BASIC Stamp's pins are inputs. Commands that rely on input pins, like PULSIN and SERIN, automatically change the specified pin to input. Writing 0s to particular bits of the variable DIRS makes the corresponding pins inputs. And then there's the INPUT command.

When a pin is an input, your program can check its state by reading the corresponding INS variable (PINS on the BS1). For example:

```
INPUT 4
Hold:
 IF  IN4  =  0  THEN  Hold                   ' Stay here until P4 is 1.
```

The code above will read the state of P4 as set by external circuitry. If nothing is connected to P4, it will alternate between states (1 or 0) apparently at random.

What happens if your program writes to the OUTS bit (PINS bit on the BS1) of a pin that is set up as an input? The value is stored in OUTS (PINS on the BS1), but has no effect on the outside world. If the pin is changed to output, the last value written to the corresponding OUTS bit (or PINS bit on the BS1) will appear on the pin. The demo program shows how this works.

Demo Program (INPUT.bas)

```
' This program demonstrates how the input/output direction of a pin is determined by
' the corresponding bit of DIRS. It also shows that the state of the pin itself (as
' reflected by the corresponding bit of PINS) is determined by the outside world when
' the pin is an input, and by the corresponding bit of PINS when it's an output. To
' set up the demo, connect a 10k resistor from +5V to P7 on the BASIC Stamp. The
' resistor to +5V puts a high (1) on the pin when it's an input. The BASIC Stamp can
' override this state by writing a low (0) to bit 7 of OUTS and changing the pin to output.
```

```
'{$STAMP  BS1}                          'STAMP directive (specifies a BS1)

INPUT 7                                 ' Make I/O pin 7 an input.
DEBUG "State of pin 7: ", #PIN7, CR

PIN7 = 0                                ' Write 0 to output latch.
DEBUG "After 0 written to OUT7: ", #PIN7, CR

OUTPUT 7                                ' Make I/O pin 7 an output.
DEBUG "After pin 7 changed to output: ", #PIN7
```

Demo Program (INPUT.bs2)

```
' This program demonstrates how the input/output direction of a pin is determined by
' the corresponding bit of DIRS. It also shows that the state of the pin itself (as
' reflected by the corresponding bit of INS) is determined by the outside world when
' the pin is an input, and by the corresponding bit of OUTS when it's an output. To
' set up the demo, connect a 10k resistor from +5V to P7 on the BASIC Stamp. The
' resistor to +5V puts a high (1) on the pin when it's an input. The BASIC Stamp can
' override this state by writing a low (0) to bit 7 of OUTS and changing the pin to output.

'{$STAMP  BS2}                          'STAMP directive (specifies a BS2)

INPUT 7                                 ' Make I/O pin 7 an input.
DEBUG "State of pin 7: ", BIN IN7, CR

OUT7 = 0                                ' Write 0 to output latch.
DEBUG "After 0 written to OUT7: ", BIN IN7, CR

OUTPUT 7                                ' Make I/O pin 7 an output.
DEBUG "After pin 7 changed to output: ", BIN IN7
```

NOTE: This is written for the BS2 but can be used for the BS2e, BS2sx and BS2p also. Locate the proper source code file or modify the STAMP directive before downloading to the BS2e, BS2sx or BS2p.

IOTERM

| BS1 | BS2 | BS2e | BS2sx | **BS2p** |

IOTERM *Port*

Function

Switch control to main I/O pins or auxiliary I/O pins (on the BS2p40 only) depending on state of *Port*.

- **Port** is a variable/constant/expression (0 – 1) that specifies which I/O port to use.

Quick Facts

Table 5.25: IOTERM Quick Facts.

	BS2p
Values for *Port*	0 = switch to main I/O group, 1 = switch to auxiliary I/O group.
I/O pin IDs	0 – 15 (after IOTERM command, all references affect physical pins 5 – 20 or 21 – 36 depending on state of *Port*).
Special notes	Both the BS2p24 and the BS2p40 accept this command, however, only the BS2p40 gives access to the auxiliary I/O pins.

Explanation

The BS2p is available in two module styles, 1) a 24-pin module (called the BS2p24) that is pin compatible with the BS2, BS2e and BS2sx and 2) a 40-pin module (called the BS2p40) that has an additional 16 I/O pins (for a total of 32). The BS2p40's I/O pins are organized into two groups, called main and auxiliary. The I/O pins in each group can be accessed in the same manner (by referencing I/O pins 0 – 15) but access is only possible within one group at a time. The IOTERM command causes the BASIC Stamp to affect either the main or auxiliary I/O pins in all further code until the MAINIO, AUXIO or another IOTERM command is reached, or the BASIC Stamp is reset or power-cycled. The value of *Port* determines which group of I/O pins will be referenced. Using 0 for *Port* will switch to the main I/O group and using 1 for *Port* will switch to the auxiliary group.

A SIMPLE IOTERM EXAMPLE.

The following example illustrates this:

```
HIGH  0
IOTERM  1
LOW  0
```

The first line of the above example will set I/O pin 0 of the main I/O pins (physical pin 5) high. Afterward, the IOTERM command tells the BASIC Stamp that all commands following it should affect the auxiliary I/O pins (*Port = 1*). The following LOW command will set I/O pin 0 of the auxiliary I/O pins (physical pin 21) low.

Note that the main I/O and auxiliary I/O pins are independent of each other; the states of the main I/O pins remain unchanged while the program affects the auxiliary I/O pins, and vice versa.

MAIN I/O AND AUXILIARY I/O PINS ARE INDEPENDENT AND UNAFFECTED BY CHANGES IN THE OPPOSITE GROUP.

Other commands that affect I/O group access are AUXIO and MAINIO.

Demo Program (AUX_MAIN_TERM.bsp)

```
' This program demonstrates the use of the AUXIO, MAINIO and IOTERM commands to
' affect I/O pins in the auxiliary and main I/O groups.

'{$STAMP BS2p}                              'STAMP directive (specifies a BS2p)

Port VAR    BIT

Loop:
  MAINIO                    'Switch to main I/O pins
  TOGGLE 0                  'Toggle state of I/O pin 0 (physical pin 5)
  PWM 1, 100, 40            'Generate PWM on I/O pin 1 (physical pin 6)

  AUXIO                     'Switch to auxiliary I/O pins
  TOGGLE 0                  'Toggle state of I/O pin 0 (physical pin 21)
  PULSOUT 1, 1000           'Generate a pulse on I/O pin 1 (physical pin 22)
  PWM 2, 100, 40            'Generate PWM on I/O pin 2 (physical pin 23)

  IOTERM Port               'Switch to main or aux I/Os (depending on Port)
  TOGGLE 3                  'Toggle state of I/O pin 3 (on main and aux, alternately)
  Port = ~Port              'Invert port (switch between 0 and 1)
  PAUSE 1000
GOTO Loop
```

NOTE: This is written for the BS2p but its effects can only be seen on the 40-pin version: the BS2p40.

LCDCMD

LCDCMD *Pin, Command*

Function

Send a command to an LCD display.

- **Pin** is a variable/constant/expression (0 – 1 or 8 – 9) that specifies which I/O pins to use. The LCD requires, at most, seven I/O pins to operate. The *Pin* argument serves a double purpose; specifying the first pin and, indirectly, the group of other required pins. See explanation below. All I/O pins will be set to output mode.
- **Command** is a variable/constant/expression (0 – 255) indicating the LCD command to send.

Quick Facts

Table 5.26: LCDCMD Quick Facts.

	BS2p
Values for *Pin*	0, 1, 8 or 9
I/O pin arrangement when *Pin* is 0 or 1	0 or 1 (depending on pin): LCD Enable (E) pin 2: LCD Read/Write (R/W) pin 3: LCD Register Select (RS) pin 4 – 7: LCD Data Buss (DB4 – DB7, respectively) pins
I/O pin arrangement when *Pin* is 8 or 9	8 or 9 (depending on pin): LCD Enable (E) pin 10: LCD Read/Write (R/W) pin 11: LCD Register Select (RS) pin 12 – 15: LCD Data Buss (DB4 – DB7, respectively) pins

Explanation

The three LCD commands (LCDCMD, LCDIN and LCDOUT) allow the BS2p to interface directly to standard LCD displays that feature a Hitachi 44780 controller (part #HD44780A). This includes many 1 x 16, 2 x 16 and 4 x 20 character LCD displays.

The Hitachi 44780 LCD controller supports a number of special instructions for initializing the display, moving the cursor, changing the default layout, etc. The LCDCMD command is used to send one of these instructions to the LCD. It is most commonly used to initialize the display upon a power-up or reset condition.

A SIMPLE LCDCMD EXAMPLE.

The following is an example of the LCDCMD command:

```
LCDCMD  1, 24
```

The above code will send the Scroll Left command (represented by the number 24) to the LCD whose enable pin is connected to I/O pin 1. This will cause the LCD display to scroll, or shift, the entire display one character to the left.

You may have noticed that the *Pin* argument in the example above was 1. The LCDCMD command actually uses more than just this I/O pin, however. The LCDCMD command requires seven I/O pins. This is because the standard LCD displays have a parallel interface, rather than a serial one. The *Pin* argument can be the numbers 0, 1, 8 or 9 and will result in the use of the I/O pins shown in Table 5.26. Figure 5.12 shows the required wiring for the above command to work.

WIRING THE BASIC STAMP TO AN LCD.

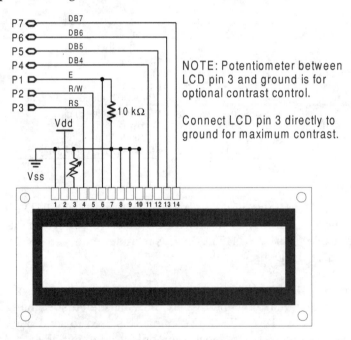

NOTE: Potentiometer between LCD pin 3 and ground is for optional contrast control.

Connect LCD pin 3 directly to ground for maximum contrast.

Figure 5.12: Example LCD Circuit. Shown with all connections necessary for the LCDCMD, LCDIN and LCDOUT commands.

Note that we could have used 0 for the *Pin* argument and moved the LCD's Enable pin (pin 6) to I/O pin 0. Similarly, using 9 for the *Pin* argument would have required us to wire the LCD's pins to I/O pins 9 through 15, rather than I/O pins 1 through 7.

When the LCD is first powered-up, it will be in an unknown state and must be properly configured before sending commands like the one

INITIALIZING THE LCD; THE MOST IMPORTANT STEP!

shown above. This process is known as initializing the LCD and is the first thing your program should do upon starting up. The following code is a good example of LCD initialization.

```
InitLCD:                    'LCD's usually take more than 500 µs to power-up.  This pause is
  PAUSE  1000               'to keep the BASIC Stamp from talking to the LCD too early.
  LCDCMD 1, 48              'Send wakeup sequence to LCD (three Wake-Up (48) commands)
  PAUSE 10                  'This pause is necessary to meet the LCD specs
  LCDCMD 1, 48
  PAUSE 1                   'This pause is necessary to meet the LCD specs
  LCDCMD 1, 48
  PAUSE 1                   'This pause is necessary to meet the LCD specs
  LCDCMD 1, 32             'Set data bus to 4-bit mode
  LCDCMD 1, 40             'Set to 2-line mode with 5x8 font
  LCDCMD 1, 8              'Turn display off
  LCDCMD 1, 12            'Turn display on without cursor
  LCDCMD 1, 6              'Set to auto-increment cursor (no display shift)
  LCDCMD 1, 1              'Clear the display
```

This initialization code is the most commonly used sequence for a 2 x 16 and 4 x 20 LCD display (the 2-line mode instruction sets the 4 x 20 to 4-line mode). The PAUSE 1000 command is optional, but only if your program takes more than approximately 700 ms before it executes the InitLCD code above. Without it, upon powering your circuit, the BASIC Stamp may talk to the LCD too early, the LCD will then miss some of the commands and the display will operate strangely, or not at all.

Do not change the "wake-up" and "4-bit mode" sequence commands. However, the commands below the line that says, "Set data bus to 4-bit mode" may be modified to set other desired modes.

COMMON LCD COMMANDS.

Table 5.27 shows the most commonly used LCD commands. Here's an example:

LCDCMD 1, 16

This will make the LCD's cursor move left by one character (16 is the Cursor Left command), even if the cursor is not visible. The next character printed on the display (with the LCDOUT command) will appear at the current cursor's location. Here's another example:

LCDCMD 1, 128 + 64

The above command will move the cursor to the first character position on the second line (on a 2 x 16 display). 128 is the Move To Display Address

LCDCMD - BASIC Stamp Command Reference

command and 64 is the location number. See the "Character Positioning" section, below, for more information.

	Command (in decimal)	Description
Do Nothing	0	Don't perform any special operation.
Clear Display	1	Clear the display and move cursor to home position.
Home Display	2	Move cursor and display to home position.
Inc Cursor	6	Set cursor direction to right, without a display shift.
Display Off	8	Turn off display (display data is retained).
Display On	12	Turn on display without cursor (display is restored).
Blinking Cursor	13	Turn on display with blinking cursor.
Underline Cursor	14	Turn on display with underline cursor.
Cursor Left	16	Move cursor left one character.
Cursor Right	20	Move cursor right one character.
Scroll Left	24	Scroll display left one character.
Scroll Right	28	Scroll display right one character.
Move To CRAM Address	64 + address	Move pointer to character RAM location
Move To DRAM Address	128 + address	Move cursor to display RAM location

Table 5.27: Common LCD Commands. These are supported by LCDs with the Hitachi 44780 controller.

While most users will only need the commands shown in Table 5.27, above, Table 5.28, below, details all of the instructions supported by the LCD (for advanced users). Many instructions are multipurpose, depending on the state of special bits. Cleaver manipulation of the instruction bits will allow for powerful control of the LCD.

A NOTE ABOUT ADVANCED LCD COMMANDS.

The last command shown above (Move To DRAM Address) is used to move the cursor to a specific position on the LCD. The LCD's DRAM (Display RAM) is a fixed size with unique position number for each character cell. The viewable portion of the DRAM depends on the LCD's logical view position (which can be altered with the Scroll Display command). The default view position is called the Home position; it means that the display's upper left character corresponds to DRAM location 0. Figure 5.13 indicates the position numbers for characters on the LCD screen.

CHARACTER POSITIONING: MOVING THE CURSOR.

Note that Figure 5.13 shows the most common DRAM mapping, though some LCD's may have organized the DRAM differently. A little experimentation with your LCD may reveal this.

Table 5.28: All LCD Commands (for advanced users). These are supported by LCDs with the Hitachi 44780 controller.

	Command Code (in binary)								Description
	7	6	5	4	3	2	1	0	
Clear Display	0	0	0	0	0	0	0	1	Clear entire display and move cursor home (address 0).
Home Display	0	0	0	0	0	0	1	0	Move cursor home and return display to home position.
Entry Mode	0	0	0	0	0	1	M	S	Sets cursor direction (M: 0=left, 1=right) and display scrolling (S: 0=no scroll, 1=scroll)
Display/Cursor	0	0	0	0	1	D	U	B	Sets display on/off (D), underline cursor (U) and blinking block cursor (B). (0=off, 1=on)
Scroll Display / Shift Cursor	0	0	0	1	C	M	0	0	Shifts display or cursor (C: 0=cursor, 1=display) left or right (M: 0=left, 1=right).
Function Set	0	0	1	B	L	F	0	0	Sets buss size (B: 0=4-bits, 1=8-bits), number of lines (L: 0=1-line, 1=2-lines) and font size (F: 0=5x8, 1=5x10)
Move To CRAM Address	0	1	A	A	A	A	A	A	Move pointer to character RAM location specified by address (A)
Move To DRAM Address	1	A	A	A	A	A	A	A	Move cursor to display RAM location specified by address (A)

On a standard 2 x 16 character display, the following command would move the cursor to the third column of the second line:

LCDCMD 1, 128 + 66

Figure 5.13: LCD Character Positions. NOTE: Many 1 x 16 displays conform to the position numbers shown on Line 1 of the 2 x 16 display.

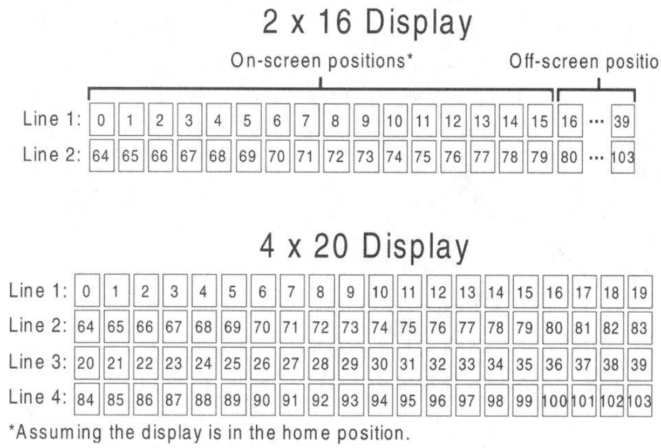

2 x 16 Display

On-screen positions*   Off-screen positions*

Line 1: | 0 | 1 | 2 | 3 | 4 | 5 | 6 | 7 | 8 | 9 | 10 | 11 | 12 | 13 | 14 | 15 | 16 | ... | 39 |

Line 2: | 64 | 65 | 66 | 67 | 68 | 69 | 70 | 71 | 72 | 73 | 74 | 75 | 76 | 77 | 78 | 79 | 80 | ... | 103 |

4 x 20 Display

Line 1: | 0 | 1 | 2 | 3 | 4 | 5 | 6 | 7 | 8 | 9 | 10 | 11 | 12 | 13 | 14 | 15 | 16 | 17 | 18 | 19 |

Line 2: | 64 | 65 | 66 | 67 | 68 | 69 | 70 | 71 | 72 | 73 | 74 | 75 | 76 | 77 | 78 | 79 | 80 | 81 | 82 | 83 |

Line 3: | 20 | 21 | 22 | 23 | 24 | 25 | 26 | 27 | 28 | 29 | 30 | 31 | 32 | 33 | 34 | 35 | 36 | 37 | 38 | 39 |

Line 4: | 84 | 85 | 86 | 87 | 88 | 89 | 90 | 91 | 92 | 93 | 94 | 95 | 96 | 97 | 98 | 99 | 100 | 101 | 102 | 103 |

*Assuming the display is in the home position.

The number 128 tells the LCD we wish to move the cursor and 66 is the location number of the desired position. Similarly, sending just 128 (128 + 0) would move the cursor to the first character of the first line (the upper left character if the display is at the home position).

You may have noticed that the 2 x 16 display has many locations that are not visible; they are to the right of the edge of the screen. These locations (16 – 39 and 80 to 103) become important for scrolling operations. For example, it is possible to move the cursor to location 16, print some text there and then issue a number of Scroll Left instructions (LCDCMD 1, 24) to slowly scroll the text onto the display from right to left. If you did so, the DRAM positions that were on the left of the screen would now be past the left edge of the screen. For example,

SCROLLING THE DISPLAY.

```
LCDCMD 1, 24
LCDCMD 1, 24
```

would cause the screen to scroll to the left by two characters. At this point, the upper-left character in the display would actually be DRAM location 2 and the lower-left character would be DRAM location 66. Locations 0, 1, 64 and 65 would be off the left edge of the LCD and would no longer be visible. Some interesting effects can be achieved by taking advantage of this feature.

The 4 x 20 LCD has a strange DRAM map. The upper-right character is location 19 and the next location, 20, appears as the first character of the third line. This strange mapping is due to constraints in the LCD controller and the manufacturers design, and unfortunately makes the scrolling features virtually useless on the 4 x 20 displays.

NOTES ON DRAM MAPPING FOR 4 X 20 LCDs.

Even though the LCD requires many pins to talk to it, only the Enable pin needs to remain dedicated to the LCD and all the other pins can be multiplexed (shared) with certain other devices (if wired carefully). In addition, the I/O pin connected to the LCD's R/W pin is only necessary if the LCDIN command will be used in the application. If the LCDIN command will not be used, LCD pin 5 (R/W pin) can be connected to ground and I/O pin 2 (shown above) may be left disconnected. I/O pin 2 will still be set to output mode for each LCDCMD and LCDOUT command executed, however.

DETAILS ON LCD WIRING.

Demo Program (LCDINIT.bsp)

```
' This program demonstrates initialization and printing on a 2 x 16 character LCD display.
' The set of "LCD constants", below, are provided as pre-defined and useful LCD commands,
' though only a few are actually used in this program.

'{$STAMP BS2p}                          'STAMP directive (specifies a BS2p)

'-----Define LCD constants-----
WakeUp            CON  %00110000  'Wake-up
FourBitMode       CON  %00100000  'Set to 4-bit mode
OneLine5x8Font    CON  %00100000  'Set to 1 display line, 5x8 font
OneLine5x10Font   CON  %00100100  'Set to 1 display line, 5x10 font
TwoLine5x8Font    CON  %00101000  'Set to 2 display lines, 5x8 font
TwoLine5x10Font   CON  %00101100  'Set to 2 display lines, 5x10 font
DisplayOff        CON  %00001000  'Turn off display, data is retained
DisplayOn         CON  %00001100  'Turn on display, no cursor
DisplayOnULCrsr   CON  %00001110  'Turn on display, with underline cursor
DisplayOnBLCrsr   CON  %00001101  'Turn on display, with blinking cursor
IncCrsr           CON  %00000110  'Auto-increment cursor, no display shift
IncCrsrShift      CON  %00000111  'Auto-increment cursor, shift display left
DecCrsr           CON  %00000100  'Auto-decrement cursor, no display shift
DecCrsrShift      CON  %00000101  'Auto-decrement cursor, shift display right
ClearDisplay      CON  %00000001  'Clear the display
HomeDisplay       CON  %00000010  'Move cursor and display to home position
ScrollLeft        CON  %00011000  'Scroll display to the left
ScrollRight       CON  %00011100  'Scroll display to the right
CrsrLeft          CON  %00010000  'Move cursor left
CrsrRight         CON  %00010100  'Move cursor right
MoveCrsr          CON  %10000000  'Move cursor to position (must add address)
MoveToCGRAM       CON  %01000000  'Move to CGRAM position (must add address)

'-----Main Routines-----

Init:
  PAUSE  1000
  GOSUB  InitLCD

Start:
  LCDOUT  1, ClearDisplay, ["Hello World!"]
  LCDOUT  1, MoveCrsr+64, ["How are you?"]
STOP

'-----Subroutines-----

InitLCD:
  LCDCMD  1, WakeUp           'Send wakeup sequence to LCD
  PAUSE  10                   'These pauses are necessary to meet the LCD specs
  LCDCMD  1, WakeUp
  PAUSE  1
  LCDCMD  1, WakeUp
  PAUSE  1
```

```
LCDCMD  1, FourBitMode          'Set buss to 4-bit mode
LCDCMD  1, TwoLine5x8Font       'Set to 2-line mode with 5x8 font
LCDCMD  1, DisplayOff           'Turn display off
LCDCMD  1, DisplayOn            'Turn display on with blinking cursor
LCDCMD  1, IncCrsr              'Set to auto-increment cursor (no display shift)
LCDCMD  1, ClearDisplay         'Clear the display
RETURN
```

LCDIN

| BS1 | BS2 | BS2e | BS2sx | **BS2p** |

LCDIN *Pin, Command, [InputData]*

Function

Receive data from an LCD display.

- **Pin** is a variable/constant/expression (0 – 1 or 8 – 9) that specifies which I/O pins to use. The LCD requires, at most, seven I/O pins to operate. The *Pin* argument serves a double purpose; specifying the first pin and, indirectly, the group of other required pins. See explanation below. All I/O pins will be set to output mode initially and the upper I/O pins (4 – 7 or 12 – 15) will be set to input mode by the end of the LCDIN command.
- **Command** is a variable/constant/expression (0 – 255) indicating the LCD command to send.
- **InputData** is a list of variables and formatters that tells LCDIN what to do with incoming data. LCDIN can store data in a variable or array, interpret numeric text (decimal, binary, or hex) and store the corresponding value in a variable, wait for a fixed or variable sequence of bytes, or ignore a specified number of bytes. These actions can be combined in any order in the *InputData* list.

Quick Facts

Table 5.29: LCDIN Quick Facts.

	BS2p
Values for *Pin*	0, 1, 8 or 9
I/O pin arrangement when *Pin* is 0 or 1	0 or 1 (depending on pin): LCD Enable (E) pin 2: LCD Read/Write (R/W) pin 3: LCD Register Select (RS) pin 4 – 7: LCD Data Buss (DB4 – DB7, respectively) pins
I/O pin arrangement when *Pin* is 8 or 9	8 or 9 (depending on pin): LCD Enable (E) pin 10: LCD Read/Write (R/W) pin 11: LCD Register Select (RS) pin 12 – 15: LCD Data Buss (DB4 – DB7, respectively) pins

Explanation

The three LCD commands (LCDCMD, LCDIN and LCDOUT) allow the BS2p to interface directly to standard LCD displays that feature a Hitachi 44780 controller (part #HD44780A). This includes many 1 x 16, 2 x 16 and 4 x 20 character LCD displays.

A SIMPLE LCDIN EXAMPLE.

The LCDIN command is used to send one instruction and then receive at least one data byte from the LCD's Character RAM or Display RAM. The following is an example of the LCDIN command:

```
Char       VAR   BYTE
LCDIN  1, 128, [Char]
```

The above code will read the character value at location 0 of the DRAM. See the "Character Positioning" section, below, for more information.

The LCDIN command actually uses more than just the I/O pin specified by the *Pin* argument. The LCDIN command requires seven I/O pins. This is because the standard LCD displays have a parallel interface, rather than a serial one. The *Pin* argument can be the numbers 0, 1, 8 or 9 and will result in the use of the I/O pins shown in Table 5.29. Please refer to the LCDCMD command description for information on properly wiring the LCD display.

TWO VERY IMPORTANT STEPS:
1) WIRING THE BS2P TO AN LCD.
2) INITIALIZING THE LCD.

When the LCD is first powered-up, it will be in an unknown state and must be properly configured before sending commands like the one shown above. This process is known as initializing the LCD and is the first thing your program should do upon starting up. Please refer to the LCDCMD command description for information on properly initializing the LCD display.

The LCDIN command's *InputData* argument is similar to the SERIN command's *InputData* argument. This means data can be received as ASCII character values, decimal, hexadecimal and binary translations and string data as in the examples below (assume the LCD display has "Value: 3A:101" starting at the first character of the first line on the screen).

RECEIVING FORMATTED DATA.

```
Value       VAR   BYTE(13)
LCDIN  1, 128, [Value]             'receive the ASCII value for "V"
LCDIN  1, 128, [DEC  Value]        'receive the number 3.
LCDIN  1, 128, [HEX  Value]        'receive the number $3A.
LCDIN  1, 128, [BIN  Value]        'receive the number %101.
LCDIN  1, 128, [STR Value\13]      'receive the string "Value: 3A:101"
```

Tables 5.30 and 5.31 list all the available conversion formatters and special formatters available to the LCDIN command. See the SERIN command for additional information and examples of their use.

Some possible uses of the LCDIN command are 1) in combination with the LCDOUT command to store and read data from the unused DRAM or CRAM locations (as extra variable space), 2) to verify that the data from a previous LCDOUT command was received and processed properly by the

LCD, and 3) to read character data from CRAM for the purposes of modifying it and storing it as a custom character.

Table 5.30: LCDIN Conversion Formatters.

Conversion Formatter	Type of Number	Numeric Characters Accepted	Notes
DEC{1..5}	Decimal, optionally limited to 1 – 5 digits	0 through 9	1
SDEC{1..5}	Signed decimal, optionally limited to 1 – 5 digits	-, 0 through 9	1,2
HEX{1..4}	Hexadecimal, optionally limited to 1 – 4 digits	0 through 9, A through F	1,3
SHEX{1..4}	Signed hexadecimal, optionally limited to 1 – 4 digits	-, 0 through 9, A through F	1,2,3
IHEX{1..4}	Indicated hexadecimal, optionally limited to 1 – 4 digits	$, 0 through 9, A through F	1,3,4
ISHEX{1..4}	Signed, indicated hexadecimal, optionally limited to 1 – 4 digits	-, $, 0 through 9, A through F	1,2,3,4
BIN{1..16}	Binary, optionally limited to 1 – 16 digits	0, 1	1
SBIN{1..16}	Signed binary, optionally limited to 1 – 16 digits	-, 0, 1	1,2
IBIN{1..16}	Indicated binary, optionally limited to 1 – 16 digits	%, 0, 1	1,4
ISBIN{1..16}	Signed, indicated binary, optionally limited to 1 – 16 digits	-, %, 0, 1	1,2,4

1 All numeric conversions will continue to accept new data until receiving either the specified number of digits (ex: three digits for DEC3) or a non-numeric character.

2 To be recognized as part of a number, the minus sign (-) must immediately precede a numeric character. The minus sign character occurring in non-numeric text is ignored and any character (including a space) between a minus and a number causes the minus to be ignored.

3 The hexadecimal formatters are not case-sensitive; "a" through "f" means the same as "A" through "F".

4 Indicated hexadecimal and binary formatters ignore all characters, even valid numerics, until they receive the appropriate prefix ($ for hexadecimal, % for binary). The indicated formatters can differentiate between text and hexadecimal (ex: ABC would be interpreted by HEX as a number but IHEX would ignore it unless expressed as $ABC). Likewise, the binary version can distinguish the decimal number 10 from the binary number %10. A prefix occurring in non-numeric text is ignored, and any character (including a space) between a prefix and a number causes the prefix to be ignored. Indicated, signed formatters require that the minus sign come before the prefix, as in -$1B45.

Special Formatter	Action
STR *ByteArray* \L {\E}	Input a character string of length L into an array. If specified, an end character E causes the string input to end before reaching length L. Remaining bytes are filled with 0s (zeros).
WAITSTR *ByteArray* {\L}	Wait for a sequence of bytes matching a string stored in an array variable, optionally limited to L characters. If the optional L argument is left off, the end of the array-string must be marked by a byte containing a zero (0).
SKIP *Length*	Ignore *Length* bytes of characters.

Table 5.31: LCDIN Special Formatters.

Demo Program (LCDIN.bsp)

```
' This program demonstrates initialization, printing and reading from a 2 x 16 character
' LCD display.
'{$STAMP BS2p}                          'STAMP directive (specifies a BS2p)

Char      VAR      BYTE(16)             'Variable for holding text read from LCD

Init:
  LCDCMD 1,48      'Send wakeup sequence to LCD
  PAUSE 10         'These pauses are necessary to meet the LCD specs
  LCDCMD 1,48
  PAUSE 1
  LCDCMD 1,48
  PAUSE 1
  LCDCMD 1,32      'Set buss to 4-bit mode
  LCDCMD 1,40      'Set to 2-line mode with 5x8 font
  LCDCMD 1,8       'Turn display off
  LCDCMD 1,12      'Turn display on with blinking cursor
  LCDCMD 1,6       'Set to auto-increment cursor (no display shift)

Start:
  LCDOUT 1,1,["Hello!"]
  GOSUB ReadLCDScreen
  PAUSE 3000
  LCDOUT 1,1,["I'm a 2x16 LCD!"]
  GOSUB ReadLCDScreen
  PAUSE 3000
GOTO Start

ReadLCDScreen:
  DEBUG "LCD Now Says: "
  LCDIN 1,128,[STR Char\16]
  DEBUG  STR Char\16,CR,CR
RETURN
```

LCDOUT

| BS1 | BS2 | BS2e | BS2sx | **BS2p** |

LCDOUT *Pin, Command, [OutputData]*

Function

Send data to an LCD display.

- **Pin** is a variable/constant/expression (0 – 1 or 8 – 9) that specifies which I/O pins to use. The LCD requires, at most, seven I/O pins to operate. The *Pin* argument serves a double purpose; specifying the first pin and, indirectly, the group of other required pins. See explanation below. All I/O pins will be set to output mode initially and the upper I/O pins (4 – 7 or 12 – 15) will be set to input mode by the end of the LCDIN command.
- **Command** is a variable/constant/expression (0 – 255) indicating an LCD command to send.
- **OutputData** is a list of variables, constants, expressions and formatters that tells LCDOUT how to format outgoing data. LCDOUT can transmit individual or repeating bytes, convert values into decimal, hex or binary text representations, or transmit strings of bytes from variable arrays. These actions can be combined in any order in the *OutputData* list.

Quick Facts

Table 5.32: LCDOUT Quick Facts.

	BS2p
Values for *Pin*	0, 1, 8 or 9
I/O pin arrangement when *Pin* is 0 or 1	0 or 1 (depending on pin): LCD Enable (E) pin 2: LCD Read/Write (R/W) pin 3: LCD Register Select (RS) pin 4 – 7: LCD Data Buss (DB4 – DB7, respectively) pins
I/O pin arrangement when *Pin* is 8 or 9	8 or 9 (depending on pin): LCD Enable (E) pin 10: LCD Read/Write (R/W) pin 11: LCD Register Select (RS) pin 12 – 15: LCD Data Buss (DB4 – DB7, respectively) pins

Explanation

The three LCD commands (LCDCMD, LCDIN and LCDOUT) allow the BS2p to interface directly to standard LCD displays that feature a Hitachi 44780 controller (part #HD44780A). This includes many 1 x 16, 2 x 16 and 4 x 20 character LCD displays.

A SIMPLE LCDOUT EXAMPLE.

The LCDOUT command is used to send one instruction followed by at least one data byte to the LCD. The data that is output is written to the

LCDOUT - BASIC Stamp Command Reference

LCD's Character RAM or Display RAM. The following is an example of the LCDOUT command:

LCDOUT 1, 1, ["Hello World!"]

The above code will clear the LCD screen and then send "Hello World!" to the screen. The first argument (1) is the starting I/O pin number and the second argument (also 1) is the LCD's instruction for Clear Screen.

The LCDOUT command actually uses more than just the I/O pin specified by the *Pin* argument. The LCDOUT command requires seven I/O pins. This is because the standard LCD displays have a parallel interface, rather than a serial one. The *Pin* argument can be the numbers 0, 1, 8 or 9 and will result in the use of the I/O pins shown in Table 5.32. Please refer to the LCDCMD command description for information on properly wiring the LCD display.

TWO VERY IMPORTANT STEPS:
1) WIRING THE BS2P TO AN LCD.
2) INITIALIZING THE LCD.

When the LCD is first powered-up, it will be in an unknown state and must be properly configured before sending commands like the one shown above. This process is known as initializing the LCD and is the first thing your program should do upon starting up. Please refer to the LCDCMD command description for information on properly initializing the LCD display.

The LCDOUT command's *OutputData* argument is exactly like that of the DEBUG and SEROUT command's *OutputData* argument. This means data can be sent as literal text, ASCII character values, repetitive values, decimal, hexadecimal and binary translations and string data as in the examples below.

SENDING AND FORMATTING DATA.

```
Value      VAR   BYTE
Value = 65
LCDOUT 1, 0, [Value]       'send the ASCII value for "A"
LCDOUT 1, 0, [REP Value\5 'send the ASCII value for "A" five time, ie: "AAAAA"
LCDOUT 1, 0, [DEC Value]   'send two characters, "6" and "5"
LCDOUT 1, 0, [HEX Value]   'send two characters, "4" and "1"
LCDOUT 1, 0, [BIN Value]   'send seven characters, "1000001"
```

Tables 5.33 and 5.34 list all the available conversion formatters and special formatters available to the LCDOUT command. See the DEBUG and SEROUT commands for additional information and examples of their use.

Table 5.33: LCDOUT Conversion Formatters.

Conversion Formatter	Type of Number	Notes
DEC{1..5}	Decimal, optionally fixed to 1 – 5 digits	1
SDEC{1..5}	Signed decimal, optionally fixed to 1 – 5 digits	1,2
HEX{1..4}	Hexadecimal, optionally fixed to 1 – 4 digits	1
SHEX{1..4}	Signed hexadecimal, optionally fixed to 1 – 4 digits	1,2
IHEX{1..4}	Indicated hexadecimal, optionally fixed to 1 – 4 digits ($ prefix)	1
ISHEX{1..4}	Signed, indicated hexadecimal, optionally fixed to 1 – 4 digits ($ prefix)	1,2
BIN{1..16}	Binary, optionally fixed to 1 – 16 digits	1
SBIN{1..16}	Signed binary, optionally fixed to 1 – 16 digits	1,2
IBIN{1..16}	Indicated binary, optionally fixed to 1 – 16 digits (% prefix)	1
ISBIN{1..16}	Signed, indicated binary, optionally fixed to 1 – 16 digits (% prefix)	1,2

1 Fixed-digit formatters like DEC4 will pad the number with leading 0s if necessary; ex: DEC4 65 sends 0065. If a number is larger than the specified number of digits, the leading digits will be dropped; ex: DEC4 56422 sends 6422.
2 Signed modifiers work under two's complement rules.

Table 5.34: LCDOUT Special Formatters.

Special Formatter	Action
?	Displays "symbol = x' + carriage return; where x is a number. Default format is decimal, but may be combined with conversion formatters (ex: BIN ? x to display "x = binary_number").
ASC ?	Displays "symbol = 'x'" + carriage return; where x is an ASCII character.
STR ByteArray {\L}	Send character string from an array. The optional \L argument can be used to limit the output to L characters, otherwise, characters will be sent up to the first byte equal to 0 or the end of RAM space is reached.
REP Byte \L	Send a string consisting of Byte repeated L times (ex: REP "X"\10 sends "XXXXXXXXXX").

USING THE *COMMAND* ARGUMENT.

The *Command* argument is useful for proceeding a set of data with a special LCD instruction. For example, the code below will move the cursor to location 64 (the first character on the second line) and print "Hi":

LCDOUT 1, 128 + 64, ["Hi"]

The next example, below, will turn on the blinking block cursor and print "Yo!":

LCDOUT 1, 13, ["Yo!"]

Occasionally, you will want to send data without preceding it with a command. To do this, simply use 0 for the *Command* argument, as in:

LCDOUT 1, 0, ["Hello there!"]

Another use for the LCDOUT command is to access and create custom characters. The Hitachi 44780 controller has a built-in character set that is similar to the ASCII character set (at least for the first 128 characters). Most of these characters are stored in ROM and are not changeable, however, the first eight characters (ASCII 0 though 7) are programmable.

CREATING CUSTOM CHARACTERS.

Each of the programmable characters is five pixels wide and eight pixels tall. It takes eight bytes to describe each character; one byte per row (the left-most three bits are ignored). For example, the character at ASCII location 0 is defined by the bit patterns stored in bytes 0 through 7 of Character RAM (CRAM). The character at ASCII location 1 is defined by the bit patterns stored in bytes 8 through 15 of CRAM, and so on.

To create a custom character, use some graph paper to plot out the bit pattern (on and off pixels) in a 5 x 8 pattern, as shown in Figure 5.14. Then calculate the corresponding binary value of the bit pattern for each of the eight rows of character data.

Character Cell Structure and Data

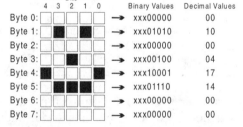

Figure 5.14: LCD Character Structure.

After the data is calculated for each character (8 byte values per character), use the LCDOUT command with the "Move To CRAM Address" instruction to insert the data into the character's CRAM locations. For example, the code below will store the character shown in Figure 5.14 into character 0's CRAM data locations. Then it will place the cursor back on the display (DRAM) and print the character on the screen.

```
LCDOUT  1, 64+0, [00, 10, 00, 04, 17, 14, 00, 00]
LCDOUT  1, 128+0, ["Custom Char: ", 0]
```

The number 64 in the *Command* argument is the LCD's "Move to CRAM Address" instruction and the 0 that is added to it is the location of the first row of data for the character 0. The LCDOUT command will write the first *OutputData* value (00) to this location, the second *OutputData* value (10) to location 1, etc. If we wanted this custom character to affect character 1, instead of 0, we'd have to adjust value of the "Move To..." command, ie: 64+8. To affect character 2, we'd use 64+16.

To try the example above, don't forget to execute the LCD initialization code (shown in the LCDCMD description) first and never forget to move the cursor back to the screen (as with the last command, above) when you're done writing the character data to CRAM.

Demo Program (LCDOUT.bsp)

```
' This program demonstrates initialization and printing on a 2 x 16 character LCD display.
' This is a modified version of the LCDINIT.bsp program.
'{$STAMP BS2p}                       'STAMP directive (specifies a BS2p)

'-----Define LCD constants-----
WakeUp          CON %00110000   'Wake-up
FourBitMode     CON %00100000   'Set to 4-bit mode
TwoLine5x8Font  CON %00101000   'Set to 2 display lines, 5x8 font
DisplayOff      CON %00001000   'Turn off display, data is retained
DisplayOn       CON %00001100   'Turn on display, no cursor
IncCrsr         CON %00000110   'Auto-increment cursor, no display shift
ClearDisplay    CON %00000001   'Clear the display
MoveCrsr        CON %10000000   'Move cursor to position (must add address)

'-----Main Routines-----
Init:
  PAUSE 1000
  GOSUB InitLCD

Start:
  LCDOUT 1, ClearDisplay, ["Hello my friend."]
  PAUSE 1000
  LCDOUT 1, MoveCrsr+64, ["How are you?"]
  PAUSE 3000
  LCDCMD 1, ClearDisplay
  LCDOUT 1, MoveCrsr+1, ["I'm doing just"]
  LCDOUT 1, MoveCrsr+70, ["fine!"]
  PAUSE 3000
GOTO Start

'-----Subroutines-----
InitLCD:
  LCDCMD 1, WakeUp        'Send wakeup sequence to LCD
  PAUSE 10                'These pauses are necessary to meet the LCD specs
  LCDCMD 1, WakeUp
  PAUSE 1
```

```
LCDCMD  1, WakeUp
PAUSE  1
LCDCMD  1, FourBitMode          'Set buss to 4-bit mode
LCDCMD  1, TwoLine5x8Font       'Set to 2-line mode with 5x8 font
LCDCMD  1, DisplayOff           'Turn display off
LCDCMD  1, DisplayOn            'Turn display on with blinking cursor
LCDCMD  1, IncCrsr              'Set to auto-increment cursor (no display shift)
LCDCMD  1, ClearDisplay         'Clear the display
RETURN
```

LOOKDOWN	BS1	BS2	BS2e	BS2sx	BS2p

1 LOOKDOWN *Target, (Value0, Value1, ...ValueN), Variable*

2 2e 2sx 2p LOOKDOWN *Target, {ComparisonOp} [Value0, Value1, ...ValueN], Variable*

Function

Compare *Target* value to a list of values and store the index number of the first value that matches into *Variable*. If no value in the list matches, *Variable* is left unaffected. On the BS2, BS2e, BS2sx and BS2p, the optional *ComparisonOp* is used as criteria for the match; the default criteria is "equal to."

1

NOTE: Expressions are not allowed as arguments on the BS1.

- **Target** is a variable/constant/expression (0 – 65535) to be compared to the values in the list.

2 2e 2sx 2p

- **ComparisonOp** is an optional comparison operator (as described in Table 5.36) to be used as the criteria when comparing values. When no *ComparisonOp* is specified, equal to (=) is assumed. This argument is not available on the BS1.

- **Values** are variables/constants/expressions (0 – 65535) to be compared to *Target*.

- **Variable** is a variable (usually a byte) that will be set to the index (0 – 255) of the matching value in the *Values* list. If no matching value is found, *Variable* is left unaffected.

Quick Facts

Table 5.35: LOOKDOWN Quick Facts.

	BS1, BS2, BS2e, BS2sx and BS2p
Limit of value entries	256
Starting index number	0
If value list contains no match...	Variable is left unaffected

Explanation

LOOKDOWN works like the index in a book. In an index, you search for a topic and get the page number. LOOKDOWN searches for a target value in a list, and stores the index number of the first match in a variable. For example:

```
SYMBOL    Value  = B0
SYMBOL    Result = B1
Value = 17
Result = 15

LOOKDOWN  Value, (26, 177, 13, 1, 0, 17, 99), Result
DEBUG "Value matches item ", #Result, "in list"
```

-- or --

```
Value      VAR  BYTE
Result     VAR  NIB
Value = 17
Result = 15

LOOKDOWN  Value, [26, 177, 13, 1, 0, 17, 99], Result
DEBUG "Value matches item ", DEC  Result, " in list"
```

DEBUG prints, "Value matches item 5 in list" because the value (17) matches item 5 of [26, 177, 13, 1, 0, 17, 99]. Note that index numbers count up from 0, not 1; that is, in this list, 26 is item 0.

THE INDEX NUMBER OF THE FIRST ITEM IS 0, NOT 1.

What happens if the value doesn't match any of the items in the list? Try changing "Value = 17" to "Value = 2." Since 2 is not on the list, LOOKDOWN leaves *Result* unaffected. Since *Result* contained 15 before LOOKDOWN executed, DEBUG prints "Value matches item 15 in list." By strategically setting the initial value of *Result*, as we have here, your program can be written to detect when an item was not found in the list.

Don't forget that text phrases are just lists of byte values, so they too are eligible for LOOKDOWN searches, as in this example:

USING TEXT IN THE VALUE LIST.

```
SYMBOL    Value  = B0
SYMBOL    Result = B1
Value = "f"
Result = 255

LOOKDOWN  Value, ("The quick brown fox"), Result
DEBUG "Value matches item ", #Result, "in list"
```

-- or --

```
Value      VAR  BYTE
Result     VAR  NIB
Value = "f"
Result = 255
```

```
LOOKDOWN  Value, ["The quick brown fox"], Result
DEBUG  "Value matches item ", DEC  Result, " in list"
```

DEBUG prints, "Value matches item 16 in list" because the character at index item 16 is "f" in the phrase, "The quick brown fox".

LOOKDOWN CAN USE VARIABLES AND EXPRESSIONS IN THE VALUE LIST.

The examples above show LOOKDOWN working with lists of constants, but it also works with variables and expressions also. Note, however, that expressions are not allowed as argument on the BS1.

USING LOOKDOWN'S COMPARISON OPERATORS.

On the BS2, BS2e, BS2sx and BS2p, the LOOKDOWN command can also use another criteria (other than "equal to") for its list. All of the examples above use LOOKDOWN's default comparison operator, =, that searches for an exact match. The entire list of *ComaprisonOps* is shown in Table 5.36. The "greater than" comparison operator (>) is used in the following example:

```
Value       VAR   BYTE
Result      VAR   NIB
Value = 17
Result = 15

LOOKDOWN  Value, >[26, 177, 13, 1, 0, 17, 99], Result
DEBUG  "Value greater than item ", DEC  Result, " in list"
```

DEBUG prints, "Value greater than item 2 in list" because the first item the value 17 is greater than is 13 (which is item 2 in the list). *Value* is also greater than items 3 and 4, but these are ignored, because LOOKDOWN only cares about the first item that matches the criteria. This can require a certain amount of planning in devising the order of the list. See the demo program below.

WATCH OUT FOR UNSIGNED MATH ERRORS WHEN USING THE COMPARISON OPERATORS.

LOOKDOWN comparison operators use unsigned 16-bit math. They will not work correctly with signed numbers, which are represented internally as two's complement (large 16-bit integers). For example, the two's complement representation of -99 is 65437. So although -99 is certainly less than 0, it would appear to be larger than zero to the LOOKDOWN comparison operators. The bottom line is: Don't used signed numbers with LOOKDOWN comparisons.

LOOKDOWN - BASIC Stamp Command Reference

ComparisonOp Symbol	Description
=	Find the first value Target is equal to
<>	Find the first value Target is not equal to
>	Find the first value Target is greater than
<	Find the first value Target is less than
>=	Find the first value Target is greater than or equal to
<=	Find the first value Target is less than or equal to

Table 5.36: LOOKDOWN Comparison Operators.

A common application for LOOKDOWN is to use it in conjunction with the BRANCH command to create selective jumps based on a simple variable input:

USING LOOKDOWN WITH BRANCH TO JUMP BASED ON VALUES.

```
Cmd          VAR  BYTE
Cmd = "M"

LOOKDOWN Cmd, ["SLMH"], Cmd
BRANCH Cmd, [_Stop, _Low, _Medium, _High]
DEBUG  "Command not in list"
END


_Stop:       DEBUG  "stop"
END


_Low:        DEBUG  "low"
END


_Medium:     DEBUG  "medium"
END


_High:       DEBUG  "high"
END
```

NOTE: For BS1's, change line 1 to:
SYMBOL Cmd = B0
And replace the [and] symbols with (and) in lines 4 and 5.

In this example, *Cmd* contains "M" (ASCII 77). LOOKDOWN finds that this is item 2 of a list of one-character commands and stores 2 into Cmd. BRANCH then goes to item 2 of its list, which is the program label "_Medium" at which point DEBUG prints "medium" on the PC screen. This is a powerful method for interpreting user input, and a lot neater than the alternative IF...THEN instructions.

Another great use of LOOKDOWN is in combination with LOOKUP to "map" non-contiguous sets of numbers together. For example, you may have an application where certain numbers are received by the BASIC Stamp and, in response, the BASIC Stamp needs to send a specific set of numbers. This may be easy to code if the numbers are contiguous, or follow some know algebraic equations... but what if they don't? The table

USING LOOKDOWN WITH LOOKUP TO "MAP" NON-CONTIGUOUS SETS OF NUMBERS.

below shows some sample, non-contiguous inputs and the corresponding outputs the BASIC Stamp needs to respond with:

Table 5.37: Non-Contiguous Number Example

Each of these values received (inputs):	Needs to result in each of these values sent (outputs):
5	16
14	17
1	18
43	24
26	10
22	12
30	11

So, if we receive the number 5, we need to output 16. If we received 43, we need to output 24, and so on. These numbers are not contiguous and they don't appear to be derived from any simple algorithm. We can solve this problem with two lines of code, as follows:

```
LOOKDOWN  Value, [5, 14, 1, 43, 26, 22, 30], Value
LOOKUP  Value, [16, 17, 18, 24, 10, 12, 11], Value
```

Assuming our received number is in *Value*, the first line (LOOKDOWN) will find the value in the list and store the index of the location that matches back into *Value*. (This step "maps" the non-contiguous numbers: 5, 14, 1, etc, to a contiguous set of numbers: 0, 1, 2, etc). The second line (LOOKUP) takes our new *Value*, finds the number at that location and stores it back into *Value*. If the received value was 14, LOOKDOWN stores 1 into *Value* and LOOKUP looks at the value at location 1 and stores 17 in *Value*. The number 43 gets mapped to 3, 3 gets mapped to 24, and so on. This is a quick and easy fix for a potentially messy problem!

Demo Program (LOOKDOWN.bas)

```
' This program uses LOOKDOWN followed by LOOKUP to map the numbers:
' 0, 10, 50, 64, 71 and 98 to 35, 40, 58, 62, 79, and 83, respectively.  All other
' numbers are mapped to 255.

'{$STAMP BS1}                             'STAMP directive (specifies a BS1)

SYMBOL    I     = W0                      ' Holds current number.
SYMBOL    Result = W1                     ' Holds mapped result.

FOR I = 0 TO 100
  Result = 255                            ' If no match in list, must be 0.
  LOOKDOWN I, (0, 10, 50, 64, 71, 98), Result
  LOOKUP Result, (35, 40, 58, 62, 79, 83), Result
  DEBUG "I= ", #I, "Result=", #Result, CR
  PAUSE 100
NEXT
```

Demo Program (LOOKDOWN.bs2)

```
' This program uses LOOKDOWN to determine the number of decimal digits in a number.
' The reasoning is that numbers less than 10 have one digit; greater than or equal
' to 10 but less than 100 have two; greater than or equal to 100 but less than 1000
' have three; greater than or equal to 1000 but less than 10000 have four; and greater
' than or equal to 10000 but less than 65535 (the largest number we can represent in
' 16-bit math) have five. There are two loopholes that we have to plug: (1) The number
' 0 does not have zero digits, and (2) The number 65535 has five digits.  To ensure that
' 0 is accorded one-digit status, we just put 0 at the beginning of the LOOKDOWN list.
' Since 0 is not less than 0, an input of 0 results in 1 as it should. At the other end
' of the scale, 65535 is not less than 65535, so LOOKDOWN will end without writing to the
' result variable, NumDig. To ensure that an input of 65535 returns 5 in NumDig, we just
' put 5 into numDig beforehand.

'{$STAMP BS2}                             'STAMP directive (specifies a BS2)

I          VAR   WORD                     ' Variable (0-65535).
NumDig     VAR   NIB                      ' Variable (0-15) to hold # of digits.

FOR I = 0 TO 1000 STEP 8
  NumDig = 5                              ' If no 'true' in list, must be 65535.
  LOOKDOWN I, <[0, 10, 100, 1000, 10000, 65535], NumDig
  DEBUG "I= ", REP " "\( 5 – NumDig ), DEC I, TAB, "digits=", DEC NumDig, CR
  PAUSE 100
NEXT
```

NOTE: This is written for the BS2 but can be used for the BS2e, BS2sx and BS2p also. Locate the proper source code file or modify the STAMP directive before downloading to the BS2e, BS2sx or BS2p.

LOOKUP

BS1	BS2	BS2e	BS2sx	BS2p

1 **LOOKUP** *Index, (Value0, Value1, ...ValueN), Variable*

2 **2e** **2sx** **2p** **LOOKUP** *Index, [Value0, Value1, ...ValueN], Variable*

Function

Find the value at location *Index* and store it in *Variable*. If *Index* exceeds the highest index value of the items in the list, *Variable* is left unaffected.

1

NOTE: Expressions are not allowed as arguments on the BS1.

- **Index** is a variable/constant/expression (0 – 255) indicating the list item to retrieve.

- **Values** are variables/constants/expressions (0 – 65535).

- **Variable** is a variable that will be set to the value at the *Index* location. If *Index* exceeds the highest location number, *Variable* is left unaffected.

Quick Facts

Table 5.38: LOOKUP Quick Facts.

	BS1, BS2, BS2e, BS2sx and BS2p
Limit of value entries	256
Starting index number	0
If index exceeds the highest location...	Variable is left unaffected

Explanation

LOOKUP retrieves an item from a list based on the item's position, *Index*, in the list. For example:

1
```
SYMBOL    Index  = B0
SYMBOL    Result = B1
Index = 3
Result = 255

LOOKUP Index, (26, 177, 13, 1, 0, 17, 99), Result
DEBUG "Item ", #Index, "is: ", #Result
```

-- or --

```
Index       VAR   NIB
Result      VAR   BYTE
Index = 3
Result = 255

LOOKUP Index, [26, 177, 13, 1, 0, 17, 99], Result
DEBUG "Item ", DEC Index, " is: ", DEC Result
```

In this example, DEBUG prints "Item 3 is: 1." Note that the first location number is 0. In the list above, item 0 is 26, item 1 is 177, etc.

If *Index* is beyond the end of the list, the result variable is unchanged. In the example above, if index were greater than 6, the message would have reported the result to be 255, because that's what *Result* contained before LOOKUP executed.

Don't forget that text phrases are just lists of byte values, so they too are eligible for LOOKUP searches, as in this example:

```
SYMBOL    Value = B0
SYMBOL    Result = B1
Index = 16
Result = " "

LOOKUP Index , ("The quick brown fox"), Result
DEBUG @Result
```

-- or --

```
Index       VAR  BYTE
Result      VAR  NIB
Index = 16
Result = " "

LOOKUP Index , ["The quick brown fox"], Result
DEBUG ASC? Result
```

DEBUG prints, "Result = 'f'" because the character at index item 16 is "f" in the phrase, "The quick brown fox".

The examples above show LOOKUP working with lists of constants, but it also works with variables and expressions also. Note, however, that expressions are not allowed as argument on the BS1.

A great use of LOOKUP is in combination with LOOKDOWN to "map" non-contiguous sets of numbers together. For example, you may have an application where certain numbers are received by the BASIC Stamp and, in response, the BASIC Stamp needs to send a specific set of numbers. This may be easy to code if the numbers are contiguous, or follow some know algebraic equations... but what if they don't? The table below shows some sample, non-contiguous inputs and the corresponding outputs the BASIC Stamp needs to respond with:

Table 5.39: Non-Contiguous Number Example.

Each of these values received (inputs):	Needs to result in each of these values sent (outputs):
5	16
14	17
1	18
43	24
26	10
22	12
30	11

So, if we receive the number 5, we need to output 16. If we received 43, we need to output 24, and so on. These numbers are not contiguous and they don't appear to be derived from any simple algorithm. We can solve this problem with two lines of code, as follows:

```
LOOKDOWN  Value, [5, 14, 1, 43, 26, 22, 30], Value
LOOKUP   Value, [16, 17, 18, 24, 10, 12, 11], Value
```

Assuming our received number is in *Value*, the first line (LOOKDOWN) will find the value in the list and store the index of the location that matches back into *Value*. (This step "maps" the non-contiguous numbers: 5, 14, 1, etc, to a contiguous set of numbers: 0, 1, 2, etc). The second line (LOOKUP) takes our new *Value*, finds the number at that location and stores it back into *Value*. If the received value was 14, LOOKDOWN stores 1 into *Value* and LOOKUP looks at the value at location 1 and stores 17 in *Value*. The number 43 gets mapped to 3, 3 gets mapped to 24, and so on. This is a quick and easy fix for a potentially messy problem!

Demo Program (LOOKDOWN.bas)

```
' This program uses Lookup to create a debug-window animation of a spinning propeller.
' The animation consists of the four ASCII characters I / - \ which, when printed rapidly
' in order at a fixed location, appear to spin. (A little imagination helps a lot here.)

'{$STAMP  BS1}                          'STAMP directive (specifies a BS1)

SYMBOL   I      = B0
SYMBOL   Frame  = B1

Rotate:
  FOR I = 0 TO 3
    LOOKUP I,("I/-\"),Frame
    DEBUG CLS, @Frame
    PAUSE 50
  NEXT
GOTO Rotate
```

Demo Program (LOOKUP.bs2)

```
' This program uses Lookup to create a debug-window animation of a spinning propeller.
' The animation consists of the four ASCII characters I / - \ which, when printed rapidly
' in order at a fixed location, appear to spin. (A little imagination helps a lot here.)

'{$STAMP  BS2}                          'STAMP directive (specifies a BS2)

I        VAR    NIB
Frame           VAR    BYTE

Rotate:
  FOR I = 0 TO 3
    LOOKUP I,["I/-\"],Frame
    DEBUG HOME, Frame
    PAUSE 50
  NEXT
GOTO Rotate
```

NOTE: This is written for the BS2 but can be used for the BS2e, BS2sx and BS2p also. Locate the proper source code file or modify the STAMP directive before downloading to the BS2e, BS2sx or BS2p.

LOW

BS1	BS2	BS2e	BS2sx	BS2p

LOW *Pin*

Function

Make the specified pin output low.

- **Pin** is a variable/constant/expression (0 – 15) that specifies which I/O pin to set low. This pin will be placed into output mode.

NOTE: Expressions are not allowed as arguments on the BS1. The range of the *Pin* argument on the BS1 is 0 – 7.

Explanation

The LOW command sets the specified pin to 0 (a 0 volt level) and then sets its mode to output. For example,

```
LOW  6
```

does exactly the same thing as:

```
OUT6 = 0
DIR6 = 1
```

Using the LOW command is faster, in this case.

Connect an LED and a resister as shown in Figure 5.15 for the demo program below.

Figure 5.15: Example LED Circuit.

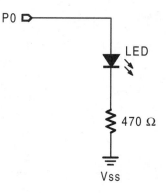

Demo Program (LOW.bs2)

```
' This simple program sets I/O pin 0 high for 1/2 second and low for 1/2 second
' in an endless loop.

'{$STAMP  BS2}                              'STAMP directive (specifies a BS2)

Loop:
  HIGH 0
  PAUSE 500
  LOW 0
  PAUSE 500
GOTO Loop
```

NOTE: This is written for the BS2 but can be used for the BS1, BS2e, BS2sx and BS2p also. Locate the proper source code file or modify the STAMP directive before downloading to the BS1, BS2e, BS2sx or BS2p.

MAINIO

BS1	BS2	BS2e	BS2sx	**BS2p**

MAINIO

Function

Switch from control of auxiliary I/O pins to main I/O pins (on the BS2p40 only).

Quick Facts

Table 5.40: MAINIO Quick Facts.

	BS2p
I/O pin IDs	0 – 15 (just like auxiliary I/O, but after MAINIO command, all references affect physical pins 5 – 20).
Special notes	Both the BS2p24 and the BS2p40 accept this command, however, only the BS2p40 gives access to the auxiliary I/O pins.

Explanation

The BS2p is available in two module styles, 1) a 24-pin module (called the BS2p24) that is pin compatible with the BS2, BS2e and BS2sx and 2) a 40-pin module (called the BS2p40) that has an additional 16 I/O pins (for a total of 32). The BS2p40's extra, or auxiliary, I/O pins can be accessed in the same manner as the main I/O pins (by using the IDs 0 to 15) but only after issuing a command called AUXIO or IOTERM. The MAINIO command causes the BASIC Stamp to affect the main I/O pins (the default) instead of the auxiliary I/O pins in all further code until the AUXIO or IOTERM command is reached, or the BASIC Stamp is reset or power-cycled.

A SIMPLE MAINIO EXAMPLE.

The following example illustrates this:

```
AUXIO
HIGH 0
MAINIO
LOW 0
```

The first line of the above example will tell the BASIC Stamp to affect the auxiliary I/O pins in the commands following it. Line 2, sets I/O pin 0 of the auxiliary I/O pins (physical pin 21) high. Afterward, the MAINIO command tells the BASIC Stamp that all commands following it should affect the main I/O pins. The last command, LOW, will set I/O pin 0 of the main I/O pins (physical pin 5) low.

MAINIO - BASIC Stamp Command Reference

Note that the main I/O and auxiliary I/O pins are independent of each other; the states of the main I/O pins remain unchanged while the program affects the auxiliary I/O pins, and vice versa.

MAIN I/O AND AUXILIARY I/O PINS ARE INDEPENDENT AND UNAFFECTED BY CHANGES IN THE OPPOSITE GROUP.

Other commands that affect I/O group access are AUXIO and IOTERM.

Demo Program (AUX_MAIN_TERM.bsp)

NOTE: This is written for the BS2p but its effects can only be seen on the 40-pin version: the BS2p40.

```
' This program demonstrates the use of the AUXIO, MAINIO and IOTERM commands to
' affect I/O pins in the auxiliary and main I/O groups.

'{$STAMP BS2p}                        'STAMP directive (specifies a BS2p)

Port VAR   BIT

Loop:
  MAINIO                  'Switch to main I/O pins
  TOGGLE 0                'Toggle state of I/O pin 0 (physical pin 5)
  PWM 1, 100, 40          'Generate PWM on I/O pin 1 (physical pin 6)

  AUXIO                   'Switch to auxiliary I/O pins
  TOGGLE 0                'Toggle state of I/O pin 0 (physical pin 21)
  PULSOUT 1, 1000         'Generate a pulse on I/O pin 1 (physical pin 22)
  PWM 2, 100, 40          'Generate PWM on I/O pin 2 (physical pin 23)

  IOTERM Port             'Switch to main or aux I/Os (depending on Port)
  TOGGLE 3                'Toggle state of I/O pin 3 (on main and aux, alternately)
  Port = ~Port            'Invert port (switch between 0 and 1)
  PAUSE 1000
GOTO Loop
```

NAP

BS1	BS2	BS2e	BS2sx	BS2p

⌷1⌷ ⌷2⌷ ⌷2e⌷ ⌷2sx⌷ ⌷2p⌷ **NAP** *Period*

Function

Enter sleep mode for a short period. Power consumption is reduced as indicated in Table 5.41 assuming no loads are being driven.

⌷1⌷
NOTE: Expressions are not allowed as arguments on the BS1.

- **Period** is a variable/constant/expression (0 – 7) that specifies the duration of the reduced-power nap. The duration is (2^*Period*) * 18 ms. Table 5.42 indicates the nap length for any given *Period*.

Quick Facts

Table 5.41: NAP Quick Facts. Note: Current measurements are based on no extra loads at 75°F.

	BS1	BS2	BS2e	BS2sx	BS2p
Current draw during run	2 mA	8 mA	25 mA	60 mA	40 mA
Current draw during NAP	20 µA	40 µA	60 µA	60 µA	60 µA
Accuracy of NAP	−50 to 100% (±10% @ 75°F with stable power supply)	−50 to 100% (±10% @ 75°F with stable power supply)	−50 to 100% (±10% @ 75°F with stable power supply)	−50 to 100% (±10% @ 75°F with stable power supply)	−50 to 100% (±10% @ 75°F with stable power supply)

Explanation

NAP uses the same shutdown/startup mechanism as SLEEP, with one big difference. During SLEEP, the BASIC Stamp automatically compensates for variations in the speed of the watchdog timer oscillator that serves as its alarm clock. As a result, longer SLEEP intervals are accurate to approximately ±1 percent.

Table 5.42: Period and Resulting Length of NAP.

Period	Length of Nap
0	18 ms
1	36 ms
2	72 ms
3	144 ms
4	288 ms
5	576 ms
6	1152 ms (1.152 seconds)
7	2304 ms (2.304 seconds)

NAP ACCURACY NOTES.

NAP intervals are directly controlled by the watchdog timer without compensation. Variations in temperature, supply voltage, and manufacturing tolerance of the BASIC Stamp's interpreter chip can cause the actual timing to vary by as much as –50, +100 percent (i.e., a *Period* of 0, NAP can range from 9 to 36 ms). At room temperature with a fresh battery or other stable power supply, variations in the length of a NAP will be less than ±10 percent.

One great use for NAP is in a battery-powered application where at least some small amount of time is spent doing nothing. For example, you may have a program that loops endlessly, performing some task, and pausing for approximately 100 ms each time through the loop. You could replace your PAUSE 100 with NAP 3, as long as the timing of the 100 ms pause was not critical. The NAP 3 would effectively pause your program for about 144 ms and, at the same time, would place the BASIC Stamp in low-power mode, which would extend your battery life.

A GREAT USE FOR NAP; FREE POWER SAVINGS.

If your application is driving loads (sourcing or sinking current through output-high or output-low pins) during a NAP, current will be interrupted for about 18 ms when the BASIC Stamp wakes up. The reason is that the watchdog-timer reset that awakens the BASIC Stamp also causes all of the pins to switch to input mode for approximately 18 ms. When the interpreter firmware regains control of the processor, it restores the I/O direction dictated by your program.

TIPS FOR DRIVING LOADS DURING NAP.

If you plan to use END, NAP, or SLEEP in your programs, make sure that your loads can tolerate these power outages. The simplest solution is often to connect resistors high or low (to +5V or ground) as appropriate to ensure a continuing supply of current during the reset glitch.

The demo program can be used to demonstrate the effects of the NAP glitch with an LED and resistor as shown in Figure 5.16.

Figure 5.16: Example LED Circuit.

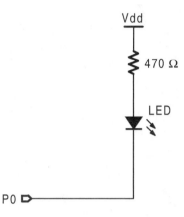

Vdd

470 Ω

LED

P0

Demo Program (NAP.bs2)

NOTE: This is written for the BS2 but can be used for the BS1, BS2e, BS2sx and BS2p also. Locate the proper source code file or modify the STAMP directive before downloading to the BS1, BS2e, BS2sx or BS2p.

```
' The program below lights an LED by placing a low on pin 0. This completes the circuit from
' +5V, through the LED and resistor, to ground. During the NAP interval, the LED stays lit, but
' blinks off for a fraction of a second. This blink is caused by the NAP wakeup mechanism
' During wakeup, all pins briefly slip into input mode, effectively disconnecting them from
' loads.

'{$STAMP BS2}                              'STAMP directive (specifies a BS2)

LOW  0            ' Turn LED on.
Snooze:
  NAP  4         ' Nap for 288 ms.
GOTO Snooze
```

OUTPUT

BS1	BS2	BS2e	BS2sx	BS2p

⌷1⌷ ⌷2⌷ ⌷2ₑ⌷ ⌷2ₛₓ⌷ ⌷2ₚ⌷ **OUTPUT** *Pin*

⌷1⌷
NOTE: Expressions are not allowed as arguments on the BS1. The range of the *Pin* argument on the BS1 is 0 – 7.

Function
Make the specified pin an output.
- *Pin* is a variable/constant/expression (0 – 15) that specifies which I/O pin to set to output mode.

Explanation
There are several ways to make a pin an output. Commands that rely on output pins, like PULSOUT and SEROUT, automatically change the specified pin to output. Writing 1s to particular bits of the variable DIRS makes the corresponding pins outputs. And then there's the OUTPUT command.

When a pin is an output, your program can change its state by writing to the corresponding bit in the OUTS variable (PINS on the BS1). For example:

OUTPUT 4
OUT4 = 1

EFFECTS OF SETTING AN INPUT PIN TO AN OUTPUT.

When your program changes a pin from input to output, whatever state happens to be in the corresponding bit of OUTS (PINS on the BS1) sets the initial state of the pin. To simultaneously make a pin an output and set its state use the HIGH and LOW commands.

⌷1⌷ **Demo Program (INOUT.bas)**
```
' This program demonstrates how the input/output direction of a pin is determined by
' the corresponding bit of DIRS. It also shows that the state of the pin itself (as
' reflected by the corresponding bit of PINS) is determined by the outside world when
' the pin is an input, and by the corresponding bit of PINS when it's an output. To
' set up the demo, connect a 10k resistor from +5V to P7 on the BASIC Stamp. The
' resistor to +5V puts a high (1) on the pin when it's an input. The BASIC Stamp can
' override this state by writing a low (0) to bit 7 of OUTS and changing the pin to output.

'{$STAMP BS1}                              'STAMP directive (specifies a BS1)

INPUT 7                                    ' Make I/O pin 7 an input.
DEBUG "State of pin 7: ", #PIN7, CR

PIN7 = 0                                   ' Write 0 to output latch.
DEBUG "After 0 written to OUT7: ", #PIN7, CR
```

```
OUTPUT 7                                ' Make I/O pin 7 an output.
DEBUG "After pin 7 changed to output: ", #PIN7
```

Demo Program (INPUT_OUTPUT.bs2)

```
' This program demonstrates how the input/output direction of a pin is determined by
' the corresponding bit of DIRS. It also shows that the state of the pin itself (as
' reflected by the corresponding bit of INS) is determined by the outside world when
' the pin is an input, and by the corresponding bit of OUTS when it's an output. To
' set up the demo, connect a 10k resistor from +5V to P7 on the BASIC Stamp. The
' resistor to +5V puts a high (1) on the pin when it's an input. The BASIC Stamp can
' override this state by writing a low (0) to bit 7 of OUTS and changing the pin to output.


'{$STAMP  BS2}                          'STAMP directive (specifies a BS2)


INPUT 7                                 ' Make I/O pin 7 an input.
DEBUG "State of pin 7: ", BIN IN7, CR


OUT7 = 0                                ' Write 0 to output latch.
DEBUG "After 0 written to OUT7: ", BIN IN7, CR


OUTPUT 7                                ' Make I/O pin 7 an output.
DEBUG "After pin 7 changed to output: ", BIN IN7
```

NOTE: This is written for the BS2 but can be used for the BS2e, BS2sx and BS2p also. Locate the proper source code file or modify the STAMP directive before downloading to the BS2e, BS2sx or BS2p.

OWIN

| BS1 | BS2 | BS2e | BS2sx | **BS2p** |

OWIN *Pin, Mode, [InputData]*

Function

Receive data from a device using the 1-wire protocol.

- *Pin* is a variable/constant/expression (0 – 15) that specifies which I/O pin to use. 1-wire devices require only one I/O pin (called DQ) to communicate. This I/O pin will be toggled between output and input mode during the OWIN command and will be set to input mode by the end of the OWIN command.
- *Mode* is a variable/constant/expression (0 – 15) indicating the mode of data transfer. The *Mode* argument controls placement of reset pulses (and detection of presence pulses) as well as byte vs. bit input and normal vs. high speed. See explanation below.
- *InputData* is a list of variables and modifiers that tells OWIN what to do with incoming data. OWIN can store data in a variable or array, interpret numeric text (decimal, binary, or hex) and store the corresponding value in a variable, wait for a fixed or variable sequence of bytes, or ignore a specified number of bytes. These actions can be combined in any order in the *InputData* list.

Quick Facts

Table 5.43: OWIN Quick Facts.

	BS2p
Receive Rate	Approximately 20 kbits/sec (low speed, not including reset pulse)
Special notes	The DQ pin (specified by *Pin*) must have a 4.7 KΩ pull-up resister.

Explanation

The 1-wire protocol is a form of asynchronous serial communication developed by Dallas Semiconductor. It only requires one I/O pin and that pin can be shared between multiple 1-wire devices. The OWIN command allows the BASIC Stamp to receive data from a 1-wire device.

A SIMPLE OWIN EXAMPLE.

The following is an example of the OWIN command:

```
Result     VAR    BYTE
OWIN 0, 1, [Result]
```

This code will transmit a "reset" pulse to a 1-wire device (connected to I/O pin 0) and then will detect the device's "presence" pulse and then receive one byte and store it in the variable *Result*.

The *Mode* argument is used to control placement of reset pulses (and detection of presence pulses) and to designate byte vs. bit input and normal vs. high speed. Figure 5.17 shows the meaning of each of the 4 bits of *Mode*. Table 5.44 shows just some of the 16 possible values and their effect.

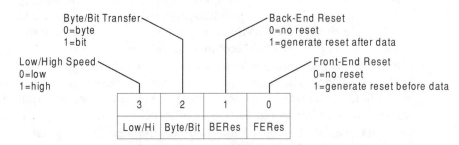

Figure 5.17: *Mode* Format.

Table 5.44: OWIN Mode Values.

Mode	Effect
0	No Reset, Byte mode, Low speed
1	Reset before data, Byte mode, Low speed
2	Reset after data, Byte mode, Low speed
3	Reset before and after data, Byte mode, Low speed
4	No Reset, Bit mode, Low speed
5	Reset before data, Bit mode, Low speed
8	No Reset, Byte mode, High speed
9	Reset before data, Byte mode, High speed

The proper value for *Mode* depends on the 1-wire device and the portion of the communication you're working on. Please consult the data sheet for the device in question to determine the correct value for *Mode*. In many cases, however, when using the OWIN command, *Mode* should be set for either No Reset (to receive data from a transaction already started by a OWOUT command) or a Back-End Reset (to terminate the session after data is received). This may vary due to device and application requirements, however.

When using the Bit (rather than Byte) mode of data transfer, all variables in the *InputData* argument will only receive one bit. For example, the following code could be used to receive two bits using this mode:

```
FirstBit    VAR    BIT
SecondBit   VAR    BIT
OWIN 0, 6, [FirstBit, SecondBit]
```

In the code above, we chose the value "6" for *Mode*. This sets Bit transfer and Back-End Reset modes. Also, we could have chosen to make the *FirstBit* and *SecondBit* variables each a byte in size, but they still would only have received one bit each in the OWIN command (due to the *Mode* we chose).

RECEIVING FORMATTED DATA.

The OWIN command's *InputData* argument is similar to the SERIN command's *InputData* argument. This means data can be received as ASCII character values, decimal, hexadecimal and binary translations and string data as in the examples below. (Assume a 1-wire device is used and that it transmits the string, "Value: 3A:101" every time it receives a Front-End Reset pulse).

```
Value       VAR    BYTE(13)
OWIN 0, 1, [Value]          'receive the ASCII value for "V"
OWIN 0, 1, [DEC Value]      'receive the number 3.
OWIN 0, 1, [HEX Value]      'receive the number $3A.
OWIN 0, 1, [BIN Value]      'receive the number %101.
OWIN 0, 1, [STR Value\13]   'receive the string "Value: 3A:101"
```

Tables 5.45 and 5.46 list all the available special formatters and conversion formatters available to the OWIN command. See the SERIN command for additional information and examples of their use.

Table 5.45: OWIN Special Formatters.

Special Formatter	Action
STR *ByteArray* \L {\E}	Input a character string of length L into an array. If specified, an end character E causes the string input to end before reaching length L. Remaining bytes are filled with 0s (zeros).
WAITSTR *ByteArray* {\L}	Wait for a sequence of bytes matching a string stored in an array variable, optionally limited to L characters. If the optional L argument is left off, the end of the array-string must be marked by a byte containing a zero (0).
SKIP *Length*	Ignore *Length* bytes of characters.

Conversion Formatter	Type of Number	Numeric Characters Accepted	Notes
DEC{1..5}	Decimal, optionally limited to 1 – 5 digits	0 through 9	1
SDEC{1..5}	Signed decimal, optionally limited to 1 – 5 digits	-, 0 through 9	1,2
HEX{1..4}	Hexadecimal, optionally limited to 1 – 4 digits	0 through 9, A through F	1,3
SHEX{1..4}	Signed hexadecimal, optionally limited to 1 – 4 digits	-, 0 through 9, A through F	1,2,3
IHEX{1..4}	Indicated hexadecimal, optionally limited to 1 – 4 digits	$, 0 through 9, A through F	1,3,4
ISHEX{1..4}	Signed, indicated hexadecimal, optionally limited to 1 – 4 digits	-, $, 0 through 9, A through F	1,2,3,4
BIN{1..16}	Binary, optionally limited to 1 – 16 digits	0, 1	1
SBIN{1..16}	Signed binary, optionally limited to 1 – 16 digits	-, 0, 1	1,2
IBIN{1..16}	Indicated binary, optionally limited to 1 – 16 digits	%, 0, 1	1,4
ISBIN{1..16}	Signed, indicated binary, optionally limited to 1 – 16 digits	-, %, 0, 1	1,2,4

Table 5.46: OWIN Conversion Formatters.

1 All numeric conversions will continue to accept new data until receiving either the specified number of digits (ex: three digits for DEC3) or a non-numeric character.

2 To be recognized as part of a number, the minus sign (-) must immediately precede a numeric character. The minus sign character occurring in non-numeric text is ignored and any character (including a space) between a minus and a number causes the minus to be ignored.

3 The hexadecimal formatters are not case-sensitive; "a" through "f" means the same as "A" through "F".

4 Indicated hexadecimal and binary formatters ignore all characters, even valid numerics, until they receive the appropriate prefix ($ for hexadecimal, % for binary). The indicated formatters can differentiate between text and hexadecimal (ex: ABC would be interpreted by HEX as a number but IHEX would ignore it unless expressed as $ABC). Likewise, the binary version can distinguish the decimal number 10 from the binary number %10. A prefix occurring in non-numeric text is ignored, and any character (including a space) between a prefix and a number causes the prefix to be ignored. Indicated, signed formatters require that the minus sign come before the prefix, as in -$1B45.

THE 1-WIRE PROTOCOL FORMAT.

The 1-wire protocol has a well-defined standard for transaction sequences. Every transaction sequence consists of four parts: 1) Initialization, 2) ROM Function Command, 3) Memory Function Command, and 4) Transaction/Data. Additionally, the ROM Function Command and Memory Function Command are always 8 bits wide (1 byte in size) and is sent least-significant-bit (LSB) first.

The Initialization part consists of a reset pulse (generated by the master) and will be followed by a presence pulse (generated by all slave devices). Figure 5.18 details the reset pulse generated by the BASIC Stamp and a typical presence pulse generated by a 1-wire slave, in response.

Figure 5.18: OWIN Reset and Presence Pulse.

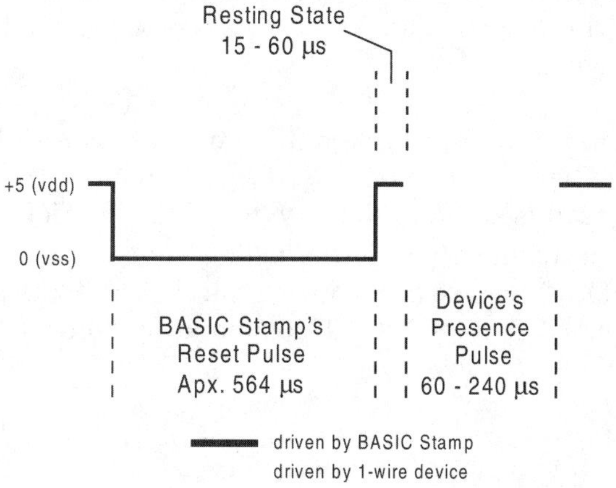

```
                              Resting State
                               15 - 60 µs

 +5 (vdd)  _____           _____           _____

 0 (vss)         |_____|

                   BASIC Stamp's      Device's
                   Reset Pulse        Presence
                   Apx. 564 µs        Pulse
                                      60 - 240 µs

                  ▬▬▬▬  driven by BASIC Stamp
                        driven by 1-wire device
```

This reset pulse is controlled by the lowest two bits of the *Mode* argument in the OWIN command. It can be made to appear before the ROM Function Command (ex: *Mode* = 1), after the Transaction/Data portion (ex: *Mode* = 2), before and after the entire transaction (ex: *Mode* = 3) or not at all (ex: *Mode* = 0). See the section on *Mode*, above, for more information.

Following the Initialization part is the ROM Function Command. The ROM Function Command is used to address the desired 1-wire device. Table 5.47 shows common ROM Function Commands. If only a single 1-wire device is connected, the Match ROM command can be used to address it. If more than one 1-wire device is attached, the BASIC Stamp will ultimately have to address them individually using the Match ROM command.

Command	Value (in Hex)	Action
Read ROM	$33	Reads the 64-bit ID of the 1-wire device. This command can only be used if there is a single 1-wire device on the line.
Match ROM	$55	This command, followed by a 64-bit ID, allows the BASIC Stamp to address a specific 1-wire device.
Skip ROM	$CC	Address a 1-wire device without its 64-bit ID. This command can only be used if there is a single 1-wire device on the line.
Search ROM	$F0	Reads the 64-bit IDs of all the 1-wire devices on the line. A process of elimination is used to distinguish each unique device.

Table 5.47: 1-wire ROM Function Commands.

The third part, the Memory Function Command, allows the BASIC Stamp to address specific memory locations, or features, of the 1-wire device. Refer to the 1-wire device's data sheet for a list of the available Memory Function Commands.

Finally, the Transaction/Data section is used to read or write data to the 1-wire device. The OWIN command will read data at this point in the transaction. A read is accomplished by generating a brief low-pulse and sampling the line within 15 µs of the falling edge of the pulse. This is called a "Read Slot." Figure 5.19 shows typical Read Slots performed by the BASIC Stamp. See the OWOUT command for information on Write Slots.

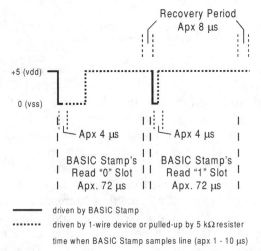

Figure 5.19: Example Read Slot.

The Demo Program uses a Dallas Semiconductor DS1820 Digital Thermometer device connected as follows. Note that the 4.7 kΩ pull-up resister is required for proper operation.

Figure 5.20: DS1820 Circuit. NOTE: The 4.7 kΩ resister is required for proper operation.

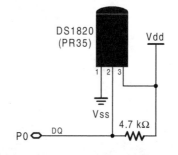

Demo Program (I2C.bsp)

```
' This program demonstrates interfacing to a Dallas Semiconductor DS1820 1-wire Digital
' Thermometer chip using the BS2p's 1-wire commands. Connect the BS2p to the DS1820
' as shown in the diagram in the OWIN or OWOUT command description.
' This code reads the Counts Remaing and Counts per Degree C registers in the DS1820
' chip in order to provide a more accurate temperature reading (down to 1/100th of a
' degree). It also calculates degrees Fahrenheit. NOTE: The algebraic equations used
' will not work properly with negative temperatures.

'{$STAMP BS2p}                'STAMP directive (specifies a BS2p)

Temp            VAR    WORD          'Holds the temperature value
CRem            VAR    BYTE          'Holds the counts remaining value
CPerC           VAR    BYTE          'Holds the Counts per degree C value

Start:
  OWOUT  0, 1, [$CC, $44]            'Send Calculate Temperature command

CheckForDone:                        'Wait until conversion is done
  PAUSE  25
  OWIN  0, 4, [Temp]                 'Here we just keep reading low pulses until
IF  Temp = 0  THEN  CheckForDone     'the DS1820 is done, then it returns high.

  OWOUT  0, 1, [$CC, $BE]            'Send Read ScratchPad command
  OWIN  0, 2, [Temp.LOWBYTE,Temp.HIGHBYTE,CRem,CRem,CRem,CRem,CRem,CPerC]

  'Calculate temperature in degrees C
  Temp = Temp>>1*100-25+((CPerC*100-(CRem*100))/CPerC)
  DEBUG  HOME, DEC3 Temp/100, ".", DEC2 Temp-(Temp/100*100), " C", CR

  'Calculate temperature in degrees F
  Temp = Temp*/461+3200
  DEBUG  DEC3 Temp/100, ".", DEC2 Temp-(Temp/100*100), " F"
GOTO  Start
```

OWOUT

| BS1 | BS2 | BS2e | BS2sx | **BS2p** |

OWOUT *Pin, Mode, [OutputData]*

Function

Send data to a device using the 1-wire protocol.

- ***Pin*** is a variable/constant/expression (0 – 15) that specifies which I/O pin to use. 1-wire devices require only one I/O pin (called DQ) to communicate. This I/O pin will be toggled between output and input mode during the OWOUT command and will be set to input mode by the end of the OWOUT command.
- ***Mode*** is a variable/constant/expression (0 – 15) indicating the mode of data transfer. The *Mode* argument controls placement of reset pulses (and detection of presence pulses) as well as byte vs. bit input and normal vs. high speed. See explanation below.
- ***OutputData*** is a list of variables and modifiers that tells OWOUT how to format outgoing data. OWOUT can transmit individual or repeating bytes, convert values into decimal, hexadecimal or binary text representations, or transmit strings of bytes from variable arrays. These actions can be combined in any order in the *OutputData* list.

Quick Facts

Table 5.48: OWOUT Quick Facts.

	BS2p
Transmission Rate	Approximately 20 kbits/sec (low speed, not including reset pulse)
Special notes	The DQ pin (specified by *Pin*) must have a 4.7 KΩ pull-up resister.

Explanation

The 1-wire protocol is a form of asynchronous serial communication developed by Dallas Semiconductor. It only requires one I/O pin and that pin can be shared between multiple 1-wire devices. The OWOUT command allows the BASIC Stamp to send data to a 1-wire device.

A SIMPLE OWOUT EXAMPLE.

The following is an example of the OWOUT command:

OWOUT 0, 1, [$4E]

This code will transmit a "reset" pulse to a 1-wire device (connected to I/O pin 0) and then will detect the device's "presence" pulse and then transmit one byte (the value $4E).

The *Mode* argument is used to control placement of reset pulses (and detection of presence pulses) and to designate byte vs. bit input and normal vs. high speed. Figure 5.21 shows the meaning of each of the 4 bits of *Mode*. Table 5.49 shows just some of the 16 possible values and their effect.

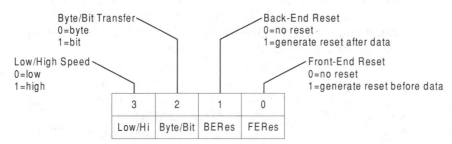

Figure 5.21: *Mode* Format.

Mode	Effect
0	No Reset, Byte mode, Low speed
1	Reset before data, Byte mode, Low speed
2	Reset after data, Byte mode, Low speed
3	Reset before and after data, Byte mode, Low speed
4	No Reset, Bit mode, Low speed
5	Reset before data, Bit mode, Low speed
8	No Reset, Byte mode, High speed
9	Reset before data, Byte mode, High speed

Table 5.49: OWOUT Common Mode Values.

The proper value for *Mode* depends on the 1-wire device and the portion of the communication you're working on. Please consult the data sheet for the device in question to determine the correct value for *Mode*. In many cases, however, when using the OWOUT command, *Mode* should be set for a Front-End Reset (to initialize the transaction). This may vary due to device and application requirements, however.

When using the Bit (rather than Byte) mode of data transfer, all variables in the *OutputData* argument will only transmit one bit. For example, the following code could be used to send two bits using this mode:

```
FirstBit     VAR   BIT
SecondBit    VAR   BIT
FirstBit = 0
SecondBit = 1
OWOUT  0, 5, [FirstBit, SecondBit]
```

In the code above, we chose the value "6" for *Mode*. This sets Bit transfer and Front-End Reset modes. Also, we could have chosen to make the *FirstBit* and *SecondBit* variables each a byte in size, but the BASIC Stamp would still only use the their lowest bit (BIT0) as the value to transmit in the OWOUT command (due to the *Mode* we chose).

SENDING AND FORMATTING DATA.

The OWOUT command's *OutputData* argument is similar to the DEBUG and SEROUT command's *OutputData* argument. This means data can be sent as literal text, ASCII character values, repetitive values, decimal, hexadecimal and binary translations and string data as in the examples below. (Assume a 1-wire device is used and that it transmits the string, "Value: 3A:101" every time it receives a Front-End Reset pulse).

```
Value        VAR   BYTE
Value = 65
OWOUT  0, 1, [Value]         'send the ASCII value for "A"
OWOUT  0, 1, [REP Value\5]   'send the ASCII value for "A" five times, ie: "AAAAA"
OWOUT  0, 1, [DEC Value]     'send two characters, "6" and "5"
OWOUT  0, 1, [HEX Value]     'send two characters, "4" and "1"
OWOUT  0, 1, [BIN Value]     'send seven characters, "1000001"
```

Tables 5.50 and 5.51 list all the available special formatters and conversion formatters available to the OWOUT command. See the DEBUG and SEROUT commands for additional information and examples of their use.

Table 5.50: OWOUT Special Formatters.

Special Formatter	Action
?	Displays "symbol = x' + carriage return; where x is a number. Default format is decimal, but may be combined with conversion formatters (ex: BIN ? x to display "x = binary_number").
ASC ?	Displays "symbol = 'x'" + carriage return; where x is an ASCII character.
STR *ByteArray* {\L}	Send character string from an array. The optional \L argument can be used to limit the output to L characters, otherwise, characters will be sent up to the first byte equal to 0 or the end of RAM space is reached.
REP *Byte* \L	Send a string consisting of *Byte* repeated L times (ex: REP "X"\10 sends "XXXXXXXXXX").

Table 5.51: OWOUT Conversion Formatters.

Conversion Formatter	Type of Number	Notes
DEC{1..5}	Decimal, optionally fixed to 1 – 5 digits	1
SDEC{1..5}	Signed decimal, optionally fixed to 1 – 5 digits	1,2
HEX{1..4}	Hexadecimal, optionally fixed to 1 – 4 digits	1
SHEX{1..4}	Signed hexadecimal, optionally fixed to 1 – 4 digits	1,2
IHEX{1..4}	Indicated hexadecimal, optionally fixed to 1 – 4 digits ($ prefix)	1
ISHEX{1..4}	Signed, indicated hexadecimal, optionally fixed to 1 – 4 digits ($ prefix)	1,2
BIN{1..16}	Binary, optionally fixed to 1 – 16 digits	1
SBIN{1..16}	Signed binary, optionally fixed to 1 – 16 digits	1,2
IBIN{1..16}	Indicated binary, optionally fixed to 1 – 16 digits (% prefix)	1
ISBIN{1..16}	Signed, indicated binary, optionally fixed to 1 – 16 digits (% prefix)	1,2

1 Fixed-digit formatters like DEC4 will pad the number with leading 0s if necessary; ex: DEC4 65 sends 0065. If a number is larger than the specified number of digits, the leading digits will be dropped; ex: DEC4 56422 sends 6422.
2 Signed modifiers work under two's complement rules.

THE 1-WIRE PROTOCOL FORMAT.

The 1-wire protocol has a well-defined standard for transaction sequences. Every transaction sequence consists of four parts: 1) Initialization, 2) ROM Function Command, 3) Memory Function Command, and 4) Transaction/Data. Additionally, the ROM Function Command and Memory Function Command are always 8 bits wide (1 byte in size) and is sent least-significant-bit (LSB) first.

The Initialization part consists of a reset pulse (generated by the master) and will be followed by a presence pulse (generated by all slave devices). Figure 5.22 details the reset pulse generated by the BASIC Stamp and a typical presence pulse generated by a 1-wire slave, in response.

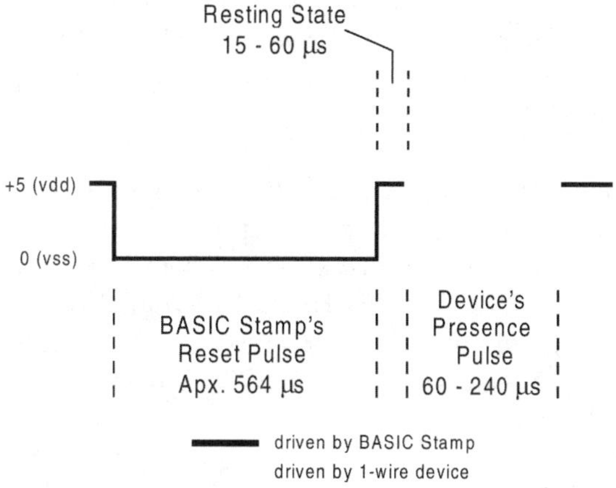

Figure 5.22: OWOUT Reset and Presence Pulse.

Resting State
15 - 60 µs

+5 (vdd)

0 (vss)

BASIC Stamp's
Reset Pulse
Apx. 564 µs

Device's
Presence
Pulse
60 - 240 µs

driven by BASIC Stamp
driven by 1-wire device

This reset pulse is controlled by the lowest two bits of the *Mode* argument in the OWOUT command. It can be made to appear before the ROM Function Command (ex: *Mode* = 1), after the Transaction/Data portion (ex: *Mode* = 2), before and after the entire transaction (ex: *Mode* = 3) or not at all (ex: *Mode* = 0). See the section on *Mode*, above, for more information.

Following the Initialization part is the ROM Function Command. The ROM Function Command is used to address the desired 1-wire device. Table 5.52 shows common ROM Function Commands. If only a single 1-wire device is connected, the Match ROM command can be used to address it. If more than one 1-wire device is attached, the BASIC Stamp will ultimately have to address them individually using the Match ROM command.

Table 5.52: OWOUT ROM Function Commands.

Command	Value (in Hex)	Action
Read ROM	$33	Reads the 64-bit ID of the 1-wire device. This command can only be used if there is a single 1-wire device on the line.
Match ROM	$55	This command, followed by a 64-bit ID, allows the BASIC Stamp to address a specific 1-wire device.
Skip ROM	$CC	Address a 1-wire device without its 64-bit ID. This command can only be used if there is a single 1-wire device on the line.
Search ROM	$F0	Reads the 64-bit IDs of all the 1-wire devices on the line. A process of elimination is used to distinguish each unique device.

The third part, the Memory Function Command, allows the BASIC Stamp to address specific memory locations, or features, of the 1-wire device. Refer to the 1-wire device's data sheet for a list of the available Memory Function Commands.

Finally, the Transaction/Data section is used to read or write data to the 1-wire device. The OWOUT command will write data at this point in the transaction. A write is accomplished by generating a low-pulse of a varying width to indicate a 0 or a 1. This is called a "Write Slot" and must be at least 60 µs wide. Figure 5.23 shows typical Write Slots performed by the BASIC Stamp. See the OWIN command for information on Read Slots.

Figure 5.23: Example Write Slots.

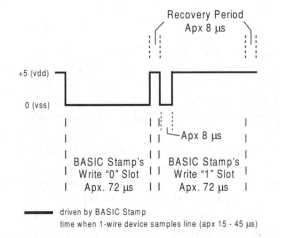

The Demo Program uses a Dallas Semiconductor DS1820 Digital Thermometer device connected as follows. Note that the 4.7 kΩ pull-up resister is required for proper operation.

Figure 5.24: DS1820 Circuit. NOTE: The 4.7 kΩ resister is required for proper operation.

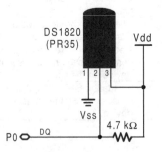

Demo Program (I2C.bsp)

```
' This program demonstrates interfacing to a Dallas Semiconductor DS1820 1-wire Digital
' Thermometer chip using the BS2p's 1-wire commands.  Connect the BS2p to the DS1820
' as shown in the diagram in the OWIN or OWOUT command description.
' This code reads the Counts Remaing and Counts per Degree C registers in the DS1820
' chip in order to provide a more accurate temperature reading (down to 1/100th of a
' degree).  It also calculates degrees Fahrenheit.  NOTE: The algebraic equations used
' will not work properly with negative temperatures.

'{$STAMP BS2p}              'STAMP directive (specifies a BS2p)

Temp            VAR    WORD         'Holds the temperature value
CRem            VAR    BYTE         'Holds the counts remaining value
CPerC           VAR    BYTE         'Holds the Counts per degree C value

Start:
  OWOUT  0, 1, [$CC, $44]           'Send Calculate Temperature command

CheckForDone:                       'Wait until conversion is done
  PAUSE  25
  OWIN  0, 4, [Temp]                'Here we just keep reading low pulses until
IF  Temp = 0  THEN CheckForDone     'the DS1820 is done, then it returns high.

  OWOUT  0, 1, [$CC, $BE]           'Send Read ScratchPad command
  OWIN  0, 2, [Temp.LOWBYTE,Temp.HIGHBYTE,CRem,CRem,CRem,CRem,CRem,CPerC]

'Calculate temperature in degrees C
Temp = Temp>>1*100-25+((CPerC*100-(CRem*100))/CPerC)
DEBUG  HOME, DEC3 Temp/100, ".", DEC2 Temp-(Temp/100*100), " C", CR

'Calculate temperature in degrees F
Temp = Temp*/461+3200
DEBUG DEC3 Temp/100, ".", DEC2 Temp-(Temp/100*100), " F"
GOTO  Start
```

PAUSE

| BS1 | BS2 | BS2e | BS2sx | BS2p |

PAUSE *Period*

NOTE: Expressions are not allowed as arguments on the BS1.

Function

Pause the program (do nothing) for the specified *Period*.

- **Period** is a variable/constant/expression (0 – 65535) that specifies the duration of the pause. The unit of time for *Period* is 1 millisecond.

Explanation

PAUSE delays the execution of the next program instruction for the specified number of milliseconds. For example:

```
Flash:
  LOW  0
  PAUSE  100
  HIGH  0
  PAUSE  100
GOTO  Flash
```

This code causes pin 0 to go low for 100 ms, then high for 100 ms. The delays produced by PAUSE are as accurate as the ceramic-resonator time base (on the BASIC Stamp modules), ±1 percent. When you use PAUSE in timing-critical applications, keep in mind the relatively low speed of the PBASIC interpreter. This is the time required for the BASIC Stamp to read and interpret an instruction stored in the EEPROM.

NOTE: This is written for the BS2 but can be used for the BS1, BS2e, BS2sx and BS2p also. Locate the proper source code file or modify the STAMP directive before downloading to the BS1, BS2e, BS2sx or BS2p.

Demo Program (PAUSE.bs2)

```
' This program demonstrates the PAUSE command's time delays. Once a second, the
' program will put the message, "paused" on the screen.

'{$STAMP BS2}                              'STAMP directive (specifies a BS2)

Again:
  DEBUG "paused", cr
  PAUSE 1000
GOTO Again
```

POLLIN

POLLIN *Pin, State*

Function

Specify a polled-input pin and active state.

- **Pin** is a variable/constant/expression (0 – 15) that specifies the I/O pin to use. This I/O pin will be set to input mode.
- **State** is a variable/constant/expression (0 – 1) that specifies whether to poll the I/O pin for a low (0) or a high (1) level.

Quick Facts

Table 5.53: POLLIN Quick Facts.

	BS2p
Available actions in response to reaching the desired State	1) Nothing, 2) Set polled-output pins to a specified state, 3) Run another program (in a specified program-slot), 4) Wait (pause program execution) until desired *State* is reached, 5) Any combination of 2, 3 and 4, above.
Special notes	• The polled-input pins are monitored (polled) in-between each command within the PBASIC code. • On the BS2p40, polled-input pins can be defined on both Main I/O and Aux I/O pins. These are all active regardless of which group the program happens to be using at the time of a polling event.

Explanation

The POLLIN command is one of a family of unique "polling" commands on the BS2p module. The other commands in this family include POLLMODE, POLLOUT, POLLRUN and POLLWAIT. The POLLIN command is used to specify an input pin to monitor, or "poll", in-between instructions during the rest of the PBASIC program. The BASIC Stamp will then perform some activity (in-between instructions) when the specified *State* is detected. The activity performed depends on the POLLMODE, POLLOUT and POLLRUN commands.

The "polling" commands allow the BASIC Stamp to respond to certain I/O pin events at a faster rate than what is normally possible through manual PBASIC programming. The term "poll" comes from the fact that the BASIC Stamp's interpreter periodically checks the state of the designated polled-input pins. It "polls" these pins after the end of each PBASIC command and before it reads the next PBASIC command from the user program; giving the appearance that it is polling "in the background".

POLLIN - BASIC Stamp Command Reference

This feature should not be confused with the concept of interrupts, as the BASIC Stamp does not support true interrupts.

The following is an example of the POLLIN command:

A SIMPLE POLLIN EXAMPLE.

```
POLLIN  0, 1
POLLMODE  2
```

The POLLIN command in the above code will cause the BASIC Stamp to set I/O pin 0 to an input mode and get ready to poll it for a high (1) state. The BASIC Stamp will not actually start polling until it is set to the appropriate mode, however. The second line, POLLMODE, initiates the polling process (see the POLLMODE description for more information). From then on, as the BASIC Stamp executes the rest of the program, it will check for a high level (logic 1) on I/O pin 0, in-between instructions.

In the code above, no obvious action will be noticed since we didn't tell the BASIC Stamp what to do when it detects a change on the I/O pin. One possible action the BASIC Stamp can be instructed to take is to change the state of an output, called a polled-output. Take a look at the next example:

SETTING ONE OF THE POSSIBLE ACTIONS: POLLED-OUTPUTS

```
POLLIN  0, 1
POLLOUT  1, 0
POLLMODE  2

Loop:
  DEBUG "Looping...", CR
GOTO Loop
```

In this example, in addition to an endless loop, we've added another polling command called POLLOUT (see the POLLOUT description for more information). Our POLLOUT command tells the BASIC Stamp to set I/O pin 1 to an output mode and set it low (0) when it detects the desired poll state. The poll state is the high (1) level on I/O pin 0 that POLLIN told it to look for. If the polled-input pin is not high, it will set polled-output pin 0 to high (1), instead.

Once the program reaches the endless loop, called *Loop*, it will continuously print "Looping..." on the PC screen. In between reading the DEBUG command and the GOTO command (and vice versa) it will check polled-input pin 0 and set polled-output pin 1 accordingly. In this case, when I/O pin 0 is set high, the BASIC Stamp will set I/O pin 1 low. When I/O pin 0 is set low, the BASIC Stamp will set I/O pin 1 high. It will continue to perform this operation, in-between each command in the loop, endlessly.

THE BASIC STAMP "REMEMBERS" THE POLLING CONFIGURATION FOR THE DURATION OF THE PBASIC PROGRAM.

It's important to note that, in this example, only the DEBUG and GOTO commands are being executed over and over again. The first three lines of code are only run once, yet their effects are "remembered" by the BASIC Stamp throughout the rest of the program.

FOR COMPARISON: ACHIEVING THE SAME EFFECTS WITHOUT THE POLLING COMMANDS.

If the polling commands were not used, the program would have to look like the one below in order to achieve the same effect.

```
INPUT 0
OUTPUT 1

Loop:
  OUT1 = ~IN0
  DEBUG "Looping...", CR
  OUT1 = ~IN0
GOTO Loop
```

In this example, we create the inverse relationship of input pin 0 and output pin 1 manually, in-between the DEBUG and GOTO lines. Though the effects are the same as when using the polling commands, this program actually takes a little longer to run and consumes 7 additional bytes of program (EEPROM) space. Clearly, using the polling commands is more efficient.

USING MULTIPLE POLLED-INPUT AND POLLED-OUTPUT PINS.

You can have as many polled-input and polled-output pins as you have available. If multiple polled-input pins are defined, any one of them can trigger changes on the polled-output pins that are also defined. For example:

```
POLLIN 0, 1
POLLIN 1, 1
POLLOUT 2, 0
POLLOUT 3, 0
POLLMODE 2

Loop:
  DEBUG "Looping...", CR
GOTO Loop
```

This code sets I/O pins 0 and 1 to polled-input pins (looking for a high (1) state) and sets I/O pins 2 and 3 to polled-output pins (with a low-active state). If either I/O pin 0 or 1 goes high, the BASIC Stamp will set I/O pins 2 and 3 low. This works similar to a logical OR operation. The truth table below shows all the possible states of these two polled-input pins and the corresponding states the BASIC Stamp will set the polled-output pins to.

Polled-Inputs		Polled-Outputs	
0	1	2	3
0	0	1	1
0	1	0	0
1	0	0	0
1	1	0	0

Table 5.54: Polled-Inputs / Polled-Outputs Truth Table.

Normally, any polled-output pins reflect the state changes continuously, as described above. The POLLMODE command supports another feature, however, where the polled-output pins will latch the active state; they will change only once (when the poll state is reached) and stay in the new state until the PBASIC program tells it to change again. See the POLLMODE description for more information.

POLLED-OUTPUTS CAN BE "LATCHED" ALSO.

Other possible actions in response to polled-input states are: 1) Running another program (in a specified program slot), 2) Waiting (pausing program execution with or without low-power mode) until the poll state is reached, or 3) Any combination of the above-mentioned actions.

Demo Program (POLINOUT.bsp)

```
' This program demonstrates the POLLIN, POLLOUT and POLLMODE commands. It
' will watch for a high signal on I/O pin 0 and then will output the opposite signal on I/O pin 1
' all while printing a message on the PC screen.

'{$STAMP  BS2p}                    'STAMP directive (specifies a BS2p)

Init:
  POLLIN  0, 1                     'Set I/O pin 0 to polled-input looking for a high
  POLLOUT 1, 0                     'Set I/O pin 1 to polled-output; opposite level a 0
  POLLMODE 2                       'Set mode to enable polled-outputs

Main:
  DEBUG  "Working...", BIN1 OUT2, CR        'Waste time writing to PC screen
  PAUSE  100
GOTO  Main
```

POLLMODE

 POLLMODE *Mode*

Function

Specify a polled command mode.

- **Mode** is a variable/constant/expression (0 – 15) that indicates the mode in which to process the polled command configuration.

Quick Facts

Table 5.55: POLLMODE Quick Facts.

	BS2p
Special notes	• Polled-output pins will either change states continuously, just once or not at all, depending on the POLLMODE command. • A poll-mode of 2 or 4 is required for a POLLWAIT command to work. • If both polled-outputs and polled-run are active, the polled-output event will occur before the polled-run event.

Explanation

The POLLMODE command is one of a family of unique "polling" commands on the BS2p module. The other commands in this family include POLLIN, POLLOUT, POLLRUN and POLLWAIT. The POLLMODE command is used to specify the mode in which polling events and activities are processed. This activity will occur in-between instructions during the rest of the PBASIC program.

The "polling" commands allow the BASIC Stamp to respond to certain I/O pin events at a faster rate than what is normally possible through manual PBASIC programming. The term "poll" comes from the fact that the BASIC Stamp's interpreter periodically checks the state of the designated polled-input pins. It "polls" these pins after the end of each PBASIC command and before it reads the next PBASIC command from the user program; giving the appearance that it is polling "in the background". This feature should not be confused with the concept of interrupts, as the BASIC Stamp does not support true interrupts.

The POLLMODE command sets one of 15 possible modes for the polling commands. It is used mainly before and/or after any POLLIN, POLLOUT and POLLRUN commands to disable and enable the polling features as desired. Table 5.56 shows the mode values and their effect.

Mode	Effect
0	Deactivate polling, clear polled-input and output configuration.
1	Deactivate polling, save polled-input and output configuration.
2	Activate polling with polled-output action (and polled-wait) only.
3[1]	Activate polling with polled-run action only.
4[2]	Activate polling with polled-output/polled-wait and polled-run actions.
5[3]	Clear polled-input configuration.
6[3]	Clear polled-output configuration.
7[3]	Clear polled-input and output configuration.
8 – 15	Same at 0 – 7 except polled-output states are latched.

Table 5.56: POLLMODE *Mode* Values.

[1] After the polled-run action occurs, the mode switches to 1 (deactivated, saved)
[2] After the polled-run action occurs, the mode switches to 2 (activated, outputs)
[3] These modes do not override the previous mode. Also, the output state of polled-outputs does not change as a result of these modes.

The polled-run modes, 3 and 4, are unique. As soon as the polled-run action occurs, the mode switches to 1 (deactivated, saved) or 2 (activated, outputs), respectively. This is so that the BASIC Stamp doesn't continuously go to the start of the designated program slot while the polled-inputs are in the desired poll state. Without this "one shot" feature, your program would appear to lock-up as long as the polled-inputs are in the designated state.

The clear configuration modes, 5, 6 and 7, are also unique. These modes do not override the previous mode. For example, if polled-inputs, polled-outputs and a polled-run configuration was set and the mode was set to 4 (activated, outputs and run) and later the program issued a POLLMODE 6 command, the polled-output configuration would be cleared but the mode would switch back to 4… still allowing the run action. This also means if, later still, the program issues a POLLOUT command, this polled-output would take effect immediately (since the mode is still 4). Also note that these modes do not change the output state of previously defined polled-output pins.

The POLLMODE command determines what action, if any, will occur in response to a polled-input event. This command works in conjunction with the POLLIN, POLLOUT and POLLRUN commands. The following is an example of the POLLMODE command:

A SIMPLE POLLMODE EXAMPLE.

```
POLLIN  0, 1
POLLOUT  1, 0
POLLMODE  2

Loop:
 DEBUG "Looping...", CR
GOTO Loop
```

In this example, the first two lines configure I/O pin 0 as a polled-input (looking for a high state) and I/O pin 1 as a polled-output (going low if I/O pin 0 goes high, and vice versa). The third line, POLLMODE, initiates the polling process and configures polled-outputs to be active. From then on, as the BASIC Stamp executes the rest of the program, it will check for a high level (logic 1) on I/O pin 0, in-between instructions and will set I/O pin 1 accordingly.

If, in the above example, the poll mode was set to 1 (which means deactivate polling but save configuration) I/O pins 0 and 1 would still be defined the same way, and I/O pin 1 would still be set to output mode, but no polling would take place during the rest of the program.

Here's another example that demonstrates mode 1 (deactivate but save configuration).

```
POLLIN  0, 1
POLLOUT  1, 0
POLLMODE  2

DEBUG "Polling configured", CR

Main:
 POLLMODE 1
 DEBUG "No polling allowed here...", CR
 PAUSE 1000
 POLLMODE 2

Loop:
 DEBUG "Polling now...", CR
GOTO Loop
```

In this case, polling is configured and activated before "Polling configured" is printed on the screen. Once we reach the *Main* routine, however, polling is disabled (via the POLLMODE 1 command) and no polling occurs during the printing of "No polling allowed here..." or during the 1 second pause afterward. Finally, polling is activated again, and since the configuration was saved (because of mode 1, before) the polling activity acts just like it did initially for the remainder of the program. The ability to temporarily disable polling, without changing the configuration, can be a powerful feature for certain "critical" parts of a program.

The following example contains two programs. The first should be downloaded into program slot 0 and the second into program slot 1. We'll assume they are called POLL0.bsp and POLL1.bsp, respectively (as defined in the STAMP directive lines).

```
' ----- program #1 (slot 0) -----
' {$STAMP BS2p, POLL1.bsp}

POLLIN 0, 1
POLLOUT 1, 1
POLLRUN 1
POLLMODE 4

Loop:
  DEBUG "Program 1", CR
GOTO Loop
```

```
' ----- program #2 (slot 1) -----
' {$STAMP BS2p}

DEBUG "Switching...", CR

Loop:
  DEBUG "Program 2", CR
GOTO Loop
```

In this example (containing two programs; one is slot 0 and the other in slot 1) program 1 (slot 0) will configure polled-input pin 0 to detect a high state and polled-output 1 to go high in response. Program 1 also configures a polled-run activity (see the POLLRUN description for more information) to run the program in slot 1. The POLLMODE setting activates the polled-output and the polled-run. Then, program 1 continuously prints "Program 1" on the PC screen.

Once I/O pin 0 goes high, however, the BASIC Stamp will set I/O pin 1 high, then execution will be switched to the program in slot 1 (program 2). Program 2 will first print "Switching..." on the PC screen and then will continuously print "Program 2". From this point forward, I/O pin 1 will continue to be set low and high in response to changes occurring on I/O pin 0, but the polled-run activity is disabled and the BASIC Stamp endlessly runs the code in program 2's *Loop* routine.

Demo Program (POLINOUT.bsp)

```
' This program demonstrates the POLLIN, POLLOUT and POLLMODE commands.  It
' will watch for a high signal on I/O pin 0 and then will output the opposite signal on I/O pin 1
' all while printing a message on the PC screen.

'{$STAMP BS2p}                          'STAMP directive (specifies a BS2p)

Init:
  POLLIN  0, 1                          'Set I/O pin 0 to polled-input looking for a high
  POLLOUT  1, 0                         'Set I/O pin 1 to polled-output; opposite level a 0
  POLLMODE  2                           'Set mode to enable polled-outputs

Main:
  DEBUG  "Working...", BIN1 OUT2, CR         'Waste time writing to PC screen
  PAUSE  100
GOTO  Main
```

POLLOUT

BS1	BS2	BS2e	BS2sx	**BS2p**

POLLOUT *Pin, State*

Function

Specify a polled-output pin and active state.

- *Pin* is a variable/constant/expression (0 – 15) that specifies the I/O pin to use. This I/O pin will be set to output mode.
- *State* is a variable/constant/expression (0 – 1) that specifies whether to set the I/O pin low (0) or high (1) when a polled-input pin changes to its poll state.

Quick Facts

Table 5.57: POLLOUT Quick Facts.

	BS2p
Special notes	• The POLLOUT command will immediately change the I/O pin to an output mode and set its level opposite to that of *State*, regardless of the polled-input states or the polled mode. • Polled-output pins will either change states continuously, just once or not at all, depending on the POLLMODE command. • On the BS2p40, polled-output pins can be defined on both Main I/O and Aux I/O pins. These are all active regardless of which group the program happens to be using at the time of a polling event. • If both polled-outputs and polled-run are active, the polled-output event will occur before the polled-run event.

Explanation

The POLLOUT command is one of a family of unique "polling" commands on the BS2p module. The other commands in this family include POLLIN, POLLMODE, POLLRUN and POLLWAIT. The POLLOUT command is used to specify an output pin that changes states in response to changes on any of the defined polled-input pins. This activity will occur in-between instructions during the rest of the PBASIC program.

The "polling" commands allow the BASIC Stamp to respond to certain I/O pin events at a faster rate than what is normally possible through manual PBASIC programming. The term "poll" comes from the fact that the BASIC Stamp's interpreter periodically checks the state of the designated polled-input pins. It "polls" these pins after the end of each PBASIC command and before it reads the next PBASIC command from the user program; giving the appearance that it is polling "in the background". This feature should not be confused with the concept of interrupts, as the BASIC Stamp does not support true interrupts.

POLLOUT - BASIC Stamp Command Reference

The POLLOUT command achieves one of three possible actions in response to a polled-input event. This command works in conjunction with the POLLIN and POLLMODE commands. The following is an example of the POLLOUT command:

A SIMPLE POLLOUT EXAMPLE.

```
POLLIN 0, 1
POLLOUT 1, 0
POLLMODE 2

Loop:
  DEBUG "Looping...", CR
GOTO Loop
```

In this example, the POLLOUT command tells the BASIC Stamp to set I/O pin 1 to an output mode and set it low (0) when it detects the desired poll state. The poll state is the high (1) level on I/O pin 0 that POLLIN told it to look for. If the polled-input pin is not high, the BASIC Stamp will set polled-output pin 0 to high (1), instead. The BASIC Stamp will not actually start polling until it is set to the appropriate mode, however. The third line, POLLMODE, initiates the polling process (see the POLLMODE description for more information). From then on, as the BASIC Stamp executes the rest of the program, it will check for a high level (logic 1) on I/O pin 0, in-between instructions.

Once the program reaches the endless loop, called *Loop*, it will continuously print "Looping..." on the PC screen. In between reading the DEBUG command and the GOTO command (and vice versa) it will check polled-input pin 0 and set polled-output pin 1 accordingly. In this case, when I/O pin 0 is set high, the BASIC Stamp will set I/O pin 1 low. When I/O pin 0 is set low, the BASIC Stamp will set I/O pin 1 high. It will continue to perform this operation, in-between each command in the loop, endlessly.

It's important to note that in this example only the DEBUG and GOTO commands are being executed over and over again. The first three lines of code are only run once, yet their effects are "remembered" by the BASIC Stamp throughout the rest of the program.

THE BASIC STAMP "REMEMBERS" THE POLLING CONFIGURATION FOR THE DURATION OF THE PBASIC PROGRAM.

If the polling commands were not used, the program would have to look like the one below in order to achieve the same effect.

FOR COMPARISON: ACHIEVING THE SAME EFFECTS WITHOUT THE POLLING COMMANDS.

```
INPUT 0
OUTPUT 1

Loop:
  OUT1 = ~IN0
  DEBUG "Looping...", CR
  OUT1 = ~IN0
GOTO Loop
```

In this example, we create the inverse relationship of input pin 0 and output pin 1 manually, in-between the DEBUG and GOTO lines. Though the effects are the same as when using the polling commands, this program actually takes a little longer to run and consumes 7 additional bytes of program (EEPROM) space. Clearly, using the polling commands is more efficient.

USING MULTIPLE POLLED-INPUT AND POLLED-OUTPUT PINS.

You can have as many polled-input and polled-output pins as you have available. If multiple polled-output pins are defined, all of them change in response to changes on the polled-input pins. For example:

```
POLLIN 0, 1
POLLOUT 1, 0
POLLOUT 2, 1
POLLOUT 3, 1
POLLMODE 2

Loop:
  DEBUG "Looping...", CR
GOTO Loop
```

This code sets up I/O pin 0 as a polled-input pin (looking for a high (1) state) and sets I/O pins 1, 2 and 3 to polled-output pins. Polled-output pin 1 is set to a low-active state and pins 2 and 3 are set to a high-active state. If I/O pin 0 goes high, the BASIC Stamp will set I/O pin 1 low and I/O pins 2 and 3 high. The table below shows the two possible states of the polled-input pin and the corresponding states the BASIC Stamp will set the polled-output pins to.

Table 5.58: POLLOUT Truth Table.

Polled-Input	Polled-Outputs		
0	1	2	3
0	1	0	0
1	0	1	1

POLLED-OUTPUTS CAN BE "LATCHED" ALSO.

Normally, any polled-output pins reflect the state changes continuously, as described above. The POLLMODE command supports another feature,

POLLOUT - BASIC Stamp Command Reference

however, where the polled-output pins will latch the active state; they will change only once (when the poll state is reached) and stay in the new state until the PBASIC program tells it to change again. See the POLLMODE description for more information.

A clever use of the "latched" feature is to set a polled-output to be the same as the polled-input. For example, suppose an application needed to respond in some way if a polled-input pin goes high, but it doesn't need to respond immediately, and the other tasks should not be interrupted. In essence, we need a way to know if the pin has gone high since the last time we checked it. Look at this example:

```
POLLOUT 0, 1                    'Set I/O 0 to polled-output, high
POLLIN 0, 1                     'Set I/O 0 back to polled-input, high
POLLMODE 10                     'Set mode to latch the polled-output

Idx  VAR   BYTE

Work:                           'Do nonsense work, but check once in a
  FOR Idx = 1 TO 20             'while to see if the polled event ever occured
    DEBUG "Working...", CR
  NEXT
  IF OUT0 = 0 THEN Work

Respond:                        'Send a different message if it did occur
  DEBUG CR, "Hey!  You set my pin high!", CR
  POLLMODE 10                   'Reset polled-output's latch function
GOTO Work
```

Here, we set I/O pin 0 to a polled-output, then immediately set it to a polled-input. Then we set the polled-mode to latch the polled-outputs. Since the POLLIN command occurred after the POLLOUT, I/O pin 0 will be an input, but the polling feature will still affect the OUT0 bit (output latch for I/O pin 0). Then, the program performs some work, and once in a while, checks the state of OUT0. If OUT0 is 0, I/O pin 0 was never seen to go high. If, however, OUT0 is 1, I/O pin 0 must have gone high while the program was doing other work, and now it can respond in the proper manner. This even works if the pin had gone high and then low again before we check it (as long as it was high at some point in between the instructions in our *Work* routine.

It is important to note that during the time between the POLLOUT and POLLIN commands, I/O pin 0 will be set to an output direction. This can cause a temporary short with the circuitry connected to I/O pin 0, so it is vital that a large enough series resister (perhaps 100 ohms or greater) be inserted on that pin to protect the external device and the BASIC Stamp.

Demo Program (POLINOUT.bsp)

```
' This program demonstrates the POLLIN, POLLOUT and POLLMODE commands.  It
' will watch for a high signal on I/O pin 0 and then will output the opposite signal on I/O pin 1
' all while printing a message on the PC screen.

'{$STAMP BS2p}                          'STAMP directive (specifies a BS2p)

Init:
  POLLIN  0, 1                          'Set I/O pin 0 to polled-input looking for a high
  POLLOUT  1, 0                         'Set I/O pin 1 to polled-output; opposite level a 0
  POLLMODE  2                           'Set mode to enable polled-outputs

Main:
  DEBUG  "Working...", BIN1  OUT2, CR          'Waste time writing to PC screen
  PAUSE  100
GOTO  Main
```

POLLRUN

BS1	BS2	BS2e	BS2sx	**BS2p**

POLLRUN *Slot*

Function

Specify a program to run upon a polled-input event.

- **Slot** is a variable/constant/expression (0 – 7) that specifies the program slot to run when a polled-input event occurs.

Quick Facts

Table 5.59: POLLRUN Quick Facts.

	BS2p
Default Slot	The default polled-run slot is 0. If no POLLRUN command is given and a poll mode of 3 or 4 is set, the program in slot 0 will run in response to a polled-input event.
Special notes	• If both polled-outputs and polled-run are active, the polled-output event will occur before the polled-run event.

Explanation

The POLLRUN command is one of a family of unique "polling" commands on the BS2p module. The other commands in this family include POLLIN, POLLMODE, POLLOUT and POLLWAIT. The POLLRUN command is used to specify a program slot to run in response to a polled event. This activity can occur in-between any two instructions within the rest of the PBASIC program.

The "polling" commands allow the BASIC Stamp to respond to certain I/O pin events at a faster rate than what is normally possible through manual PBASIC programming. The term "poll" comes from the fact that the BASIC Stamp's interpreter periodically checks the state of the designated polled-input pins. It "polls" these pins after the end of each PBASIC command and before it reads the next PBASIC command from the user program; giving the appearance that it is polling "in the background". This feature should not be confused with the concept of interrupts, as the BASIC Stamp does not support true interrupts.

A SIMPLE POLLRUN EXAMPLE.

The following is a simple example of the POLLRUN command.

```
POLLIN 0, 1
POLLRUN 1
POLLMODE 3

Loop:
 DEBUG "Waiting in Program Slot 0...", CR
GOTO Loop
```

The first line of the above code will set up I/O pin 0 as a polled-input pin looking for a high (1) state. The second line, POLLRUN, tells the BASIC Stamp that when I/O pin 0 goes high, it should switch execution over to the program residing in program slot 1. The third line, POLLMODE, activates the polled-run configuration.

Once the BASIC Stamp reaches the *Loop* routine, it will continuously print "Waiting in Program Slot 0..." on the PC screen. In between reading the DEBUG and GOTO commands, however, the BASIC Stamp will poll I/O pin 0 and check for a high or low state. If the state of pin 0 is low, it will do nothing and continue as normal. If the state of pin 1 is high, it will switch execution over to the program in slot 1 (the second program is not shown in this example). The switch to another program slot works exactly like with the RUN command; the designated program is run and the BASIC Stamp does not "return" to the previous program (similar to a GOTO command).

Note that in order for the polled-run activity to occur, the poll mode must be set to either 3 or 4 (the two modes that activate polled-run). Also note, that the polled-run modes, 3 and 4, are unique. As soon as the polled-run action occurs, the mode switches to 1 (deactivated, saved) or 2 (activated, outputs), respectively. This is so that the BASIC Stamp doesn't continuously go to the start of the designated program slot while the polled-inputs are in the desired poll state. Without this "one shot" feature, your program would appear to lock-up as long as the polled-inputs are in the designated state.

After the program switch takes place, the *Slot* value is maintained. Any future change to poll mode 3 or 4, without another POLLRUN command, will result in the previously defined program slot being used.

Demo Program (POLLRUN0.bsp)

```
' This program demonstrates the POLLRUN command.  It is intended to be downloaded
' to program slot 0, and the program called PROGRUN1.BSP should be downloaded to
' program slot 1.  I/O pin 0 is set to watch for a high signal.  Once the Loop routine
' starts running, the program constant prints it's program slot number to the screen.  If I/O
' pin 0 goes high, the program in program slot 1 (which should be POLLRUN1.BSP) is run.

'{$STAMP  BS2p, PollRun1.bsp}          'STAMP directive (specifies a BS2p)

ProgSlot  VAR      BYTE

Init:
  POLLIN  0, 1                         'Set I/O 0 to polled-input looking for a high
  POLLRUN  1                           'Set polled-run to program slot 1
  POLLMODE  3                          'Set mode to enable polled-outputs and polled wait

Loop:
  GET  127, ProgSlot
  DEBUG  "Running Program #", DEC  ProgSlot.LOWNIB, CR
GOTO  Loop
```

Demo Program (POLLRUN1.bsp)

```
' This program demonstrates the POLLRUN command.  It is intended to be downloaded
' to program slot 1, and the program called PROGRUN0.BSP should be downloaded to
' program slot 0.  This program is run when program 0 detects a high on I/O pin 0
' via the polled commands.

ProgSlot    VAR    BYTE

Loop:
  GET  127, ProgSlot
  DEBUG  "Running Program #", DEC  ProgSlot.LOWNIB, CR
GOTO  Loop
```

POLLWAIT

BS1	BS2	BS2e	BS2sx	**BS2p**

POLLWAIT *Period*

Function

Pause program execution, in a low-power mode, in units of *Period* until any polled-input pin reaches the desired poll state.

- **Period** is a variable/constant/expression (0 – 8) that specifies the duration of the low-power state. The duration is $(2^\wedge Period) * 18$ ms. Table 5.61 indicates the low-power length for any give *Period*. Using 8 as the *Period* is a special case; the BS2p will not go into low-power mode and will respond quicker to polled-inputs.

Quick Facts

Table 5.60: POLLWAIT Quick Facts.

	BS2p
Current draw during POLLWAIT	60 µA
Response time with *Period* set to 8	Less than 160 µS
Special notes	• Poll mode must be 2 or 4 and at least one polled-input must be set to activate POLLWAIT (POLLWAIT will be ignored otherwise). • If both polled-wait and polled-run are active, the polled-run event will occur immediately after the polled-wait detects an event.

Explanation

The POLLWAIT command is one of a family of unique "polling" commands on the BS2p module. The other commands in this family include POLLIN, POLLMODE, POLLOUT and POLLRUN. The POLLWAIT command is used to pause program execution and go into a low-power state until any polled-input pin reaches the desired poll state.

The "polling" commands allow the BASIC Stamp to respond to certain I/O pin events at a faster rate than what is normally possible through manual PBASIC programming. The term "poll" comes from the fact that the BASIC Stamp's interpreter periodically checks the state of the designated polled-input pins. It "polls" these pins after the end of each PBASIC command and before it reads the next PBASIC command from the user program; giving the appearance that it is polling "in the background". This feature should not be confused with the concept of interrupts, as the BASIC Stamp does not support true interrupts.

The POLLWAIT command is unique among the polling commands in that it actually causes execution to halt, until a polled-input pin event occurs. The *Period* argument is similar to that of the NAP command; using the values 0 to 7 specifies the duration of the low-power period. After the low-power period is over, the BASIC Stamp polls the polled-input pins and determines if any meet the desired poll state. If no polled-input is in the desired state (as set by POLLIN command) the BASIC Stamp goes back into low-power mode, again, for the same duration as before. If any polled-input is in the desired state, however, the BASIC Stamp will continue execution with the next line of code.

A *Period* of 8, makes the BASIC Stamp pause execution in normal running mode (not low-power mode) until a polled-input event occurs. The response time is indicated in Table 5.60. Since the response time is so fast, this feature can be used to synchronize a portion of PBASIC code to an incoming pulse.

Period	Length of Low-Power Mode
0	18 ms
1	36 ms
2	72 ms
3	144 ms
4	288 ms
5	576 ms
6	1152 ms (1.152 seconds)
7	2304 ms (2.304 seconds)
8	No power-down

Table 5.61: *Period* values and associated low-power modes.

The following is a simple example of the POLLWAIT command.

A SIMPLE POLLWAIT EXAMPLE.

```
POLLIN  0, 1

Loop:
  POLLWAIT  0
  TOGGLE  1
GOTO  Loop
```

In this example, the POLLIN command sets I/O pin 0 to be a polled-input pin looking for a high (1) state. The *Loop* routine immediately runs a POLLWAIT command and specifies a *Period* of 0 (with results in a low-power state of 18 ms). This means that every 18 ms, the BASIC Stamp wakes-up and checks I/O pin 0 for a high. If I/O pin 0 is low, it goes back to sleep for another 18 ms. If I/O pin 0 is high, it runs the next line of code, which toggles the state of I/O pin 1. Then the loop starts all over again. Note: Due to the nature of low-power mode, I/O pin 1 may toggle between high and low (at 18 ms intervals in this case) even if I/O pin 0 stays low. This is an artifact of the "reset" condition in the interpreter chip that occurs when the chip wakes up from a low-power state. Upon this "reset" condition, all the I/O pins are switched to inputs for apx. 18 ms. It is the switching to inputs that will cause I/O pin 1 to appear to toggle. See the NAP or SLEEP commands for more information.

If low-power mode is not required, change the POLLWAIT command in the example above to "POLLWAIT 8" instead. This will have the effect of keeping the BASIC Stamp in normal running mode (ie: no low-power glitches) and will also cause the TOGGLE command to execute in a much shorter amount of time after a polled-input event occurs.

Demo Program (POLLWAIT.bsp)

```
' This program demonstrates the POLLWAIT command.  I/O pin 0 is set to watch for a
' high signal.  Once the Loop routine starts running, the POLLWAIT command causes the
' program to halt until the polled event happens (I/O pin is high) then it prints
' a message on the PC screen.  It will do nothing until I/O pin is high.

'{$STAMP BS2p}              'STAMP directive (specifies a BS2p)


POLLIN 0, 1                'Set I/O 0 to polled-input looking for a high
POLLMODE 2                 'Set mode to enable polled-outputs and polled wait

Loop:
  POLLWAIT 8                 'Wait for polled event (in normal power mode)
  DEBUG "I/O 0 is HIGH!", CR                'Print to the screen when polled event occurs
GOTO Loop
```

POT

BS1	BS2	BS2e	BS2sx	BS2p

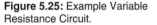 **POT** *Pin, Scale, Variable*

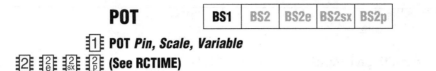 **(See RCTIME)**

Function

Read a 5 kΩ to 50 kΩ potentiometer, thermistor, photocell, or other variable resistance.

- *Pin* is a variable/constant (0 – 7) that specifies the I/O pin to use. This pin will be set to output mode initially, then to input mode.

- *Scale* is a variable/constant (0 – 255) used to scale the command's internal 16-bit result. See Explanation below for steps to finding the scale value to use for your circuit.

- *Variable* is a variable (usually a byte) where the final result of the reading will be stored. Internally, the POT command calculates a 16-bit value, which is scaled down to an 8-bit value.

Explanation

POT reads a variable resistance and returns a value (0 – 255) representing the amount of time it took to discharge the capacitor through the resistance. *Pin* must be connected to one side of the variable resistance, whose other side is connected through a capacitor to ground, as shown in Figure 5.25.

Figure 5.25: Example Variable Resistance Circuit.

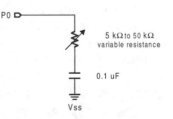

P0 ▷

5 kΩ to 50 kΩ variable resistance

0.1 uF

Vss

HOW POT REALLY WORKS.

POT works by first setting the specified I/O pin to an output and setting its state high. This step places +5 volts on one side of the capacitor (see Figure 5.25) and ground (0 volts) on the other side, which charges the capacitor. POT waits for 10 ms and then sets the I/O pin to an input mode and starts its timer. Initially the I/O pin will see a high (1) that will eventually drop to a low (0) when the capacitor discharges past the 1.4-volt threshold. The timer stops once the low is seen. The value of the variable resistor affects the time it takes to discharge the capacitor from 5 volts to approximately 1.4 volts.

The 16-bit reading is multiplied by (*Scale*/256), so a scale value of 128 would reduce the range by approximately 50%, a scale of 64 would reduce to 25%, and so on. The amount by which the internal value must be scaled varies with the size of the resistor being used.

Finding the best *Scale* value:

STEPS TO FIND THE BEST SCALE VALUE.

1. Build the circuit shown in Figure 5.25 and plug the BS1 into the PC.
2. In the DOS editor (stamp.exe) press ALT-P. A special calibration window appears, allowing you to find the best value.
3. The window asks for the number of the I/O pin to which the variable resistor is connected. Select the appropriate pin (0-7).
4. The editor downloads a short program to the BS1 (this overwrites any program already stored in the BS1).
5. Another window appears, showing two numbers: scale and value. Adjust the resistor until the smallest number is shown for scale (assuming you can adjust the resistor, as with a potentiometer).
6. Once you've found the smallest number for scale, you're done. This number should be used for the *Scale* in the POT command.
7. Optionally, you can verify the scale number found above by pressing the spacebar. This locks the scale and causes the BS1 to read the resistor continuously. The window displays the value. If the scale is good, you should be able to adjust the resistor, achieving a 0–255 reading for the value (or as close as possible). To change the scale value and repeat this step, just press the spacebar. Continue this process until you find the best scale.

Demo Program (POT.bas)

```
' This program demonstrates the PAUSE command's time delays. Once a second, the
' program will put the message, "paused" on the screen.

'{$STAMP  BS1}                        'STAMP directive (specifies a BS1)


Loop:
  POT  0, 100, B2                     ' Read potentiometer on pin 0.
  SEROUT 1, N300, (B2)                ' Send potentiometer reading
                                      ' over serial output.

GOTO  Loop
```

PULSIN

| BS1 | BS2 | BS2e | BS2sx | BS2p |

PULSIN *Pin, State, Variable*

Function

Measure the width of a pulse on *Pin* described by *State* and store the result in *Variable*.

NOTE: Expressions are not allowed as arguments on the BS1. The range of the *Pin* argument on the BS1 is 0 – 7.

- **Pin** is a variable/constant/expression (0 – 15) that specifies the I/O pin to use. This pin will be set to input mode.

- **State** is a variable/constant/expression (0 – 1) that specifies whether the pulse to be measured is low (0) or high (1). A low pulse begins with a 1-to-0 transition and a high pulse begins with a 0-to-1 transition.

- **Variable** is a variable (usually a word) in which the measured pulse duration will be stored. The unit of time for *Variable* is described in Table 5.62.

Quick Facts

Table 5.62: PULSIN Quick Facts.

	BS1	BS2	BS2e	BS2sx	BS2p
Units in Variable	10 µs	2 µs	2 µs	0.8 µs	0.75 µs
Maximum pulse width	655.35 ms	131.07 ms	131.07 ms	52.428 ms	49.125 ms

Explanation

PULSIN is like a fast stopwatch that is triggered by a change in state (0 or 1) on the specified pin. The entire width of the specified pulse (high or low) is measured, in units shown in Table 5.62, and stored in *Variable*.

Many analog properties (voltage, resistance, capacitance, frequency, duty cycle) can be measured in terms of pulse durations. This makes PULSIN a valuable form of analog-to-digital conversion.

SPECIFICS OF PULSIN'S OPERATION. PULSIN will wait, for the desired pulse, for up to the maximum pulse width it can measure, shown in Table 5.62. If it sees the desired pulse, it measures the time until the end of the pulse and stores the result in *Variable*. If it never sees the start of the pulse, or the pulse is too long (greater than the Maximum Pulse Width shown in Table 5.62) PULSIN "times out" and store 0 in *Variable*. This operation keeps your program from locking-up should the desired pulse never occur.

Regardless of the size of *Variable*, PULSIN internally uses a 16-bit timer. Unless the pulse widths are known to be short enough to fit in an 8-bit result, it is recommended using a word-sized variable. Not doing so may result in strange and misleading results as the BASIC Stamp will only store the lower 8-bits into a byte variable.

HOW THE RESULT IS REPORTED.

Demo Program (PULSIN.bas)

```
' This program uses PULSIN to measure a pulse generated by discharging a 0.1 uF capacitor
' through a 1k resistor (see the figure in the description of PULSIN in the manual).
' Pressing the switch generates the pulse, which should ideally be approximately 120 us
' (12 PULSIN units of 10 us) long. Variations in component values may produce results that
' are up to 10 units off from this value. For more information on calculating
' resistor-capacitor timing, see the RCTIME command.

'{$STAMP BS1}                        'STAMP directive (specifies a BS1)

SYMBOL   Time   =   W0

Again:
  PULSIN 7, 1, Time         ' Measure positive pulse.
  IF  Time = 0  THEN  Again  ' If 0, try again.
  DEBUG CLS, Time           ' Otherwise, display result.
GOTO Again
```

Demo Program (PULSIN.bs2)

```
' This program uses PULSIN to measure a pulse generated by discharging a 0.1 µF capacitor
' through a 1k resistor (see the figure in the description of PULSIN in the manual).
' Pressing the switch generates the pulse, which should ideally be approximately 120 µs
' (60 PULSIN units of 2 µs) long. Variations in component values may produce results that
' are up to 10 units off from this value. For more information on calculating
' resistor-capacitor timing, see the RCTIME command.

'{$STAMP BS2}                        'STAMP directive (specifies a BS2)

TimeVAR   WORD

Again:
  PULSIN 7, 1, Time         ' Measure positive pulse.
  IF  Time = 0  THEN  Again  ' If 0, try again.
  DEBUG  CLS, DEC ? Time              ' Otherwise, display result.
GOTO Again
```

NOTE: This is written for the BS2 but can be used for the BS2e, BS2sx and BS2p also. Locate the proper source code file or modify the STAMP directive before downloading to the BS2e, BS2sx or BS2p. Keep in mind that the unit of time may be different than what appears in the comments here.

PULSOUT

BS1	BS2	BS2e	BS2sx	BS2p

PULSOUT *Pin, Period*

NOTE: Expressions are not allowed as arguments on the BS1. The range of the *Pin* argument on the BS1 is 0 – 7.

Function

Generate a pulse on *Pin* with a width of *Period*.

- **Pin** is a variable/constant/expression (0 – 15) that specifies the I/O pin to use. This pin will be set to output mode.

- **Period** is a variable/constant/expression (0 – 65535) that specifies the duration of the pulse. The unit of time for *Period* is described in Table 5.63.

Quick Facts

Table 5.63: PULSOUT Quick Facts.

	BS1	BS2	BS2e	BS2sx	BS2p
Units in *Period*	10 µs	2 µs	2 µs	0.8 µs	1.18 µs
Maximum pulse width	655.35 ms	131.07 ms	131.07 ms	52.428 ms	55.479 ms

Explanation

PULSOUT sets *Pin* to output mode, inverts the state of that pin; waits for the specified *Period*; then inverts the state of the pin again; returning the bit to its original state. The unit of *Period* is described in Table 5.63. The following example will generate a 100 us pulse on I/O pin 5 (of the BS2):

```
PULSOUT 5, 50      ' Generate a pulse on pin 5.
```

CONTROLLING THE POLARITY OF THE PULSE.

The polarity of the pulse depends on the state of the pin before the command executes. In the example above, if pin 5 was low, PULSOUT would produce a positive pulse. If the pin was high, PULSOUT would produce a negative pulse.

WATCH OUT FOR UNDESIRABLE PULSE GLITCHES.

If the pin is an input, the output state bit, OUT5 (PIN5 on the BS1) won't necessarily match the state of the pin. What happens then? For example: pin 7 is an input (DIR7 = 0) and pulled high by a resistor as shown in Figure 5.26a. Suppose that pin 7 is low when we execute the instruction:

```
PULSOUT 7, 5       ' Generate a pulse on pin 7.
```

Figure 5.26b shows the sequence of events on that pin. Initially, pin 7 is high. Its output driver is turned off (because it is in input mode), so the

10k resistor sets the state on the pin. When PULSOUT executes, it turns on the output driver, allowing OUT7 (PIN7 on the BS1) to control the pin.

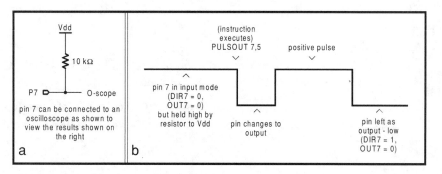

Figure 5.26: Example Pulse Diagram.

Since OUT7 (PIN7 on the BS1) is low, the pin goes low. After a few microseconds of preparation, PULSOUT inverts the state of the pin; from low to high. It leaves the pin in that state for the specified time (10μs if using a BS2) and then inverts it again, leaving the pin in its original state.

Demo Program (PULSOUT.bas)

' This program blinks an LED on for 10ms at 1-second intervals. Connect the LED to I/O
' pin 0 as shown in the figure within the NAP command description of the manual.

```
'{$STAMP  BS1}                     'STAMP directive (specifies a BS1)

HIGH  0                            ' Set the pin high (LED off).
Again:
  PULSOUT  0, 1000                 ' Flash the LED for 10 ms.
  PAUSE  1000                      ' Wait one second.
GOTO  Again                        ' Repeat endlessly.
```

Demo Program (PULSOUT.bs2)

' This program blinks an LED on for 10ms at 1-second intervals. Connect the LED to I/O
' pin 0 as shown in the figure within the NAP command description of the manual.

```
'{$STAMP  BS2}                     'STAMP directive (specifies a BS2)

HIGH  0                            ' Set the pin high (LED off).
Again:
  PULSOUT  0, 5000                 ' Flash the LED for 10 ms.
  PAUSE  1000                      ' Wait one second.
GOTO  Again                        ' Repeat endlessly.
```

NOTE: This is written for the BS2 but can be used for the BS2e, BS2sx and BS2p also. Locate the proper source code file or modify the STAMP directive before downloading to the BS2e, BS2sx or BS2p. Keep in mind that the unit of time may be different than what appears in the comments here.

PUT

BS1	BS2	BS2e	BS2sx	BS2p

PUT *Location, Value*

Function
Put *Value* into Scratch Pad RAM *Location*.
- **Location** is a variable/constant/expression (0 – 63: BS2e/BS2sx, 0 - 127: BS2p) that specifies the Scratch Pad RAM location to write to.
- **Value** is a variable/constant/expression (0 - 255) to store in RAM.

Quick Facts

Table 5.64: PUT Quick Facts.

	BS2e, BS2sx	BS2p
Scratch Pad RAM size and organization	64 bytes (0 – 63). Organized as bytes only.	128 bytes (0 – 127). Organized as bytes only.
General-purpose locations	0 – 62	0 – 126
Special use location	Current program slot number in read-only location 63.	Current program slot number in lowest nibble of read-only location 127. Current read/write slot number in highest nibble of location 127.

Explanation
The PUT command writes a byte-sized value into the specified Scratch Pad RAM location. All values in the general-purpose locations can be written to from within any of the 8 program slots.

USES FOR SCRATCH PAD RAM.

Scratch Pad RAM is useful for passing data to programs in other program slots and for additional workspace. It is different than regular RAM in that symbol names cannot be assigned directly to locations and each location is always configured as a byte only. The following code will write the value 100 to location 25, read it back out with GET, and display it:

```
Temp     VAR    BYTE
PUT 25, 100
GET 25, Temp
DEBUG DEC Temp
```

SCRATCH PAD RAM LOCATIONS AND THEIR PURPOSE.

Most Scratch Pad RAM locations are available for general use. The highest location (63 for BS2e/BS2sx and 127 for BS2p) is a special, read-only, location that always contains the number of the currently running program slot. On the BS2p, the upper nibble of location 127 also contains the current program slot that will be used for the READ and WRITE commands. Any values written to this location will be ignored.

Demo Program (GETPUT1.bsx)

```
' This example demonstrates the use of the GET and PUT commands. First, location 63
' is read using GET to display the currently running program number. Then a set of
' values are written (PUT) into locations 0 to 9. Afterwards, program number 1 is run.
' This program is a BS2sx project consisting of GETPUT1.bsx and GETPUT2.bsx. See the
' BASIC Stamp Project section in the manual for more information.

'{$STAMP BS2sx, GETPUT2.BSX}          'STAMP directive (specifies a BS2sx and
                                      'a second program, GETPUT2.BSX)


Value       VAR   BYTE
Index       VAR   BYTE

GET 63, Value
DEBUG "Program #",DEC Value, CR

FOR Index = 0 TO 9
  Value = (Index + 3) * 8
  PUT Index, Value
  DEBUG "  Writing: ", DEC2 Value, " to location: ", DEC2 Index, CR
NEXT

RUN 1
```

NOTE: This is written for the BS2sx but can be used for the BS2e, and BS2p also. Locate the proper source code file or modify the STAMP directive before downloading to the BS2e, or BS2p.

Demo Program (GETPUT2.bsx)

```
' This example demonstrates the use of the GET and PUT commands. First, location 63
' is read using GET to display the currently running program number. Then a set of
' values are read (GET) from locations 0 to 9 and displayed on the screen for verification.
' This program is a BS2sx project consisting of GETPUT1.bsx and GETPUT2.bsx. See the
' BASIC Stamp Project section in the manual for more information.

'{$STAMP BS2sx}                       'STAMP directive (specifies a BS2sx)

Value       VAR   BYTE
Index       VAR   BYTE

GET 63, Value
DEBUG CR, "Program #",DEC Value, CR

FOR Index = 0 TO 9
  GET Index, Value
  DEBUG "  Reading: ", DEC2 Value, " from location: ", DEC2 Index, CR
NEXT

STOP
```

NOTE: This is written for the BS2sx but can be used for the BS2e, and BS2p also. Locate the proper source code file or modify the STAMP directive before downloading to the BS2e, or BS2p.

PWM

BS1	BS2	BS2e	BS2sx	BS2p

⌷1⌷ ⌷2⌷ ⌷2e⌷ ⌷2sx⌷ ⌷2p⌷ **PWM** *Pin, Duty, Cycles*

⌷1⌷
NOTE: Expressions are not allowed as arguments on the BS1. The range of the *Pin* argument on the BS1 is 0 – 7.

Function

Convert a digital value to analog output via pulse-width modulation.

- **Pin** is a variable/constant/expression (0 – 15) that specifies the I/O pin to use. This pin will be set to output mode initially then set to input mode when the command finishes.

- **Duty** is a variable/constant/expression (0 - 255) that specifies the analog output level (0 to 5V).

- **Cycles** is a variable/constant/expression (0 - 255) that specifies the duration of the PWM signal.

Quick Facts

Table 5.65: PWM Quick Facts.

	BS2	BS2e	BS2sx	BS2p
Units in *Cycles*	1 ms	1 ms	400 µs	652 µs
Average voltage equation	Average Voltage = (Duty / 255) * 5 volts			
Require charge time (*Cycles*) equation	Charge time = 4 * R * C			
Special notes	*Pin* is set to output initially, and set to input at end			

Explanation

Pulse-width modulation (PWM) allows the BASIC Stamp (a purely digital device) to generate an analog voltage. The basic idea is this: If you make a pin output high, the voltage at that pin will be close to 5V. Output low is close to 0V. What if you switched the pin rapidly between high and low so that it was high half the time and low half the time? The average voltage over time would be halfway between 0 and 5V (2.5V). PWM emits a burst of 1s and 0s whose ratio is proportional to the duty value you specify.

DETERMINING AVERAGE VOLTAGE FOR A PARTICULAR DUTY CYCLE.

The proportion of 1s to 0s in PWM is called the duty cycle. The duty cycle controls the analog voltage in a very direct way; the higher the duty cycle the higher the voltage. In the case of the BASIC Stamp, the duty cycle can range from 0 to 255. Duty is literally the proportion of 1s to 0s output by the PWM command. To determine the proportional PWM output voltage, use this formula: $(Duty/255) * 5V$. For example, if *Duty* is 100, $(100/255) * 5V = 1.96V$; PWM outputs a train of pulses whose average voltage is 1.96V.

In order to convert PWM into an analog voltage we have to filter out the pulses and store the average voltage. The resistor/capacitor combination in Figure 5.27 will do the job. The capacitor will hold the voltage set by PWM even after the instruction has finished. How long it will hold the voltage depends on how much current is drawn from it by external circuitry, and the internal leakage of the capacitor. In order to hold the voltage relatively steady, a program must periodically repeat the PWM instruction to give the capacitor a fresh charge.

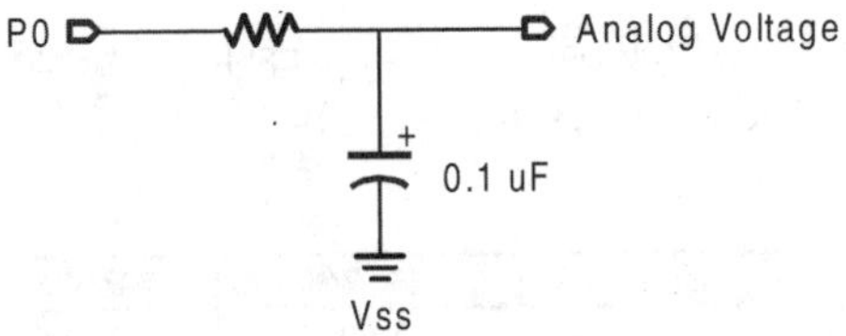

FILTERING THE PWM SIGNAL.

Figure 5.27: Example PWM Filter Circuit.

Just as it takes time to discharge a capacitor, it also takes time to charge it in the first place. The PWM command lets you specify the charging time in terms of PWM cycles. The period of each cycle is shown in Table 5.65. So, on the BS2, to charge a capacitor for 5ms, you would specify 5 cycles in the PWM instruction.

DETERMINING THE APPROPRIATE CYCLE TIME FOR YOUR CIRCUIT.

How do you determine how long to charge a capacitor? Use this rule-of-thumb formula: Charge time = 4 * R * C. For instance, Figure 5.27 uses a 10k (10×10^3 ohm) resistor and a 1 µF (1×10^{-6} F) capacitor:

Charge time = $4 * 10 \times 10^3 * 1 \times 10^{-6} = 40 \times 10^{-3}$ seconds, or 40 ms.

Since, on the BS2, each cycle is approximately a millisecond, it would take at least 40 cycles to charge the capacitor. Assuming the circuit is connected to pin 0, here's the complete PWM instruction:

```
PWM  0, 100, 40        ' Put a 1.96V charge on capacitor.
```

After outputting the PWM pulses, the BASIC Stamp leaves the pin in input mode (0 in the corresponding bit of DIRS). In input mode, the pin's output driver is effectively disconnected. If it were not, the steady output state of the pin would change the voltage on the capacitor and undo the voltage setting established by PWM. Keep in mind that leakage currents of up to 1 µA can flow into or out of this "disconnected" pin. Over time, these small currents will cause the voltage on the capacitor to drift. The same applies for leakage current from an op-amp's input, as well as the capacitor's own internal leakage. Executing PWM occasionally will reset the capacitor voltage to the intended value.

PWM charges the capacitor; the load presented by your circuit discharges it. How long the charge lasts (and therefore how often your program should repeat the PWM command to refresh the charge) depends on how much current the circuit draws, and how stable the voltage must be. You may need to buffer PWM output with a simple op-amp follower if your load or stability requirements are more than the passive circuit of Figure 5.27 can handle.

HOW PULSE-WIDTH-MODULATION IS GENERATED.

The term "PWM" applies only loosely to the action of the BASIC Stamp's PWM command. Most systems that output PWM do so by splitting a fixed period of time into an on time (1) and an off time (0). Suppose the interval is 1 ms and the duty cycle is 100 / 255. Conventional PWM would turn the output on for 0.39 ms and off for 0.61 ms, repeating this process each millisecond. The main advantage of this kind of PWM is its predictability; you know the exact frequency of the pulses (in this case, 1 kHz), and their widths are controlled by the duty cycle.

BASIC Stamp's PWM does not work this way. It outputs a rapid sequence of on/off pulses, as short as 1.6 µs in duration, whose overall proportion over the course of a full PWM cycle of approximately a millisecond is equal to the duty cycle. This has the advantage of very quickly zeroing in on the desired output voltage, but it does not produce the neat, orderly pulses that you might expect. The BS2, BS2e, BS2sx and BS2p also uses this high-speed PWM to generate pseudo-sine wave tones with the DTMFOUT and FREQOUT instructions.

Demo Program (PWM.bs2)

```
' Connect a voltmeter (such as a digital multimeter set to its voltage range) to the output of
' the circuit shown in the figure for the PWM command (in the manual).  Run the program
' and observe the readings on the meter. They should come very close to 1.96V, then
' decrease slightly as the capacitor discharges. Try varying the interval between PWM
' bursts (by changing the PAUSE value) and the number of PWM cycles to see their effect.

'{$STAMP  BS2}                           'STAMP directive (specifies a BS2)

Again:
 PWM  0, 100, 40                         ' 40 cycles of PWM at 100/255 duty
 PAUSE  1000                             ' Wait a second.
GOTO  Again                              ' Repeat
```

NOTE: This is written for the BS2 but can be used for the BS1, BS2e, BS2sx and BS2p also. Locate the proper source code file or modify the STAMP directive and the *Cycles* value of PWM before downloading to the BS1, BS2e, BS2sx or BS2p.

RANDOM

BS1	BS2	BS2e	BS2sx	BS2p

RANDOM *Variable*

Function

Generate a pseudo-random number.

- **Variable** is a variable (usually a word) whose bits will be scrambled to produce a random number. *Variable* acts as RANDOM's input and its result output. Each pass through RANDOM stores the next number, in the pseudorandom sequence, in *Variable*.

Explanation

RANDOM generates pseudo-random numbers ranging from 0 to 65535. They're called "pseudo-random" because they appear random, but are generated by a logic operation that uses the initial value in *Variable* to "tap" into a sequence of 65535 essentially random numbers. If the same initial value, called the "seed", is always used, then the same sequence of numbers is generated. The following example demonstrates this:

```
SYMBOL    Result = W0

Loop:
  Result = 11000              ' Set initial "seed" value
  RANDOM  Result              ' Generate random number.
  DEBUG  Result               ' Show the result on screen.
GOTO  Loop
```

-- or --

```
Result      VAR    WORD

Loop:
  Result  = 11000             ' Set initial "seed" value
  RANDOM  Result              ' Generate random number
  DEBUG  DEC ? Result         ' Show the result on screen.
GOTO  Loop
```

In this example, the same number would appear on the screen over and over again. This is because the same seed value was used each time; specifically, the first line of the loop sets *Result* to 11,000. The RANDOM command really needs a different seed value each time. Moving the "Result =" line out of the loop will solve this problem, as in:

```
SYMBOL    Result = W0
Result = 11000                        ' Set initial "seed" value

Loop:
  RANDOM Result                       ' Generate random number.
  DEBUG Result                        ' Show the result on screen.
GOTO Loop
```

⌷1⌷

-- or --

```
Result      VAR    WORD
Result = 11000                        ' Set initial "seed" value

Loop:
  RANDOM Result                       ' Generate random number
  DEBUG DEC ? Result                  ' Show the result on screen.
GOTO Loop
```

⌷2⌷ ⌷2e⌷ ⌷2sx⌷ ⌷2p⌷

Here, *Result* is only initialized once, before the loop. Each time through the loop, the previous value of *Result*, generated by RANDOM, is used as the next seed value. This generates a more desirable set of pseudorandom numbers.

In applications requiring more apparent randomness, it's necessary to "seed" RANDOM with a more random value every time. For instance, in the demo program below, RANDOM is executed continuously (using the previous resulting number as the next seed value) while the program waits for the user to press a button. Since the user can't control the timing of button presses very accurately, the results approach true randomness. Another possibility is to take advantage of the "floating" effect of unused input pins. Because any I/O pin that is an input, and is not electrically connected to anything, tends to "float" randomly between 0 and 1, this is a good source of a potential seed value. For example, if the upper 8 pins on a BS2 are not being used, leave them as inputs and don't electrically connect them (leave them "floating"). Then, use something like the following code to initialize the seed value:

⌷1⌷

```
Result = INH * 256 + INH             ' Fill high and low byte with current, floating,
                                     ' value of I/O pins 8 - 15
```

NOTE: BS1's only have 8 I/O pins. There may not be enough unused pins to do something similar, but if so, use the PINS variable, rather than INH.

Figure 5.28: RANDOM Button Circuit.

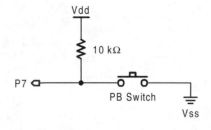

🔲 Demo Program (RANDOM.bas)

```
' Connect a button to I/O pin 7 as shown in the figure in the RANDOM command description
' (in the manual) and run this program. This program uses RANDOM to simulate a coin toss.
' After 100 trials, it reports the total number of heads and tails thrown.

'{$STAMP  BS1}                              'STAMP directive (specifies a BS1)

SYMBOL    Flip      =    W0                 ' The random number.
SYMBOL    Coin      =    BIT0               ' A single bit of the random number.
SYMBOL    Trials    =    B2                 ' Number of flips.
SYMBOL    Heads     =    B3                 ' Number of throws that came up heads.
SYMBOL    Tails     =    B4                 ' Number of throws that came up tails.
SYMBOL    Btn       =    B5                 ' Workspace for Button instruction.

Start:
  DEBUG CLS, "Press button to start"

FOR Trials = 1 TO 100                       ' 100 tosses of the coin.
Hold:
    RANDOM Flip                             ' While waiting for button, randomize.
    BUTTON 7, 0, 250, 100, Btn, 0, Hold     ' Wait for button.
    BRANCH Coin,(Head,Tail)                 ' If 0 then head; if 1 then tail.
Head:
    DEBUG CR, "HEADS"                       ' Show heads.
    Heads = Heads + 1                       ' Increment heads counter.
    GOTO TheNext                            ' Next flip.
Tail:
    DEBUG CR, "TAILS"                       ' Show tails.
    Tails = Tails + 1                       ' Increment tails counter.
TheNext:                                    ' Next flip.
NEXT
' When done, show the total number of heads and tails.
DEBUG CR, CR, "Heads: ", # Heads, " Tails: ", #Tails
```

RANDOM - BASIC Stamp Command Reference

Demo Program (RANDOM.bs2)

```
' Connect a button to I/O pin 7 as shown in the figure in the RANDOM command description
' (in the manual) and run this program. This program uses RANDOM to simulate a coin toss.
' After 100 trials, it reports the total number of heads and tails thrown.

'{$STAMP  BS2}                           'STAMP directive (specifies a BS2)

Flip       VAR   WORD                    ' The random number.
Coin       VAR   Flip.BIT0               ' A single bit of the random number.
Trials     VAR   BYTE                    ' Number of flips.
Heads      VAR   BYTE                    ' Number of throws that came up heads.
Tails      VAR   BYTE                    ' Number of throws that came up tails.
Btn        VAR   BYTE                    ' Workspace for Button instruction.

Start:
  DEBUG CLS, "Press button to start"

FOR Trials = 1 TO 100                    ' 100 tosses of the coin.
Hold:
    RANDOM Flip                          ' While waiting for button, randomize.
    BUTTON 7, 0, 250, 100, Btn, 0, Hold  ' Wait for button.
    branch coin,[head,tail]              ' If 0 then head; if 1 then tail.
Head:
    DEBUG CR, "HEADS"                    ' Show heads.
    Heads = Heads + 1                    ' Increment heads counter.
    GOTO TheNext                         ' Next flip.

Tail:
    DEBUG CR, "TAILS"                    ' Show tails.
    Tails = Tails + 1                    ' Increment tails counter.
TheNext:                                 ' Next flip.
NEXT
' When done, show the total number of heads and tails.
DEBUG CR, CR, "Heads: ", DEC Heads, " Tails: ", DEC Tails
```

NOTE: This is written for the BS2 but can be used for the BS2e, BS2sx and BS2p also. Locate the proper source code file or modify the STAMP directive before downloading to the BS2e, BS2sx or BS2p.

RCTIME

BS1	BS2	BS2e	BS2sx	BS2p

1 (See POT)

2 2e 2sx 2p **RCTIME *Pin, State, Variable***

Function

Measure time while *Pin* remains in *State*; usually to measure the charge/discharge time of resistor/capacitor (RC) circuit.

- ***Pin*** is a variable/constant/expression (0 – 15) that specifies the I/O pin to use. This pin will be placed into input mode.
- ***State*** is a variable/constant/expression (0 - 1) that specifies the desired state to measure. Once *Pin* is not in *State*, the command ends and stores the result in *Variable*.
- ***Variable*** is a variable (usually a word) in which the time measurement will be stored. The unit of time for *Variable* is described in Table 5.66.

Quick Facts

Table 5.66: RCTIME Quick Facts.

	BS2	BS2e	BS2sx	BS2p
Units in *Variable*	2 µs	2 µs	0.8 µs	0.9 µs
Maximum pulse width	131.07 ms	131.07 ms	52.428 ms	58.982 ms

Explanation

RCTIME can be used to measure the charge or discharge time of a resistor/capacitor circuit. This allows you to measure resistance or capacitance; use R or C sensors such as thermistors or capacitive humidity sensors or respond to user input through a potentiometer. In a broader sense, RCTIME can also serve as a fast, precise stopwatch for events of very short duration.

HOW RCTIME'S TIMER WORKS.

When RCTIME executes, it starts a counter (who's unit of time is shown in Table 5.66). It stops this counter as soon as the specified pin is no longer in *State* (0 or 1). If pin is not in *State* when the instruction executes, RCTIME will return 1 in *Variable*, since the instruction requires one timing cycle to discover this fact. If pin remains in *State* longer than 65535 timing cycles RCTIME returns 0.

RCTIME - BASIC Stamp Command Reference

Figure 5.29 shows suitable RC circuits for use with RCTIME. The circuit in 5.29a is preferred, because the BASIC Stamp's logic threshold is approximately 1.5 volts. This means that the voltage seen by the pin will start at 5V then fall to 1.5V (a span of 3.5V) before RCTIME stops. With the circuit of 5.29b, the voltage will start at 0V and rise to 1.5V (spanning only 1.5V) before RCTIME stops. For the same combination of R and C, the circuit shown in 5.29a will yield a higher count, and therefore more resolution than 5.29b.

Suitable RCTime circuits.

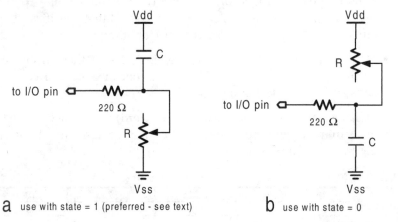

Figure 5.29: Example RC Circuits. Use A (left) with *State* = 1. Use B (right) with *State* = 0.

a use with state = 1 (preferred - see text)   b use with state = 0

Before RCTIME executes, the capacitor must be put into the state specified in the RCTIME instruction. For example, with figure 5.29a, the capacitor must be discharged until both plates (sides of the capacitor) are at 5V. It may seem counterintuitive that discharging the capacitor makes the input high, but remember that a capacitor is charged when there is a voltage difference between its plates. When both sides are at +5V, the cap is considered discharged.

Don't forget to discharge the capacitor before executing RCTIME.

Here's a typical sequence of instructions for 5.29a (assuming I/O pin 7 is used):

```
Result  VAR  WORD      ' Word variable to hold result.
HIGH  7                ' Discharge the cap
PAUSE 1                ' for 1 ms.
RCTIME  7,1,Result     ' Measure RC charge time.
DEBUG  ? Result        ' Show value on screen.
```

Using RCTIME is very straightforward, except for one detail: For a given R and C, what value will RCTIME return? It's easy to figure, based on a

Predicting the returned value.

value called the RC time constant, or tau (τ) for short. Tau represents the time required for a given RC combination to charge or discharge by 63 percent of the total change in voltage that they will undergo. More importantly, the value τ is used in the generalized RC timing calculation. Tau's formula is just R multiplied by C:

$$\tau = R \times C$$

CALCULATING CHARGE AND DISCHARGE TIME.

The general RC timing formula uses τ to tell us the time required for an RC circuit to change from one voltage to another:

$$time = -\tau * (\ln (V_{final} / V_{initial}))$$

In this formula ln is the natural logarithm; it's a key on most scientific calculators. Let's do some math. Assume we're interested in a 10 k resistor and 0.1 μF cap. Calculate τ:

$$\tau = (10 \times 10^3) \times (0.1 \times 10^{-6}) = 1 \times 10^{-3}$$

The RC time constant is 1×10^{-3} or 1 millisecond. Now calculate the time required for this RC circuit to go from 5V to 1.5V (as in Figure 5.29a):

$$Time = -1 \times 10^{-3} * (\ln(5.0v / 1.5v)) = 1.204 \times 10^{-3}$$

THE RC TIME EQUATION.

On the BS2, the unit of time is 2μs (See Table 5.66), that time (1.204×10^{-3}) works out to 602 units. With a 10 k resistor and 0.1 μF cap, RCTIME would return a value of approximately 600. Since $V_{initial}$ and V_{final} doesn't change, we can use a simplified rule of thumb to estimate RCTIME results for circuits like 5.29a:

$$RCTIME\ units = 600 \times R\ (in\ k\Omega) \times C\ (in\ \mu F)$$

DETERMINING HOW LONG TO CHARGE OR DISCHARGE THE CAPACITOR BEFORE EXECUTING RCTIME.

Another handy rule of thumb can help you calculate how long to charge/discharge the capacitor before RCTIME. In the example above that's the purpose of the HIGH and PAUSE commands. A given RC charges or discharges 98 percent of the way in 4 time constants ($4 \times R \times C$). In Figure 5.29, the charge/discharge current passes through the 220 Ω series resistor and the capacitor. So if the capacitor were 0.1 μF, the minimum charge/discharge time should be:

Charge time = 4 x 220 x (0.1 x 10^{-6}) = 88 x 10^{-6}

So it takes only 88 µs for the cap to charge/discharge, meaning that the 1 ms charge/discharge time of the example is plenty.

A final note about Figure 5.29: You may be wondering why the 220 Ω resistor is necessary at all. Consider what would happen if resistor R in Figure 5.29a were a pot, and were adjusted to 0 Ω. When the I/O pin went high to discharge the cap, it would see a short direct to ground. The 220 Ω series resistor would limit the short circuit current to 5V/220 Ω = 23 mA and protect the BASIC Stamp from damage. (Actual current would be quite a bit less due to internal resistance of the pin's output driver, but you get the idea.)

NOTES ABOUT 220 Ω RESISTER IN THE RC CIRCUITS.

Demo Program (RCTIME1.bs2)

```
' This program shows the standard use of the RCTIME instruction measuring an RC
' charge/discharge time. Use the circuit in the RCTIME description (in the manual)
' with R = 10 k pot and C = 0.1 µf. Connect the circuit to pin 7 and run the program.
' Adjust the pot and watch the value shown on the Debug screen change.

'{$STAMP  BS2}                         'STAMP directive (specifies a BS2)

Result      VAR    WORD                  'Word variable to hold result.

Again:
  HIGH 7                              'Discharge the cap
  PAUSE 1                             'for 1 ms.
  RCTIME 7, 1, Result                 'Measure RC charge time.
  DEBUG CLS, DEC Result                'Show value on screen.
GOTO Again
```

NOTE: This is written for the BS2 but can be used for the BS2e, BS2sx and BS2p also. Locate the proper source code file or modify the STAMP directive before downloading to the BS2e, BS2sx or BS2p.

Figure 5.30: Relay circuit for Demo Program 2.

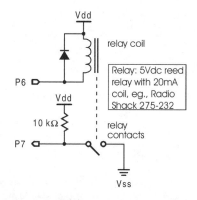

Demo Program (RCTIME2.bs2)

' This program illustrates the use of RCTIME as a fast stopwatch. The program energizes
' a relay coil, then measures how long it takes for the relay contacts to close. Figure 5.30
' shows the circuit. Note that RCTIME doesn't start timing instantly.

```
'{$STAMP  BS2}                           'STAMP directive (specifies a BS2)

Result       VAR    WORD

Again:
  Low 6                                  'Energize relay coil.
  RCTIME 7, 1, Result                    'Measure time to contact closure.
  DEBUG "Time to close: ", DEC Result, CR
  HIGH 6                                 'Release the relay.
  PAUSE 1000                             'Wait a second.
GOTO Again                                  'Do it again.
```

READ | BS1 | BS2 | BS2e | BS2sx | BS2p |

🔲1🔲 🔲2🔲 🔲2e🔲 🔲2sx🔲 🔲2p🔲 **READ** *Location, Variable*

Function

🔲1🔲

NOTE: Expressions are not allowed as arguments on the BS1.

Read value at *Location* in EEPROM and store the result in result in *Variable*.

- **Location** is a variable/constant/expression (0 – 255 on BS1, 0 – 2047 on all other BASIC Stamps) that specifies the EEPROM address to read from.

- **Variable** is a variable (usually a byte) where the value is stored.

Quick Facts

Table 5.67: READ Quick Facts.

	BS1	BS2, BS2e, BS2sx	BS2p
Range of EEPROM locations	0 to 255	0 to 2047	0 to 2047 (see notes below)
Special notes	n/a	READ only works with current program slot on BS2e and BS2sx.	READ works with any program slot as set by the STORE command.

Explanation

The EEPROM is used for both program storage (which builds downward from address 255 on BS1, 2047 on all other BASIC Stamps) and data storage (which builds upward from address 0). The READ instruction retrieves a byte of data from any EEPROM address and stores that byte in *Variable*. Any location within the EEPROM can be read (including your PBASIC program's tokens) at run-time. This feature is mainly used to retrieve long-term data from EEPROM; data stored in EEPROM is not lost when the power is removed.

A SIMPLE READ COMMAND.

The following READ command retrieves the value at location 100 and stores it into the variable called *Result*:

🔲1🔲
```
SYMBOL    Result = B0

READ  100, Result
```

--or--

🔲2🔲 🔲2e🔲 🔲2sx🔲 🔲2p🔲
```
Result    VAR    BYTE

READ  100, Result
```

READ - BASIC Stamp Command Reference

The EEPROM is organized as a sequential set of byte-sized memory locations. The READ command only retrieves byte-sized values from EEPROM. This does not mean that you can't read word-sized values, however. A word consists of two bytes, called a low-byte and a high-byte. If you wanted to read a word-sized value, you'll need to use two READ commands and a word-size variable (along with some handy modifiers). For example,

READING WORD VALUES VS. BYTE VALUES.

```
SYMBOL    Result       = W0      'The full word-sized variable
SYMBOL    Result_Low   = B0      'B0 happens to be the low-byte of W0
SYMBOL    Result_High  = B1      'B1 happens to be the high-byte of W0
EEPROM    (101, 4)              'Store word-sized value in locations 0 and 1

READ      0, Result_Low
READ      1, Result_High
DEBUG     #Result
```

--or--

```
Result    VAR   WORD
DATA      word 1125            'Store word-sized value in locations 0 and 1

READ      0, Result.LOWBYTE
READ      1, Result.HIGHBYTE
DEBUG     DEC Result
```

This code uses the EEPROM or DATA directive to write the low-byte and high-byte of the number 1125 into locations 0 and 1 during download. When the program runs, the two READ commands will read the low-byte and high-byte out of EEPROM (reconstructing it in a word-size variable) and then display the value on the screen.

Note that the EEPROM and DATA directives store data in the EEPROM before the program runs, however, the WRITE command can be used to store data while the program is running. Additionally, the EEPROM locations can be read an unlimited number of times, but EEPROM locations can be worn out by excessive writes. See the WRITE command for more information.

SPECIAL NOTES FOR EEPROM USAGE.

When using the READ and WRITE commands, take care to ensure that your program doesn't overwrite itself. On the BS1, location 255 holds the address of the last instruction in your program. Therefore, your program can use any space below the address given in location 255. For example, if location 255 holds the value 100, then your program can use locations 0–99 for data.

On other BASIC Stamps, you'll need to view the Memory Map of the program before you download it, to determine the last EEPROM location used. See the "Memory Map Function" section in Chapter 3.

On the BS2p, the READ and WRITE commands can affect locations in any program slot as set by the STORE command. See the STORE command for more information.

Demo Program (READ.bas)

```
' This program reads a string of data stored in EEPROM. The EEPROM data is downloaded
' to the BS1 at compile-time and remains there (even with the power off) until
' overwritten. Put ASCII characters into EEPROM, followed by 0, which will serve as the
' end-of-message marker.

'{$STAMP BS1}                                    'STAMP directive (specifies a BS1)

EEPROM ("BS1 EEPROM Storage!",0)

SYMBOL    StrAddr   = W0
SYMBOL    Char      = B2

StrAddr = 0                    'Set address to start of Message.

StringOut:
  READ StrAddr,Char                             'Get a byte from EEPROM.
  IF Char <> 0 THEN Cont                         'Not end? Continue.
END                                             'Stop here when done.

Cont:
  DEBUG @Char                                    'Show character on screen.
  StrAddr = StrAddr + 1                          'Point to next character.
GOTO StringOut                                   'Get next character.
```

Demo Program (READ.bs2)

NOTE: This is written for the BS2 but can be used for the BS2e, BS2sx and BS2p also. Locate the proper source code file or modify the STAMP directive before downloading to the BS2e, BS2sx or BS2p.

```
' This program reads a string of data stored in EEPROM. The EEPROM data is downloaded
' to the BS2 at compile-time and remains there (even with the power off) until
' overwritten. Put ASCII characters into EEPROM, followed by 0, which will serve as the
' end-of-message marker.

'{$STAMP BS2}                                    'STAMP directive (specifies a BS2)

Message    DATA  "BS2 EEPROM Storage!",0
StrAddr    VAR   WORD
Char       VAR   BYTE
```

```
StrAddr = Message                       'Set address to start of Message.

StringOut:
  READ  StrAddr,Char                    'Get a byte from EEPROM.
  IF  Char <> 0  THEN  Cont             'Not end? Continue.
Stop                                    'Stop here when done.

Cont:
  DEBUG  Char                           'Show character on screen.
  StrAddr = StrAddr + 1                 'Point to next character.
GOTO  StringOut                         'Get next character.
```

RETURN

BS1	BS2	BS2e	BS2sx	BS2p

⟦1⟧ ⟦2⟧ ⟦2e⟧ ⟦2sx⟧ ⟦2p⟧ **RETURN**

Function
Return from a subroutine, assuming there was a previous GOSUB executed.

Quick Facts

Table 5.68: RETURN Quick Facts.

	BS1, BS2, BS2e, BS2sx and BS2p
Maximum number of RETURNS per program	Unlimited. However, the number of GOSUBs are limited. See GOSUB for more information.

Explanation

⟦1⟧

NOTE: On the BS1, a RETURN without a GOSUB will return the program to the last GOSUB (or will end the program if no GOSUB was executed).

RETURN sends the program back to the address (instruction) immediately following the most recent GOSUB. If RETURN is executed without a prior GOSUB, the BASIC Stamp will return to the first executable line of the program; usually resulting in a logical bug in the code. See the GOSUB command for more information.

The example below will start out by GOSUB'ing to the section of code beginning with the label *Hello*. It will print "Hello my friend." on the screen then RETURN to the line after the GOSUB... which prints "How are you?" and ENDs.

```
GOSUB  Hello
DEBUG "How are you?"
END

Hello:
  DEBUG "Hello my friend.", CR
RETURN
```

WATCH OUT FOR SUBROUTINES THAT YOUR PROGRAM CAN "FALL INTO."

There's another interesting lesson here; what would happen if we removed the END command from this example? Since the BASIC Stamp reads the code from left to right / top to bottom (like the English language) once it had returned to and run the "How are you?" line, it would naturally "fall into" the *Hello* routine again. Additionally, at the end of the *Hello* routine, it would see the RETURN again (although it didn't GOSUB to that routine this time) and because there wasn't a previous place to return to, the BASIC Stamp will start the entire program over again. This would cause an endless loop. The important thing to remember here is to always make sure your program doesn't allow itself to "fall into" a subroutine.

Demo Program (RETURN.bs2)

```
' This program demonstrates a potential bug caused by allowing a program to 'fall into' a
' subroutine.  The program was intented to indicate that it is "Starting...", then
' 'Executing Subroutine', then 'Returned...' from the subroutine and stop.  Since we
' left out the END command (indicated in the comments), the program then falls into the
' subroutine, displays 'Executing..." again and then RETURNs to the start of the program
' and runs continuously in an endless loop.

'{$STAMP  BS2}                          'STAMP directive (specifies a BS2)

DEBUG "Starting Program",CR            'Indicate the start of the program

Main:
  PAUSE  1000
  GOSUB  DemoSub                        'Call the subroutine
  PAUSE  1000
  DEBUG  "Returned from Subroutine", CR 'Indicate the return from the subroutine
  PAUSE  1000

                                       '<-- Forgot to put an 'END' command here

DemoSub:
  DEBUG  " Executing Subroutine", CR    'Indicate the execution of the subroutine
RETURN
```

NOTE: This is written for the BS2 but can be used for the BS1, BS2e, BS2sx and BS2p also. Locate the proper source code file or modify the STAMP directive before downloading to the BS1, BS2e, BS2sx or BS2p.

REVERSE

BS1	BS2	BS2e	BS2sx	BS2p

REVERSE *Pin*

NOTE: Expressions are not allowed as arguments on the BS1. The range of the *Pin* argument on the BS1 is 0 – 7.

Function

Reverse the data direction of the specified pin.

- ***Pin*** is a variable/constant/expression (0 – 15) that specifies the I/O pin to use. This pin will be placed into the mode opposite of its current input/output mode.

Explanation

REVERSE is convenient way to switch the I/O direction of a pin. If the pin is an input, REVERSE makes it an output; if it's an output, REVERSE makes it an input.

Remember that "input" really has two meanings: (1) Setting a pin to input makes it possible to check the state (1 or 0) of external circuitry connected to that pin. The current state is in the corresponding bit of the INS register (PINS on the BS1). (2) Setting a pin to input also disconnects the output driver, the corresponding bit of OUTS (PINS on the BS1).

The demo program below illustrates this second fact with a two-tone LED blinker.

Figure 5.31: LED circuit for Demo Programs.

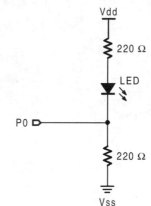

Demo Program (REVERSE.bas)

```
' Connect the circuit shown in the REVERSE command description to I/O pin 0 and run this
' program.  The LED will alternate between two states, dim and bright. The BASIC Stamp is
' using the REVERSE command to toggling I/O pin 0 between input and output states. When
' pin 0 is an input, current flows through R1, through the LED, through R2 to ground. Pin 0 is
' effectively disconnected and doesn't play a part in the circuit. The total resistance
' encountered by current flowing through the LED is R1 + R2 = 440 Ohms. When pin 0 is
' reversed to an output, current flows through R1, through the LED, and into pin 0 to ground
' (because of the 0 written to PIN0). The total resistance encountered by current flowing
' through the LED is R1, 220 Ohms. With only half the resistance, the LED glows brighter.

'{$STAMP BS1}                           'STAMP directive (specifies a BS1)

PIN0 = 0           ' Put a low in the pin 0 output driver.

Again:
   PAUSE 200        ' Brief (1/5th second) pause.
   REVERSE 0        ' Invert pin 0 I/O direction.
GOTO Again          ' Repeat forever.
```

Demo Program (REVERSE.bs2)

NOTE: This is written for the BS2 but can be used for the BS2e, BS2sx and BS2p also. Locate the proper source code file or modify the STAMP directive before downloading to the BS2e, BS2sx or BS2p.

```
' Connect the circuit shown in the REVERSE command description to I/O pin 0 and run this
' program.  The LED will alternate between two states, dim and bright. The BASIC Stamp is
' using the REVERSE command to toggling I/O pin 0 between input and output states. When
' pin 0 is an input, current flows through R1, through the LED, through R2 to ground. Pin 0 is
' effectively disconnected and doesn't play a part in the circuit. The total resistance
' encountered by current flowing through the LED is R1 + R2 = 440 Ohms. When pin 0 is
' reversed to an output, current flows through R1, through the LED, and into pin 0 to ground
' (because of the 0 written to OUT0). The total resistance encountered by current flowing
' through the LED is R1, 220 Ohms. With only half the resistance, the LED glows brighter.

'{$STAMP BS2}                           'STAMP directive (specifies a BS2)

OUT0 = 0           ' Put a low in the pin 0 output driver.

Again:
   PAUSE 200        ' Brief (1/5th second) pause.
   REVERSE 0        ' Invert pin 0 I/O direction.
GOTO Again          ' Repeat forever.
```

RUN

| BS1 | BS2 | BS2e | BS2sx | BS2p |

RUN *Program*

Function

Switches execution to another BASIC Stamp program (in a different program slot).

• *Program* is a variable/constant/expression (0 – 7) that specifies the program slot to run.

Quick Facts

Table 5.69: RUN Quick Facts.

	BS2e	BS2sx	BS2p
Number of program slots	8 (numbered 0 to 7)		
Time delay to switch between program slots	770 µs	300 µs	250 µs
Special notes	RUN is similar to a GOTO… you can not "return" from a RUN		

Explanation

The BS2e, BS2sx and BS2p have a total of 16k bytes of code space. This code space is organized into eight slots of 2 kbytes each. Up to eight different programs can be downloaded to the BASIC Stamp (one program per slot). When the BASIC Stamp powers up, or is reset, the program in slot 0 is executed.

The RUN command allows you to activate another program and causes the BASIC Stamp to stay in the newly activated program until it receives another RUN command, or until a power-down or reset condition occurs. The RUN command is similar to a GOTO command in that it allows you to "goto" another program. Normally a master-type program will be used in program slot 0 (since slot 0 runs first) and will control initial execution of the other programs.

A SIMPLE EXAMPLE OF RUN.

Look at the following example (there are two programs here, make sure to download them into program slots 0 and 1, respectively):

```
' Download the following two lines into program slot 0
DEBUG "Hello "
RUN  1

' Download the following three lines into program slot 1
DEBUG "World!", CR
PAUSE 0
RUN  0
```

The above two programs (assuming they have been downloaded into program slots 0 and 1, respectively) will display "Hello World!" on the screen. Program 0 is the first to run and it displays "Hello ", then issues a RUN 1 command. The BASIC Stamp then starts execution of program 1, from its first line of code, which causes "World!" to be displayed. Program 1 then pauses for 1 second and the runs program 0 again.

The I/O pins retain their current state (directions and output latches) and all Variable and Scratch Pad RAM locations retain their current data during a transition between programs with the RUN command. If sharing data between programs within Variable RAM, make sure to keep similar variable declarations (defined in the same order) in all programs so that the variables align themselves on the proper word, byte, nibble and bit boundaries across programs.

WHAT HAPPENS TO I/O PINS AND RAM WHEN USING RUN?

Any program number specified above 7 will wrap around and result in running one of the 8 programs (RUN 8 will run program 0, RUN 9 will run program 1, etc).

Review the BASIC Stamp Project section for more information on downloading multiple programs to a BS2e, BS2sx or BS2p.

Demo Program (RUN1.bsx)

```
' This example demonstrates the use of the RUN command.  First, location 63 is read
' using the GET command to display the currently running program number.  Then a set
' of values (based on the program number) are displayed on the screen.  Afterwards,
' program number 1 is run. This program is a BS2sx project consisting of RUN1.bsx and
' RUN2.bsx.  See the BASIC Stamp Project section in the manual for more information.

'{$STAMP  BS2sx, RUN2.BSX}            'STAMP directive (specifies a BS2sx and
                                      'a second program, RUN2.BSX)

DATA       100, 40, 80, 35, 91
```

NOTE: This is written for the BS2sx but can be used for the BS2e, and BS2p also. Locate the proper source code file or modify the STAMP directive before downloading to the BS2e, or BS2p.

```
DATA        200, 65, 23, 70, 90

ProgNum   VAR   BYTE
Value     VAR   BYTE
Index     VAR   BYTE

GET 63, ProgNum
DEBUG "Program #", DEC ProgNum, CR

FOR Index = 0 TO 4
  READ  ProgNum*5+Index, Value
  DEBUG DEC3 Value, " "
NEXT
DEBUG CR
PAUSE 1000

RUN 1
```

NOTE: This is written for the BS2sx but can be used for the BS2e, and BS2p also. Locate the proper source code file or modify the STAMP directive before downloading to the BS2e, or BS2p.

Demo Program (RUN2.bsx)

```
' This example demonstrates the use of the RUN command.  First, location 63 is read
' using the GET command to display the currently running program number.  Then a set
' of values (based on the program number) are displayed on the screen.  Afterwards,
' program number 0 is run. This program is a BS2sx project consisting of RUN1.bsx and
' RUN2.bsx.  See the BASIC Stamp Project section in the manual for more information.

'{$STAMP BS2sx}                          'STAMP directive (specifies a BS2sx and
                                         'a second program, RUN2.BSX)

DATA        100, 40, 80, 35, 91
DATA        200, 65, 23, 70, 90

ProgNum   VAR   BYTE
Value     VAR   BYTE
Index     VAR   BYTE

GET 63, ProgNum
DEBUG "Program #", DEC ProgNum, CR

FOR Index = 0 TO 4
  READ  ProgNum*5+Index, Value
  DEBUG DEC3 Value, " "
NEXT
DEBUG CR
PAUSE 1000

RUN 0
```

SERIN

BS1	BS2	BS2e	BS2sx	BS2p

[1] SERIN *Rpin, Baudmode, { (Qualifier),} {#} InputData*

[2] [2e] [2sx] [2p] SERIN *Rpin {\Fpin}, Baudmode, {Plabel,} {Timeout, Tlabel,} [InputData]*

Function

Receive asynchronous serial data (e.g., RS-232 data).

[1]
NOTE: Expressions are not allowed as arguments on the BS1. The range of the Rp*in* argument on the BS1 is 0 – 7.

- **Rpin** is a variable/constant/expression (0 – 16) that specifies the I/O pin through which the serial data will be received. This pin will be set to input mode. On the BS2, BS2e, BS2sx and BS2p, if Rpin is set to 16, the BASIC Stamp uses the dedicated serial-input pin (SIN, physical pin 2), which is normally used by the Stamp Editor during the download process.

- **Fpin** is an optional variable/constant/expression (0 – 15) that specifies the I/O pin to indicate flow control status on. This pin will be set to output mode.

- **Baudmode** is variable/constant/expression (0 – 7 on the BS1, 0 – 65535 on all other BASIC Stamps) that specifies serial timing and configuration.

- **Qualifier** is an optional variable/constant (0 – 255) indicating data that must be received before execution can continue. Multiple qualifiers can be indicated with commas separating them.

- **Plabel** is an optional label indicating where the program should go in the event of a parity error. This argument should only be provided if *Baudmode* indicates 7 bits, and even parity.

- **Timeout** is an optional variable/constant/expression (0 – 65535) that tells SERIN how long to wait for incoming data. If data does not arrive in time, the program will jump to the address specified by *Tlable*.

- **Tlabel** is an optional label that must be provided along with *Timeout*, indicating where the program should go in the event that data does not arrive within the period specified by *Timeout*.

[1]
NOTE: The BS1's *InputData* argument can only be a list of variables and the optional decimal modifier (#).

- **InputData** is list of variables and formatters that tells SERIN what to do with incoming data. SERIN can store data in a variable or array, interpret numeric text (decimal, binary, or hex) and store the corresponding value in a variable, wait for a fixed or variable sequence of bytes, or ignore a specified number of bytes. These actions can be combined in any order in the *InputData* list.

Quick Facts

	BS1	BS2	BS2e	BS2sx	BS2p
Units in *Timeout*	n/a	1 ms	1 ms	400 µs	400 µs
Baud Range	300, 600, 1200, and 2400 only	243 to 50K	243 to 50K	608 to 115K	608 to 115K
Baud Limit with Flow Control	n/a	19.2K	19.2K	19.2K	19.2K
Limit to Qualifiers	Unlimited	6 (in WAIT formatter)			
I/O Pins Available	0 - 7	0 - 15	0 - 15	0 - 15	0 – 15 (in current I/O block)
Other Serial Port Pins	n/a	SIN pin (physical pin 2) when *Rpin* = 16			

Table 5.70: SERIN Quick Facts.

Explanation

One of the most popular forms of communication between electronic devices is serial communication. There are two major types of serial communication; asynchronous and synchronous. The SERIN and SEROUT commands are used to receive and send asynchronous serial data. See the SHIFTIN and SHIFTOUT command for information on the synchronous method.

SERIAL COMMUNICATION BACKGROUND.

SERIN can wait for, filter and convert incoming data in powerful ways. SERIN deserves some lengthy discussion, below, since all this power brings some complexity.

The term asynchronous means "no clock." More specifically, "asynchronous serial communication" means data is transmitted and received without the use of a separate "clock" wire. Data can be sent using as little as two wires; one for data and one for ground. The PC's serial ports (also called COM ports or RS-232 ports) use asynchronous serial communication. Note: the other kind of serial communication, synchronous, uses at least three wires; one for clock, one for data and one for ground.

PHYSICAL AND ELECTRICAL DETAILS.

RS-232 is the electrical specification for the signals that PC serial ports use. Unlike normal logic, where a 5 volts is a logic 1 and 0 volts is logic 0, RS-232 uses -12 volts for logic 1 and +12 volts for logic 0. This specification allows communication over longer wire lengths without amplification.

Most circuits that work with RS-232 use a line driver/receiver. This component does two things: (1) it converts the ±12 volts of RS-232 to TTL-compatible 0 to 5-volt levels and (2) it inverts the relationship of the voltage levels, so that 5 volts = logic 1 and 0 volts = logic 0.

USING THE BUILT-IN SERIAL PORT ON THE BS2, BS2E, BS2SX AND BS2P.

All BASIC Stamps (except the BS1) have a line receiver on its SIN pin (*Rpin* = 16). See the "Hardware" section of the "Introduction to the BASIC Stamps" chapter. The SIN pin goes to a PC's serial data-out pin on the DB9 connector built into BASIC Stamp development boards. The connector is wired to allow both programming and run-time serial communication (unless you are using the Stamp 2 Carrier Board which is only designed for programming). For the built-in serial port set the *Rpin* argument to 16 in the SERIN command.

All BASIC Stamps (including the BS1) can also receive RS-232 data through any of their I/O pins (*Rpin* = 0 – 7 for BS1, *Rpin* = 0 – 15 on all other BASIC Stamps). The I/O pins don't need a line receiver, just a 22 kΩ resistor. The resistor limits current into the I/O pins' built-in clamping diodes, which keep input voltages within a safe range. See Figure 5.32

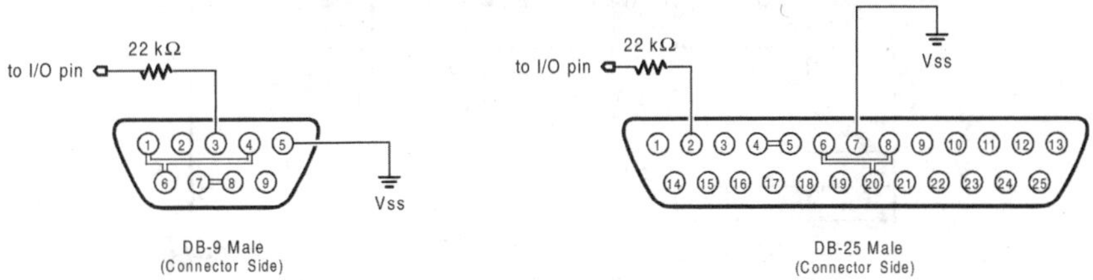

Figure 5.32: Serial Port Diagram Showing Correct Connections to a BASIC Stamp's I/O pin. NOTE: The 22 kΩ resister is not required if connecting to the SIN pin.

Function	DB9	DB25
Data Carrier Detect (DCD)	1	8
Receive Data (RD)	2	3
Transmit Data (TD)	3	2
Data Terminal Ready (DTR)	4	20
Signal Ground (SG)	5	7
Data Set Ready (DSR)	6	6
Request to Send (RTS)	7	4
Clear to Send (CTS)	8	5

NOTE: The connections shown with double-lines are normally not necessary. They indicate optional connections to disable hardware handshaking (DTR-DSR-DCD and RTS-CTS). This is only necessary if you are using software or hardware that expects hardware handshaking.

Figure 5.32 shows the pinouts of the two styles of PC serial ports and how to connect them to the BASIC Stamp's I/O pin (the 22K resister is not needed if connecting to the SIN pin). Though not normally needed, the figure also shows loop back connections that defeat hardware handshaking used by some PC software. Note that PC serial ports are always male connectors. The 25-pin style of serial port (called a DB25) looks similar to a printer (parallel) port except that it is male, whereas a parallel port is female.

Asynchronous serial communication relies on precise timing. Both the sender and receiver must be set for identical timing, usually expressed in bits per second (bps) called baud.

SERIAL TIMING AND MODE (BAUDMODE).

On all BASIC Stamps, SERIN requires a value called *Baudmode* that tells it the important characteristics of the incoming serial data; the bit period, number of data and parity bits, and polarity.

On the BS1, serial communication is limited to: no-parity, 8-data bits and 1-stop bit at one of four different speeds: 300, 600, 1200 or 2400 baud. Table 5.71 indicates the *Baudmode* value or symbols to use when selecting the desired mode.

Baudmode Value	Symbol	Baud Rate	Polarity
0	T2400	2400	TRUE
1	T1200	1200	TRUE
2	T600	600	TRUE
3	T300	300	TRUE
4	N2400	2400	INVERTED
5	N1200	1200	INVERTED
6	N600	600	INVERTED
7	N300	300	INVERTED

Table 5.71: BS1 Baudmode values.

On the BS2, BS2e, BS2sx and BS2p, serial communication is very flexible. The *Baudmode* argument for SERIN accepts a 16-bit value that determines its characteristics: 1-stop bit, 8-data bits/no-parity or 7-data bits/even-parity and virtually any speed from as low as 300 baud to greater than 100K baud (depending on the BASIC Stamp). Table 5.72

shows how *Baudmode* is calculated and Tables 5.73, 5.74 and 5.75 show common baud modes for standard serial baud rates.

Table 5.72: BS2, BS2e, BS2sx and BS2p *Baudmode* calculation. Add the results of steps 1, 2 and 3 to determine the proper value for the *Baudmode* argument.

Step 1: Determine the bit period (bits 0 – 11)	BS2 and BS2e: = INT(1,000,000 / baud rate) – 20 BS2sx: = INT(2,500,000 / baud rate) – 20 BS2p: = INT(2,500,000 / baud rate) – 20 Note: INT means 'convert to integer;' drop the numbers to the right of the decimal point.
Step 2: Set data bits and parity (bit 13)	8-bit/no-parity = 0 7-bit/even-parity = 8192
Step 3: Select polarity (bit 14)	True (noninverted) = 0 Inverted = 16384

Table 5.73: BS2 and BS2e common baud rates and corresponding *Baudmodes*.

Baud Rate	8-bit no-parity inverted	8-bit no-parity true	7-bit even-parity inverted	7-bit even-parity true
300	19697	3313	27889	11505
600	18030	1646	26222	9838
1200	17197	813	25389	9005
2400	16780	396	24972	8588
4800*	16572	188	24764	8380
9600*	16468	84	24660	8276

*The BASIC Stamp 2 and BASIC Stamp 2e may have trouble synchronizing with the incoming serial stream at this rate and higher due to the lack of a hardware input buffer. Use only simple variables and no formatters to try to solve this problem.

Table 5.74: BS2sx common baud rates and corresponding *Baudmodes*.

Baud Rate	8-bit no-parity inverted	8-bit no-parity true	7-bit even-parity inverted	7-bit even-parity true
1200	18447	2063	26639	10255
2400	17405	1021	25597	9213
4800	16884	500	25076	8692
9600*	16624	240	24816	8432

*The BASIC Stamp 2sx may have trouble synchronizing with the incoming serial stream at this rate and higher due to the lack of a hardware input buffer. Use only simple variables and no formatters to try to solve this problem.

Table 5.75: BS2p common baud rates and corresponding *Baudmodes*.

Baud Rate	8-bit no-parity inverted	8-bit no-parity true	7-bit even-parity inverted	7-bit even-parity true
1200	18447	2063	26639	10255
2400	17405	1021	25597	9213
4800	16884	500	25076	8692
9600*	16624	240	24816	8432

*The BASIC Stamp 2p may have trouble synchronizing with the incoming serial stream at this rate and higher due to the lack of a hardware input buffer. Use only simple variables and no formatters to try to solve this problem.

If you're communicating with existing software or hardware, its speed(s) and mode(s) will determine your choice of baud rate and mode. In general, 7-bit/even-parity (7E) mode is used for text, and 8-bit/no-parity (8N) for byte-oriented data. Note: the most common mode is 8-bit/no-parity, even when the data transmitted is just text. Most devices that use a 7-bit data mode do so in order to take advantage of the parity feature. Parity can detect some communication errors, but to use it you lose one data bit. This means that incoming data bytes transferred in 7E (even-parity) mode can only represent values from 0 to 127, rather than the 0 to 255 of 8N (no-parity) mode.

CHOOSING THE PROPER BAUD MODE.

Usually a device requires only 1 stop bit per byte. Occasionally, however, you may find a device that requires 2 or more stop bits. Since a stop bit is really just a delay between transmitted bytes (leaving the line in a resting state) the BASIC Stamp can receive transmissions with multiple stop bits per byte without any trouble. In fact, sometimes it is desirable to have multiple stop bits (see the "SERIN Troubleshooting" section, below, for more information).

The example below will receive a single byte through I/O pin 1 at 2400 baud, 8N1, inverted:

A SIMPLE FORM OF SERIN.

```
Symbol    SerData   = B0
SERIN  1, N2400, SerData
```

--or--

```
SerData    VAR    BYTE
SERIN  1, 16780, [SerData]
```

This is written with the BS2's *BaudMode* value. Be sure to adjust the value for your BASIC Stamp.

Here, SERIN will wait for and receive a single byte of data through pin 1 and store it in the variable *SerData*. If the BASIC Stamp were connected to a PC running a terminal program (set to the same baud rate) and the user pressed the "A" key on the keyboard, after the SERIN command executed, the variable *SerData* would contain 65, the ASCII code for the letter "A" (see the ASCII character chart in the appendix).

What would happen if, using the example above, the user pressed the "1" key? The result would be that *SerData* would contain the value 49 (the ASCII code for the character "1"). This is a critical point to remember: every time you press a character on the keyboard, the computer receives the ASCII value of that character. It is up to the receiving side (in serial

A SIMPLE NUMERIC CONVERSION; ASCII TEXT TO DECIMAL.

communication) to interpret the values as necessary. In this case, perhaps we actually wanted *SerData* to end up with the value 1, rather than the ASCII code 49.

The SERIN command provides a formatter, called the decimal formatter, which will interpret this for us. Look at the following code:

```
Symbol     SerData   = B0
SERIN  1, N2400, #SerData
```

--or--

```
SerData    VAR   BYTE
SERIN  1, 16780, [DEC  SerData]
```

THIS IS WRITTEN WITH THE BS2'S *BAUDMODE* VALUE. BE SURE TO ADJUST THE VALUE FOR YOUR BASIC STAMP.

Notice the decimal formatter in the SERIN command. It is the "#" (for the BS1) or "DEC" (for the other BASIC Stamps) that appears just to the left of the *SerData* variable. This tells SERIN to convert incoming text representing decimal numbers into true-decimal form and store the result in *SerData*. If the user running the terminal software pressed the "1", "2" and then "3" keys followed by a space or other non-numeric text, the value 123 will be stored in *SerData*. Afterwards, the program can perform any numeric operation on the number just like with any other number. Without the decimal formatter, however, you would have been forced to receive each character ("1", "2" and "3") separately, and then would still have to do some manual conversion to arrive at the number 123 (one hundred twenty three) before you can do the desired calculations on it.

DECIMAL FORMATTER SPECIFICS.

The decimal formatter is designed to seek out text that represents decimal numbers. The characters that represent decimal numbers are the characters "0" through "9". Once the SERIN command is asked to use the decimal formatter for a particular variable, it monitors the incoming serial data, looking for the first decimal character. Once it finds the first decimal character, it will continue looking for more (accumulating the entire multi-digit number) until is finds a non-decimal numeric character. Keep in mind that it will not finish until it finds at least one decimal character followed by at least one non-decimal character.

To further illustrate this, consider the following examples (assuming we're using the same code example as above):

1) **Serial input:** ABC
   Result: The BASIC Stamp halts at the SERIN command, continuously waiting for decimal text.

2) **Serial input:** 123 (with no characters following it)
   Result: The BASIC Stamp halts at the SERIN command. It recognizes the characters "1", "2" and "3" as the number one hundred twenty three, but since no characters follow the "3", it waits continuously, since there's no way to tell whether 123 is the entire number or not.

3) **Serial input:** 123 (followed by a space character)
   Result: Similar to example 2, above, except once the space character is received, the BASIC Stamp knows the entire number is 123, and stores this value in *SerData*. The SERIN command then ends, allowing the next line of code, if any, to run.

4) **Serial input:** 123A
   Result: Same as example 3, above. The "A" character, just like the space character, is the first non-decimal text after the number 123, indicating to the BASIC Stamp that it has received the entire number.

5) **Serial input:** ABCD123EFGH
   Result: Similar to examples 3 and 4 above. The characters "ABCD" are ignored (since they're not decimal text), the characters "123" are evaluated to be the number 123 and the following character, "E", indicates to the BASIC Stamp that it has received the entire number.

Of course, as with all numbers in the BASIC Stamp, the final result is WATCH OUT FOR ROLLOVER ERRORS. limited to 16 bits (up to the number 65535). If a number larger than this is received by the decimal formatter, the end result will look strange because the result rolled-over the maximum 16-bit value.

The BS1 is limited to the decimal formatter shown above, however the BS2, BS2e, BS2sx and BS2p have many more conversion formatters available for the SERIN command. If not using a BS1, see the "Additional Conversion Formatters" section below for more information.

USING SERIN TO WAIT FOR SPECIFIC DATA BEFORE PROCESSING.

The SERIN command can also be configured to wait for specified data before it retrieves any additional input. For example, suppose a device that is attached to the BASIC Stamp is known to send many different sequences of data, but the only data you desire happens to appear right after the unique characters, "XYZ". The BS1 has optional *Qualifier* arguments for this purpose. On the BS2, BS2e, BS2sx and BS2p a special formatter called WAIT can be used for this.

```
Symbol     SerData   = B0
SERIN  1, N2400, ("XYZ"), #SerData
```

--or--

THIS IS WRITTEN WITH THE BS2'S BAUDMODE VALUE. BE SURE TO ADJUST THE VALUE FOR YOUR BASIC STAMP.

```
SerData     VAR    BYTE
SERIN  1, 16780, [WAIT("XYZ"), DEC SerData]
```

The above code waits for the characters "X", "Y" and "Z" to be received, in that order, and then it looks for a decimal number to follow. If the device in this example were to send the characters "XYZ100" followed by a carriage return or some other non-decimal numeric character, the *SerData* variable would end up with the number 100 after the SERIN line finishes. If the device sent some data other than "XYZ" followed by a number, the BASIC Stamp would continue to wait at the SERIN command.

The BS1 will accept an unlimited number of *Qualifiers*. The BS2, BS2e, BS2sx and BS2p will only accept up to six bytes (characters) in the WAIT formatter.

USING ASCII CODES AND CASE SENSITIVITY.

Keep in mind that when we type "XYZ" into the SERIN command, the BASIC Stamp actually uses the ASCII codes for each of those characters for its tasks. We could also have typed: 88, 89, 90 in place of "XYZ" and the code would run the same way since 88 is the ASCII code for the "X" character, 89 is the ASCII code for the "Y" character, and so on. Also note, serial communication with the BASIC Stamp is case sensitive. If the device mentioned above sent, "xYZ" or "xyZ", or some other combination of lower and upper-case characters, the BASIC Stamp would have ignored it because we told it to look for "XYZ" (all capital letters).

The BS1's SERIN command is limited to above-mentioned features. If you are not using a BS1, please continue reading about the additional features below.

The decimal formatter is only one of a whole family of conversion formatters available with SERIN on the BS2, BS2e, BS2sx and BS2p. See Table 5.76 for a list of available conversion formatters. All of the conversion formatters work similar to the decimal formatter (as described in the "Decimal Formatter Specifics" section, above).   The formatters receive bytes of data, waiting for the first byte that falls within the range of characters they accept (e.g., "0" or "1" for binary, "0" to "9" for decimal, "0" to "9" and "A" to "F" for hex, and "+" or "-" for signed variations of any type). Once they receive a numeric character, they keep accepting input until a non-numeric character arrives or (in the case of the fixed length formatters) the maximum specified number of digits arrives.

ADDITIONAL CONVERSION FORMATTERS.

While very effective at filtering and converting input text, the formatters aren't completely foolproof. As mentioned before, many conversion formatters will keep accepting text until the first non-numeric text arrives, even if the resulting value exceeds the size of the variable. After SERIN, a byte variable will contain the lowest 8 bits of the value entered and a word would contain the lowest 16 bits. You can control this to some degree by using a formatter that specifies the number of digits, such as DEC2, which would accept values only in the range of 0 to 99.

ONCE AGAIN, PAY ATTENTION TO POTENTIAL ROLLOVER ERRORS.

The BS2, BS2e, BS2sx and BS2p also have special formatters for handling a string of characters, a sequence of characters and undesirable characters. See Table 5.77 for a list of these special formatters.   Also, see Appendix C for example serial inputs and the result of using these formatters.

Table 5.76: BS2, BS2e, BS2sx and BS2p Conversion Formatters.

Conversion Formatter	Type of Number	Numeric Characters Accepted	Notes
DEC{1..5}	Decimal, optionally limited to 1 – 5 digits	0 through 9	1
SDEC{1..5}	Signed decimal, optionally limited to 1 – 5 digits	-, 0 through 9	1,2
HEX{1..4}	Hexadecimal, optionally limited to 1 – 4 digits	0 through 9, A through F	1,3
SHEX{1..4}	Signed hexadecimal, optionally limited to 1 – 4 digits	-, 0 through 9, A through F	1,2,3
IHEX{1..4}	Indicated hexadecimal, optionally limited to 1 – 4 digits	$, 0 through 9, A through F	1,3,4
ISHEX{1..4}	Signed, indicated hexadecimal, optionally limited to 1 – 4 digits	-, $, 0 through 9, A through F	1,2,3,4
BIN{1..16}	Binary, optionally limited to 1 – 16 digits	0, 1	1
SBIN{1..16}	Signed binary, optionally limited to 1 – 16 digits	-, 0, 1	1,2
IBIN{1..16}	Indicated binary, optionally limited to 1 – 16 digits	%, 0, 1	1,4
ISBIN{1..16}	Signed, indicated binary, optionally limited to 1 – 16 digits	-, %, 0, 1	1,2,4

1 All numeric conversions will continue to accept new data until receiving either the specified number of digits (ex: three digits for DEC3) or a non-numeric character.

2 To be recognized as part of a number, the minus sign (-) must immediately precede a numeric character. The minus sign character occurring in non-numeric text is ignored and any character (including a space) between a minus and a number causes the minus to be ignored.

3 The hexadecimal formatters are not case-sensitive; "a" through "f" means the same as "A" through "F".

4 Indicated hexadecimal and binary formatters ignore all characters, even valid numerics, until they receive the appropriate prefix ($ for hexadecimal, % for binary). The indicated formatters can differentiate between text and hexadecimal (ex: ABC would be interpreted by HEX as a number but IHEX would ignore it unless expressed as $ABC). Likewise, the binary version can distinguish the decimal number 10 from the binary number %10. A prefix occurring in non-numeric text is ignored, and any character (including a space) between a prefix and a number causes the prefix to be ignored. Indicated, signed formatters require that the minus sign come before the prefix, as in -$1B45.

Special Formatter	Action
STR *ByteArray* \L {\E}	Input a character string of length L into an array. If specified, an end character E causes the string input to end before reaching length L. Remaining bytes are filled with 0s (zeros).
WAIT (*Value*)	Wait for a sequence of bytes specified by value. Value can be numbers separated by commas or quoted text (ex: 65, 66, 67 or "ABC"). The WAIT formatter is limited to a maximum of six characters.
WAITSTR *ByteArray* {\L}	Wait for a sequence of bytes matching a string stored in an array variable, optionally limited to L characters. If the optional L argument is left off, the end of the array-string must be marked by a byte containing a zero (0).
SKIP *Length*	Ignore *Length* bytes of characters.

Table 5.77: BS2, BS2e, BS2sx and BS2p Special Formatters.

The string formatter is useful for receiving a string of characters into a byte array variable. A string of characters is a set of characters that are arranged or accessed in a certain order. The characters "ABC" could be stored in a string with the "A" first, followed by the "B" and then followed by the "C." A byte array is a similar concept to a string; it contains data that is arranged in a certain order. Each of the elements in an array is the same size. The string "ABC" could be stored in a byte array containing three bytes (elements). See the "Defining Arrays" section in Chapter 4 for more information on arrays.

THE STR (STRING) FORMATTER.

Here is an example that receives nine bytes through I/O pin 1 at 9600 bps, N81/inverted and stores them in a 10-byte array:

```
SerString   VAR   BYTE(10)        ' Make a 10-byte array.
SerString(9) = 0                  ' Put 0 in last byte.
SERIN 1, 16468, [STR SerString\9] ' Get 9-byte string.
DEBUG  STR SerString              ' Display the string.
```

NOTE: The rest of the code examples for this section are written for the BS2, using the BS2's *BaudMode* and *Timeout* values. Be sure to adjust the value for your BASIC Stamp.

Why store only 9 bytes in a 10-byte array? We want to reserve space for the 0 byte that many BASIC Stamp string-handling routines regard as an end-of-string marker. This becomes important when dealing with variable-length arrays. For example, the STR formatter (see Table 5.77) can accept an additional parameter telling it to end the string when a particular byte is received, or when the specified length is reached, whichever comes first. An example:

```
SerString   VAR   BYTE(10)            ' Make a 10-byte array.
SerString(9) = 0                      ' Put 0 in last byte.
SERIN 1, 16468, [STR SerString\9\"*"] ' Stop at "*" or 9 bytes.
DEBUG  STR SerString                  ' Display the string.
```

If the serial input were "hello*" DEBUG would display "hello" since it collects bytes up to (but not including) the end character. It fills the unused bytes up to the specified length with 0s. DEBUG's normal STR formatter understands a 0 to mean end-of-string. However, if you use DEBUG's fixed-length string modifier, STR *ByteArray*\L, you will inadvertently clear the DEBUG screen. The fixed-length specification forces DEBUG to read and process the 0s at the end of the string, and 0 is equivalent to DEBUG's CLS (clear-screen) instruction! Be alert for the consequences of mixing fixed- and variable-length string operations.

MATCHING A SEQUENCE OF CHARACTERS WITH WAIT.

As shown before, SERIN can compare incoming data with a predefined sequence of bytes using the WAIT formatter. The simplest form waits for a sequence of up to six bytes specified as part of the *InputData* list, like so:

```
SERIN 1, 16468, [WAIT ("SESAME")]        'Wait for word SESAME.
DEBUG "Password accepted"
```

SERIN will wait for that word, and the program will not continue until it is received. Since WAIT is looking for an exact match for a sequence of bytes, it is case-sensitive—"sesame" or "SESAmE" or any other variation from "SESAME" would be ignored.

MATCHING A SEQUENCE OF CHARACTERS WITH WAITSTR.

SERIN can also wait for a sequence that matches a string stored in an array variable with the WAITSTR formatter. In the example below, we'll capture a string with STR then have WAITSTR look for an exact match:

```
SerString   VAR   BYTE(10)                ' Make a 10-byte array.
SerString(9) = 0                          ' Put 0 in last byte.
SERIN 1, 16468, [STR SerString\9\"!"]     ' Get the string
DEBUG "Waiting for: ", STR SerString, CR
SERIN 1, 16468, [WAITSTR SerString]       'Wait for a match
DEBUG "Password accepted!", CR
```

You can also use WAITSTR with fixed-length strings as in the following example:

```
SerString   VAR   BYTE(4)              ' Make a 4-byte array.
DEBUG  "Enter a 4 character password", CR
SERIN 1, 16468, [STR SerString\4]      ' Get the string
DEBUG  "Waiting for: ", STR SerString\4, CR
SERIN 1, 16468, [WAITSTR SerString\4]  'Wait for a match
DEBUG  "Password accepted!", CR
```

SERIN's *InputData* can be structured as a sophisticated list of actions to perform on the incoming data. This allows you to process incoming data in powerful ways. For example, suppose you have a serial stream that contains "pos: xxxx yyyy" (where xxxx and yyyy are 4-digit numbers) and you want to capture just the decimal y value. The following code would do the trick:

BUILDING COMPOUND *INPUTDATA* STATEMENTS.

```
YOffset    VAR   WORD
SERIN 1, 16468, [WAIT ("pos: "), SKIP 4, DEC yOffset]
DEBUG ? yOffset
```

The items of the *InputData* list work together to locate the label "pos: ", skip over the four-byte x data, then convert and capture the decimal y data. This sequence assumes that the x data is always four digits long; if its length varies, the following code would be more appropriate:

```
YOffset    VAR   WORD
SERIN 1, 16468, [WAIT ("pos: "), DEC yOffset, DEC yOffset]
DEBUG ? yOffset
```

The unwanted x data is stored in yOffset then replaced by the desired y data. This is a sneaky way to filter out a number of any size without using an extra variable. With a little creativity, you can combine the *InputData* modifiers to filter and extract almost any data.

Parity is a simple error-checking feature. When a serial sender is set for even parity (the mode the BASIC Stamps support) it counts the number of 1s in an outgoing byte and uses the parity bit to make that number even. For instance, if it is sending the 7-bit value: %0011010, it sets the parity bit to 1 in order to make an even number of 1s (four).

USING PARITY AND HANDLING PARITY ERRORS.

The receiver also counts the data bits to calculate what the parity bit should be. If it matches the parity bit received, the serial receiver assumes that the data was received correctly. Of course, this is not necessarily true, since two incorrectly received bits could make parity seem correct when the data was wrong, or the parity bit itself could be bad when the rest of the data was OK.

Many systems that work exclusively with text use (or can be set for) 7-bit/even-parity mode. Tables 5.73, 5.74 and 5.75 show appropriate *BaudMode* settings for different BASIC Stamps. For example, with the BS2, to receive one data byte through pin 1 at 9600 baud, 7E, inverted:

```
SerData    VAR    BYTE
SERIN  1, 24660, [SerData]
```

That instruction will work, but it doesn't tell the BS2 what to do in the event of a parity error. Here's an improved version that uses the optional *Plabel* argument:

```
SerData    VAR    BYTE
 SERIN  1, 24660, BadData, [SerData]
 DEBUG  ?  SerData
STOP

BadData:
 DEBUG  "parity error"
```

If the parity matches, the program continues at the DEBUG instruction after SERIN. If the parity doesn't match, the program goes to the label BadData. Note that a parity error takes precedence over other *InputData* specifications (as soon as an error is detected, SERIN aborts and goes to the *Plabel* routine).

USING THE SERIAL TIME-OUT FEATURE.

In all the examples above, the only way to end the SERIN instruction (other than RESET or power-off) is to give SERIN the serial data it wants. If no serial data arrives, the program is stuck. However, you can tell the BASIC Stamp to abort SERIN if it doesn't receive data within a specified number of milliseconds. For instance, to receive a decimal number through pin 1 at 9600 baud, 8N, inverted and abort SERIN after 2 seconds (2000 ms) if no data arrives:

```
Result    VAR    BYTE
SERIN  1, 16468, 2000, NoData, [DEC  Result]
Debug CLS, ? Result
STOP

NoData:
 DEBUG  CLS, "timed out"
```

If no data arrives within 2 seconds, the program aborts SERIN and continues at the label NoData.

Here's a very important concept: this timeout feature is not picky about the kind of data SERIN receives; if any serial data is received, it prevents the timeout. In the example above, SERIN wants a decimal number. But even if SERIN received letters "ABCD..." at intervals of less than two seconds, it would never abort.

REMEMBER: *TIMEOUT* DOES NOT CARE WHAT KIND OF DATA IS RECEIVED, ONLY THAT DATA IS RECEIVED OR NOT!

You can combine parity and serial timeouts. Here is an example for the BS2 designed to receive a decimal number through pin 1 at 2400 baud, 7E, inverted with a 10-second timeout:

COMBINING PARITY AND TIME-OUT.

```
Result     VAR   BYTE

Again:
  SERIN  1, 24660, BadData, 10000, NoData, [DEC  Result]
  DEBUG  CLS, ? Result
GOTO  Again

NoData:
  DEBUG  CLS, "timed out"
GOTO  Again

BadData:
  DEBUG  CLS, "parity error"
GOTO  Again
```

When you design an application that requires serial communication between BASIC Stamps, you have to work within these limitations:

CONTROLLING DATA FLOW.

- When the BASIC Stamp is sending or receiving data, it can't execute other instructions.
- When the BASIC Stamp is executing other instructions, it can't send or receive data. The BASIC Stamp does not have a serial buffer as there is in PCs. At most serial rates, the BASIC Stamp cannot receive data via SERIN, process it, and execute another SERIN in time to catch the next chunk of data, unless there are significant pauses between data transmissions.

These limitations can sometimes be addressed by using flow control; the *Fpin* option for SERIN and SEROUT (at baud rates of up to the limitation shown in Table 5.70). Through *Fpin*, SERIN can tell a BASIC Stamp sender when it is ready to receive data. (For that matter, *Fpin* flow control follows the rules of other serial handshaking schemes, but most computers other than the BASIC Stamp cannot start and stop serial transmission on a byte-by-byte basis. That's why this discussion is limited to communication between BASIC Stamps.)

Here's an example using flow control on the BS2 (data through I/O pin 1, flow control through I/O pin 0, 9600 baud, N8, noninverted):

```
SerData     VAR    BYTE
SERIN  1\0, 84, [SerData]
```

When SERIN executes, I/O pin 1 (*Rpin*) is made an input in preparation for incoming data, and I/O pin 0 (*Fpin*) is made output low, to signal "go" to the sender. After SERIN finishes receiving, I/O pin 0 goes high to tell the sender to stop. If an inverted *BaudMode* had been specified, the *Fpin's* responses would have been reversed. Here's the relationship of serial polarity to *Fpin* states.

Table 5.78: BS2, BS2e, BS2sx and BS2p flow control pin states in relation to polarity (inverted or non-inverted).

	Ready to Receive ("Go")	Not Ready to Receive ("Stop")
Inverted	Fpin is High (1)	Fpin is Low (0)
Non-inverted	Fpin is Low (0)	Fpin is High (1)

See the Demo Program, below, for a flow control example using two BS2s. In the demo program example, without flow control, the sender would transmit the whole word "HELLO!" in about 6 ms. The receiver would catch the first byte at most; by the time it got back from the first 1-second PAUSE, the rest of the data would be long gone. With flow control, communication is flawless since the sender waits for the receiver to catch up.

In Figure 5.33, I/O pin 0, *Fpin*, is pulled to ground through a 10k resistor. This is to ensure that the sender sees a stop signal (0 for inverted communications) when the receiver is being programmed.

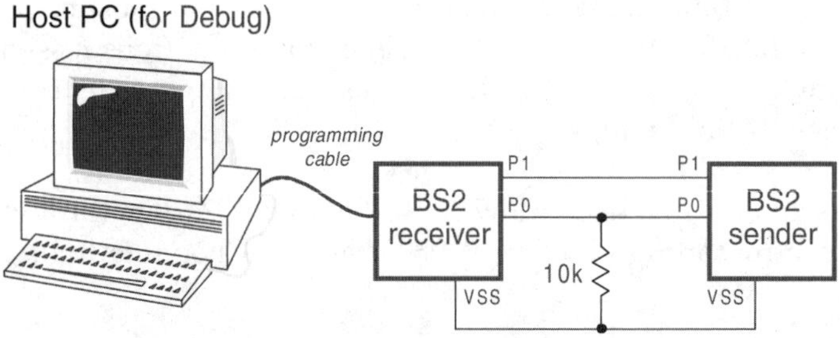

Host PC (for Debug)

Figure 5.33: Flow-Control Example Circuit.

Serial communication, because of its complexity, can be very difficult to work with at times. Please follow these guidelines when developing a project using the SERIN and SEROUT commands:

SERIN TROUBLESHOOTING.

1. Always build your project in steps.
    a. Start with small, manageable pieces of code, that deals with serial communication) and test them, one at a time.
    b. Add more and more small pieces, testing them each time, as you go.
    c. Never write a large portion of code that works with serial communication without testing its smallest workable pieces first.
2. Pay attention to timing.
    a. Be very careful to calculate and overestimate the amount of time operations should take within the BASIC Stamp. Misunderstanding the timing constraints is the source of most problems with code that communicate serially.
    b. If the serial communication in your project is bi-directional, the above statement is even more critical.
3. Pay attention to wiring.
    a. Take extra time to study and verify serial communication wiring diagrams. A mistake in wiring can cause strange problems in communication, or no communication at all. Make sure to connect the ground pins (Vss) between the devices that are communicating serially.
4. Verify port setting on the PC and in the SERIN/SEROUT commands.
    a. Unmatched settings on the sender and receiver side will cause garbled data transfers or no data transfers. If the

data you receive is unreadable, it is most likely a baud rate setting error.

5. If receiving data from another device that is not a BASIC Stamp, try to use baud rates of 4800 and below.

   a. Because of additional overhead in the BASIC Stamp, and the fact that the BASIC Stamp has no hardware receive buffer for serial communication, received data may sometimes be missed or garbled. If this occurs, try lowering the baud rate (if possible), adding extra stop bits, and not using formatters in the SERIN command. Using simple variables (not arrays) and no formatters will increase the chance that the BASIC Stamp can receive the data properly.

6. Be sure to study the effects of SERIN formatters.

   a. Some formatters have specific requirements that may cause problems in received data. For example, the DEC formatter requires a non-decimal-numeric character to follow the received number before it will allow the BASIC Stamp to continue. See Appendix C for example input data and the effects on formatters.

⌗1⌗ Demo Program (SERIN.bas)

```
' This program waits for the characters "A", "B", "C" and "D" to arrive serially
' (Inverted 2400 baud, N81) on I/O pin 0, followed by a number and a carriage return
' (or some other non-number).  It then displays the received number on the DEBUG screen.

'{$STAMP BS1}                                    'STAMP directive (specifies a BS1)

SYMBOL  Result = W0

Loop:
  SERIN  0, N2400, ("ABCD"), #Result
  DEBUG  #Result, CR
GOTO  Loop
```

Demo Program (SERIN-OUT_SENDER.bs2 & SERIN-OUT_RECEIVER.bs2)

```
' Using two BS2-IC's, connect the circuit shown in the SERIN command description and run
' this program on the BASIC Stamp designated as the Sender. This program demonstrates
' the use of Flow Control (FPin). Without flow control, the sender would transmit the
' whole word "HELLO!" in about 6 ms. The receiver would catch the first byte at most; by
' the time it got back from the first 1-second PAUSE, the rest of the data would be long
' gone. With flow control, communication is flawless since the sender waits for the
' receiver to catch up.

'{$STAMP BS2}                            'STAMP directive (specifies a BS2)

Loop:
  SEROUT  1\0, 16468, ["HELLO!"]         ' Send the greeting.
  PAUSE 2500
GOTO Loop
```

NOTE: This is written for the BS2 but can be used for the BS2e, BS2sx and BS2p also (with modifications). Locate the proper source code file or modify the STAMP directive and the *Baudmode* before downloading to the BS2e, BS2sx or BS2p.

```
' Using two BS2-IC's, connect the circuit shown in the SERIN command description and run
' this program on the BASIC Stamp designated as the Receiver.  This program demonstrates
' the use of Flow Control (FPin).  Without flow control, the sender would transmit the
' whole word "HELLO!" in about 6 ms. The receiver would catch the first byte at most; by
' the time it got back from the first 1-second PAUSE, the rest of the data would be long
' gone. With flow control, communication is flawless since the sender waits for the
' receiver to catch up.

Letter         VAR   BYTE
Again:
  SERIN  1\0, 16468, [Letter]            ' Get 1 byte.
  DEBUG  Letter                          ' Display on screen.
  PAUSE  1000                            ' Wait a second.
GOTO  Again

Case2:
     DEBUG "Branched to Case2",cr
GOTO Start
```

SEROUT | BS1 | BS2 | BS2e | BS2sx | BS2p |

〔1〕 SEROUT *Tpin, Baudmode, ({#} OutputData)*

〔2〕 〔2e〕 〔2sx〕 〔2p〕 SEROUT *Tpin {\Fpin}, Baudmode, {Pace,} {Timeout, Tlabel,} [InputData]*

Function

Transmit asynchronous serial data (e.g., RS-232 data).

〔1〕
NOTE: Expressions are not allowed as arguments on the BS1. The range of the R*pin* argument on the BS1 is 0 – 7.

- ***Tpin*** is a variable/constant/expression (0 – 16) that specifies the I/O pin through which the serial data will be transmitted. This pin will be set to output mode. On the BS2, BS2e, BS2sx and BS2p, if Tpin is set to 16, the BASIC Stamp uses the dedicated serial-output pin (SOUT, physical pin 1), which is normally used by the Stamp Editor during the download process.

- ***Fpin*** is an optional variable/constant/expression (0 – 15) that specifies the I/O pin to monitor for flow control status. This pin will be set to input mode. NOTE: Fpin must be specified to use the optional *Timeout* and *Tlabel* arguments in the SEROUT command.

- ***Baudmode*** is variable/constant/expression (0 – 7 on the BS1, 0 – 65535 on all other BASIC Stamps) that specifies serial timing and configuration.

- ***Pace*** is an optional variable/constant/expression (0 – 65535) that determines the length of the pause between transmitted bytes. NOTE: Pace cannot be used simultaneously with *Timeout*.

- ***Timeout*** is an optional variable/constant/expression (0 – 65535) that tells SEROUT how long to wait for *Fpin* permission to send. If permission does not arrive in time, the program will jump to the address specified by *Tlable*. NOTE: Fpin must be specified to use the optional *Timeout* and *Tlabel* arguments in the SEROUT command.

- ***Tlabel*** is an optional label that must be provided along with *Timeout*. Tlabel indicates where the program should go in the event that permission to send data is not granted within the period specified by *Timeout*.

〔1〕
NOTE: The BS1's *OutputData* argument can only be a list of variables and the optional decimal modifier (#).

- ***OutputData*** is list of variables, constants, expressions and formatters that tells SEROUT how to format outgoing data. SEROUT can transmit individual or repeating bytes, convert values into decimal, hex or binary text representations, or transmit strings of bytes from variable arrays. These actions can be combined in any order in the *OutputData* list.

Quick Facts

	BS1	BS2	BS2e	BS2sx	BS2p
Units in *Pace* and *Timeout*	n/a	1 ms	1 ms	400 µs	400 µs
Baud range	300, 600, 1200, and 2400 only	243 to 50K	243 to 50K	608 to 115.2K	608 to 115.2K
Baud limit with flow control	n/a	19.2K	19.2K	19.2K	19.2K
I/O pins available	0 - 7	0 – 15	0 - 15	0 - 15	0 – 15 (in current I/O block)
Other serial port pins	n/a	SOUT pin (physical pin 1) when *Rpin* = 16			
Special cases	n/a	*Fpin* must be specified to use *Timeout* and *Tlabel*. *Pace* cannot be specified at the same time as *Timeout*.			

Table 5.79: SEROUT Quick Facts.

Explanation

One of the most popular forms of communication between electronic devices is serial communication. There are two major types of serial communication; asynchronous and synchronous. The SERIN and SEROUT commands are used to receive and send asynchronous serial data. See the SHIFTIN and SHIFTOUT command for information on the synchronous method.

SERIAL COMMUNICATION BACKGROUND.

The following information is supplemental to what is discussed in the SERIN command section. Please read through the SERIN command section for additional information.

All BASIC Stamps (except the BS1) have a line driver on its SOUT pin (*Tpin* = 16). See the "Hardware" section of the "Introduction to the BASIC Stamps" chapter. The SOUT pin goes to a PC's serial data-in pin on the DB9 connector built into BASIC Stamp development boards. The connector is wired to allow both programming and run-time serial communication (unless you are using the Stamp 2 Carrier Board which is only designed for programming). For the built-in serial port set the *Tpin* argument to 16 in the SEROUT command.

USING THE BUILT-IN SERIAL PORT ON THE BS2, BS2E, BS2SX AND BS2P.

All BASIC Stamps (including the BS1) can also transmit RS-232 data through any of their I/O pins (*Tpin* = 0 – 7 for BS1, *Tpin* = 0 – 15 on all other BASIC Stamps). The I/O pins only provide a 0 to +5 volt swing (outside of RS-232 specs) and may need to be connected through a line driver for proper operation with all serial ports. Most serial ports are able to recognize a 0 to +5 volt swing, however. See Figure 5.34 for sample wiring.

Figure 5.34: Serial port diagram showing correct connections to a BASIC Stamp's I/O pin. NOTE: A line driver may have to be used between the I/O pin and the receiving serial port to ensure proper communication.

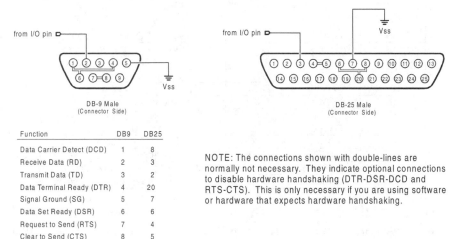

Function	DB9	DB25
Data Carrier Detect (DCD)	1	8
Receive Data (RD)	2	3
Transmit Data (TD)	3	2
Data Terminal Ready (DTR)	4	20
Signal Ground (SG)	5	7
Data Set Ready (DSR)	6	6
Request to Send (RTS)	7	4
Clear to Send (CTS)	8	5

NOTE: The connections shown with double-lines are normally not necessary. They indicate optional connections to disable hardware handshaking (DTR-DSR-DCD and RTS-CTS). This is only necessary if you are using software or hardware that expects hardware handshaking.

Figure 5.34 shows the pinouts of the two styles of PC serial ports and how to connect them to the BASIC Stamp's I/O pin. Though not normally needed, the figure also shows loop back connections that defeat hardware handshaking used by some PC software. Note that PC serial ports are always male connectors. The 25-pin style of serial port (called a DB25) looks similar to a printer (parallel) port except that it is male, whereas a parallel port is female.

SERIAL TIMING AND MODE (BAUDMODE).

Asynchronous serial communication relies on precise timing. Both the sender and receiver must be set for identical timing, usually expressed in bits per second (bps) called baud.

On all BASIC Stamps, SEROUT requires a value called *Baudmode* that tells it the important characteristics of the outgoing serial data; the bit period, number of data and parity bits, and polarity.

On the BS1, serial communication is limited to: no-parity, 8-data bits and ▐1▌ 1-stop bit at one of four different speeds: 300, 600, 1200 or 2400 baud. Table 5.80 indicates the *Baudmode* value or symbols to use when selecting the desired mode.

Baudmode Value	Symbol	Baud Rate	Polarity and Output Mode
0	T2400	2400	TRUE (always driven)
1	T1200	1200	TRUE (always driven)
2	T600	600	TRUE (always driven)
3	T300	300	TRUE (always driven)
4	N2400	2400	INVERTED (always driven)
5	N1200	1200	INVERTED (always driven)
6	N600	600	INVERTED (always driven)
7	N300	300	INVERTED (always driven)
8	OT2400	2400	TRUE (open drain, driven high)
9	OT1200	1200	TRUE (open drain, driven high)
10	OT600	600	TRUE (open drain, driven high)
11	OT300	300	TRUE (open drain, driven high)
12	ON2400	2400	INVERTED (open source, driven low)
13	ON1200	1200	INVERTED (open source, driven low)
14	ON600	600	INVERTED (open source, driven low)
15	ON300	300	INVERTED (open source, driven low)

Table 5.80: BS1 Baudmode Values.

On the BS2, BS2e, BS2sx and BS2p, serial communication is very flexible. ▐2▌ ▐2e▌ ▐2sx▌ ▐2p▌ The *Baudmode* argument for SEROUT accepts a 16-bit value that determines its characteristics: 1-stop bit, 8-data bits/no-parity or 7-data bits/even-parity and virtually any speed from as low as 300 baud to greater than 100K baud (depending on the BASIC Stamp). Table 5.81 shows how *Baudmode* is calculated and Tables 5.82, 5.83 and 5.84 show common baud modes for standard serial baud rates.

Step 1: Determine the bit period (bits 0 – 11)	BS2 and BS2e:	=	INT(1,000,000 / baud rate) – 20
	BS2sx:	=	INT(2,500,000 / baud rate) – 20
	BS2p:	=	INT(2,500,000 / baud rate) – 20
	Note: INT means 'convert to integer;' drop the numbers to the right of the decimal point.		
Step 2: Set data bits and parity (bit 13)	8-bit/no-parity	=	0
	7-bit/even-parity	=	8192
Step 3: Select polarity (bit 14)	True (noninverted)	=	0
	Inverted	=	16384
Step 4: Select driven or open output (bit 15)	Driven	=	0
	Open	=	32768

Table 5.81: BS2, BS2e, BS2sx and BS2p *Baudmode* calculation. Add the results of steps 1, 2, 3 and 4 to determine the proper value for the *Baudmode* argument.

Table 5.82: BS2 and BS2e common baud rates and corresponding *Baudmodes*.

Baud Rate	8-bit no-parity inverted	8-bit no-parity true	7-bit even-parity inverted	7-bit even-parity true
300	19697	3313	27889	11505
600	18030	1646	26222	9838
1200	17197	813	25389	9005
2400	16780	396	24972	8588
4800	16572	188	24764	8380
9600	16468	84	24660	8276

NOTE: For "open" baudmodes used in networking, add 32768 to the values from the table above. If the dedicated serial port (*Tpin*=16) is used, the data is inverted and driven regardless of the baudmode setting.

Table 5.83: BS2sx common baud rates and corresponding *Baudmodes*.

Baud Rate	8-bit no-parity inverted	8-bit no-parity true	7-bit even-parity inverted	7-bit even-parity true
1200	18447	2063	26639	10255
2400	17405	1021	25597	9213
4800	16884	500	25076	8692
9600	16624	240	24816	8432

NOTE: For "open" baudmodes used in networking, add 32768 to the values from the table above. If the dedicated serial port (*Tpin*=16) is used, the data is inverted and driven regardless of the baudmode setting.

Table 5.84: BS2p common baud rates and corresponding *Baudmodes*.

Baud Rate	8-bit no-parity inverted	8-bit no-parity true	7-bit even-parity inverted	7-bit even-parity true
1200	18447	2063	26639	10255
2400	17405	1021	25597	9213
4800	16884	500	25076	8692
9600	16624	240	24816	8432

NOTE: For "open" baudmodes used in networking, add 32768 to the values from the table above. If the dedicated serial port (*Tpin*=16) is used, the data is inverted and driven regardless of the baudmode setting.

CHOOSING THE PROPER BAUD MODE.

If you're communicating with existing software or hardware, its speed(s) and mode(s) will determine your choice of baud rate and mode. See the SERIN command description for more information.

A SIMPLE FORM OF SEROUT.

The example below will transmit a single byte through I/O pin 1 at 2400 baud, 8N1, inverted:

SEROUT - BASIC Stamp Command Reference

SEROUT 1, N2400, (65)

--or--

SEROUT 1, 16780, [65]

Here, SEROUT will transmit a byte equal to 65 (the ASCII value of the character "A") through pin 1. If the BASIC Stamp were connected to a PC running a terminal program (set to the same baud rate) the character "A" would appear on the screen (see the ASCII character chart in the appendix).

What if you really wanted the value 65 to appear on the screen? If you remember from the discussion in the SERIN command, "It is up to the receiving side (in serial communication) to interpret the values…" In this case, the PC is interpreting the byte-sized value to be the ASCII code for the character "A". Unless you're also writing the software for the PC, you can't change how the PC interprets the incoming serial data, so to solve this problem, the data needs to be translated before it is sent.

The SEROUT command provides a formatter, called the decimal formatter, which will translate the value 65 to two ASCII codes for the characters "6" and "5" and then transmit them. Look at the following code:

SEROUT 1, N2400, (#65)

--or--

SEROUT 1, 16780, [DEC 65]

Notice the decimal formatter in the SEROUT command. It is the "#" (for the BS1) or "DEC" (for the other BASIC Stamps) that appears just to the left of the number 65. This tells SEROUT to convert the number into separate ASCII characters which represent the value in decimal form. If the value 65 in the code were changed to 123, the SEROUT command would send three bytes (49, 50 and 51) corresponding to the characters "1", "2" and "3".

The BS2, BS2e, BS2sx and BS2p have many more conversion formatters available for the SEROUT command. See the "Additional Conversion Formatters" section below for more information.

This is written with the BS2's *BaudMode* value. Be sure to adjust the value for your BASIC Stamp.

A SIMPLE NUMERIC CONVERSION; DECIMAL TO ASCII NUMERIC TEXT.

This is written with the BS2's *BaudMode* value. Be sure to adjust the value for your BASIC Stamp.

The SEROUT command sends quoted text exactly as it appears in the *OutputData* list:

[1]
```
SEROUT  1, N2400, ( "HELLO", CR )
SEROUT  1, N2400, ( "Num = ", #100 )
```

--or--

[2] [2e] [2sx] [2p]
```
SEROUT  1, 16780, [ "HELLO", CR ]
SEROUT  1, 16780, [ "Num = ", DEC 100 ]
```

This is written with the BS2's *BaudMode* value. Be sure to adjust the value for your BASIC Stamp.

The above code will display "HELLO" on one line and "Num = 100" on the next line. Notice that you can combine data to output in one SEROUT command, separated by commas. In the example above, we could have written it as one line of code, with "HELLO", CR, "Num = ", DEC 100 in the *OutputData* list.

[1] The BS1's SEROUT command is limited to above-mentioned features. If you are not using a BS1, please continue reading about the additional features below.

[2] [2e] [2sx] [2p]

USING SEROUT'S *PACE* ARGUMENT TO INSERT DELAYS BETWEEN TRANSMITTED BYTES.

NOTE: The rest of the code examples for this section are written for the BS2, using the BS2's *BaudMode* and *Timeout* values. Be sure to adjust the value for your BASIC Stamp.

The SEROUT command can also be configured to pause between transmitted bytes. This is the purpose of the optional *Pace* argument. For example (9600 baud N8, inverted):

```
SEROUT  1, 16468, 1000, [ "Slowly" ]
```

Here, the BASIC Stamp transmits the word "Slowly" with a 1 second delay between each character. See Table 5.79 for units of the *Pace* argument. One good reason to use the *Pace* feature is to support devices that require more than one stop bit. Normally, the BASIC Stamp sends data as fast as it can (with a minimum of 1 stop bit between bytes). Since a stop bit is really just a resting state in the line (no data transmitted), using the *Pace* option will effectively add multiple stop bits. Since the requirement for 2 or more stop bits (on some devices) is really just a "minimum" requirement, the receiving side should receive this data correctly.

USING ASCII CODES.

Keep in mind that when we type something like "XYZ" into the SEROUT command, the BASIC Stamp actually uses the ASCII codes for each of those characters for its tasks. We could also typed: 88, 89, 90 in place of "XYZ" and the program would run the same way since 88 is the ASCII code for the "X" character, 89 is the ASCII code for the "Y" character, and so on.

The decimal formatter is only one of a whole family of conversion formatters available with SERIN on the BS2, BS2e, BS2sx and BS2p. See Table 5.85 for a list of available conversion formatters. All of the conversion formatters work similar to the decimal formatter. The formatters translate the value into separate bytes of data until the entire number is translated or until the indicated number of digits (in the case of the fixed length formatters) is translated.

ADDITIONAL CONVERSION FORMATTERS.

The BS2, BS2e, BS2sx and BS2p also have special formatters for outputting a string of characters, repeated characters and undesirable characters. See Table 5.86 for a list of these special formatters.

Conversion Formatter	Type of Number	Notes
DEC{1..5}	Decimal, optionally fixed to 1 – 5 digits	1
SDEC{1..5}	Signed decimal, optionally fixed to 1 – 5 digits	1,2
HEX{1..4}	Hexadecimal, optionally fixed to 1 – 4 digits	1
SHEX{1..4}	Signed hexadecimal, optionally fixed to 1 – 4 digits	1,2
IHEX{1..4}	Indicated hexadecimal, optionally fixed to 1 – 4 digits ($ prefix)	1
ISHEX{1..4}	Signed, indicated hexadecimal, optionally fixed to 1 – 4 digits ($ prefix)	1,2
BIN{1..16}	Binary, optionally fixed to 1 – 16 digits	1
SBIN{1..16}	Signed binary, optionally fixed to 1 – 16 digits	1,2
IBIN{1..16}	Indicated binary, optionally fixed to 1 – 16 digits (% prefix)	1
ISBIN{1..16}	Signed, indicated binary, optionally fixed to 1 – 16 digits (% prefix)	1,2

Table 5.85: BS2, BS2e, BS2sx and BS2p Conversion Formatters.

1 Fixed-digit formatters like DEC4 will pad the number with leading 0s if necessary; ex: DEC4 65 sends 0065. If a number is larger than the specified number of digits, the leading digits will be dropped; ex: DEC4 56422 sends 6422.
2 Signed modifiers work under two's complement rules.

Table 5.86: BS2, BS2e, BS2sx and BS2p Special Formatters.

Special Formatter	Action
?	Displays "symbol = x' + carriage return; where x is a number. Default format is decimal, but may be combined with conversion formatters (ex: BIN ? x to display "x = binary_number").
ASC ?	Displays "symbol = 'x'" + carriage return; where x is an ASCII character.
STR *ByteArray* {\L}	Send character string from an array. The optional \L argument can be used to limit the output to L characters, otherwise, characters will be sent up to the first byte equal to 0 or the end of RAM space is reached.
REP *Byte* \L	Send a string consisting of *Byte* repeated L times (ex: REP "X"\10 sends "XXXXXXXXXX").

THE STR (STRING) FORMATTER.

The string formatter is useful for transmitting a string of characters from a byte array variable. A string of characters is a set of characters that are arranged or accessed in a certain order. The characters "ABC" could be stored in a string with the "A" first, followed by the "B" and then followed by the "C." A byte array is a similar concept to a string; it contains data that is arranged in a certain order. Each of the elements in an array is the same size. The string "ABC" could be stored in a byte array containing three bytes (elements). See the "Defining Arrays" section in Chapter 4 for more information on arrays.

Here is an example that transmits five bytes (from a byte array) through I/O pin 1 at 9600 bps, N81/inverted:

```
SerString    VAR    BYTE(5)                   ' Make a 5-byte array.
SerString(0) = "H"
SerString(1) = "E"
SerString(2) = "L"
SerString(3) = "L"
SerString(4) = "O"
SEROUT  1, 16468, [ STR  SerString\5 ]        ' Send 5-byte string.
```

Note that we use the optional \L argument of STR. If we didn't specify this, the BASIC Stamp would try to keep sending characters until it found a byte equal to 0. Since we didn't specify a last byte of 0 in the array, we chose to tell it explicitly to only send 5 characters.

USING PARITY AND HANDLING PARITY ERRORS.

Parity is a simple error-checking feature. When the SEROUT command's *Baudmode* is set for even parity it counts the number of 1s in the outgoing byte and uses the parity bit to make that number even. For instance, if it is sending the 7-bit value: %0011010, it sets the parity bit to 1 in order to make an even number of 1s (four).

The receiver also counts the data bits to calculate what the parity bit should be. If it matches the parity bit received, the serial receiver assumes that the data was received correctly. Of course, this is not necessarily true, since two incorrectly received bits could make parity seem correct when the data was wrong, or the parity bit itself could be bad when the rest of the data was OK. Parity errors are only detected on the receiver side. Generally, the receiver determines how to handle the error. In a more robust application, the receiver and transmitter might be set up such that the receiver can request a re-send of data that was received with a parity error.

When you design an application that requires serial communication CONTROLLING DATA FLOW. between BASIC Stamps, you have to work within these limitations:
- When the BASIC Stamp is sending or receiving data, it can't execute other instructions.
- When the BASIC Stamp is executing other instructions, it can't send or receive data. The BASIC Stamp does not have a serial buffer as there is in PCs. At most serial rates, the BASIC Stamp cannot receive data via SERIN, process it, and execute another SERIN in time to catch the next chunk of data, unless there are significant pauses between data transmissions.

These limitations can sometimes be addressed by using flow control; the *Fpin* option for SERIN and SEROUT (at baud rates of up to the limitation shown in Table 5.79). Through *Fpin*, SERIN can tell a BASIC Stamp sender when it is ready to receive data and SEROUT (on the sender) will wait for permission to send. (For that matter, *Fpin* flow control follows the rules of other serial handshaking schemes, but most computers other than the BASIC Stamp cannot start and stop serial transmission on a byte-by-byte basis. That's why this discussion is limited to communication between BASIC Stamps.)

Here's an example using flow control on the BS2 (data through I/O pin 1, flow control through I/O pin 0, 9600 baud, N8, noninverted):

⌷2⌷ ⌷2e⌷ ⌷2sx⌷ ⌷2p⌷ SerData   VAR   BYTE
SEROUT 1\0, 84, [SerData]

When SEROUT executes, I/O pin 1 (*Tpin*) is made an output, and I/O pin 0 (*Fpin*) is made an input, to wait for the "go" signal from the receiver. Here's the relationship of serial polarity to *Fpin* states.

Table 5.87: BS2, BS2e, BS2sx and BS2p flow control pin states in relation to polarity (inverted or non-inverted).

	Ready to Receive ("Go")	Not Ready to Receive ("Stop")
Inverted	Fpin is High (1)	Fpin is Low (0)
Non-inverted	Fpin is Low (0)	Fpin is High (1)

See the Demo Program, below, for a flow control example using two BS2s. In the demo program example, without flow control, the sender would transmit the whole word "HELLO!" in about 6 ms. The receiver would catch the first byte at most; by the time it got back from the first 1-second PAUSE, the rest of the data would be long gone. With flow control, communication is flawless since the sender waits for the receiver to catch up.

In Figure 5.35, I/O pin 0, *Fpin*, is pulled to ground through a 10k resistor. This is to ensure that the sender sees a stop signal (0 for inverted communications) when the receiver is being programmed.

USING THE SERIAL TIME-OUT FEATURE.

In the flow control examples above, the only way the SEROUT instruction will end (other than RESET or power-off) is if the receiver allows it to send the entire *OutputData* list. If *Fpin* permission never occurs, the program is stuck. However, you can tell the BASIC Stamp to abort SEROUT if it doesn't receive *Fpin* permission within a specified time period. For instance, to transmit a decimal number through pin 1 at 9600 baud, 8N, inverted and abort SEROUT after 2 seconds (2000 ms) if no *Fpin* permission arrives on I/O pin 0:

⌷2⌷ ⌷2e⌷ ⌷2sx⌷ ⌷2p⌷ SEROUT 1\0, 16468, 2000, NoPermission, [DEC 150]
STOP

NoPermission:
  DEBUG CLS, "timed out"

If no *Fpin* permission arrives within 2 seconds, the program aborts SEROUT and continues at the label NoPermission.

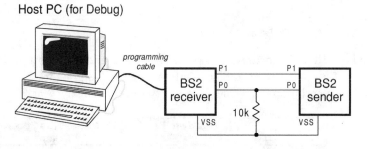

Host PC (for Debug)

Figure 5.35: Flow-Control Example Circuit.

The SEROUT command supports open-drain and open-source output, which makes it possible to network multiple BASIC Stamps on a single pair of wires. These "open baudmodes" only actively drive the *Tpin* in one state (for the other state, they simply disconnect the pin; setting it to an input mode). If two BASIC Stamps in a network had their SEROUT lines connected together (while a third device listened on that line) and the BASIC Stamps were using always-driven baudmodes, they could simultaneously output two opposite states (ie: +5 volts and ground). This would create a short circuit. The heavy current flow would likely damage the I/O pins or the BASIC Stamps themselves. Since the open baudmodes only drive in one state and float in the other, there's no chance of this kind of short.

USING OPEN BAUDMODES FOR NETWORKING BASIC STAMPS.

The polarity selected for SEROUT determines which state is driven and which is open as in Table 5.88.

	State (0)	State (1)	Resister Pulled to
Inverted	Open	Driven	Gnd (Vss)
Non-inverted	Driven	Open	+5V (Vdd)

Table 5.88: BS2, BS2e, BS2sx and BS2p Open Baudmode States.

Since open baudmodes only drive to one state, they need a resistor to pull the networked line into the other state, as shown in Table 5.88 and in Figures 5.36 and 5.37.

Open baudmodes allow the BASIC Stamp to share a line, but it is up to your program to resolve other networking issues such as who talks when and how to detect, prevent and fix data errors.

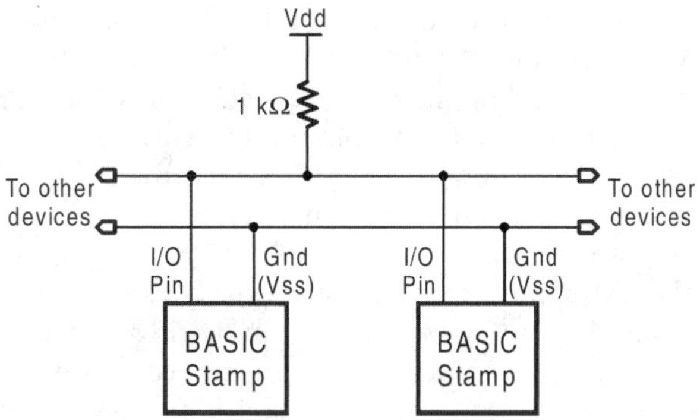

Figure 5.36: SEROUT Open-Drain Circuit. This circuit is for use with the Open, Non-inverted baudmode.

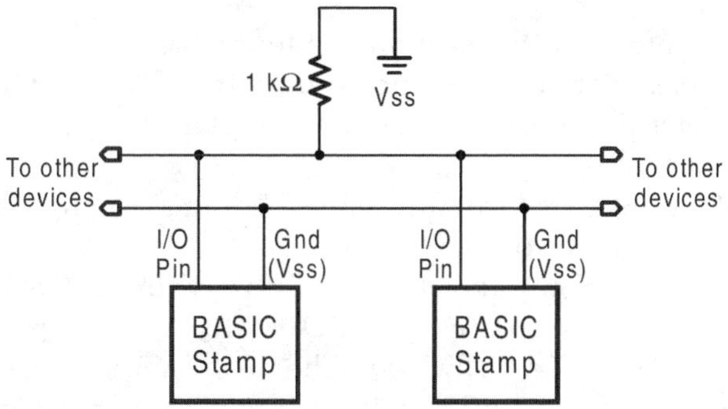

Figure 5.37: SEROUT Open-Source Circuit. This circuit is for use with the Open, Inverted baudmode.

SEROUT TROUBLESHOOTING.

Serial communication, because of its complexity, can be very difficult to work with at times. Please follow these guidelines (and those in the "SERIN Troubleshooting" section of the SERIN command description) when developing a project using the SERIN and SEROUT commands:

1. Always build your project in steps.
   a. Start with small, manageable pieces of code, that deals with serial communication) and test them, one at a time.
   b. Add more and more small pieces, testing them each time, as you go.
   c. Never write a large portion of code that works with serial communication without testing its smallest workable pieces first.

2. Pay attention to timing.
   a. Be very careful to calculate and overestimate the amount of time operations should take within the BASIC Stamp. Misunderstanding the timing constraints is the source of most problems with code that communicate serially.
   b. If the serial communication in your project is bi-directional, the above statement is even more critical.
3. Pay attention to wiring.
   a. Take extra time to study and verify serial communication wiring diagrams. A mistake in wiring can cause strange problems in communication, or no communication at all. Make sure to connect the ground pins (Vss) between the devices that are communicating serially.
4. Verify port setting on the PC and in the SERIN/SEROUT commands.
   a. Unmatched settings on the sender and receiver side will cause garbled data transfers or no data transfers. If the data you receive is unreadable, it is most likely a baud rate setting error.
5. If data transmitted to the Stamp Editor's Debug Terminal is garbled, verify the output format.
   a. A common mistake is to send data with SEROUT in ASCII format. For example, SEROUT 16, 84, [0] instead of SEROUT 16, 84, [DEC 0]. The first example will send a byte equal to 0 to the PC, resulting in the Debug Terminal clearing the screen (since 0 is the control character for a clear-screen action).

Demo Program (SEROUT.bas)

' This program transmits the characters "A", "B", "C" and "D" (Inverted 2400 baud, N81) on
' I/O pin 0, followed by a number and a carriage return.

```
'{$STAMP BS1}                          'STAMP directive (specifies a BS1)

SYMBOL  Result = W0

Result = 1500
Loop:
  SERIN 0, N2400, ("ABCD"), #Result
  PAUSE 1000
GOTO Loop
```

NOTE: This is written for the BS2 but can be used for the BS2e, BS2sx and BS2p also (with modifications). Locate the proper source code file or modify the STAMP directive and the *Baudmode* before downloading to the BS2e, BS2sx or BS2p.

Demo Program (SERIN-OUT_SENDER.bs2 & SERIN-OUT_RECEIVER.bs2)

```
' Using two BS2-IC's, connect the circuit shown in the SEROUT command description and
' run this program on the BASIC Stamp designated as the Sender. This program
' demonstrates the use of Flow Control (FPin).  Without flow control, the sender would
' transmit the whole word "HELLO!" in about 6 ms. The receiver would catch the first byte at
' most; by the time it got back from the first 1-second PAUSE, the rest of the data would be
' long gone. With flow control, communication is flawless since the sender waits for the
' receiver to catch up.

'{$STAMP  BS2}                                    'STAMP directive (specifies a BS2)

Loop:
  SEROUT  1\0, 16468, ["HELLO!"]                  ' Send the greeting.
  PAUSE 2500
GOTO Loop


' Using two BS2-IC's, connect the circuit shown in the SEROUT command description and
' run this program on the BASIC Stamp designated as the Receiver.  This program
' demonstrates the use of Flow Control (FPin).  Without flow control, the sender would
' transmit the whole word "HELLO!" in about 6 ms. The receiver would catch the first byte at
' most; by the time it got back from the first 1-second PAUSE, the rest of the data would be
' long gone. With flow control, communication is flawless since the sender waits for the
' receiver to catch up.

Letter          VAR    BYTE
Again:
  SERIN  1\0, 16468, [Letter]                     ' Get 1 byte.
  DEBUG  Letter                                   ' Display on screen.
  PAUSE  1000                                     ' Wait a second.
GOTO  Again

Case2:
      DEBUG "Branched to Case2",cr
GOTO Start
```

SHIFTIN | BS1 | BS2 | BS2e | BS2sx | BS2p |

SHIFTIN *Dpin, Cpin, Mode, [Variable {\Bits} {, Variable {\Bits}...}]*

Function

Shift data in from a synchronous serial device.

- **Dpin** is a variable/constant/expression (0 – 15) that specifies the I/O pin that will be connected to the synchronous serial device's data output. This pin will be set to input mode.

- **Cpin** is a variable/constant/expression (0 – 15) that specifies the I/O pin that will be connected to the synchronous serial device's clock input. This pin will be set to output mode.

- **Mode** is a variable/constant/expression (0 – 3), or one of four predefined symbols, that tells SHIFTIN the order in which data bits are to be arranged and the relationship of clock pulses to valid data. See Table 5.90 for value and symbol definitions.

- **Variable** is a variable in which incoming data bits will be stored.

- **Bits** is an optional variable/constant/expression (1 – 16) specifying how many bits are to be input by SHIFTIN. If no *Bits* entry is given, SHIFTIN defaults to 8 bits.

Quick Facts

Table 5.89: SHIFTIN Quick Facts.

	BS2	BS2e	BS2sx	BS2p
Timing of T_h and t_i	14 µs / 46 µs	14 µs / 46 µs	5.6 µs / 18 µs	5.6 µs / 18.8 µs
Transmission Rate	~16 kbits/sec	~16 kbits/sec	~42 kbits/sec	~42 kbits/sec

Explanation

SHIFTIN and SHIFTOUT provide an easy method of acquiring data from synchronous serial devices. Synchronous serial differs from asynchronous serial (like SERIN and SEROUT) in that the timing of data bits (on a data line) is specified in relationship to clock pulses (on a clock line). Data bits may be valid after the rising or falling edge of the clock line. This kind of serial protocol is commonly used by controller peripherals like ADCs, DACs, clocks, memory devices, etc.

At their heart, synchronous-serial devices are essentially shift-registers; trains of flip-flops that pass data bits along in a bucket brigade fashion to a single data output pin. Another bit is output each time the appropriate edge (rising or falling, depending on the device) appears on the clock line.

The SHIFTIN instruction first causes the clock pin to output low and the data pin to switch to input mode. Then, SHIFTIN either reads the data pin and generates a clock pulse (PRE mode) or generates a clock pulse then reads the data pin (POST mode). SHIFTIN continues to generate clock pulses and read the data pin for as many data bits as are required.

SHIFTIN OPERATION.

Making SHIFTIN work with a particular device is a matter of matching the mode and number of bits to that device's protocol. Most manufacturers use a timing diagram to illustrate the relationship of clock and data. Items to look for include: 1) which bit of the data arrives first; most significant bit (MSB) or least significant bit (LSB) and 2) is the first data bit ready before the first clock pulse (PRE) or after the first clock pulse (POST). Table 5.90 shows the values and symbols available for the *Mode* argument and Figure 5.38 shows SHIFTIN's timing.

Symbol	Value	Meaning
MSBPRE	0	Data is msb-first; sample bits before clock pulse
LSBPRE	1	Data is lsb-first; sample bits before clock pulse
MSBPOST	2	Data is msb-first; sample bits after clock pulse
LSBPOST	3	Data is lsb-first; sample bits after clock pulse

Table 5.90: SHIFTIN Mode Values and Symbols.

(Msb is most-significant bit; the highest or leftmost bit of a nibble, byte, or word. Lsb is the least-significant bit; the lowest or rightmost bit of a nibble, byte, or word.)

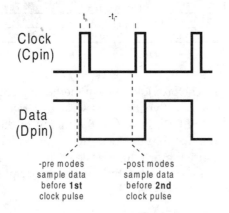

Figure 5.38: SHIFTIN Timing Diagram. Refer to the SHIFTIN Quick Answers table for timing information on t_h and t_l.

Clock (Cpin)

Data (Dpin)

-pre modes sample data before **1st** clock pulse

-post modes sample data before **2nd** clock pulse

A SIMPLE SHIFTIN EXAMPLE.

Here is a simple example:

```
Result     VAR   BYTE
SHIFTIN 0, 1, MSBPRE, [ Result ]
```

Here, the SHIFTIN command will read I/O pin 0 (the *Dpin*) and will generate a clock signal on I/O 1 (the *Cpin*). The data that arrives on the *Dpin* depends on the device connected to it. Let's say, for example, that a shift register is connected and has a value of $AF (10101111) waiting to be sent. Additionally, let's assume that the shift register sends out the most significant bit first, and the first bit is on the *Dpin* before the first clock pulse (MSBPRE). The SHIFTIN command above will generate eight clock pulses and sample the data pin (*Dpin*) eight times. Afterward, the *Result* variable will contain the value $AF.

CONTROLLING THE NUMBER OF BITS RECEIVED.

By default, SHIFTIN acquires eight bits, but you can set it to shift any number of bits from 1 to 16 with the *Bits* argument. For example:

```
Result     VAR   BYTE
SHIFTIN 0, 1, MSBPRE, [ Result \4 ]
```

Will only input the first 4 bits. In the example discussed above, the *Result* variable will be left with %1010.

Some devices return more than 16 bits. For example, most 8-bit shift registers can be daisy-chained together to form any multiple of 8 bits; 16, 24, 32, 40... To solve this, you can use a single SHIFTIN instruction with multiple variables. Each variable can be assigned a particular number of bits with the *Bits* argument. As in:

```
ResultLow  VAR   WORD
ResultHigh VAR   NIB
SHIFTIN  0, 1, MSBPRE, [ ResultHigh\4 , ResultLow\16]
```

The above code will first shift in four bits into *ResultHigh* and then 16 bits into *ResultLow*. The two variables together make up a 20 bit value.

Demo Program (SHIFTIN.bs2)

```
' This program uses the SHIFTIN instruction to interface with the ADC0831 8-bit
' analog-to-digital converter from National Semiconductor.

'{$STAMP BS2}                           'STAMP directive (specifies a BS2)

ADres     VAR   BYTE                    'A-to-D result: one byte.
CS        CON   0                       'Chip select is pin 0.
AData     CON   1                       'ADC data output is pin 1.
CLK       CON   2                       'Clock is pin 2.


HIGH  CS                                'Deselect ADC to start.

' In the loop below, just three lines of code are required to read the ADC0831. The
' SHIFTIN command does most of the work.  The mode argument in the SHIFTIN command
' specifies msb or lsb-first and whether to sample data before or after the clock.
' In this case, we chose msb-first, post-clock. The ADC0831 precedes its data output
' with a dummy bit, which we take care of by specifying 9 bits of data instead of 8.

Again:
  LOW  CS                               'Activate the ADC0831.
  SHIFTIN AData, CLK, MSBPOST, [ADres\9] 'Shift in the data.
  HIGH  CS                              'Deactivate ADC0831.
  DEBUG  ? ADres                        'Show us the conversion result.
  PAUSE  1000                           'Wait a second.
GOTO  Again                             'Do it again.
```

NOTE: This is written for the BS2 but can be used for the BS2e, BS2sx and BS2p also. Locate the proper source code file or modify the STAMP directive before downloading to the BS2e, BS2sx or BS2p.

SHIFTOUT

BS1	BS2	BS2e	BS2sx	BS2p

SHIFTOUT *Dpin, Cpin, Mode, [OutputData {\Bits} {,OutputData {\Bits}...}]*

Function

Shift data out to a synchronous serial device.

- **Dpin** is a variable/constant/expression (0 – 15) that specifies the I/O pin that will be connected to the synchronous serial device's data input. This pin will be set to output mode.

- **Cpin** is a variable/constant/expression (0 – 15) that specifies the I/O pin that will be connected to the synchronous serial device's clock input. This pin will be set to output mode.

- **Mode** is a variable/constant/expression (0 – 1), or one of two predefined symbols, that tells SHIFTOUT the order in which data bits are to be arranged. See Table 5.92 for value and symbol definitions.

- **OutputData** is a variable/constant/expression containing the data to be sent.

- **Bits** is an optional variable/constant/expression (1 – 16) specifying how many bits are to be output by SHIFTOUT. If no *Bits* entry is given, SHIFTOUT defaults to 8 bits.

Quick Facts

Table 5.91: SHIFTOUT Quick Facts.

	BS2	BS2e	BS2sx	BS2p
Timing of t_1, t_2, t_a and t_b	14 µs / 46 µs	14 µs / 46 µs	5.6 µs / 18 µs	5.6 µs / 18.8 µs
Transmission Rate	~16 kbits/sec	~16 kbits/sec	~42 kbits/sec	~42 kbits/sec

Explanation

SHIFTIN and SHIFTOUT provide an easy method of acquiring data from synchronous serial devices. Synchronous serial differs from asynchronous serial (like SERIN and SEROUT) in that the timing of data bits (on a data line) is specified in relationship to clock pulses (on a clock line). Data bits may be valid after the rising or falling edge of the clock line. This kind of serial protocol is commonly used by controller peripherals like ADCs, DACs, clocks, memory devices, etc.

SHIFTOUT - BASIC Stamp Command Reference

At their heart, synchronous-serial devices are essentially shift-registers; trains of flip-flops that receive data bits in a bucket brigade fashion from a single data input pin. Another bit is input each time the appropriate edge (rising or falling, depending on the device) appears on the clock line.

The SHIFTOUT instruction first causes the clock pin to output low and the data pin to switch to output mode. Then, SHIFTOUT sets the data pin to the next bit state to be output and generates a clock pulse. SHIFTOUT continues to generate clock pulses and places the next data bit on the data pin for as many data bits as are required for transmission.

SHIFTOUT OPERATION.

Making SHIFTOUT work with a particular device is a matter of matching the mode and number of bits to that device's protocol. Most manufacturers use a timing diagram to illustrate the relationship of clock and data. One of the most important items to look for is which bit of the data should be transmitted first; most significant bit (MSB) or least significant bit (LSB). Table 5.92 shows the values and symbols available for the *Mode* argument and Figure 5.39 shows SHIFTOUT's timing.

Symbol	Value	Meaning
LSBFIRST	0	Data is shifted out lsb-first
MSBFIRST	1	Data is shifted out msb-first

Table 5.92: SHIFTOUT Mode Values and Symbols.

(Msb is most-significant bit; the highest or leftmost bit of a nibble, byte, or word. Lsb is the least-significant bit; the lowest or rightmost bit of a nibble, byte, or word.)

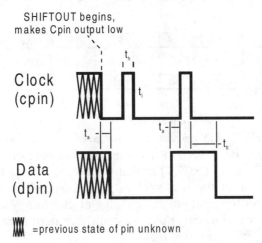

SHIFTOUT begins, makes Cpin output low

Clock (cpin)

Data (dpin)

t_h t_i t_a t_b

▓▓▓ =previous state of pin unknown

Figure 5.39: SHIFTOUT Timing Diagram. Refer to the SHIFTOUT Quick Answers table for timing information on t_h, t_i, t_a and t_b.

A SIMPLE SHIFTOUT EXAMPLE.

Here is a simple example:

SHIFTOUT 0, 1, MSBFIRST, [250]

Here, the SHIFTOUT command will write to I/O pin 0 (the *Dpin*) and will generate a clock signal on I/O 1 (the *Cpin*). The SHIFTOUT command will generate eight clock pulses while writing each bit (of the 8-bit value 250) onto the data pin (*Dpin*). In this case, it will start with the most significant bit first as indicated by the *Mode* value of MSBFIRST.

CONTROLLING THE NUMBER OF BITS TRANSMITTED.

By default, SHIFTOUT transmits eight bits, but you can set it to shift any number of bits from 1 to 16 with the *Bits* argument. For example:

SHIFTOUT 0, 1, MSBFIRST, [250 \4]

Will only output the lowest 4 bits (%0000 in this case).

Some devices require more than 16 bits. To solve this, you can use a single SHIFTOUT command with multiple values. Each value can be assigned a particular number of bits with the *Bits* argument. As in:

SHIFTOUT 0, 1, MSBFIRST, [250\4 , 1045\16]

The above code will first shift out four bits of the number 250 (%1111) and then 16 bits of the number 1045 (%0000010000010101). The two values together make up a 20 bit value.

SHIFTOUT ACCEPTS VARIABLES AND EXPRESSIONS FOR *OUTPUTDATA* AND *BITS* ARGUMENTS.

In the examples above, specific numbers were entered as the data to transmit, but, of course, the SHIFTOUT command will accept variables and expressions for the *OutputData* and even for the *Bits* argument.

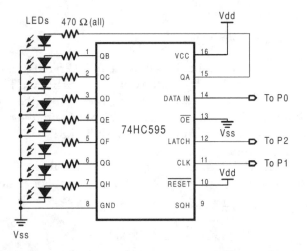

Figure 5.40: SHIFTOUT Timing Diagram. Refer to the SHIFTOUT Quick Answers table for timing information on t_h, t_l, t_a and t_b.

Demo Program (SHIFTOUT.bs2)

```
' This program uses the SHIFTOUT command to interface to the 74HC595 shift register as an
' 8-bit output port.  The '595 requires a minimum of three inputs: data, clock, and latch. See
' the figure in the SHIFTOUT command description in the manual for wiring information.
' SHIFTOUT automatically handles the data and clock, pulsing the clock to shift data bits into
' the '595. An extra step (pulsing the latch input) is required to move the shifted bits in parallel
' onto the '595's output pins. Note: this code does not control the output-enable or reset lines
' of the '595. This means that before the BASIC Stamp first sends, the '595's output latches
' are turned on and may contain random data. In critical applications, you should hold
' output-enable high (disabled) until the BASIC Stamp can take control.

'{$STAMP  BS2}                        'STAMP directive (specifies a BS2)

DataP           CON   0              ' Data pin to 74HC595.
Clock           CON   1              ' Shift clock to 74HC595.
Latch           CON   2              ' Moves data from register to output latch.
Counter   VAR   BYTE                 ' Counter for demo program.

' This loop moves the 8-bit value 'counter' onto the output lines of the '595, pauses, then
' increments counter and repeats.  The data is shifted msb first so that the msb appears on
' pin QH and the lsb on QA. Changing 'msbfirst' to 'lsbfirst' causes the data to
' appear backwards on the outputs.

Again:
  SHIFTOUT DataP,Clock,MSBFIRST,[Counter]      ' Send the bits.
  PULSOUT Latch,1                              ' Transfer to outputs.
  PAUSE 50                                     ' Wait briefly.
  Counter = Counter + 1                        ' Increment counter.
GOTO Again                                     ' Do it again.
```

NOTE: This is written for the BS2 but can be used for the BS2e, BS2sx and BS2p also. Locate the proper source code file or modify the STAMP directive before downloading to the BS2e, BS2sx or BS2p.

SLEEP

BS1	BS2	BS2e	BS2sx	BS2p

SLEEP *Period*

Function

Put the BASIC Stamp into low-power mode for a specified time.

NOTE: Expressions are not allowed as arguments on the BS1.

- *Period* is a variable/constant/expression (1 – 65535) that specifies the duration of sleep. The unit of time for *Period* is 1 second, though the BASIC Stamp rounds up to the nearest multiple of 2.3 seconds.

Quick Facts

Table 5.93: SLEEP Quick Facts.

	BS1	BS2	BS2e	BS2sx	BS2p
Current draw during run	2 mA	8 mA	25 mA	60 mA	40 mA
Current draw during SLEEP	20 µA	40 µA	60 µA	60 µA	60 µA
Accuracy of SLEEP	±1% @ 75°F with stable power supply	±1% @ 75°F with stable power supply	±1% @ 75°F with stable power supply	±1% @ 75°F with stable power supply	±1% @ 75°F with stable power supply

Explanation

SLEEP allows the BASIC Stamp to turn itself off, then turn back on after a programmed period of time. The length of SLEEP can range from 2.3 seconds to slightly over 18 hours. Power consumption is reduced to the amount described in Table 5.93, assuming no loads are being driven. The resolution of the SLEEP instruction is 2.304 seconds. SLEEP rounds the specified number of seconds up to the nearest multiple of 2.304. For example, SLEEP 1 causes 2.3 seconds of sleep, while SLEEP 10 causes 11.52 seconds (5 x 2.304) of sleep.

Pins retain their previous I/O directions during SLEEP. However, outputs are interrupted every 2.3 seconds during SLEEP due to the way the chip keeps time. The alarm clock that wakes the BASIC Stamp up is called the watchdog timer. The watchdog is a resistor/capacitor oscillator built into the interpreter chip. During SLEEP, the chip periodically wakes up and adjusts a counter to determine how long it has been asleep. If it isn't time to wake up, the chip "hits the snooze bar" and goes back to sleep.

To ensure accuracy of SLEEP intervals, the BASIC Stamp periodically compares the watchdog timer to the more-accurate resonator time base. It calculates a correction factor that it uses during SLEEP. As a result, longer SLEEP intervals are accurate to approximately ±1 percent.

If your application is driving loads (sourcing or sinking current through output-high or output-low pins) during SLEEP, current will be interrupted for about 18 ms when the BASIC Stamp wakes up every 2.3 seconds. The reason is that the watchdog-timer reset that awakens the BASIC Stamp also causes all of the pins to switch to input mode for approximately 18 ms. When the interpreter firmware regains control of the processor, it restores the I/O directions dictated by your program.

If you plan to use END, NAP, or SLEEP in your programs, make sure that your loads can tolerate these periodic power outages. The simplest solution is often to connect resistors high or low (to +5V or ground) as appropriate to ensure a continuing supply of current during the reset glitch.

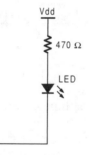

Figure 5.41: SLEEP Example LE▶ Circuit.

The demo program can be used to demonstrate the effects of the SLEEP glitch with an LED and resistor as shown in Figure 5.41.

Demo Program (SLEEP.bs2)

```
' This program lights an LED and then goes to sleep. Connect an LED to pin 0 as shown in
' the description of SLEEP in the manual and run the program. The LED will turn on, then
' the BASIC Stamp will go to sleep. During sleep, the LED will remain on, but will blink
' at intervals of approximately 2.3 seconds due to the watchdog timeout and reset.

'{$STAMP BS2}                            'STAMP directive (specifies a BS2)

LOW  0              ' Turn LED on
Snooze:
  SLEEP  10        ' Sleep for 10 seconds.
GOTO Snooze
```

NOTE: This is written for the BS2 but can be used for the BS1, BS2e▶ BS2sx and BS2p also. Locate the proper source code file or modify the STAMP directive before downloading to the BS1, BS2e, BS2sx or BS2p.

SOUND

| BS1 | BS2 | BS2e | BS2sx | BS2p |

 SOUND *Pin, (Note, Period {, Note, Period...})*

(See FREQOUT)

Function

Generate square-wave tones for a specified period.

- ***Pin*** is a variable/constant (0 – 7) that specifies the I/O pin to use. This pin will be set to output mode.

- ***Note*** is a variable/constant (0 – 255) specifying the type and frequency of the tone. 1 – 127 are ascending tones and 128 – 255 are ascending white noises ranging from buzzing (128) to hissing (255).

- ***Period*** is a variable/constant (1 - 255) specifying the amount of time to generate the tone(s). The unit of time for *Period* is 12 ms.

Explanation

SOUND generates one of 255 square-wave frequencies on an I/O pin. The output pin should be connected as shown in Figure 5.42.

The tones produced by SOUND can vary in frequency from 94.8 Hz (1) to 10,550 Hz (127). If you need to determine the frequency corresponding to a given note value, or need to find the note value that will give you best approximation for a given frequency, use the equations below.

$$Note = 127 - (((1/Frequency)-0.000095)/0.000083)$$

--and--

$$Frequency = (1/(0.000095 + ((127-Note)*0.000083))$$

Note, in the above equations, Frequency is in Hertz (Hz).

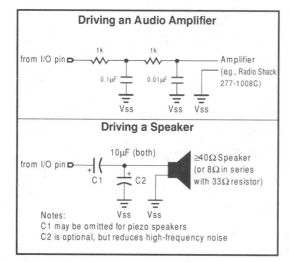

Figure 5.42: Example RC filter circuits for driving and audio amplifier or a speaker.

Demo Program (SOUND.bas)

```
' This program generates a constant tone 25 followed by an ascending tones. Both the tones
' have the same period (duration).

'{$STAMP BS1}                          'STAMP directive (specifies a BS1)

SYMBOL    Tone = B0

FOR Tone = 0  TO 255
     SOUND  1, (25, 10, Tone, 10)
NEXT
```

STOP

BS1	BS2	BS2e	BS2sx	BS2p

STOP

Function
Stop program execution.

Explanation
STOP prevents the BASIC Stamp from executing any further instructions until it is reset. The following actions will reset the BASIC Stamp:

1. Pressing and releasing the RESET button on the development board.
2. Driving the RES pin low then letting it float (high).
3. Downloading a new program
4. Disconnecting then reconnecting the power.

STOP differs from END in two respects:

1. Stop does not put the BASIC Stamp into low-power mode. The BASIC Stamp draws just as much current as if it were actively running program instructions.
2. The output glitch that occurs after a program has "ended" does not occur after a program has "stopped."

NOTE: This is written for the BS2 but can be used for the BS2e, BS2sx and BS2p also. Locate the proper source code file or modify the STAMP directive before downloading to the BS2e, BS2sx or BS2p.

Demo Program (STOP.bs2)

```
' This program is similar to SLEEP.bs2 except that the LED will not blink since the BASIC
' Stamp does not go into low power mode.  Use the circuit shown in the description of the
' SLEEP command for this example.

'{$STAMP BS2}                              'STAMP directive (specifies a BS2)

LOW  0              ' Turn LED on
STOP               ' Stop the program forever
```

STORE

| BS1 | BS2 | BS2e | BS2sx | **BS2p** |

STORE *ProgramSlot*

Function

Designate a program slot for the READ/WRITE instructions to operate upon.

- **ProgramSlot** is a variable/constant/expression (0 – 7) that specifies the program slot to use for READ and WRITE instructions.

Explanation

STORE tells the BS2p which program slot to use when a READ or WRITE instruction is executed. The STORE command only affects the READ and WRITE instructions.

The STORE command allows a program to access all EEPROM locations that exist on the BS2p, regardless of which program is running or which program slot is active. The READ and WRITE commands can only access locations 0 to 2047 within a single program slot. The STORE command switches the program slot that the READ and WRITE commands operate on.

The default program slot that the READ and WRITE instructions operate on is the currently running program. The STORE command can be used to temporarily change this, to any program slot. The change will remain in effect until another STORE command is issued, or until another program slot is executed.

Demo Program (STORE0.bsp)

```
' This program demonstrates the STORE command and how it affects the READ and WRITE
' commands. This program "STORE0.BSP" is intended to be downloaded into program
' slot 0. It is meant to work with STORE1.BSP and STORE2.BSP. Each program is very
' similar (they display the current Program Slot and Read/Write Slot numbers and the
' values contained in the first five EEPROM locations. Each program slot will have
' different data due to different DATA commands in each of the programs downloaded.

'{$STAMP BS2p, Store1.bsp, Store2.bsp}        'STAMP directive (specifies a BS2p)

DATA @0, 1, 2, 3, 4, 5

Idx        VAR    WORD
Value      VAR    BYTE
```

```
' ------------------------- Main Routines -------------------------

Main:
  GOSUB  DisplaySlotsAndReadData
  PAUSE 2000
  STORE 1                                    'Switch to READ/WRITE slot 1
  GOSUB  DisplaySlotsAndReadData
  PAUSE 2000
  RUN 1                    'Switch to program 1

' ------------------------- Subroutines -------------------------
DisplaySlotsAndReadData:
  GET  127, Value
  DEBUG  CR, "Prog Slot: ", DEC1 Value.LOWNIB
  DEBUG  "  R/W Slot: ", DEC1 Value.HIGHNIB, CR, CR

  FOR  Idx = 0  TO  4
    READ  Idx, Value
    DEBUG "Location: ", DEC  Idx, " Value: ", DEC3  Value, CR
  NEXT
RETURN
```

Demo Program (STORE1.bsp)

```
DATA  @0, 6, 7, 8, 9, 10

Idx          VAR   WORD
Value        VAR   BYTE

' ------------------------- Main Routines -------------------------
Main:
  GOSUB  DisplaySlotsAndReadData
  PAUSE 2000
  STORE 0                                    'Switch to READ/WRITE slot 0
  GOSUB  DisplaySlotsAndReadData
  PAUSE 2000
  RUN 2                                      'Switch to program 2

' ------------------------- Subroutines -------------------------
DisplaySlotsAndReadData:
  GET  127, Value
  DEBUG  CR, "Prog Slot: ", DEC1 Value.LOWNIB
  DEBUG  "  R/W Slot: ", DEC1 Value.HIGHNIB, CR, CR

  FOR  Idx = 0  TO  4
    READ  Idx, Value
    DEBUG "Location: ", DEC  Idx, " Value: ", DEC3  Value, CR
  NEXT
RETURN
```

Demo Program (STORE2.bsp)

```
DATA @0, 11, 12, 13, 14, 15

Idx          VAR   WORD
Value        VAR   BYTE

' ------------------------- Main Routines -------------------------
Main:
  GOSUB DisplaySlotsAndReadData
  PAUSE 2000
  STORE 0                                    'Switch to READ/WRITE slot 0
  GOSUB DisplaySlotsAndReadData
  STOP                                       'Stop execution

' ------------------------- Subroutines -------------------------
DisplaySlotsAndReadData:
  GET 127, Value
  DEBUG CR, "Prog Slot: ", DEC1 Value.LOWNIB
  DEBUG "  R/W Slot: ", DEC1 Value.HIGHNIB, CR, CR

  FOR Idx = 0 TO 4
    READ Idx, Value
    DEBUG "Location: ", DEC Idx, " Value: ", DEC3 Value, CR
  NEXT
RETURN
```

The next Demo Program, StoreAll.bsp, is not related to the previous three programs. StoreAll.bsp demonstrates the use of the STORE command to treat contiguous program slots as one block of memory (14 kbytes). This illustrates one of the most powerful uses of the STORE command.

Demo Program (STOREALL.bsp)

```
' This program demonstrates the STORE command and how it can be used to "flatten"
' the EEPROM space for applications requiring a lot of storage. This program
' writes to EEPROM locations within program slots 1 though 7 and, thus, has access
' to 14 kbytes of space.

'{$STAMP BS2p}                 'STAMP directive (specifies a BS2p)

Idx          VAR   WORD
Value        VAR   WORD

' ------------------------- Main Routines -------------------------
Main:
  DEBUG "Writing...", CR
  PAUSE 2000
  FOR Idx = 2048 TO 16383 STEP 32            'Write values to EEPROM
```

```
  Value = Idx – 2048 * 2                    'Use different numbers in each location
    GOSUB  WriteWordToEEPROM
    DEBUG  "Location: ", DEC5 Idx, " Value: ", DEC5 Value, CR
  NEXT

  DEBUG  "Reading...", CR
  PAUSE  2000
  FOR  Idx = 2048  TO  16383  STEP  32       'Read values from EEPROM
    GOSUB  ReadWordFromEEPROM
    DEBUG  "Location: ", DEC5 Idx, " Value: ", DEC5 Value, CR
  NEXT
STOP

' ---------------------- Subroutines ------------------------
WriteWordToEEPROM:
  'NOTE: This routine is written to work only when Idx is an even-byte boundary
  STORE  Idx >> 11           'Set to proper READ/WRITE slot (upper 3-bits of address)
  WRITE  Idx,  Value.LOWBYTE
  WRITE  Idx+1,  Value.HIGHBYTE
RETURN

ReadWordFromEEPROM:
  'NOTE: This routine is written to work only when Idx is an even-byte boundary
  STORE  Idx >> 11            'Set to proper READ/WRITE slot (upper 3-bits of address)
  READ  Idx,  Value.LOWBYTE
  READ  Idx+1,  Value.HIGHBYTE
RETURN
```

TOGGLE

BS1	BS2	BS2e	BS2sx	BS2p

TOGGLE *Pin*

NOTE: Expressions are not allowed as arguments on the BS1. The range of the *Pin* argument on the BS1 is 0 – 7.

Function

Invert the state of an output pin.

- **Pin** is a variable/constant/expression (0 – 15) that specifies which I/O pin to set high. This pin will be placed into output mode.

Explanation

TOGGLE sets a pin to output mode and inverts the output state of the pin, changing 0 to 1 and 1 to 0.

In some situations TOGGLE may appear to have no effect on a pin's state. For example, suppose pin 2 is in input mode and pulled to +5V by a 10k resistor. Then the following code executes:

```
DIR2 = 0        ' Pin 2 in input mode.
PIN2 = 0        ' Pin 2 output driver low.
DEBUG ? PIN2    ' Show state of pin 2 (1 due to pullup).
TOGGLE 2        ' Toggle pin 2 (invert PIN2, put 1 in DIR2).
DEBUG ? PIN2    ' Show state of pin 2 (1 again).
```

--or--

```
DIR2 = 0        ' Pin 2 in input mode.
OUT2 = 0        ' Pin 2 output driver low.
DEBUG ? IN2     ' Show state of pin 2 (1 due to pullup).
TOGGLE 2        ' Toggle pin 2 (invert OUT2, put 1 in DIR2).
DEBUG ? IN2     ' Show state of pin 2 (1 again).
```

The state of pin 2 doesn't change; it's high (due to the resistor) before TOGGLE, and it's high (due to the pin being output high) afterward. The point is that TOGGLE works on the OUTS register, which may not match the pin's state when the pin is initially an input. To guarantee that the state actually changes, regardless of the initial input or output mode, do this:

```
PIN2 = PIN2' Make output driver match pin state.
TOGGLE 2 ' Then toggle.
```

--or—

```
OUT2 = IN2 ' Make output driver match pin state.
TOGGLE 2 ' Then toggle.
```

TOGGLE - BASIC Stamp Command Reference

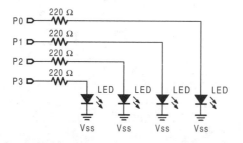

Figure 5.43: Example LED circuit for TOGGLE demo programs.

Demo Program (TOGGLE.bas)

```
' Connect LEDs to pins 0 through 3 as shown in the TOGGLE command description in the
' manual and run this program. The TOGGLE command will treat you to a light show. You
' may also run the demo without LEDs. The debug window will show you the states of pins 0
' through 3.

'{$STAMP BS1}                        'STAMP directive (specifies a BS1)

SYMBOL    ThePin = B0                ' Variable to count 0-3.
Again:
  FOR ThePin = 0 TO 3               ' Pins 0 to 3 driving LEDs.
    TOGGLE ThePin                   ' Toggle each pin.
    DEBUG CLS, #PINS                ' No LEDs? Watch debug screen.
    PAUSE 200                       ' Brief delay.
  NEXT                              ' Next pin
GOTO Again                          ' Repeat endlessly.
```

Demo Program (TOGGLE.bs2)

```
' Connect LEDs to pins 0 through 3 as shown in the TOGGLE command description in the
' manual and run this program. The TOGGLE command will treat you to a light show. You
' may also run the demo without LEDs. The debug window will show you the states of pins 0
' through 3.

'{$STAMP BS2}                        'STAMP directive (specifies a BS2)

ThePin    VAR   NIB                 ' Variable to count 0-3.
Again:
  FOR ThePin = 0 TO 3               ' Pins 0 to 3 driving LEDs.
    TOGGLE ThePin                   ' Toggle each pin.
    DEBUG CLS, BIN4 INA             ' No LEDs? Watch debug screen.
    PAUSE 200                       ' Brief delay.
  NEXT                              ' Next pin
GOTO Again                          ' Repeat endlessly.
```

NOTE: This is written for the BS2 but can be used for the BS2e, BS2sx and BS2p also. Locate the proper source code file or modify the STAMP directive before downloading to the BS2e, BS2sx or BS2p.

WRITE

| BS1 | BS2 | BS2e | BS2sx | BS2p |

WRITE *Location, DataItem*

Function

Write *DataItem* into *Location* in EEPROM.

- **Location** is a variable/constant/expression (0 – 255 on BS1, 0 – 2047 on all other BASIC Stamps) that specifies the EEPROM address to write to.

- **DataItem** is a variable/constant/expression specifying the value to be stored.

NOTE: Expressions are not allowed as arguments on the BS1.

Quick Facts

Table 5.94: WRITE Quick Facts.

	BS1	BS2	BS2e, BS2sx	BS2p
Range of EEPROM locations	0 to 255	0 to 2047	0 to 2047	0 to 2047 (see notes below)
Maximum number of writes per location	10 million	10 million	100,000	100,000
Special notes	n/a	n/a	WRITE only works with current program slot on BS2e and BS2sx.	WRITE works with any program slot as set by the STORE command.

Explanation

The EEPROM is used for both program storage (which builds downward from address 255 on BS1, 2047 on all other BASIC Stamps) and data storage (which builds upward from address 0). The WRITE instruction stores a byte of data to any EEPROM address. Any location within the EEPROM can be written to (including your PBASIC program's locations) at run-time. This feature is mainly used to store long-term data from EEPROM; data stored in EEPROM is not lost when the power is removed.

A SIMPLE WRITE COMMAND.

The following WRITE command stores the value 245 at location 100:

WRITE 100, 245

--or--

WRITE 100, 245

WRITING WORD VALUES VS. BYTE VALUES.

The EEPROM is organized as a sequential set of byte-sized memory locations. The WRITE command only stores byte-sized values into EEPROM. This does not mean that you can't write word-sized values, however. A word consists of two bytes, called a low-byte and a high-byte. If you wanted to write a word-sized value, you'll need to use two WRITE commands and a word-size value or variable (along with some handy modifiers). For example,

```
SYMBOL    Value        = W0      'The full word-sized variable
SYMBOL    Value_Low    = B0      'B0 happens to be the low-byte of W0
SYMBOL    Value_High   = B1      'B1 happens to be the high-byte of W0

Value = 1125

WRITE     0, Value_Low
WRITE     1, Value_High
```

--or--

```
Value     VAR    WORD

WRITE     0, Value.LOWBYTE
WRITE     1, Value.HIGHBYTE
```

When this program runs, the two WRITE commands will store the low-byte and high-byte of the number 1125 into EEPROM.

EEPROM differs from RAM, the memory in which variables are stored, in several respects:

SPECIAL NOTES FOR EEPROM USAGE.

1. Writing to EEPROM takes more time than storing a value in a variable. Depending on many factors, it may take several milliseconds for the EEPROM to complete a write. RAM storage is nearly instantaneous.
2. The EEPROM can only accept a finite number of write cycles per location before it wears out. Table 5.94 indicates the guaranteed number of writes before failure. If a program frequently writes to the same EEPROM location, it makes sense to estimate how long it

might take to exceed the guaranteed maximum. For example, on the BS2, at one write per second (86,400 writes/day) it would take nearly 116 days of continuous operation to exceed 10 million.

3. The primary function of the EEPROM is to store programs (data is stored in leftover space). If data overwrites a portion of your program, the program will most likely crash.

Check the program's memory map to determine what portion of memory your program occupies and make sure that EEPROM writes cannot stray into this area. You may also use the DATA directive on the BS2, BS2e, BS2sx and BS2p to set aside EEPROM space.

On the BS1, location 255 holds the address of the last instruction in your program. Therefore, your program can use any space below the address given in location 255. For example, if location 255 holds the value 100, then your program can use locations 0–99 for data.

On other BASIC Stamps, you'll need to view the Memory Map of the program before you download it, to determine the last EEPROM location used. See the "Memory Map Function" section in Chapter 3.

On the BS2p, the READ and WRITE commands can affect locations in any program slot as set by the STORE command. See the STORE command for more information.

Demo Program (WRITE.bas)

```
' This program writes a few bytes to EEPROM and then reads them back out and displays
' them on the screen.

'{$STAMP BS1}                                    'STAMP directive (specifies a BS1)

SYMBOL    ValAddr    = B0
SYMBOL    Value      = B1

WriteItOut:
  WRITE 0, 100                                   'Write some data to location 0 through 3
  WRITE 1, 200
  WRITE 2, 45
  WRITE 3, 28

ReadItOut:
  FOR ValAddr = 0 TO 3                           'Read all four locations and display the
    READ ValAddr, Value                          'value on the screen
    DEBUG ? Value
```

NEXT

Demo Program (WRITE.bs2)
' This program writes a few bytes to EEPROM and then reads them back out and displays
' them on the screen.

```
'{$STAMP BS2}                          'STAMP directive (specifies a BS2)

ValAddr     VAR  BYTE
Value       VAR  BYTE

WriteItOut:
  WRITE 0, 100                         'Write some data to location 0 through 3
  WRITE 1, 200
  WRITE 2, 45
  WRITE 3, 28

ReadItOut:
  FOR  ValAddr = 0  TO  3              'Read all four locations and display the
    READ  ValAddr, Value              'value on the screen
    DEBUG  ? Value
  NEXT
```

NOTE: This is written for the BS2 but can be used for the BS2e, BS2sx and BS2p also. Locate the proper source code file or modify the STAMP directive before downloading to the BS2e, BS2sx or BS2p.

XOUT

| BS1 | BS2 | BS2e | BS2sx | BS2p |

⌧2 ⌧2e ⌧2sx ⌧2p **XOUT** *Mpin, Zpin, [House\Command {\Cycles} {, House\Command {\Cycles}...}]*

Function

Send an X-10 power-line control command (through the appropriate power-line interface).

- **Mpin** is a variable/constant/expression (0 – 15) that specifies the I/O pin to output X-10 signals (modulation) to the power-line interface device. This pin will be set to output mode.

- **Zpin** is a variable/constant/expression (0 – 15) that specifies the I/O pin that inputs the zero-crossing signal from the power-line interface device. This pin will be set to input mode.

- **House** is a variable/constant/expression (0 – 15) that specifies the X-10 house code (values 0 - 15 representing letters A through P).

- **Command** is a variable/constant/expression (0 – 30) that specifies the command to send. Values 0 – 15 correspond to unit codes 1 – 16. Other commands are shown in Table 5.96.

- **Cycles** is an optional variable/constant/expression (1 – 255) specifying the number of times to transmit a given key or command. If no *Cycles* entry is used, XOUT defaults to two. The *Cycles* entry should be used only with the DIM and BRIGHT command codes

Quick Facts

Table 5.95: XOUT Quick Facts.

	BS2, BS2e, BS2sx and BS2p
Compatible power-line interfaces	PL-513 and TW-523
Special notes	The XOUT command will stop the BASIC Stamp program until it is able to send the transmission. If there is no AC power to the power-line interface, the BASIC Stamp program will halt forever.

Explanation

XOUT lets you control appliances via signals sent through household AC wiring to X-10 modules. The appliances plugged into these modules can be switched on or off; lights may also be dimmed. Each module is assigned a house code and unit code by setting dials or switches on the module. To talk to a particular module, XOUT sends the appropriate house code and unit code. The module with the corresponding code listens for its house code again followed by a command (on, off, dim, or bright).

X-10 signals are digital codes imposed on a 120 kHz carrier that is transmitted during zero crossings of the AC line. To send X-10 commands, a controller must synchronize to the AC line frequency with 50 μs precision, and transmit an 11-bit code sequence representing the command.

X-10 PROTOCOL DETAILS.

XOUT interfaces to the AC power-line through an approved interface device such as a PL-513 or TW-523, available from Parallax or X-10 dealers. The hookup requires a length of four-conductor phone cable and a standard modular phone-base connector (6P4C type). Connections are shown in Figure 5.44.

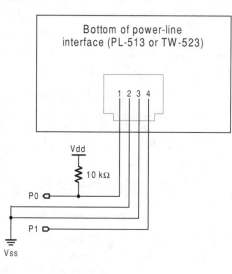

Figure 5.44: XOUT Power-Line Interface Circuit.

Table 5.96 lists the XOUT command codes and their functions:

Table 5.96: XOUT Commands and Their Function.

Command	Value	Function
UnitOn	%10010	Turn on the currently selected unit.
UnitOff	%11010	Turn off the currently selected unit.
UnitsOff	%11100	Turn off all modules in this house code.
LightsOn	%10100	Turn on all lamp modules in this house code.
Dim	%11110	Reduce brightness of currently selected lamp.
Bright	%10110	Increase brightness of currently selected lamp.

Note: In most applications, it's not necessary to know the code for a given X-10 instruction. Just use the command constant (UnitOn, Dim, etc.) instead. But knowing the codes leads to some interesting possibilities. For example, XORing a UnitOn command with the value %1000 turns it into a UnitOff command, and vice-versa. This makes it possible to write the equivalent of an X-10 "toggle" instruction.

A SIMPLE XOUT EXAMPLE: TURNING AN APPLIANCE ON.

Here is an example of the XOUT instruction:

```
Zpin      CON   0   ' Zpin is P0.
Mpin      CON   1   ' Mpin is P1.
HouseA    CON   0   ' House code A = 0.
Unit1     CON   0   ' Unit code 1 = 0.

XOUT  Mpin, Zpin, [HouseA\Unit1]        ' Get unit 1's attention..
XOUT  Mpin, Zpin, [HouseA\UnitOn]       ' ..and tell it to turn on.
```

COMBINING MULTIPLE COMMANDS.

You can combine those two XOUT instructions into one like so:

```
XOUT  Mpin, Zpin, [HouseA\Unit1\2, HouseA\UnitOn]' Unit 1 on.
```

Note that to complete the attention-getting code HouseA\Unit1 we tacked on the normally optional cycles entry \2 to complete the command before beginning the next one. Always specify two cycles in multiple commands unless you're adjusting the brightness of a lamp module.

DIMMING LIGHTS.

Here is an example of a lamp-dimming instruction:

```
Zpin      CON   0   ' Zpin is P0.
Mpin      CON   1   ' Mpin is P1.
HouseA    CON   0   ' House code A = 0.
Unit1     CON   0   ' Unit code 1 = 0.

XOUT  Mpin, Zpin, [HouseA\Unit1]                     'Get unit 1's attention..
XOUT  Mpin, Zpin, [HouseA\UnitOff\2, HouseA\Dim\10] 'Dim halfway.
```

The dim/bright commands support 19 brightness levels. Lamp modules may also be turned on and off using the standard UnitOn and UnitOff commands. In the example instruction above, we dimmed the lamp by first turning it completely off, then sending 10 cycles of the Dim command. This may seem odd, but it follows the peculiar logic of the X-10 system.

Demo Program (X10.bs2)

```
' This program--really two program fragments--demonstrates the syntax and use of the XOUT
' command. XOUT works like pressing the buttons on an X-10 control box; first you press one
' of 16 keys to identify the unit you want to control, then you press the key for the action you
' want that unit to take (turn ON, OFF, Bright, or Dim). There are also two group-action keys,
' Lights ON and All OFF. Lights ON turns all lamp modules on without affecting appliance
' modules. All OFF turns off all modules, both lamp and appliance types.  Connect the BASIC
' Stamp to a power-line interface as shown in the XOUT command description in the manual.

'{$STAMP BS2}                                'STAMP directive (specifies a BS2)

Zpin          CON   0    ' Zero-crossing-detect pin from TW523 or PL513.
Mpin          CON   1    ' Modulation-control pin to TW523 or PL513.
HouseA        CON   0    ' House code: 0=A, 1=B... 15=P
Unit1         CON   0    ' Unit code: 0=1, 1=2... 15=16
Unit2         CON   1    ' Unit code 1=2.

' This first example turns a standard (appliance or non-dimmer lamp) module ON, then OFF.
' Note that once the Unit code is sent, it need not be repeated--subsequent instructions are
' understood to be addressed to that unit.

XOUT  Mpin, Zpin, [HouseA\Unit1\2, HouseA\UnitOn]' Talk to Unit 1. Turn it ON.
PAUSE 1000                                  ' Wait a second.
XOUT  Mpin, Zpin, [HouseA\UnitOff]          ' Tell it to turn OFF.

' The next example talks to a lamp module using the dimmer feature. Dimmers go from full
' ON to dimmed OFF in 19 steps. Because dimming is relative to the current state of the
' lamp, the only guaranteed way to set a predefined brightness level is to turn the dimmer fully
' OFF, then ON, then dim to the  desired level.

XOUT  Mpin, Zpin, [HouseA\Unit2]            ' Talk to Unit 2.

' This example shows the use of the optional Cycles argument.  Here we Dim for 10 cycles.

XOUT  Mpin, Zpin, [HouseA\UnitOff\2, HouseA\Dim\10]

STOP
```

NOTE: This is written for the BS2 but can be used for the BS2e, BS2sx and BS2p also. Locate the proper source code file or modify the STAMP directive before downloading to the BS2e, BS2sx or BS2p.

ASCII Chart (first 128 characters)

Dec	Hex	Char	Name / Function
0	00	NUL	Null
1	01	SOH	Start Of Heading
2	02	STX	Start Of Text
3	03	ETX	End Of Text
4	04	EOT	End Of Transmit
5	05	ENQ	Enquiry
6	06	ACK	Acknowledge
7	07	BEL	Bell
8	08	BS	Backspace
9	09	HT	Horizontal Tab
10	0A	LF	Line Feed
11	0B	VT	Vertical Tab
12	0C	FF	Form Feed
13	0D	CR	Carriage Return
14	0E	SO	Shift Out
15	0F	SI	Shift In
16	10	DLE	Data Line Escape
17	11	DC1	Device Control 1
18	12	DC2	Device Control 2
19	13	DC3	Device Control 3
20	14	DC4	Device Control 4
21	15	NAK	Non Acknowledge
22	16	SYN	Synchronous Idle
23	17	ETB	End Transmit Block
24	18	CAN	Cancel
25	19	EM	End Of Medium
26	1A	SUB	Substitute
27	1B	ESC	Escape
28	1C	FS	File Separator
29	1D	GS	Group Separator
30	1E	RS	Record Separator
31	1F	US	Unit Separator

Dec	Hex	Char
32	20	space
33	21	!
34	22	"
35	23	#
36	24	$
37	25	%
38	26	&
39	27	'
40	28	(
41	29	)
42	2A	*
43	2B	+
44	2C	,
45	2D	-
46	2E	.
47	2F	/
48	30	0
49	31	1
50	32	2
51	33	3
52	34	4
53	35	5
54	36	6
55	37	7
56	38	8
57	39	9
58	3A	:
59	3B	;
60	3C	<
61	3D	=
62	3E	>
63	3F	?

Dec	Hex	Char
64	40	@
65	41	A
66	42	B
67	43	C
68	44	D
69	45	E
70	46	F
71	47	G
72	48	H
73	49	I
74	4A	J
75	4B	K
76	4C	L
77	4D	M
78	4E	N
79	4F	O
80	50	P
81	51	Q
82	52	R
83	53	S
84	54	T
85	55	U
86	56	V
87	57	W
88	58	X
89	59	Y
90	5A	Z
91	5B	[
92	5C	\
93	5D	]
94	5E	^
95	5F	_

Dec	Hex	Char
96	60	`
97	61	a
98	62	b
99	63	c
100	64	d
101	65	e
102	66	f
103	67	g
104	68	h
105	69	i
106	6A	j
107	6B	k
108	6C	l
109	6D	m
110	6E	n
111	6F	o
112	70	p
113	71	q
114	72	r
115	73	s
116	74	t
117	75	u
118	76	v
119	77	w
120	78	x
121	79	y
122	7A	z
123	7B	{
124	7C		
125	7D	}
126	7E	~
127	7F	delete

Note that the control codes (lowest 32 ASCII characters) have no standardized screen symbols. The characters listed for them are just names used in referring to these codes. For example, to move the cursor to the beginning of the next line of a printer or terminal often requires sending line feed and carriage return codes. This common pair is referred to as "LF/CR."

Reserved Words

BS1		BS2			BS2e/sx (same as BS2 plus below)	BS2p (same as BS2 plus below)
AND	ON2400	ABS	HOME	OUTL	GET	AUXIO
B0..B13	OR	AND	IHEX	OUTPUT	PUT	GET
BIT0..BIT15	OT300	ASC	IHEX1..IHEX4	OUTS	RUN	I2CIN
BRANCH	OT600	B0..B25	IF	PAUSE		I2COUT
BSAVE	OT1200	BELL	IN0..IN15	RCTIME		IOTERM
BUTTON	OT2400	BKSP	INA	REV		LCDCMD
DEBUG	OUTPUT	BIN	INB	PULSIN		LCDIN
DIR0..DIR7	PAUSE	BIN1..BIN4	INC	PULSOUT		LCDOUT
DIRS	PIN0..PIN7	BIT	IND	PWM		MAINIO
EEPROM	PINS	BIT0..BIT15	INH	RANDOM		OWIN
END	PORT	BRANCH	INL	READ		OWOUT
FOR	POT	BRIGHT	INPUT	REP		POLLIN
GOSUB	PULSIN	BUTTON	INS	REVERSE		POLLOUT
GOTO	PULSOUT	BYTE	ISBIN	SBIN		POLLMODE
HIGH	PWM	CLS	ISBIN1..ISBIN16	SBIN1..SBIN16		POLLRUN
IF	RANDOM	CON	ISHEX	SDEC		POLLWAIT
INPUT	READ	COS	ISHEX1..ISHEX4	SDEC1..SDEC5		PUT
LET	REVERSE	COUNT	LIGHTSON	SERIN		RUN
LOOKDOWN	SERIN	CR	LOOKDOWN	SEROUT		STORE
LOOKUP	SEROUT	DATA	LOOKUP	SHEX		
LOW	SLEEP	DCD	LOW	SHEX1..SHEX4		
MAX	SOUND	DEBUG	LOWBIT	SHIFTIN		
MIN	STEP	DEC	LOWNIB	SHIFTOUT		
N300	SYMBOL	DEC1..DEC5	LSBFIRST	SIN		
N600	T300	DIG	LSBPOST	SKIP		
N1200	T600	DIM	LSBPRE	SLEEP		
N2400	T1200	DIR0..DIR15	MAX	STEP		
NAP	T2400	DIRA	MIN	STOP		
NEXT	THEN	DIRB	MSBFIRST	STR		
ON300	TOGGLE	DIRC	MSBPOST	SQR		
ON600	W0..W6	DIRD	MSBPRE	TAB		
ON1200	WRITE	DIRH	NAP	THEN		
		DIRL	NCD	TO		
		DIRS	NEXT	TOGGLE		
		DTMFOUT	NIB	UNITOFF		
		END	NIB0..NIB3	UNITON		
		FOR	NOT	UNITSOFF		
		FREQOUT	NUM	VAR		
		GOSUB	OR	W0..W12		
		GOTO	OUT0..OUT15	WAIT		
		HEX	OUTA	WAITSTR		
		HEX1..HEX4	OUTB	WORD		
		HIGH	OUTC	WRITE		
		HIGHBIT	OUTD	XOR		
		HIGHNIB	OUTH	XOUT		

Reserved Words

Appendix C: Conversion Formatters

Conversion Formatters

This appendix lists the Conversion Formatters available for the commands SERIN, I2CIN, LCDIN, and OWIN and demonstrates, though various input/output data examples, exactly what will be received when using these formatters.

Decimal Formatters	Characters Received						
	⊗	123	123⊗	-123⊗	⊗123⊗	12345⊗	65536⊗	255255⊗
DEC	--	--	123	123	123	12345	0	58647
DEC1	--	1	1	1	1	1	6	2
DEC2	--	12	12	12	12	12	65	25
DEC3	--	123	123	123	123	123	655	255
DEC4	--	--	123	123	123	1234	6553	2552
DEC5	--	--	123	123	123	12345	0	25525
SDEC	--	--	123	-123	123	12345	0	-6889
SDEC1	--	1	1	-1	1	1	6	2
SDEC2	--	12	12	-12	12	12	65	25
SDEC3	--	123	123	-123	123	123	655	255
SDEC4	--	--	123	-123	123	1234	6553	2552
SDEC5	--	--	123	-123	123	12345	0	25525

⊗ Means any non-decimal-numeric characters such as letters, spaces, minus signs, carriage returns, control characters, etc. (Decimal numerics are: 0,1,2,3,4,5,6,7,8 and 9).

-- Means no valid data (or not enough valid data) was received so the SERIN command will halt forever (unless the *Timeout* argument is used).

Hexadecimal Formatters	Characters Received						
	⊗	1F	1F⊗	-1F⊗	⊗1F⊗	15AF⊗	10000⊗	3E517⊗
HEX	--	--	1F	1F	1F	15AF	0	E517
HEX1	--	1	1	1	1	1	1	3
HEX2	--	1F	1F	1F	1F	15	10	3E
HEX3	--	--	1F	1F	1F	15A	100	3E5
HEX4	--	--	1F	1F	1F	15AF	1000	3E51
SHEX	--	--	1F	-1F	1F	15AF	0	-1AE9
SHEX1	--	1	1	-1	1	1	1	3
SHEX2	--	1F	1F	-1F	1F	15	10	3E
SHEX3	--	--	1F	-1F	1F	15A	100	3E5
SHEX4	--	--	1F	-1F	1F	15AF	1000	3E51

NOTE: The HEX formatters are not case sensitive. For example, 1F is the same as 1f.

⊗ Means any non-hexadecimal-numeric characters such as letters (greater than F), spaces, minus signs, carriage returns, control characters, etc. (Hexadecimal numerics are: 0,1,2,3,4,5,6,7,8,9,A,B,C,D,E,F).

-- Means no valid data (or not enough valid data) was received so the SERIN command will halt forever (unless the *Timeout* argument is used).

Conversion Formatters

Additional Hexadecimal Formatters	Characters Received							
	⊗	1F	1F⊗	$1F	$1F⊗	-$1F⊗	⊗$1F⊗	$15AF⊗
IHEX	--	--	--	--	1F	1F	1F	15AF
IHEX1	--	--	--	1	1	1	1	1
IHEX2	--	--	--	1F	1F	1F	1F	15
IHEX3	--	--	--	--	1F	1F	1F	15A
IHEX4	--	--	--	--	1F	1F	1F	15AF
ISHEX	--	--	--	--	1F	-1F	1F	15AF
ISHEX1	--	--	--	1	1	-1	1	1
ISHEX2	--	--	--	1F	1F	-1F	1F	15
ISHEX3	--	--	--	--	1F	-1F	1F	15A
ISHEX4	--	--	--	--	1F	-1F	1F	15AF

NOTE: The HEX formatters are not case sensitive. For example, 1F is the same as 1f.

⊗ Means any non-hexadecimal-numeric characters such as letters (greater than F), spaces, minus signs, carriage returns, control characters, etc. (Hexadecimal numerics are: 0,1,2,3,4,5,6,7,8,9,A,B,C,D,E,F).

-- Means no valid data (or not enough valid data) was received so the SERIN command will halt forever (unless the *Timeout* argument is used).

Binary Formatters	Characters Received						
	⊗	11	11⊗	-11⊗	⊗11⊗	101⊗	3E517⊗
BIN	--	--	11	11	11	101	1
BIN1	--	1	1	1	1	1	1
BIN2	--	11	11	11	11	10	1
BIN3 – BIN16	--	--	11	11	11	101	1
SBIN	--	--	11	-11	11	101	1
SBIN1	--	1	1	-1	1	1	1
SBIN2	--	11	11	-11	11	10	1
SBIN3 – SBIN16	--	--	11	-11	11	101	1

⊗ Means any non-binary-numeric characters such as letters, spaces, minus signs, carriage returns, control characters, etc. (Binary numerics are: 0 and 1).

-- Means no valid data (or not enough valid data) was received so the SERIN command will halt forever (unless the *Timeout* argument is used).

Additional Binary Formatters	Characters Received						
	⊗	11	11⊗	%11	%11⊗	-%11⊗	⊗%11⊗	%101⊗
IBIN	--	--	--	--	11	11	11	101
IBIN1	--	--	--	1	1	1	1	1
IBIN2	--	--	--	11	11	11	11	10
IBIN3 – IBIN16	--	--	--	--	11	11	11	101
ISBIN	--	--	--	--	11	-11	11	101
ISBIN1	--	--	--	1	1	-1	1	1
ISBIN2	--	--	--	11	11	-11	11	10
ISBIN3 – ISBIN16	--	--	--	--	11	-11	11	101

⊗ Means any non-binary-numeric characters such as letters, spaces, minus signs, carriage returns, control characters, etc. (Binary numerics are: 0 and 1).

-- Means no valid data (or not enough valid data) was received so the SERIN command will halt forever (unless the *Timeout* argument is used).

Conversion Formatters

Index

Index

Index